Crisis and Sequels

Studies in Critical Social Sciences Book Series

Haymarket Books is proud to be working with Brill Academic Publishers (www.brill.nl) to republish the *Studies in Critical Social Sciences* book series in paperback editions. This peer-reviewed book series offers insights into our current reality by exploring the content and consequences of power relationships under capitalism, and by considering the spaces of opposition and resistance to these changes that have been defining our new age. Our full catalog of *SCSS* volumes can be viewed at https://www.haymarketbooks.org/series_collections/4-studies-in-critical-social-sciences.

Crisis and Sequels

Capitalism and the New Economic Turmoil since 2007

Edited by
Martin Thomas

Haymarket Books
Chicago, IL

First published in 2017 by Brill Academic Publishers, The Netherlands.

Published in paperback in 2018 by
Haymarket Books
P.O. Box 180165
Chicago, IL 60618
773-583-7884
www.haymarketbooks.org

ISBN: 978-1-60846-086-1

Trade distribution:
In the U.S. through Consortium Book Sales, www.cbsd.com
In the UK, Turnaround Publisher Services, www.turnaround-uk.com
In Canada, Publishers Group Canada, www.pgcbooks.ca
All other countries, Ingram Publisher Services International, ips_intlsales@ingramcontent.com

Cover design by Jamie Kerry and Ragina Johnson.

This book was published with the generous support of Lannan Foundation and the Wallace Action Fund.

Printed in United States.

10 9 8 7 6 5 4 3 2 1

Library of Congress Cataloging-in-Publication Data is available.

Contents

Acknowledgements IX
List of Illustrations X
About the Discussants XI

Introduction 1

PART 1
After 2007

Introduction to Part 1

1 The Long Trends of Profit (March 2008) 45
Discussion with Fred Moseley

2 A New Sort of Financial Crisis (April 2008) 50
Discussion with Costas Lapavitsas

3 The Crisis Depends on the Fightback (April 2008) 57
Discussion with Leo Panitch

4 An Era of Rampant Inequality (May 2008) 68
Discussion with Simon Mohun

5 The Imbalances are Unsustainable (June 2008) 72
Discussion with Trevor Evans

6 The Inventiveness of Capital (July 2008) 80
Discussion with Dick Bryan

7 A Systemic Crisis, both Global and Long-Lasting (July 2008) 89
Discussion with Michel Husson

PART 2
After September 2008

Introduction to Part 2

8 The Crisis of Neoliberal Capitalism (December 2008) 102
Discussion with Michel Husson

9 The Debacle of Financialised Capitalism (January 2009) 105
Discussion with Costas Lapavitsas

10 The Level of Debt is Astronomical (December 2008) 112
Discussion with Andrew Kliman

11 The Chain Broke at the Weakest Link (December 2008) 119
Discussion with Leo Panitch

12 The Bondholders and the Taxpayers (December 2008) 124
Discussion with Fred Moseley

13 The Neoliberal Model is Bust (January 2009) 128
Discussion with Simon Mohun

14 The Economy in a World of Trouble (April 2009) 134
Robert Brenner interviewed by Seongjin Jeong

15 The Underlying Contradictions of Capitalist Finance (June 2009) 149
Discussion with Dick Bryan

PART 3
After 2009

Introduction to Part 3

16 The Falling Rate of Profit (July 2011) 158
Barry Finger

17 The Banks' Crisis and the Left's Crisis (August 2011) 163
Leo Panitch

18 Nationalise the Banks! (September 2011) 169
Michel Husson

19 The Endless Bail-out of Europe (November 2011) 171
Michel Husson

20 Europe: The Bankers vs the People (June 2012) 176
Discussion with Daniela Gabor

PART 4
After 2010

Introduction to Part 4

21 No Choice but to Change (June 2012) 184
Discussion with Hugo Radice

22 The World of Neoliberalism (October 2013) 188
Paul Hampton and Martin Thomas

23 An Alternative View on the World of Neoliberalism (January 2014) 196
Barry Finger

24 The Resilience of Neoliberalism (June 2016) 201
Discussion with Andrew Gamble

PART 5
After 2015

Introduction to Part 5

25 The Coming Crisis (October 2015) 212
Michel Husson

26 **Too Much Debt in Relation to Income (January 2016)** 224
Discussion with Fred Moseley

27 **The Situation Has Long Been Unsustainable (January 2016)** 227
Discussion with Andrew Kliman

28 **We Become a Hedge Fund of Our Own Lives (January 2016)** 240
Discussion with Dick Bryan

29 **The Globalisation of Elites (January 2016)** 248
Discussion with Hugo Radice

30 **The Great Recession Is Not Going Away (January 2016)** 255
Discussion with Leo Panitch

31 **A Protracted Transition (June 2016)** 261
Discussion with Simon Mohun

32 **Brazil and Neoliberalism (July–August 2016)** 268
Discussion with Alfredo Saad-Filho

Afterword: 2016 278

Appendices

Appendix 1: Marx on Capitalist Crises 289
Appendix 2: Ruinous Competition 300
Appendix 3: The Tendency of the Rate of Profit to Fall 310

List of Previously Published Articles 315
Bibliography 318
Index 324

Acknowledgements

I owe thanks to the contributors who made time for the discussions recorded here, and often for reworking or correcting the transcripts. I thank my colleagues on the editorial staff of the socialist newspaper *Solidarity* and of the associated website *Workers' Liberty*, where many of the texts included here first appeared. I also express my gratitude to *Against the Current* and *The Bullet*, for permission to use texts that were previously published with them. Much of the material for this book was previously collected at the blog *Sense of* GFC (https://senseofgfc.wordpress.com/), August 2016.

List of Illustrations

16.1 Economy-wide Return on Invested Capital (ROIC), USA, 1965–2012 161
19.1 Growth gap between countries of the South and the North of Europe 172
23.1 Corporate profits before taxes against corporate assets valued at historical cost for the non-financial sector of the US economy, 1940–2012 200
25.1 Central bank official interest rates. Germany, USA, Japan 214
25.2 Global stock of debt 215
25.3 Tendencies in growth of labour productivity 219
25.4 Rates of profit, 2007–2015 220
25.5 Two episodes of recession in the Eurozone: Investment 221
25.6 Two episodes of recession in the Eurozone: Wage share 222

About the Discussants

Robert Brenner
is a professor at UCLA, a member of the US socialist group Solidarity, and author of *The Economics of Global Turbulence* (1998 and 2006).

Dick Bryan
is the co-author with Michael Rafferty of a book, *Capitalism with Derivatives* (2006), and of several articles, in which he argues that the recent rise of financial derivatives marks a fundamental new stage in capitalist development, and especially in the development of what functions as "money" in capitalism. He is emeritus professor of political economy at the University of Sydney.

Trevor Evans
is a professor at the Berlin School of Economics and Law, and has also worked in Nicaragua and other countries. He has written especially on the interrelation between finance and capitalist crises.

Barry Finger
is the business manager of the US socialist journal *New Politics*, and a member of its editorial board.

Daniela Gabor
is a professor of economics at the University of the West of England and an expert on the economics of banking, editor (with Charles Goodhart and others) of *Central Banking at a Crossroads: Europe and Beyond* (2014).

Andrew Gamble
is emeritus professor of politics at Cambridge University and author of two books on the turmoil following 2007–8, *The Spectre at the Feast* (2009) and *Crisis Without End?* (2014).

Paul Hampton
is a trade-union researcher, a regular contributor to the socialist weekly *Solidarity*, and author of *Workers and Trade Unions for Climate Solidarity* (2015).

Michel Husson
is a Marxist economist well-known on the French left, author of many books including *Un pur capitalisme* (2008).

Andrew Kliman
is the author of *Reclaiming Marx's "Capital"* (2007); *The Failure of Capitalist Production: Underlying Causes of the Great Recession* (2011); and many articles, and is a professor of economics at Pace University, USA.

Costas Lapavitsas
is a Marxist economist specialising in the study of financial systems. His writings include *Profiting Without Producing* (2013), and he is a professor at the School of Oriental and African Studies in London.

Simon Mohun
has done extensive research on the development of productive and unproductive labour (in the Marxist sense, i.e. labour which does or does not produce surplus value), especially in the USA. He is emeritus professor of economics at Queen Mary University of London, and author of *Debates in Value Theory* (1994) and many articles.

Fred Moseley
is the author of a distinctive Marxist account of the decline in profit rates which brought crisis in the 1970s and 80s, one has spawned a whole series of further studies. He is professor of economics at Mount Holyoke College in Massachusetts, USA. His books include *The Falling Rate of Profit in the Postwar United States Economy* (1991), and, most recently, *Money and Totality: A Macro-Monetary Interpretation of Marx's Logic in Capital and the End of the 'Transformation Problem'* (2015).

Leo Panitch
has been editor of the annual *Socialist Register* in recent years, and has written many books and articles, several with Sam Gindin, former research director for the Canadian Auto Workers Union (CAW), and notably *The Making of Global Capital* (2013). He is active in the Socialist Project group, http://www.socialistproject.ca/, and is a professor at York University, Toronto.

Hugo Radice
is the author of *Global Capitalism: Selected Essays* (2014) and a Life Fellow of the School of Politics and International Studies at Leeds University.

Alfredo Saad-Filho
is the author of books including (with Ben Fine) *Marx's Capital* (sixth edition 2016); editor of other books including (with Deborah Johnston) *Neoliberalism: A Critical Reader* (2014) and (with Lecio Morais) *Brazil: Neoliberalism versus Democracy* (2017); and professor of political economy at the School of Oriental and African Studies in London.

Introduction

Since 2008 I have conducted a series of discussions and interviews with left-minded economists and political economists about the economic crisis of 2007–8 and its sequels, some published over those years,[1] some published here for the first time. The collated discussions form a unique resource, documenting real-time investigation of and debate about the economic turmoil in a form accessible to readers without technical training in economics. Where I've been able to, I've interviewed the same person at different times over those years, so that the discussion includes their criticism and correction of their own previous views as well as their disputes with other economists. I've sought to interview a variety of writers, to get a variety of views and angles. I thank those who took part, and apologise for the shortcomings: I've not been able to get every interview I sought; the selection is biased towards economists writing in English, and grossly gender-imbalanced.

The discussions are presented (with a few exceptions) chronologically: as the reader moves through the book, she or he has the economic developments of the time indicated by way of the comments and discussion of the time, and also she or he can see the development in our thinking and our debates, as issues which at an early time seem central fade or are resolved, and new questions are posed, or questions are posed in new ways. I have divided the sessions into five periods of time. Each part starts with a brief guidepost text, followed by the different interviews during that period of time. Finally, the afterword sums up, as of 2016.

In this general introduction, I will summarise the story of the crisis and its sequels since 2007–8, give my own views on some of the debated issues, and summarise some of what is said about those issues in the interviews.

The Story of the Crisis

The story started in finance. In June 2005 mortgage interest rates in the USA started rising sharply. They levelled off and declined after July 2006, but in the meantime house prices had reversed their giddy rise of previous years. House prices would continue to fall until January 2012, when they would be on average 33% down on their May 2006 peak.

From mid-2006 the proportion of delinquent mortgagees (those with payments seriously overdue) rose, and it would keep rising until early 2010. By 2011

1 http://www.workersliberty.org/story/2008/05/02/marxist-economists-analyse-crisis.

eleven million households in the USA owed more on their home mortgage than their house was worth (Mian and Sufi 2015), and by late 2015 around six million households would have their homes foreclosed (CoreLogic 2015). Unlike for example the UK house-price crash of 1989–92 (in which about 188,000 homes were repossessed), the US mortgage crash fed into a financial, industrial, and international crash. It revealed that "the bond bubble [had been] by no means limited to mortgages. It was ubiquitous". Building on the mortgage bubble, "risk spreads were irrationally small", i.e. small extra revenues had been needed to attract buyers to risky securities, and so once financiers realised those securities were risky, their prices were likely to drop sharply. (Blinder 2013, pp. 45–46, 90–91).

On 9 August 2007, a French bank, BNP, told holders of stakes in three of its investment funds that they could not have their money back. The bank held mortgage-backed securities – bits of paper which entitled holders to a slice of the income from payments on mortgages made in the USA – and now, as one financier put it, those "securities... simply [could]n't be priced because there [was] no trading in them. There [were] no bids for them. Asset-backed securities, mortgage loans, especially subprime loans, [did]n't have any buyers" (Bloomberg 2007).

The freezing of credit flows between banks escalated. On 14 September 2007 queues of people fearing collapse and wanting to get their money out formed at the branches of a British bank, Northern Rock; the British government nationalised the bank in February 2008. On 14 March 2008, the US investment bank Bear Stearns collapsed; the US government helped J P Morgan to take it over. On 15 September 2008, the USA's fourth largest investment bank, Lehman Brothers, collapsed, and was not bailed out. The collapse triggered panic in financial markets. Many countries, including the USA under the avowedly free-market presidency of George W Bush, nationalised or did public bail-outs of big banks. Central banks, notably the USA's Federal Reserve and the Bank of England, cut the interest rates at which they lend money to commercial banks to record lows and, in effect, printed larger amounts of cash in order to stop the total stock of money (cash plus bank accounts) shrinking.

From Crunch to Slump

US industry and services had started receding already, before the Lehman crash. In the USA, the mass of corporate profits had been rising tidily since late 2000, but it fell from 2006 quarter 3 (reaching bottom soon, in 2008 Q4, and then recovering slowly). US private non-residential fixed investment peaked in 2007 Q4, and had declined 20% by its low point, 2009 Q4. US industrial production fell from November 2007 by 17% to a low point in June 2009; US real GDP, from 2007 Q4 to 2009 Q2; US consumer spending, from November 2007 to June 2009.

Industrial slump came a bit later in other countries, but quite soon. UK industrial production, which had been stagnant, fell sharply from April 2008 by 13% to a low point in August 2009; after recovering a little it would fall again from January 2011 to October 2012. German industrial production fell slowly from January 2008 and more rapidly from September 2008, and would be 25% down by a low point in April 2009.

China's industrial production (excluding construction) did not fall, but its official annualised rate of growth decreased from 18% in 2007 Q2 to 6% in 2008 Q4, and has decreased again since 2009 Q4, despite the Chinese government organising a vast construction and investment boom to offset the decline in China's export markets. India's GDP fell in only one quarter, 2009 Q1, but was stagnant throughout 2008.

Brazilian economist Ruy Quadros reported in November 2008: "The global financial crisis... [has] hit a Brazilian economy in its most prosperous moment in 30 years... The exposure of large firms to hedge operations and the foreign credit crunch have led major Brazilian banks to initially paralyse consumer and corporate credit lines, a movement which has been partially circumvented after the intervention of the Central Bank... The jump in the price of the US dollar and the choking of export credit rapidly taught policy-makers and the press that there is no possible shield which would be able to protect a very internationalised economy from a global crisis" (Quadros 2008). Brazil's GDP fell from 2008 Q3 to 2009 Q1.

World trade fell by almost 20% in the nine months from April 2008 to January 2009, and continued falling until June 2009; world industrial production fell about 13% in the eleven months from April 2008 (Almunia 2010). 2009 became the only year since World War II in which slump was so generalised that total world output declined.

From Banks to Governments to "Emerging Economies"

In capitalist economies, not every financial crisis snowballs into an economy-wide crisis. The October 1987 crash of many stock markets round the world – bigger than the more famous New York stock market crash of October 1929 – caused no great slump in industry or services. The US "Savings and Loans" crisis at the end of the 1980s, in which about a quarter of the USA's "savings and loans" companies (savings banks specialising in mortgage loans) collapsed, was accompanied only by a small industrial recession in the USA.

The difference in 2007–8 was not that industry and services were already in a downturn or painful stagnation, and the financial disarray pushed them down the slope. Some writers argue something like that, but I am not convinced. There was no garish boom underway in 2006, but profits and even investment were mostly buoyant by recent standards, and the level of debt held by non-financial businesses was modest in relation to their incomes. Yet the financial crash in 2007–8 was much bigger and more far-reaching than the previous ones, because it dug deeper into a bigger-than-ever spiral-built edifice of credit built upon credit built upon credit. The spirals had become so interwoven that in the crash "concerns over $400 billion subprime lending in the US housing market led to the wiping-off of about $40 trillion in global asset markets" (Palma 2009).

Its repercussions have rolled through one sector after another. The next wave of disorder hit governments, while the credit system was still limping. Some small countries depended heavily on credit supplied to households and businesses through foreign-owned banks. Other governments were caught in a spiral of death with their commercial banks. The governments depended on the banks to buy their government IOUs (bonds); the banks depended on the governments to make the bonds they held solid enough to count as assets to borrow on. Iceland, Hungary, and Latvia sought IMF or IMF-EU rescues in September-October 2008, October 2008, and February 2009. From 2010 a new wave of disarray centred on the debt crises of Eurozone governments. UK and Eurozone industrial production declined in 2011–2, though US recovery continued, slowly. Newer industrial powers like China, India, and Brazil, were at first reputed to have lost little in the crisis: they had been hailed since 2001, under the portmanteau-name "BRIC" (or "BRICS", from 2010), as the great new force in the world economy. Recovery in the first two waves (credit between banks, government debt crises) remains slight into 2016. As of July 2016, central banks are still propping up their states' commercial banks by lending to them at ultra-low interest rates and by other exceptional measures: the top 50 central banks cut their official interest rates a total of 672 times between September 2008 and July 2016, often to record-low levels, and rarely increased them (*Financial Times*, 28/07/16). Italy's banks were reported in "turmoil", with "€360bn of gross non-performing loans" in July 2016 (*Financial Times* 28/07/16). But since about 2012 a third wave of hurt has hit the "emerging economies". World trade has grown only slowly since 2011, and fell 13% (in US-dollars measure) in 2015. Primary commodity prices, which soared speculatively in 2008, slumped in 2009, and then recovered in 2009–11, have fallen since 2011. Oil prices started slumping dramatically from mid-2014. Persistently stagnant demand, and maybe also expectations of raised interest rates, are factors here. Although official interest rates remain at record lows in Europe and Japan, the US Federal

Reserve, after much speculation and advance signalling, raised its federal-funds rate in December 2015, for the first time since 2006. A flood of "anything up to US $7 trillion of so-called quantitative easing (QE) funds" (Palma 2015) into "emerging markets" since 2008 has generated an oppressive debt overhang for corporations in those "emerging economies". According to the Purchasing Managers' Index compiled by Markit, Chinese manufacturing industry was stagnant or declining from the second half of 2011 through to mid-2016. From June 2015 China suffered a stock market crash. China's exports fell 1.8% in 2015, and its imports 13.2%. Container traffic through Singapore fell 8.7%, and through Hong Kong, 9.5%. Industrial production and investment in India stagnated from early 2012 to early 2014, though it has recovered since. GDP in Brazil has been falling from early 2014. China's huge infrastructure investment surge from 2009 has slowed; it could not continue forever while China's export markets were sagging; some calculations, admittedly lurid rounding-up exercises, categorise over 30% of it as wasted on bridges to nowhere and empty flats (Economist, 28/11/14); and certainly, it has brought China a big debt overhang.

Global Finance

Finance had grown hugely in proportion to industry and services over the three or four decades before 2007–8. On Palma's calculations (Palma 2009), between 1980 and 2007, the total of financial assets increased from the equivalent of 1.2 years' world output to 4.4. On Bain & Co's figures (Bain 2012) financial assets now total three times as much as non-financial assets, and ten times as much as a year's global output. Finance had also grown hugely in its global interconnectedness (and speed of transactions). Paradoxically, it had both become more of a world of its own, and more connected to non-financial capital.

Giant multinationals increasingly organise production on a world scale. "Value chains administered in various ways by transnational corporations now account for 80 per cent of the $20 trillion in [world] trade each year", according to UNCTAD (February 2013). These corporations borrow money in one currency, make investments in another, buy supplies in yet others, and get revenues in others again. They do those things in a capitalist world where, even before 2007–8, financial uncertainty was great. They need to juggle collections of diverse financial assets, to hold reserves for crises, and to buy insurance where they can against unexpected movements of relative prices of financial assets.

With those needs, rooted in global production, has come the rise of finance, and the increasing financialisation of non-financial corporations. On top of the necessities of trade and production has been built a vast superstructure of intra-financial dealing. Banks and other financial firms do many more transactions with each other than with non-financial corporations. Redistributing funds for non-financial corporations to invest in equipment and buildings is in fact a small part of their operation; in the richer countries (though not necessarily in the "emerging economies"), most of those funds for productive investment come from corporations' retained profits.

Each firm wanted a balanced mix of safer assets with (so that they could maximise gains) riskier high-yielding financial assets carrying diverse and little-correlated risks. Paradoxically, the desire for safer assets generated an explosion of invention of allegedly-safe assets, many of which proved not so safe after all. "In January 2008", according to Lloyd Blankfein of Goldman Sachs, "there were 12 triple A-rated companies in the world [i.e. whose debt was rated triple-A-safe]. At the same time, there were 64,000 structured finance instruments [bits of paper giving title to combinations of revenue streams] rated triple A" (Blankfein 2009).

As early as 2007, another Goldman Sachs official exclaimed that "we were seeing things that were 25 standard-deviation moves, several days in a row" (*Financial Times*, 13/08/07). If the risks were as calculated, and financial assets labelled safe were safe, then such outlandish shifts would be unlikely to occur even once in the whole life of the universe, let alone days in a row. The risks were calculated not as they really were partly because the financiers didn't know, and partly because a halfway-plausible calculation of relatively low risk was profitable.

Rather than being limited to a particular segment of finance dealing with mortgages in the USA, the US mortgage crash spread into a global financial crash. The mortgage revenues had been packaged into millions of securities (bits of paper giving title to revenues) which had been traded across the world. What had been accredited as safe, proved risky. What was thought uncorrelated, proved to be correlated. What else was risky, and how risky, no-one knew. Back in October 2007 Federal Reserve chair Ben Bernanke had said, about much of the paper circulating in the financial markets: "I would like to know what those damn things are worth" (Bernanke 2007). Financiers didn't know, either, but if they could still find someone willing to pay a price for "those damn things", then they could make money by dealing in them. Two years later, in November 2009, Bernanke said: "I'd still like to know what the stuff is worth". In between times, financiers had frozen, no longer willing to buy, or lend on the strength of, paper whose worth they didn't know.

By 2005 over 50% of US non-financial corporations' total assets were financial assets, and those assets were matched by soaring financial liabilities. The proportion was 28% in 1982; had risen steadily over the next two decades; and is back over 50% now, after dipping below that figure as financial assets lost value in the financial crisis. They were "financialised" enough that a financial crash was a crash for them, too. The financial crisis also affected their markets, as consumers lost credit. Consumer spending fell sharply from November 2007, though it then partially recovered for a few months in early 2008 before plummeting. The fall in consumer spending started some six months before the sharp rise in unemployment.

The car industry went down especially hard. General Motors and Chrysler went bankrupt, and were restructured with government aid; Ford only narrowly escaped bankruptcy. "Realising that GM was running out of cash, Fritz Henderson, then the chief financial officer, sought to raise $3 billion through a sale of bonds or shares. When it became clear after the collapse of Lehman Brothers in September that there was no chance of success, he attempted to sell some non-core assets. That too failed" (*The Economist*, 4/6/09). Sales in the USA of US-made cars had halved between November 2007 and January 2009, and then didn't regain their November 2007 level until January 2013. It was harder for buyers to get credit, and moreover they were deterred by rapidly-rising fuel prices. World oil prices more than doubled between June 2007 and June 2008. This rise was attributed to increased demand for oil from China and India, but since it was followed by an even quicker fall in oil prices in the second half of 2008, speculation must have been a big factor.

The Keynesian Moment, and Reverting to Type

The spiralling competitive rush for profit in the financial sector, which stimulated each competitor to outdo the others in ingenious or shady speculations and financial inventions, had crashed as such spirals in capitalism habitually crash; and it had brought down industry and services with it. Once the slump got going in 2008, it snowballed. Unemployment and lay-offs reduced consumer demand, which in turn reduced output further. Firms shut down. Investment plans were cancelled or postponed. Debts were called in. Finally, the cost-cutting reached a point where the surviving firms could sell off inventories and begin to raise output again.

The decline in industrial production in the USA was bigger than in 1973–5, and the global simultaneity of the slump was greater than ever before. After mid-1929, US industrial production fell for three years straight before it turned around. In 2008–9, as in 1973–5, decline levelled off more quickly, after about 18 months. Or quicker in some countries: Japan levelled off in January 2009, after industrial production started falling sharply in January 2008; Germany in April 2009, after a similar start. Brazil, India, and China all recovered faster in 2009, though they have slumped again since.

Capital owed this levelling-off to government intervention. Governments nationalised or bailed out banks. Governments nudged central banks into lowering the interest rates at which they would lend to commercial banks and into (effectively) printing more money. Governments pumped up public spending and cut taxes to offset the slump. They did that on top of the "automatic stabilisers" by which governments with large social programs pump extra demand into the economy in recessions because spending on items like unemployed benefit rises and tax revenues shrink.

The first G20 summit, convened in the heat of the crisis in November 2008, included as the most specific commitment in its declaration: "within the next 12 months, we will refrain from raising new barriers to investment or to trade in goods and services, imposing new export restrictions, or implementing World Trade organisation (WTO) inconsistent measures to stimulate exports". The governments largely stuck to that. There have been some protectionist measures since 2008, but nothing drastic yet. The governments applied the lessons about offsetting slumps taught by monetarists (pump up the money supply) and by Keynesians (pump up government budget deficits). Yet the bottoming-out of the crash in 2009 was not followed by a smart revival.

The Toronto G20 summit in June 2010 said, in terms unusually precise for such declarations: "Advanced economies have committed to fiscal plans that will at least halve deficits by 2013 and stabilize or reduce government debt-to-GDP ratios by 2016". Its recommendations for future economic growth prioritised "labour market reforms... wage bargaining systems to support employment... strengthening competition in the service sector... further reducing the barriers to foreign competition... enhancing foreign investment opportunities".

This sharp turn to neoliberal cuts policies came not when revival seemed assured, but at around the same time that the government debt crises in Eurozone countries exploded. In May 2010, Greece; in December 2010, Ireland; in May 2011, Portugal; and in May 2013, Cyprus, became unable to get fresh loans in the global financial markets to meet their debt repayments, and went for "bail-outs" from the European Central Bank, the EU, and the IMF. The "bail-out" loans in fact served to pay off the international banks who held debt from those countries, so that the countries ended up still in debt, but to the international capitalist public agencies. In return for this double-edged service, the countries' governments were required to chop social spending, privatise, and introduce "structural reforms" in labour markets to curb workers' rights. In all the affected countries, the governments first entering the "bail-outs" fell, and sometimes their replacements fell too. But all their governments, including those formed by parties which had previously criticised "bail-out" terms, ended up enforcing those terms. Even the Syriza government elected in Greece in January 2015 did that.

In summer 2011 Spain and Italy came near having to apply for similar "bail-outs". Those governments became able to function again by borrowing on global markets only after the European Central Bank, in July 2012, announced that it was willing to buy up bonds of Eurozone governments and would do "whatever it takes to preserve the euro". Nevertheless, they had to carry out cuts similar to those imposed on the governments in "bail-out" programs and, like them, suffered economic depression.

As early as summer 2009, Germany adopted a balanced-budget amendment to its constitution (though with provision for it to be flouted in emergency). In March 2012, the Eurozone formally adopted a Fiscal Stability Treaty requiring its member states to run almost-balanced budgets.

The Obama administration in the USA shifted to social cuts not so clearly through ideological decision, but rather as an outcome of its battles with the Republicans in Congress in summer 2011 over increasing the USA's ceiling, set by law, on federal debt. State governments had been making cuts long before that, despite the federal government's Keynesian stimulus policy. As I wrote in *Solidarity*,[2] "Standard and Poor's, Fitch, and Moody's have got their way. Three relatively small New York finance companies have strong-armed the mighty US government into big cuts in social spending." Standard and Poor's, Fitch, and Moody's are the "ratings agencies" which had threatened to mark down the US government's IOUs (bonds) to less than 100% good-as-gold. Their threat was so powerful that it pulled into line both the right-wing "Tea Party" Republicans who wanted a financial panic so that they could force even bigger social cuts, and Obama and the Democrats, who preferred smaller social cuts and reversal of the tax cuts for the rich brought in by George W Bush. The ratings agencies have intervened powerfully in the Eurozone crisis, too. Greek government IOUs (bonds) have had no chance of being rated good-as-gold, but the European Union, the European Central Bank and the Eurozone governments laboured hard to avoid having the IOUs labelled "in default" (outright rubbish).

"Why are Standard and Poor's, Fitch, and Moody's so powerful? Because, in capitalism, the market is god. The market god sometimes speaks more directly, though just as brutally, as the gods of old religions. Sometimes, as when it's a matter of the trustworthiness of IOUs, the market god needs Popes, Ayatollahs, Bishops, or High Priests to speak for it. For IOUs, the ratings agencies serve as the Popes of the market god. As with the Pope in the Catholic Church, so with the ratings agencies in the Market Church (capitalism), there is a public convention to see them as infallible even though privately everyone knows they are human. Like a Pope preaching anathema to infidels after he has been found

2 "Popes of the market curse the USA's poor" *Solidarity*, 3 August 2011, page 5 (http://www.workersliberty.org/files/213.pdf).

out collaborating with Nazis or conniving in Vatican financial misdeeds, the ratings agencies are revered now only three years after they were shown up in 2008 as having rated lots of bank IOUs good-as-gold when in fact they were dodgy. The agencies' mistakes were a big factor in the 2008 crash.

"The governments agree to treat the ratings agencies as the voice of the market god because they think that agreed fiction is necessary for 'market discipline' to work – just as an agreement to hear the Pope as inspired by god is necessary for the Catholic Church to work. Actually, over $5 trillion of the US government's $14.3 trillion IOUs are I-owe-me's – debts owed to other bits of the USA's public authorities, the Federal Reserve, the USA's social security fund, and so on. There was no real problem about increasing the USA's legal debt limit. The debt limit row gave the ratings agencies the chance to step in as the voice of the market god, and to enforce social cuts for the poor in a USA where inequality has already been spiralling for decades".

Thus, the chief capitalist governments, only months after the initial economic crash had levelled off, set aside the "Keynesian" deficit-budget policies which they had so recently used. They continued monetary policies which were unusual, but in line with the long-sketched analysis by right-wing economists Milton Friedman and Anna Schwartz of the 1930s depression (Friedman and Schwartz 2016): low official interest rates, printing extra money, and "quantitative easing" (buying up financial paper from banks and thus supplying them with extra cash: detailed analysis has found that this policy increases economic inequality. Montecino and Epstein 2015.) The governments shelved the criticisms of pre-2007 economic-policy orthodoxy which had flourished in 2008–9.

And they did that with broad consensus at the top of capitalist politics, despite criticism from middle-of-the-road economists. The Social Democrats in Germany governed in coalition with Angela Merkel from 2005 to 2009 and again from 2013. Francois Hollande in France spoke of higher taxes on the rich and similar policies in his 2012 presidential election campaign, but then went for social cuts and new laws to repeal worker rights. In Britain, Gordon Brown, as Labour prime minister, denied that the crisis called for social cuts until September 2009, and then stressed that the cuts should be small and delayed. Ed Balls, who would be Labour shadow chancellor from October 2010 to May 2015, made a speech on 27 August 2010 arguing for a "classic Keynesian response" and no cuts until renewed growth was "fully secured" (Balls, 2010). Then, when his 2010 argument against the Tory government's economic policy was confirmed in practice, Balls moved to supporting the Tory cuts and pay freezes with only small reservations.

The exception among major capitalist governments is the Abe administration in Japan, which from December 2012 declared a program of tax cuts, increases in money supply from the central bank, and public spending, designed to restore modest price inflation and growth. Japan has run budget deficits of about 8% of GDP since then, and in fact since 2009. Profits in Japan have increased somewhat, while they have remained low in the Eurozone; but GDP has grown only modestly, and in April 2016 industrial production was still 3% lower than in 2010.

"Safe to Invest"

Analysis of the reasons for the shift by capitalist governments back to cuts, marketising, and privatising takes us into an examination of the underlying patterns of world capitalism, and thus into theorising about the crisis. The official explanation for this shift was summarised by British Chancellor George Osborne in his Mansion House speech of 16 June 2010: "What business will invest with confidence if they fear ever higher deficits will lead to ever higher taxes? What family will spend with confidence if they fear ever higher debts mean ever higher interest rates? That is why we have moved at a brisk pace in the six weeks since the general election". He strengthened his argument by citing Greece as a scarecrow. "We see now with countries like Greece that what began as a crisis of liquidity and then solvency in banking systems, has been succeeded by market fears about the solvency of some of the governments that stand behind them. I do not want that question ever to be asked of Britain..." Obviously, Britain was nowhere near Greece's plight. Osborne's gist was this: cuts could be expansionary because of their good effect on business confidence. The cuts would increase the confidence of capitalists that in this country they could be sure not to have to deal with tax rises or debt crises. Osborne, and those who thought like him, were patient about when the regained confidence would produce growth, for they stuck to their cuts plans when, in the Eurozone and in Britain, the short-term results were stagnation.

The core idea was stated more briefly by German Chancellor Angela Merkel at the end of 2011, as she was steering the Eurozone towards the Fiscal Stability Treaty. The priority, she said, was to "show that Europe is a 'safe place to invest'." (*Financial Times*, 5/12/11).

Here we have the principle of capitalist government in the era of vastly mobile global capital and fast-mutating global production chains. As New Labour's ex-CBI minister Digby Jones put it, the job of a government is to fashion its country as a "product" attractive to the global wealthy seeking sites for their operations (Guardian, 8 February 2008). Academics sum it up in such terms as: "The prevailing view of the role of government is more facilitative than interventionist" (Dunning and Lundan 2008, p. 399). Or: "The role of... governments today is to establish the infrastructure that will attract the factors of production. Only by doing so will their economy receive the investments that are central to economic development" (Simerly 2000). Or: "Neoliberalism rationalised the transfer of state capacity to allocate resources inter-temporally (the balance between investment and consumption) and inter-sectorally (the distribution of investment, employment and output) towards an increasingly internationally integrated (and US-led) financial sector" (Saad-Filho and Johnston 2005, p. 4). Or: "the burden on all states to create 'a good business climate' to attract and retain geographically mobile capital" (Harvey 2005 p. 117).

To build or nurture an integrated industrial base within the country, which was central in previous eras, is no longer central. Growth, in and of itself, and in measurable short terms, is not central either. The new doctrine is not classic laissez faire. The government must develop and regulate infrastructure and education; organise a "flexible" labour market, with an adequate level of unemployment to keep it boss-friendly; manage social peace; keep social overheads low and regulation light though at least minimally stabilising; open doors for foreign direct investment; create new investment openings by privatisation; maintain its currency as a reliable, easily-traded token in global markets; and ensure that its government bonds figure in markets as reliable and easily-traded. There is more than one choice it can make between priorities in that package (not all governments cover all priorities), and there is more than one way it can serve each priority. There is scope for governments moving a different way from their first choices, and they may be forced to do that by democratic mobilisation. The PT (Workers' Party) administration in Brazil in 2002–10 reduced inequality significantly (Saad-Filho and Morais, 2014), even though it operated within a neoliberal framework. The flight of the PT (under Dilma Rousseff) in November 2014 to neoliberal austerity, and the way a new right-wing surge in Brazil overtook that flight with the "impeachment" coup of May 2016, shows the limits. The resilient, consensus-commanding, hard-core principle is: run things so as to make the country an attractive site for global capital.

Global capitalists were willing to see drastic "Keynesian" measures in 2008–9 when otherwise, as US president George W Bush put it in September 2008, "this sucker could go down". They were especially willing since many of them were direct beneficiaries of the "Keynesian" measures, and the others could see that if their weaker brothers and sisters collapsed dramatically, then there would be no markets for them. Contrary to some comment from the left, the bourgeoisie was not pixilated by strict neo-liberal doctrine. But once the immediate crash was over, the very fact of economic dysfunction spurred governments to revert to the neoliberal norms, and big business to support that move. Another element was summed up by Rahm Emanuel, president Obama's chief of staff.

"You never want a serious crisis to go to waste," he told a *Wall Street Journal* conference of corporate bosses (WSJ, 21 November 2008). The crisis provided an opportunity to rush through long-desired erosions of workers' rights, privatisations, marketisations.

In 2008 critics of neoliberal high theory had been confident, and its defenders evasive. Asked about his famous "efficient markets hypothesis", Eugene Fama replied that "it did quite well in this episode". Then, asked what had caused the recession if markets were so efficient, he replied: "That's where economics has always broken down. We don't know what causes recessions... We've never known... Economics is not very good at explaining swings in economic activity" (*New Yorker*, 13 January 2010). Robert Lucas, another of the most celebrated neoliberal economists, airily declared that it was impossible for economics to forecast "sudden falls in the value of financial assets, like the declines that followed the failure of Lehman Brothers in September" (*The Economist*, 6 August 2009). The tight bonding in today's global capitalism between uncontrolled global markets, intricate and mutating global production chains, and government priorities, and the concentrated power of high finance as a strategic lobby, explains why so soon neoliberalism was more strident than ever.

Greg Mankiw, author of the world's most influential economics textbook and chair of George W Bush's Council of Economic Advisers in 2003–5, had commented ruefully even before the crash: "New classical [Lucas's school] and new Keynesian [Mankiw's own] research has had little impact on practical macroeconomists who are charged with the messy task of conducting actual monetary and fiscal policy" (Mankiw 2006, p. 44). The more leftish Joseph Stiglitz retorted, later, that "these models... in mindset... have had too much influence", and called for a reassembly of the orthodox economic research of "the past 30 years" into a "new macroeconomics" (Stiglitz 2011, p. 636). As the crisis broke, Mankiw wrote in the *New York Times* (28/11/08): "If you were going to turn to only one economist to understand the problems facing the economy, there is little doubt that the economist would be John Maynard Keynes". In the *Economist* article cited above, Lucas too invoked Keynes, commenting approvingly that governments had "drawn on the ideas and research of Keynes from the 1930s" to deal with the crash in 2008.

Our picture of bourgeois economic thinking around the crisis is skewed if we think that neoliberalism and Keynesianism are polar opposites. Many neoliberal economists acknowledge Keynes. Despite the panicked Labour Party leader Jim Callaghan telling the Labour Party conference in 1976: "We used to think that you could spend your way out of a recession... I tell you in all candour that that option no longer exists", most neoliberal economists think that deficit spending is mandatory for governments in acute crises like 2008. What they reject are elements latched on to Keynes's economics in the 1960s: the idea (born of bourgeois overconfidence after a period of fairly smooth expansion) that deficit spending could be "fine-tuned" so as to eliminate crises, and (to varying extents, and not all of them) the social welfare philosophy (imprinted on orthodox bourgeois thinking by the strength of the labour movement).

Reason, analysis of the 1930s, and comparison of the stagnant Eurozone and its drastic budget-balancing with the slacker regime and greater growth in the USA indicate that the turn back to tight neoliberalism has played a big part in the depression since 2010. It cannot be explained by the hegemony of neoliberal economic theory; rather, social and political conditions explain the resilience of the apparently-shattered intellectual hegemony. We need to look deeper into the anatomy of capitalism, of crises, of depressions, and of today's capitalism. Here I move away from narrative and into debate and dispute with the writers whose views are collected here.

Crises and Finance

A debate about the rate of profit runs across the different contributions in this book. Some contributors argue that the rate of profit has been on a downward trend since the 1970s or earlier, and that the crisis of 2008 came fundamentally from that trend, or from the breakdown of untenable temporary fixes which stalled the trend for a while. Others argue that the rate of profit recovered, on the whole, despite setbacks and an increase in the febrility of the system, from 1982 through to the 2000s. Some see it as more or less mandatory for Marxists to explain crises, or depressions, by declining profit rates: to do otherwise is not just (they believe) empirically wrong, but theoretically un-Marxist.

The balance of evidence and debate indicates to me that profits did recover after about 1982, that the 2008 crash was not set off by declining profit rates, and, indeed, that declining profit rates are not usually or generally the trigger of crisis. Crises are endemic to capitalism. They are sudden imbalances between different economic flows which, rather than being quickly corrected by adjustments in supply, demand, or price, escalate, creating a spiral of imbalances and blockages and thus general economic decline. Crises, therefore, cannot be read off from "snapshot" ratios in the capitalist economy, whether between profits and capital-stock (as in some falling-rate-of-profit theories of crisis) or between wage-bill and total product (as in some "underconsumption" theories of crisis). They develop from imbalances in time.

As Marx put it: "There would be no overproduction, if demand and supply corresponded to each other, if the capital were distributed in such proportions in all spheres of production, that the production of one article involved the consumption of the other, and thus its own consumption... Since, however, capitalist production can allow itself free rein only in certain spheres, under certain conditions, there could be no capitalist production at all if it had to develop simultaneously and evenly in all spheres. Because absolute over-production takes place in certain spheres, relative over-production occurs also in the spheres where there has been no over-production...

"If production were proportionate, there would be no over-production. The same could be said if demand and supply corresponded to each other, or if all spheres provided equal opportunities for capitalist production and its expansion... over-production takes place because all these pious wishes are not fulfilled. Or, in even more abstract form: There would be no over-production in one place, if overproduction took place to the same extent everywhere...

"[Bourgeois denial of the possibility of general overproduction] rests on abstracting from money and from the fact that we are not concerned with the exchange of products, but with the circulation of commodities, an essential part of which is the separation of purchase and sale... In world market crises, all the contradictions of bourgeois production erupt collectively; in particular crises (particular in their content and in extent) the eruptions are only sporadical, isolated and one-sided. Over-production is specifically conditioned by the general law of the production of capital: to produce to the limit set by the productive forces, that is to say, to exploit the maximum amount of labour with the given amount of capital, without any consideration for the actual limits of the market or the needs backed by the ability to pay..." (Marx 1969 p. 532, 534–535).

In good times capital, by its very nature, tends to self-expand out of proportion to markets, or at least to some markets. In those good times capitalists race to compete to invest first in new fields. From the race follows a flood of potential output from the new investments, and a hesitation to invest more since capacity and costs (interest, wages) are now relatively high. The race falters. Debt, which has soared in the upturn, now bites. Some capitalists who have stretched their credit cannot meet the payments they have already committed themselves to. The race goes into sharp reverse: capitalists scrabble for cash, restrict credit, postpone investments, lay off workers, shut down operations, in a snowballing process, until eventually the cost-cutting from crisis reaches the point where the stronger capitalists, who have survived the crash, can expand again and start a new cycle. As well as these cyclical crises, there are also longer periods in which the cyclical upturns are weaker, and the cyclical downturns sharper; others, in which the cyclical upturns are stronger, and the downturns milder.

In terms of this general scheme, the unusual feature of the 2008 crisis is that there was no giddy surge of productive investment and associated debt, not even in particular sectors, leading up to the crisis. US total non-residential real fixed investment had risen from 2003 Q1 (after its slump following the 2001 dot com crisis) to 2008 Q1 before falling 20% to 2009 Q4, but at a historically modest 6% p.a. US non-financial corporate business's investment in industrial equipment rose until 2007 Q3 (after which it fell 28% to 2010 Q1), but again modestly. Real gross private domestic fixed investment in nonresidential structures rose faster, at 13% p.a., from 2005 Q4 to 2007 Q4, before slowing down and then falling, from 2008 Q2 to 2010 Q1, by 34%; but non-financial corporations' debt burden had recently been, if anything, declining, at least up to 2006 Q3.

As James Crotty notes, "Marx's criticisms of schools of thought that see all crises as imposed by 'irresponsible' financial activity on an otherwise crisis-free capitalism have been frequently misinterpreted as an argument that the financial system is an unimportant aspect of his crisis theory" (Crotty 1985). It is an important aspect. The expansion of finance is endemic to capital. Marx explained some of the dynamic in *Capital* volume 2. As capitalist production becomes more layered and concatenated, and as circulation speeds up, capitalist firms more and more need cash-in-hand to see them through and evade delays. On the basis of those needs in production, inevitably, a vast secondary market develops, in which financiers trade the bits of paper which represent the firms' pledges of revenues in return for cash advanced.

A capitalist crisis is not a quiet trend, like a rate of profit drifting downwards or a slow rate of growth: it is a sudden convulsion. Capitalists rush to get cash, but can't get it; credit dries up; some capitalists can't even make the payments due on past credit transactions. All that is financial.

Normal, "respectable", "productive" capitalism organically and usually generates "abnormal", "irresponsible", swindle-packed finance. In Marx's terms, capitalist production organically drives beyond its own inbuilt limits and hence into crises; but it is "banking and credit [which] become the most potent means" of doing so, and "the most effective vehicles of crises and swindle".

To say this is not at all to say that capitalism can be made healthy by regulation of finance. Regulated finance can limit slumps. At the limit, it can produce something like the Khrushchev-Brezhnev USSR, where all credit was nominally under the control of the central government, and the result was a stop-go lurching between sneaky bit-by-bit expansion of credit beyond central government wishes, followed by exasperated reinings-in, which gave the economy slow growth and a varying but constantly disproportionate number of unproductive half-finished projects. Even in western Europe and the USA, the 1930s, as governments intervened more, produced continued depression rather than new financial crashes. The sharp downturn of May 1937 in the USA was triggered by Federal Reserve restrictions on credit and US government cuts in spending and increases in taxes, rather than by a financial-sector crash (Romer 2009).

That does not mean that capitalism would be stable and prosperous if only it had better financial regulation. In the first place, to get from here to that tight regulation would require a great raising of economic barriers between countries, and a consequent great depression. In second place, if and when the system got there, it would only be to a stumbling shuffle. And, third, stricter financial regulation, especially if not coupled with comprehensive state control over all large-scale economic activity, as in the USSR, is likely to stimulate recourse to shady off-the-books expedients which lead to pissing into the capitalist tent from outside.

Minsky vs Marx?

Debates about the dynamics of capitalist crisis are sometimes posed in terms of "Marx versus Minsky". The writings of the maverick Keynesian economist Hyman Minsky are, indeed, slight compared to Marx's. There is nothing there about how economic life comes to be shaped by the drive for profit, how the relation between workers and capitalists develops, how the technology and organisation of production is shaped, or indeed about the dynamics of how capitalism becomes inherently "financialised". There is, however, discussion of how the capitalist financial system can become the vehicle of crisis, more rounded discussion than was possible for Marx, and with empirical reference to a capitalism much more "financialised" than Marx could know. There is nothing un-Marxist about seeing 2008 as a "Minsky moment".

Minsky came from a Menshevik émigré family background. As a school student in the late 1930s he was a member of the American Socialist Party youth group, where he probably came across Trotskyists. He studied with Oskar Lange, Henry Simons, Frank Knight, and Josef Schumpeter, and became an economics lecturer at the University of California, Berkeley, from 1957 to 1965. He supported the 1964–5 Free Speech Movement at Berkeley, a big starting-point for late-1960s student radicalism; or, at least, he was one of only two lecturers who tried to intervene to stop a mass arrest of the protesting students (*Columbia Daily Spectator*, 18 December 1964). He was active in the left-liberal Americans for Democratic Action.

In 1965 he moved from Berkeley to a smaller, quieter university, and remained in a quiet academic world until his death in 1996. According to one biographer, he moved because he decided to focus on academic research rather than political activism. His economic writings were convoluted and opaque. Despite his family background, and although he referred to Marx as a great pioneer comparable to Darwin or Einstein, he saw Marxism as a "sterile theorising" that "within a capitalist economy nothing useful could be done to counteract depressions". His writings suggest he never studied Marx seriously. He rejected "complete socialism" by equating it to Stalinism. He favoured "a humane, decentralised socialism", "an economy in which leading sectors are socialised, communal consumption satisfies a large proportion of private needs... taxation of income and wealth is designed to decrease inequality". He saw the British Labour Party as conservative relative to that program (Minsky 1975, pp. 6–7, 145, 164, 156). His writings give no signal that he saw his version of socialism as connected to working-class struggle.

Minsky argued "an analysis of investment under conditions of uncertainty and with capitalist financial usages is the core of... theory". "There are really two systems of prices in a capitalist economy – one for current output and the other for capital assets", which are bought and sold not for use but for their capacity to yield future revenues. The evolution of the asset-price level is decisively shaped by uncertainty. "Uncertainty" here means what Keynes called "irreducible uncertainty", and others call "Knightian uncertainty". The outcome of tossing a coin is uncertain, but we know the probability of heads: ½. Whether the euro will survive another decade is uncertain in the more radical sense that we cannot even confidently calculate a probability.

In capitalist booms the indefiniteness of uncertainty, and the capacity of banks to create new money in response to investors' demands, works to expand debt faster than the future revenues-from-assets which must cover it. As Mian and Sufi put it, more crisply than Minsky, "debt enhances the buying power of optimists", and pessimists are willing to lend because they have well-founded confidence in the collateral or because of systematically "neglected risks" (new ones, or ones from which financiers systematically over-create new securities just because the risks are "neglected") (Mian and Sufi 2015). The price level of revenue-yielding assets rises faster than the current-goods price level. In their market "a rise in the relative prices of some set of financial instruments or capital assets may very well increase the quantity demanded". An "euphoric economy" develops.

"Stability is destabilising", and even more so if there is a "socialisation of risks", i.e. adventurous capitalists know that public authorities are likely to bail them out if things go bad. "The tendency to transform doing well into a speculative investment boom is the basic instability in a capitalist economy". An increasing number of "Ponzi units" develops – businesses which rely not just on near-future assured revenues, but on being able to sell assets at high prices, to meet their bills (Minsky, 2008).

Eventually interest rates rise. The boom continues for a while, but some previously non-Ponzi units are now Ponzi, because debt-service payments are bigger, and Ponzi units have to sell more and more assets. The price level for revenue-yielding assets drops. Ponzi units go bust. Interest rates rise further. Credit contracts. Capitalists rush for liquidity. There is a "Minsky moment". A crash.

If the economy has a fast-rising current-goods price level (i.e. high inflation), and the central bank and the government respond judiciously, then liquidity recovers quite fast. There will be a reasonably rapid general recovery, but at a low level of growth (stagflation). If the current-goods price level is not fast-rising, then the slump will worsen further, through deflation of financial-asset prices, before it mends.

Minsky's argument, I submit, is an extension of an idea sketched by Marx in an unfinished form. Marx wrote no even provisionally "finished" theory of crisis. In his most sustained discussion of crises, in his 1861–3 drafts for *Capital*, he argued that: "The real crisis can only be educed from the real movement of capitalist production, competition, and credit". He insisted that crises must be analysed in the interaction between production and circulation – on the money side as well as the commodity side, and on the financial-assets side as well as the current-output side – and not in production alone (Marx 1969, p. 512, 507, 513, etc.).

He saw crises being generated by booms in a pattern similar to Minsky's. Thus in the run-up to the crisis of 1846: "The enticingly high profits had led to far more extensive operations than justified by the available liquid resources. Yet there was credit – easy to obtain and cheap... All inland quotations [share prices] were higher than ever before. Why then allow this splendid opportunity to escape? Why not go in for all one was worth?"

"Banking and credit... become the most potent means of driving capitalist production beyond its own limits, and one of the most effective vehicles of crises and swindle". "The credit system appears as the main lever of over-production and over-speculation in commerce... the reproduction process, which is elastic by nature, is here forced to its extreme limits... The credit system accelerates the material development of the productive forces and the establishment of the world-market... At the same time credit accelerates the violent eruptions of this contradiction – crises – and thereby the elements of disintegration of the old mode of production" (Marx 1977, p. 407, 607, 441).

Phases

According to Robert Brenner, the "golden age" of European, US, and Japanese capitalism, between the Korean war boom and the early 1970s, was based on a "highly dynamic, but ultimately highly unstable, symbiosis". "Both the German and Japanese economies prospered to no small degree by virtue of their ability to dynamise rapidly progressing regional economic blocs in Europe and East Asia by supplying them with increasingly high-powered capital goods. Still, it was the ability of German and Japanese manufacturers to wrest ever greater shares of the world market from US (and UK) producers that ultimately made possible their post-war economic 'miracles'. Again, however, this capacity to seize market share could only come into play because of the willingness of the US government to tolerate not only the broad opening of the US economy to overseas penetration, but even a certain decline in US manufacturing competitiveness in the interests of US military and political hegemony, international economic stability, and the rapid expansion overseas of US multinational corporations and banks" (Brenner 1998).

That benign imbalance was possible only because the US economy, hugely dominant in the capitalist world market of 1945, faltered so little. Its growth was slower than the other advanced capitalist countries (except the UK), it was wobbly before the Korean war boom of the early 1950s, and it suffered a downturn in 1957–8 sharper than other advanced capitalist countries had in the 1950s and 60s. Yet it grew fairly fast and steadily, without a downturn equivalent to those of 1974–5, 1980–2, 1908, or 1893–4, let alone the 1930s or after 2008.

There were high rates of profit in the US at the end of World War II, resulting from the compression of wages in the 1930s slump and in wartime. But World War I was followed in the US by a boom which ended in the crash of 1929. Why was it not the same after World War II? The slump-dampening, demand-sustaining role of high military spending, and higher state spending generally, was a relative stabiliser. The international framework was also important. After 1945 the US capitalist class, trying to learn from the experiences of 1917–29, deliberately set about reconstructing Europe, and the framework of international trade, on different lines. Instead of the crippling reparations payments demanded from Germany after World War I, there was the Marshall Plan. And there was the Bretton Woods system of gradually-freer international trade, based on a dollar guaranteed against gold. The gradual freeing of trade between the big capitalist powers had a dynamising effect on those economies. Although the US was losing markets (relatively) to German, Japanese (etc.) capital, it still dominated. Its exports rose. Almost every year until 1976, the US ran a trade surplus, and every year until 1966, a large one. When markets in the US slumped, US corporations could find other markets overseas. They were also cushioned by a steadily-rising flow of income from their expanding assets overseas. The dollar's role as world money allowed the US to send overseas, in military spending, aid to client governments, and investments, much larger sums that warranted by its trade surplus. As early as 1962, according to the Federal Reserve's estimates, over 40% of US-dollar notes and coins were held outside the USA: it's now probably over 70% (Judson 2012). Finance was still "repressed" by capitalist governments, and mostly boxed in to national frameworks; but, effectively, the USA supplied credit to the world market by printing dollars. It held the ring for a dynamising but ultimately destabilising revival of autonomous and globally-traded finance. Until it was troubled by its huge spending abroad on the Vietnam war in the late 1960s, the US government did not have to worry about its balance of payments. It was not condemned to "stop-go" like British governments.

At the watershed of the late 1960s and early 70s, the conditions broke down for the "highly dynamic symbiosis" of unevenly-developing segments of the advanced capitalist world. Although politically and strategically the US remained hegemonic, its industrial advantage had been whittled back. The combined effects of that fact, of the economic drain of the Vietnam war, and of the steadily-accumulating mass of "Eurodollars" at large (both actual dollar notes, and dollar-denominated bank deposits), broke the Bretton Woods framework. The dollar was devalued.

"Globalist", internationalised, interests, growing over the decades, had achieved dominance in the various ruling classes. Despite considerable pressures for protectionism, the big capitalist governments maintained fairly free trade. They set exchange rates to float freely, but managed them carefully even at the expense of immediate domestic imperatives. This would be demonstrated most spectacularly under the Thatcher government in Britain in the early 1980s, when one-quarter of all manufacturing employment was trashed through an economic policy whose main pay-back was the scope it gave to big UK-based firms to buy many assets overseas.

In the new regime of floating exchange rates the multinational corporations whose power had expanded in the great upswing wanted freedom to move funds from one country to another at will. Otherwise they would risk huge losses on funds held in the "wrong" form in the "wrong" country at the "wrong" time. Exchange controls were scrapped, and global financial markets expanded dizzily. The US now needed to bother about its balance of payments and the level of the dollar, which dived alarmingly in the late 1970s. Its balance of trade went into deficit.

Many Marxists write of the "failure" of Keynesian policies in the 1970s. However, to argue that the Keynesian "fine-tuning" briefly fashionable in the 1960s was an illusion, or that Keynesian policies (the state acting to sustain effective demand in the economy) cannot ensure an indefinite smooth capitalist upswing is one thing. It is another to contend that they can play no role in dampening recessions, not even in the big capitalist national economies of the 1950s and 60s, more protected than today from external destabilising pressures. Marx, discussing the 1846–7 crisis in Britain in *Capital* volume 3, identified a government measure, the suspension of the 1844 Bank Act, as the turning-point to capitalist recovery. He argued that the crash had been "carried more or less to extremes by mistaken legislation". He did not argue that capitalist crises were more-or-less automatic processes, immune to being made deeper by inept, or shallower by astute, capitalist government policies. Keynesian policies did not fail – from the point of view of their capitalist promoters – in the 1970s. They engineered a recovery from the 1973–5 slump within about 18 months, and sufficient revival to avert a further radicalisation of the workers' movements – all at a cost, but the bourgeoisie had no way of doing those things without cost. Their success prepared the conditions for capitalist governments to shift to the aggressive "opening-up-to-world-competition" policies of the 1980s and 90s. The relatively stabilising effect for capitalism of large state expenditures remains. In 2008–9, too, the "Keynesian moment" of crisis management was effective. It could not stop the 2008 crash, or stop the recovery from 2009 being slow and erratic; it could brake the crash before it fell as far as in the early 1930s.

Finance, which in the great upswing had been the handmaiden of industry, stepped forward in the 1970s, and more in the 1980s. Where the reserves of the world's central banks (excluding gold) had risen by a modest 3.4% a year between 1950 and 1969, they surged by 21% a year between 1970 and 1979. For non-financial corporations in the US, in the 1960s, net interest accounted for less than a tenth of the amount of profits from production; by the 1980s and 90s, for 30 or 40% as much as profits directly from production. A much bigger proportion of total profits appears as the profits of financial rather than non-financial enterprises. Many of us had thought US hegemony was already declining, and set to decline further, by the late 1960s. In fact, at least until now, US hegemony has continued, pivoted now on its central role in global financial markets. Despite the 2008 crash hitting the USA first, it generated a rush of wealth not out of US Treasury paper and dollars, but into them, as the safest and most liquid forms available.

It is not the case that the new rise of finance directly depresses output by diverting capital from production to speculation. A doubling, or trebling, of "fictitious capital" swirling round the financial markets means more "fiction" spun out of the underlying labour processes and expectations of revenue, not less capital in production. Financial speculators cannot work just by swindling each other, but only by vying to siphon revenues from the real production of goods and services. The domination of finance does give a depressive bias to the economy. Holding cash to make good promised revenues from financial assets takes precedence over productive expansion. Since the early 1980s business investment has increased much less than profits; corporations have paid out much more in dividends and share buybacks (and pay-outs to top bosses); the luxury consumption-goods sector has exploded. The top 13% of households in the USA buy as much in consumer goods and services as the bottom 50% (calculated from BLS 2014). "Patrimonial" wealth is resurgent, as Thomas Piketty's book on *Capital in the 21st Century* has shown. Its political power is resurgent too. The new surge of financialisation enables financial capitalists to develop a "second exploitation", drawing surplus-value directly from workers' budgets through debt charges, and recalling Marx's comment in the *Communist Manifesto*: "No sooner is the exploitation of the labourer by the manufacturer, so far, at an end, that he receives his wages in cash, then he is set upon by the other portions of the bourgeoisie, the landlord, the shopkeeper, the pawnbroker, etc." Financial capitalists have also been able to siphon much surplus-value from industrial capital: they and their allies used "neoliberalism as a new technology of power to help transform capitalism into a rentiers' delight" (Palma 2009). "The result of this cocktail of changes, greater inequality, greater power for the wealthy at unchanged levels of inequality, and greater political utility of the thing the wealthy had most of – money – [has, in the USA] created a new form of 'inequality multiplier': as inequality increased the rich were able to push government regulation and policy in their favour, thus creating even more inequality" (Acemoglu and Robinson 2012).

It is often said that the expansion of household debt also kept consumer demand buoyant. In the hectic mortgage market in the USA from about 1997 to 2006, many people "used their houses as ATMs", remortgaging in order to cash in on rising house prices and then spending the cash. Yet other households had lower consumer demand because so much of their income was siphoned off in debt payments. J W Mason finds: "The rise in [household] debt [in the USA] in the 1980s is explained by a rise in non-demand expenditures [i.e. expenditures which do not generate consumer demand]. Specifically, it is entirely due to the rise in interest payments, which doubled from 3–4 percent of household income in the 1950s and 1960s to over 8 percent in the late 1980s. Interest payments continued around this level up to the Great Recession, falling somewhat only in the past few years" (Mason 2014; Mason and Jayadev 2014). Bank of England research for the UK found that "increases in debt did not provide significant support to consumption" between 1992 and 2007 (Bunn and Rostum 2014). Thus, over any long-ish period, the expansion of household debt does not boost consumer demand. It only boosts the appropriation of revenues by financial capitalists.

Particular periods of exceptionally rapid growth of household debt may boost consumer demand. Periods when household credit stalls certainly depress consumer demand. That depression of demand feeds through to lower incomes, and so the brake on household credit may reduce the ratio of household debt to income only a little, or not at all. Since the crash of 2008, household debt has declined only modestly relative to household income in the UK and most other richer capitalist countries, declined a bit more in the USA, and actually increased in some. Higher household debt, generally, is a destabilising factor (Mian and Sufi 2015), not one which stabilises by propping up consumer demand. Business investment demand, and luxury consumer demand, have always been vulnerable to sudden crashes; in an economy with high household debt, mass consumer demand can be volatile too.

The new structure of capitalism is unstable, and maybe not so much because of its particularities as because of its generalities – because it represents the nearest yet to "a pure capitalism" (in Michel Husson's term). It no longer has the quirky but for-a-period-helpful imbalances, or the benignly increasing flexibility given by a gradually loosening repression of finance, of the upswing of the 1950s and 60s. The world market, more and more important for individual capitalists, is increasingly synchronised. The world market has only the flimsiest of stabilisers in the IMF and the World Bank and coordinated action through the G7 or G20 – even assuming those bodies do not act to accentuate slumps, as the IMF is widely reckoned to have done in Asia in 1997–8. A movement from protectionism and "financial repression" to free trade and fast global flows of finance tends to dynamise a capitalist world; the free-trade regime, once arrived at, tends to destabilise it.

That business investment has increased much less than profits in the neoliberal era, and that banks and corporations have tended to keep bigger and bigger cash reserves, is a puzzle (except for some writers who argue that, rightly calculated, profits have not increased). The trend for corporations to hold relatively bigger cash reserves dates back to the early 1980s, in the USA anyway, but has increased since the crash. (Bates 2006, Graham 2015, Mason 2015).

Husson (2008) explains the problem as a lack of profitable investment outlets. He refers to "exhaustion of productivity gains" as a cause of that lack of investment outlets. He contrasts today's "drift of social demand from manufactured goods to services" with the role played in the 1950s and 1960s by the car industry, where productivity rose and where the industry's expansion generated expansion of road-building and other associated industries. Although on many issues I think I have learned more from Husson than others, I do not find his argument here convincing.

For a start, world car production has continued to rise. For a long time, the rise was below the peak expansion rate of the 1960s (6.2% per annum increase in production of cars and commercial vehicles, 1961–71). But it was still a rise: 3.4% p.a. 1971–81, 2.1% p.a. 1981–91, 3.1% 1991–2001. Then production rose at 5.8% p.a. 2001–7. It crashed in 2008–9, and after recovering in 2010 stagnated in 2011 and 2012, but rose by 7.0% p.a. 2012–14 (US government figures[3]). More fundamentally, why does there have to be just one industry which is the focus of investment, and why do profitable industries have to be those in which productivity is rising? For example, healthcare and education have been expanding. Healthcare is highly profitable where it is private, e.g. in the USA. Even when healthcare and education are publicly-run or non-profit, they generate big multipliers in pharmaceutical industries, biotech, care homes, construction, information technology. IT has rising productivity and, again, many multipliers. Or transport and logistics. In fact, these expansive sectors have not been weighty enough to lift overall investment levels, but just the fact that they are several (rather than one core industry) does not explain that.

An alternative explanation for low investment is structural "short-termism", which both feeds and is fed by "financialisation" and economic volatility. If General Motors or IBM made a big investment in the 1950s or 60s, they could feel fairly sure of long-term returns. The bosses of GM or IBM in the 1950s and 60s were "corporation men" (almost all men) who measured their success by the growth and long-term profits of the corporation, rather than year-by-year dividend payouts; by the growth of that particular complex of capital, not the mathematical expansion, in calculable time-scales, of the general form of wealth as wealth. Today "capital's ceaseless striving towards the general form of wealth", as Marx put it, takes a more direct and short-sighted form. Thus, the priority given to "shareholder value". Increasing "financialisation" and a more febrile regime, giving capitalist corporations fewer assurances about steadily-expanding markets and a stable share in those markets, have changed the strategies of productive capital and the way capitalist management is organised, with bosses moving more and more often from one corporation and being more and more focused on short-term returns. "In the name of 'creating shareholder value', the [1980s and 90s] witnessed a marked shift in the strategic orientation of top corporate managers in the allocation of corporate resources and returns away from 'retain and reinvest' and towards 'downsize and distribute'. Under the new regime, top managers downsize the corporations they control, with a particular emphasis on cutting the size of the labour forces they employ, in an attempt to increase the return on equity". (Lazonick & O'Sullivan

3 http://www.rita.dot.gov/bts/sites/rita.dot.gov.bts/files/publications/national_transportation_statistics/html/table_01_23.html_mfd.

2000. See also Mason 2015, and Dallery 2009 on "finance-oppressed accumulation"). Simultaneously, "the functioning capitalists" (as Marx put it: the captains of industry or commerce) became MBA-ised, converted into a cadre for "running business" (i.e. coining profits) in general, with relatively few roots in or ties to specific trades. MBA or MBA-type degrees per year have multiplied in the USA from 26,000 in 1970 to 168,000 in 2009, and since the 1960s the MBA (previously limited to the USA, since its origin in the early 1900s) has spread worldwide.

Profits and Crises

"It is only in so far as the appropriation of ever more and more wealth in the abstract becomes the sole motive of his operations, that [the wealth-owner] functions as a capitalist, that is, as capital personified and endowed with consciousness and a will. Use-values must therefore never be looked upon as the real aim of the capitalist; neither must the profit on any single transaction. The restless never-ending process of profit-making alone is what he aims at" (Marx, *Capital* volume 1 Chapter 4).

In capitalism, a crisis is when that "boundless greed after riches" is suddenly choked – when capitalists can no longer expand profit-making; when expansion would fail to produce profits, not only on single transactions or groups of transactions, but for a period; or when expansion is impossible because they cannot meet the payments due on past expansions. It is all about profit. But it is not about profit-rates dropping below some set level, or about gradual falls in the rate of profit. Crises are not signalled by prior sharp falls in the rate of profit, either. Usually crises set off sharp falls in the rate of profit, rather than vice versa.

What is a "low" rate of profit? Just as there is no mathematical rule stating some minimum share for workers in national income below which "underconsumption" will ruin capitalism, so also there is no rule setting a minimum rate (20%? 10%? 5%? what?) below which crisis breaks out. It is arguable that a "low" rate of profit will tend to make the system more fragile, by making industrialists quicker to cut inventories and investments when they see trouble, but that depends on them seeing the rate as "low" (by comparison with recent years, presumably) and seeing trouble. If the rate of profit gradually sinks, then, all else equal, capitalists' expectations of profit, and the rate of return they demand before making new investments, will also sink, so that demand remains buoyant. A falling rate of profit can be – and Marx argues that it generally will be – accompanied by an increased mass of profit, so the falling rate of profit still yields increasing riches to the capitalist magnates. "And thus the river of capital rolls on... or its accumulation does, not in proportion to the rate of profit, but in proportion to the impetus it already possesses" (Marx 1977, p. 245). Even if a "tendency of the rate of profit to fall", as traditionally understood by Marxists, operates most straightforwardly, it will not explain crises.

Or maybe the tendency operates strongly in booms, so the rate of profit falls relatively fast in booms until its fall precipitates a crisis? In the slump, the counter-tendencies take over and the rate of profit is restored in the downturn, only to pave the way for a new boom? Then in the business cycle profit rates would generally be highest at the very start of the recovery, and decline at increasing speed as the expansion proceeds. It is not so. Profit rates may level off or drop slightly in the last stages of the expansion, before the crisis, but that is distinguishable only with hindsight from a wobble during expansion, and during most of the expansion they rise. "Business always appears almost excessively sound right on the eve of a crash... Business is always thoroughly sound and the campaign in full swing, until suddenly the debacle takes place" (Marx 1977, p. 484).

Only one month before the BNP announcement of August 2007 which signalled that a global crisis in high finance was brewing, researchers at the Bank of International Settlements reported: "Profits growth has been strong in many developed economies in recent years, and the profit share – the share of factor income going to capital – has been high compared with historical experience. This paper shows that, rather than being a recent phenomenon, profit shares have trended upwards since about the mid 1980s in most developed economies for which comparable data are available" (Ellis and Smith, 2007).

Wages have been squeezed since the early 1980s, more tightly in the USA than elsewhere, but in all the old industrial countries, and more production has been moved to lower-wage countries. Unions have generally been weakened, and "flexibility" has been imposed on capitalist terms.

IT equipment prices have been cut by technical change, and that cheapens equipment incorporating IT, as most complex equipment does these days. Industrial equipment has generally become more compact. Industrial buildings are usually more compact, too. Even in China, where there are many giant factories like the Foxconn campus in Shenzhen, "smaller plants are replacing the vertically integrated behemoths that defined Chinese manufacturing in the early 2000s" (*Australian Financial Review*, 16 April 2015). All in all, the "cheapening of constant capital" has probably proceeded apace. Statistics for the USA suggest that, too, though some researchers detect a rising trend in relative prices of capital goods after 2004 (Basu and Vasudevan 2011, pp. 38–39). And the turnover of capital has speeded up.

Thus, the increasing trend in profit rates (modest for non-financial business, larger for financial businesses) shown by official statistics from the early 1980s to the eve of the 2007–8 crash is plausible (Basu and Vasudevan 2011, Daly and Broadbent 2009). Indeed, the official US statistics may underestimate the rise. An increasing and sizeable chunk of what should properly be reckoned as profit has been paid to top bosses as ever-multiplying "wages". For tax reasons, US corporations make inflated claims for depreciation allowances. And they hide a lot of profits in tax havens (Kincaid 2016, p. 3).

Many Marxist analysts agree that profit rates have generally risen since around 1982 (Husson 2010, Kincaid 2016). There is scope for argument, because the definition of profit rates is slippery.

Should we include the profits of financial businesses along with those of non-financial businesses? I would say yes, since those financial businesses are also part of capital. A much increased proportion of total profit has ended up in their hands; that is an important shift within capital, but not the same as a decline in the profit rate. Should we include the profits of "unincorporated" business in the USA as well as corporate? Yes, if we can get reliable figures. A not-negligible portion of surplus value goes to consultants and such. Should we count only profits on operations in the USA, or global profits? (US economic statistics are better than other countries', so much of the debate centres on US statistics). Global, because otherwise our results are likely to be skewed by transfer-pricing and tax-avoidance tactics.

Should we measure capital stock by replacement cost or by historical cost? By replacement cost, so as to get a measure of capital's self-expansion as an ongoing process. Otherwise reduced inflation automatically reduces measured profit rates. Historical-cost calculation seems right if we reckon capitalist enterprise as a one-off operation. In fact, it is ongoing. Suppose one capitalist spends £1 million on equipment, gets £1.6 million in revenues net of current costs over the life of the equipment, and then folds because equivalent equipment now costs £2 million. Another (in another time) spends £1 million, gets £1.4 million in net revenues over the equipment's lifetime, but then can continue on double the scale with two lots of equipment equivalent to the first costing £0.5 million each and keep £0.4 million for mansions, watches, yachts, etc. On historical-cost calculations the first capitalist is successfully profitable, and the second has failed. A replacement-cost calculation tracks capitalist self-expansion more accurately.

Should we measure percentage profits as a ratio to corporations' total assets, or only to capital used in production? To capital used in production. Non-financial corporations have become "financialised". Between 1932 and the early 1980s, corporations' total of equities and bonds rose broadly in line with the replacement cost of fixed assets; then "from the early 1980s until the 2007 crisis, the annual real rate of growth of corporate capitalisation nearly trebled that of the replacement cost of fixed assets" (Palma 2009, p. 47). Corporations hold more financial assets and financial liabilities. They cannot show a rate of profit on those financial assets similar to the rate on capital used in production: only capital used in production directly commands surplus value, and what we want to measure is its capacity to do so. Textbooks on accounting and corporate finance usually mention the ratio of profits to total assets, but they give more attention to other ways of calculating profit rates, which they consider "more useful" for measuring capitalist performance (Damodaran 2001, p. 95).

Figures published by Deloitte's "Centre for the Edge" (or CtfE) management consultancy show profit rates in the USA as declining steadily and dramatically since 1965 (Hagel 2013). But those figures are published, not for economic or social research, but to alarm bosses – especially in IT-heavy industries, which CtfE describes as suffering worse than others – and incite them to buy CtfE's management advice. CtfE describes the decline as due not to deep tendencies of capital, but to the spread of IT. Since (it says) IT brings constant improvements in performance, every firm is at constant risk of being outpaced. The cure, it says, is for bosses to find ways to pull in knowledge from outside the firm, especially from workers at the "edge" of the firm, and to increase workers' "passion" for their jobs. The CtfE measure varies widely and long-term between sectors, without generating any tendency for capital to move from low-CtfE-measure sectors to high-CtfE-measure sectors.

CtfE does not deny that the mass-of-profits has increased, and kept pace or better with overall output and with the mass of productive capital. It recognises that in recent decades there has been what Marxists would call "a cheapening of constant capital": industrial equipment has become cheaper. It does not deny the trends described by Marxists as an increased rate of exploitation. It denies none of the trends in production which would make Marxists expect a rise in profit rates.

On CtfE's own account, and study of the US Federal Reserve's Flow of Funds reports confirms this, the trend underlying the decline of its measure is the steady rise of financial assets as a proportion of non-financial corporations' assets. CtfE's figures essentially measure increased financialisation rather than changes in conditions of production. The very neatness of CtfE's figures should also cause doubt. Their graph shows their profit rate decreasing in a dead straight line – with only small temporary wobbles one way or another – for 47 years, just the same in one decade as the next, and with no effect from shifts in class forces or (despite CtfE's claim that IT innovation is at the root of the trend) from variations in technical change. Extrapolate the graph, and

US big business will be extinct by 2025, because by then average profits will become negative.

I conclude that on the definitions best suited to gauging profit rates as understood by Marxists and by working capitalists, profit rates were generally rising (though with serious dips at times) over the quarter-century 1982 to 2007. In any case, and this is important, the consensus of the bourgeoisie was that profit rates were rising. The mechanisms which might be set in train by the bourgeoisie panicking over plunging profit rates were not being set off around 2007.

Okishio

Marx never referred to a tendency of the rate of profit to fall in anything he readied for publication, and nor did Engels in any of his writings. Marx did not mention a tendency of the rate of profit to fall in his most sustained discussion of capitalist crises, in the notes published in *Theories of Surplus Value* part 2.

However, there was a consensus among economists in Marx's day, and later days too, that the rate of profit tended to decrease from one decade to the next. Adam Smith said the decrease was due to the diminishing "scarcity of capital". As late as the 1930s, John Maynard Keynes would accept this theory of Smith's. David Ricardo argued that there could be no such thing as an absolute abundance (non-scarcity) of capital, and that the decrease in the rate of profit was due to expanding population pushing agriculture onto less and less favourable land, thus raising the labour-time socially necessary to produce food and increasing money (though not real) wages and landlords' rent, at the expense of the capitalists. "Adam Smith, Ricardo, Marx, alike with Bohm-Bawerk and Wicksell [neo-classical economists] predicted a steady fall in the rate of profit with technical progress" (Kaldor, in Hague 1961, p. 179).

Marx demolished both Smith's and Ricardo's theories, and considered the fall in the rate of the profit to be not so "steady", but a tendency with many counter-tendencies. He did not dispute the broad idea that the rate of profit tended to fall. In the unfinished notes later published as the *Grundrisse* and *Capital* volume 3 he essayed a different explanation.

The share of variable capital in productive capital tends to fall because of increasing use of machines to replace living labour (so he argued); but profits are always based on variable capital, representing as they do the extra hours which the capitalist can get the workers to work (up to 40-odd hours a week, or whatever has become the normal working week) above the hours in which they produce the value-equivalent of their wages (maybe only 12 or 20 hours).

If the ratio of variable capital to total productive capital declines, then the ratio of profits to total productive capital – i.e. the rate of profit – must tend to decline. Cheapening of constant capital, and increase of the rate of exploitation, generally operate as counter-tendencies, and so, Marx wrote, "the law acts only as a tendency. And it is only under certain circumstances and only after long periods that its effects become strikingly pronounced" (Marx 1977 p. 237). He thought that the counter-tendencies were bound to be subordinate in the long run. There are good reasons to think that, in fact, in general, the counter-tendencies are at least as strong as the tendency.

The counter-mechanism had been explained by Marx himself in his chapter on relative surplus-value in *Capital* volume 1. Suppose capitalist A introduces new technology to produce product B. She or he will only do it if they calculate that the new technology will enable cheaper production. They can still sell B at the prices charged by the old-technology firms, so they make extra profits.

Bit by bit, the new technology spreads. The price which can be charged for B declines (or, if there is general inflation, declines relative to other prices). What is the effect of that decline on other capitalists? Maybe B is a production input. Then the other capitalists get a reduction of costs. Maybe B is a wage-good. Then capitalists can make workers' money-wages lag while leaving the workers' real wages intact or even improved. Either way, the other capitalists enjoy a reduction (or relative reduction) of costs. The only case in which other capitalists do not enjoy a reduction of costs is if B is something consumed only as a luxury by capitalists (or the state). In general, then, the bit-by-bit decline in the extra profits of capitalist A and the price of B is also a boost to the profits of other capitalists. Eventually the decline in A's profit rate and the risein other capitalists' profit rates meet – but at a higher profit rate than before. A dozen reasons can make profit rates fall at a time when new technologies are coming on stream; but none of them is the technological change as such.

The "image" conjured up by the conventional presentation of Marx's account of the tendency of rate of profit to fall is of a constantly more gigantic mass of fixed capital. In Marx's day and for decades following, the factory equipment generally became bulkier; even today, when it often becomes more compact, it becomes more complex and impressive. Won't the mass of value embodied in that equipment also constantly rise? Not quite as fast, but pretty fast? Marx, writing at a time when large machinery was new in almost all industries, and lacking access to systematic statistics, thought it would. "The capital-value employed today in spinning is 7/8 constant and 1/8 variable, whilst at the beginning of the 18th century it was ½ constant and ½ variable…", he wrote, apparently thinking that typical and a trend continuing into the future (Marx 1970, p. 623).

But the mass of value embodied in industrial buildings and equipment cannot rise as fast as first impressions suggest. Industrial equipment does not last forever. In periods of capitalist boom and rapid technical change it may get scrapped faster. In any case, the fixed capital actually existing at any time, in value terms, can only be a portion of the surplus value produced in a finite range of recent years, depreciated somewhat by its wear and tear and by intervening technical changes which have made it possible to produce that equipment by less labour-time.

If the mass of surplus value tends to increase – and Marx argues it will – then the ratio of that mass of surplus value to fixed capital, i.e. to a portion of a finite range of past years' masses of surplus value, will have some tendency to rise. Many offsetting factors can operate so as to raise the ratio of stock of fixed capital to flow of output. But it is unlikely for that ratio to rise hugely and continuously.

The best surrogate in available statistics for the ratio of capital stock to flow of labour costs is the capital-output ratio. There are many controversies over its evaluation and how well it reflects the ratio Marx had in mind. Ascension Mejorado, a writer arguing that reduced profitability contributed heavily to the 2008 crash, and that an increased capital-output ratio had "great significance" there, finds that the capital-output ratio in the USA, after increasing from the mid-60s (a trend to which much attention was given in Marxist discussions of the early 70s), then decreased from about 1982 to about 2000. Long-term, she finds a slight trend increase in capital-output ratio from 1.2 in 1900 to 1.5 in 2010 (Mejorado 2013, p. 150). Marx's argument about relative surplus value in Capital volume 1 indicates a trend for the rate of surplus value, s/v, to increase with technical change. If the long-term rise in capital-output ratios resulting from technical change is as modest as the figures suggest, then the "trend" increases in the rate of surplus value could easily outweigh it.

The argument made above, about how a technological change adopted by capitalists as profit-increasing cannot in and of itself reduce overall profit rates, was formalised mathematically in 1961 by a Japanese Marxist, Nobuo Okishio, and is known as "Okishio's Theorem" (Bowles 1981). The mathematics (the Perron-Frobenius theorem of 1907–12 about eigenvalues of square matrices with non-negative entries) was similar to that used in Piero Sraffa's book *Production of Commodities by Means of Commodities*. Many have seen the "theorem" as linked to the critique of Marx developed by some writers following

Sraffa (not by Sraffa himself), though in fact the substantive argument does not depend on any grand claim for the mathematical formalisation, or any of the post-Sraffian critique. Dozens of articles have claimed to refute Okishio; unconvincingly, I think. Andrew Kliman (1996) usefully summarises a number of those attempted refutations as well as offering his own.

Kliman's argument is built on his interpretation of value and price theory, in which values and prices of commodities are not determined by labour-times and market exchanges "simultaneously", but sequentially. "Input prices differ from output prices, and input values differ from output values. [And] the price paid to acquire an input is the sum of value advanced for it". So, prices of commodities, as inputs, are their values; their prices as outputs are determined by adding labour-times and then taking account of the equalisation of the rate of profit (Kliman 1998).

Kliman then constructs a model in which inputs and outputs are commensurable in physical units, and both outputs and constant-capital inputs grow faster than living-labour inputs. For each period, the price of physical units as outputs (ergo, as inputs for the next period) is lower than their price as inputs for the given period. A bit of algebra shows that the price of physical units dwindles towards zero.

Kliman's model, however, does not allow for depreciation, and evaluates all fixed capital at historic costs. The fixed-capital stock thus "rises without limit", pushing down the rate of profit. Even the mass of profit declines. They decline even if the real wage remains constant (and thus the money wage dwindles towards zero) and the rate of exploitation rises without limit. Kliman writes that Okishio's result may be true for one-off technical change, but cannot be true for continuous technical change.

Kliman has surely "proved" too much. In contemporary capitalism, prices do not decline continually. Capitalist governments make sure they rise, though modestly. Even in the time of gold-standard currencies, prices declined only modestly over long periods. Marx argued that the tendency of the rate of profit to fall would be accompanied by a trend for the mass of surplus-value to increase, but Kliman seems to have "proved" that the mass will decrease. In Kliman's argument, the tendency of the rate of profit to fall results not from social trends (as it does with Marx) but simply from Kliman's assumptions about the formation of prices.

Kliman's "temporal single-system" scheme for values and prices is unconvincing in three ways. Firstly, it assumes values and prices commensurable, although they are formed at different levels, in the labour process and in the market. Marx's argument was that price was the only "phenomenal" expression of value. "Money as a measure of value is the phenomenal form that must of necessity be assumed by that measure of value which is immanent in commodities, labour-time" (*Capital* volume 1, Chapter 3). In the nature of capitalist economy, labour-time cannot pop up in a different and direct phenomenal form as an intermediary between input prices and output prices.

Moreover, all commodities in a capitalist economy are in fact simultaneously inputs and outputs, and they have the same price both ways. All calculations about values and prices of production are based on the abstraction of a relative balance. To replace them by supposed "disequilibrium" calculations is to jump incoherently between the abstract and the concrete. If it is a matter of price-formation in "disequilibrium", then neither labour-times nor equalisation of the rate of profit will work regularly, and sequentially-calculated prices based on the assumption that they do work are likely to diverge further and further from reality. The "temporal single-system" scheme is intended to address difficulties with Marx's arguments, but in fact only sidesteps those difficulties by creating a scheme to abolish them by fiat and enable the schematisers to "prove" many results by including them in their assumptions. (The criticisms by Mongiovi 2002 have force, despite the reply by Kliman 2002, and even without accepting Mongiovi's neo-Sraffian approach).

The exclusion of depreciation and the insistence on measuring the rate of profit against a mass of fixed capital which, by definition, must increase indefinitely and without limit, surely helps to "prove" that the rate of profit must fall. But even then, surely, a greenfield capitalist, purchasing buildings and equipment at current (low) prices, would get a better rate of profit? The dilemma would be solved by all firms (not just some) collapsing after only a few years and being replaced by new starts.

As Kliman points out, other critiques of the Okishio argument show essentially only that factors other than technical change can come with technical change to reduce profit rates. That is true, but not a reply to the argument that profit-maximising technical change in and of itself will not drive down the rate of profit.

If real wages rise sufficiently alongside the technical change – because the technical change has cheapened workers' consumer goods, and they are able to resist the capitalists' drive to limit that benefit – then profit rates will fall. But then the driver of profit-depression is the wage push, not the technical change in and of itself.

If technical change is so rapid that installed technologies must again and again be scrapped earlier than planned, then that too can depress profit rates. But there is no evidence that (outside exceptional sectors) technical change is so rapid. And, if there were such evidence, the driver of profit-depression would be the unexpectedly rapid and accelerating character of technical change, not technical change in general.

If capitalist competition is so cut-throat as to drive capitalists into "premature" technical change – paying upfront for new equipment even if it will bring a better return on current costs than the old technique only when prices have been forced down so low that production with the old technique is barely viable – then, again, that cut-throat competition will depress profit rates. But in fact, 50-year-old sewing machines are still being used in factories round the world. It remains to be shown that capitalism does actually "over-innovate" as described, rather than often retaining old techniques because, with low wages, they are still more profitable than paying out to save labour-time. If capitalism does "over-innovate" as described, then the new ultra-cut-throat competition (not technical change as such) drives profit-depression.

Okishio himself, in one of his last papers, argued that in capitalism, if there is no technical change and no increase in labour supply, the rate of surplus value will converge to zero because expansion bids up the real wage to a profit-abolishing rate (Okishio 2000). Actual profits require "incessant technical change". He concludes that his theorem, based on comparing equilibrium prices before and after a single technical change, was "questionable". But this argument hits, at most, the mathematical formalisation, not the underlying argument about technical change tending to reduce costs. Any "tendency to fall" based on this argument by Okishio relies on wage rises, not changed composition of capital, to drive it.

In sum: a general tendency in capitalism for the rate of profit to fall would not explain crises, and in any case, there is no such general tendency. And "imperialism" – if we use the term to denote the hierarchical structures of the world economy, whether in the older ages of colonial plunder or the newer age of world-market compulsions[4] – develops by its own logic, not as a reflex to an imagined general slide of profit rates.

Ruinous Competition

Robert Brenner, in his study of "the economics of global turbulence" first sketched in 1998 (Brenner 1998), and in subsequent comments (Brenner 2006

4 This is not the only way the term is used. In political discourse "imperialism" often signifies extra-economic conquest, coercion, threats (see, e.g., Matgamna, *The Left in Disarray*, pp.112ff; cf ibid p.217). In 1900–14 and 1914–18 Marxist and liberal writings, the characteristic forms of "political" imperialism (wars to redivide colonies, arms races, tariffs) were linked tightly to economic hierarchies. Both the economic and the political forms, and the interrelations, have changed since then.

and the interview included here) has developed an account of a "long downturn" based on a "deep, and lasting, decline of the rate of return on capital investment since the end of the 1960s". Brenner rejects the traditional scheme of "the tendency of the rate of profit to fall" (Brenner 1998, pp. 1–12, Brenner 2006, pp. 14–15), but his outline picture of events now comes very close to that of the most ardent proponents of the tendency as iron law.

Aside from the argument about whether the rate of profit really did continue to decline after the early 1980s, surveyed above, there are other problems with Brenner's scheme. In the interview included here he said: "The basic source of today's crisis is the declining vitality of the advanced economies since 1973". But are crises necessarily correlated with a prior decline in vitality? Engels commented on British capitalism in the Great Depression between 1873 and the 1890s that low vitality – a dull long-term depression – seemed to have replaced sharp slumps. On the other hand, the crisis of 1907–8 in the USA produced a fall in real GDP of 8% between 1907 and 1908, a bigger fall than in 2008–9, yet came after a period of capitalist vitality, with 6% p.a. real growth between 1894 and 1906. In capitalism, vitality is often not the opposite of crisis, but its forerunner.

Brenner's core argument is that ruinous competition brought down profit rates in the mid-60s, as the regrowth of industry in Germany and Japan, and the speeding of trade flows round the world, quickly sharpened competition in manufactured-goods markets. He follows up by arguing that this ruinous competition still bites a half-century later, because of "a persistent tendency to overcapacity in global manufacturing industries". Nothing short of a drastic shake-out and scrapping of overcapacity can break the curse.

Yet on anecdotal evidence the rate of industrial scrapping has been much higher since the 1970s than in the 1930s. In the 1930s, existing capacity like Ford River Rouge, or Trafford Park in Manchester, or the Coats mills in Paisley, or ICI Billingham, or the big shipyards, was often idle through lay-offs, but not scrapped. Since the 1970s large industrial areas have become rustbelts. If demand is sluggish, capacity utilisation will be low, and if there are sharp crises, average capacity utilisation over the cycle will be low; but isn't it then a circular argument to explain crises and depression from overcapacity which comes from depression or crises? In any case, over the whole period 1967–98, US manufacturing capacity utilisation averaged 81.2%, only slightly down from its 1948–65 average of 82.4%. Capacity utilisation declined in the 2000–1 downturn, and had recovered only to 79.4% in 2007 before it plunged again in the turmoil that started in 2007–8 and continues; but that reads more like crises generating low capacity-utilisation than low capacity-utilisation generating crisis.

The Resilience of Neoliberalism

In his 2009 interview, Brenner also asserted that "the crisis has revealed the total bankruptcy of the neoliberal mode of economic organisation". In the sense that no-one believes the claims of a Great Moderation any longer, that millions have come to hate neoliberal doctrines as hocus-pocus rationalisations of increasing inequality, and that new chances have opened up for the left, he was right. And maybe he meant no more than that.

But, as Lenin remarked at the Second Congress of the Communist International: "There are no absolutely hopeless situations. The bourgeoisie... are committing one stupidity after another, thus making the situation worse and accelerating their own downfall. This is true, but... the attempt to 'prove' in advance the 'absolute' hopelessness of their position is sheer pedantry, a game with ideas and words" (Degras 1956, p. 114). In the same way, the bankruptcy of neoliberalism will become "total" only when political action breaks it up. Neoliberal governments are tracing slow, stumbling, painful ways out of the crisis, but they still govern, and they still have alternative-neoliberal governments as their ready replacements. The mainstream parties are again aggressively pushing neoliberal policies, and the main dissident voices among the ruling classes are far-right parties or leftish academics with little influence. Even in emergent left-wing groupings like Syriza and Podemos, or the Corbyn surge in Britain and the Sanders movement in the USA, challenges to neoliberalism have so far been muted, subdued, tangential rather than head-on. That needs to be understood. Socialists who believe that neoliberalism is already in full ideological collapse; or that capitalism is in such unfixable trouble that its leaders are sure to switch from neoliberalism soon; or that, consequently, even a modest push from the left is will topple neoliberalism and surely bring more benign capitalist regime, lack evidence for their views, and may fail badly in the socialist task of dissecting, disputing, and refuting the widespread hold of neoliberalism in all its many variants and of the dangerous right-wing challenges to it from Trump and his like.

Neoliberalism is not just a doctrine. It is a world regime. It is the product of bourgeois class-revanchism and labour-movement defeats in the late 1970s and early 80s and of the intellectual resurgence of hard-line economic doctrines of "sound money" and government-must-serve-markets in the wake of the stagflation of the 1970s. It has a softer, but insidious, ideological underpinning in post-modernism (since 1975). But it is also the codification of many global economic developments: (1) of the incremental conversion of the capitalist world economy towards free trade between 1945 and the 1970s; (2) of the great cheapening of international transactions via containerisation and microelectronics; (3) of the incremental growth in the same period of global production chains; (4) of the anti-colonial revolutions following World War II and then the conversion (over decades, but especially from 1960 onwards) of some, and then more, ex-colonial states from primary-product-dominated economies weighed down by many pre-capitalist structures into at least semi-industrialised bourgeois forms; (5) of the rise of capitalist corporations to the size where they can take on, "privatised", what previously only states had the scale to do; (6) of the expansion of global financial markets via the "euro-dollar" (1960s) and "petrodollar" (1970s) surges.

In their turn, neoliberal policies have pushed those world-scale developments further. Neoliberalism made a big step forward when, after China's turn to the world market in the 1980s and the collapse of Stalinism in Russia and Europe in 1989–91, it proved resilient enough to set terms for integrating vast new areas into capitalist world markets. At the same time, because of the extent of Stalinist ideological seepage even into anti-Stalinist left movements over the previous decades, the collapse of Stalinism also brought a wide collapse of the credibility of "socialism" (as commonly understood) and disorientation and demoralisation in labour movements. In the long term, the clearing-away of Stalinist debris improves the prospects for the authentic socialist left; but that long term is a long time coming. The web of international institutions, rationalising and organising increasingly potent, far-reaching, and fast-paced world markets, which had built up on the US side of the Cold War, and which were mostly lynch-pinned by the USA – IMF, WTO, G7, World Bank, NATO, European Union – proved strong and flexible enough to integrate vast new territories over the 1980s and 90s. They were able to do that despite the follies of the free-market ideologues who advised the ex-Stalinist state leaders on how to transform their economies; despite the pauperisation of many millions in the process; despite, or maybe in part thanks to, the shocks of the various financial crises in those decades.

The G7 ("Group of Seven" leading states) was set up in 1975. It brought in Russia to become the G8 in 1998, but suspended that expansion in 2014 after Russia annexed Crimea. The World Trade Organisation was set up, as a higher-powered successor to the old General Agreement on Tariffs and Trade, in 1995, with 76 members. By 2003 it had 145 members; in July 2016, it has 163, and 19 others seeking to join. By 2003, the IMF included 184 member states, up from 150 in the mid-1980s. NATO expanded in late 2002 to 26 members (it had been 16). The European Union clinched its Single Market in 1993, introduced a single currency in much of its territory from January 2002, and expanded (three new members in 1995; ten in 2004; two in 2007; one in 2013). Those 27 member states codified neoliberal rules in the Treaty of Lisbon (2007). Though Harvey

(2005) tends to summarise neoliberalism much more narrowly as bourgeois class-revanchism, his Chapter 4 (pp. 96ff) chronicles the "progress of neoliberalisation on the world stage" in terms of state responses to the constraints of integration into the world markets. Those state responses then further develop world markets on neoliberal lines. Neoliberalism is an era of huge quicksilver world financial markets and fast-mutating global production chains, in which the regulating principle for each state is to make its territory accessible, secure, and attractive for globally-mobile capital, rather than to build an integrated national industrial base. It is also an era of recurrent financial crises (Allen and Gale 2007). Dysfunction makes the neoliberal imperative bite more, not less, sharply. Paradoxically, dysfunction – so long it is within some limits, as long as no political initiative or gyration breaks the bones of neoliberalism – tends to be "functional" for neoliberalism. The crash of 2008 threw governments into disarray; confounded and discomforted neoliberal doctrinaires; and stirred up opposition movements like Occupy (2011). But once the governments had recovered themselves, if only partially, the dysfunction tended to make politicians repeat and increase the neoliberal dose, rather than seeking different ways. States pursue policies which ease or push the envelope of neoliberalism more readily when neoliberalism is relatively stable and thriving than when it is in trouble.

Thus the June 2010 Toronto G20 declaration. Thus the moves in the EU for balanced-budget rules and for stepped-up "labour market reform" and privatisation. Thus Dilma Rousseff's move, in Brazil, to appoint a hardline neoliberal as Finance Minister weeks after winning the October 2014 presidential election on a pledge to defend social programs against neoliberal attack. Thus Francois Hollande's steady move, after being elected president of France in 2012 on a leftish platform, to harsher and harsher neoliberal policies, and the almost-as-steady gains from the neofascist Front National. Thus the background to the shift in recent years to more right-wing and authoritarian regimes in many areas: India, Turkey, Brazil, almost the entire Eastern periphery of the EU. And now the right-wing shift which may be so drastic as to disrupt neoliberalism from its very centre: the election of Donald Trump as president of the USA.

PART 1

After 2007

∴

INTRODUCTION TO PART 1

"Those of us who have looked to the self-interest of lending institutions to protect shareholders' equity (myself especially) are in a state of shocked disbelief"*

From mid-2007 the housing-market slump in the USA was leading into a financial crisis in the USA, with international repercussions. No-one yet knew how dramatic the financial crisis would be. No-one knew whether it would be bigger than, comparable to, or smaller than other financial crises of the neoliberal era, such as the US Savings and Loan crisis of the late 80s and early 90s, the "Asian crisis" of 1997–8, the "dot.com" slump of 2000–1, and so on. Fred Moseley reviewed his research on the rate of profit, concluded that it had risen somewhat since the 1980s, and was not suddenly crashing. This was "more of a Minsky crisis than a Marx crisis". Its repercussions were unpredictable. Costas Lapavitsas summarised his work on the growing autonomy of finance, and concluded "the world of finance has always created crises out of its own operations. In the last thirty years, the scope for this has become greater": it could hit real accumulation.

Leo Panitch, having researched the strength of the central role of the USA in the "making of global capitalism", was sceptical of talk of uncontrollable global imbalances. He thought that the governments' anti-crisis measures might shift capitalist regimes in a decidedly more state-interventionist direction long-term as well as short-term. Simon Mohun would later suggest the same possibilities, but in early 2008 thought governments would rescue the financiers sufficiently to avoid a full-scale crash in the "real" economy.

Trevor Evans thought the financial sector had been "breeding trouble" and unsustainable imbalances since the early 2000s. Dick Bryan, however, thought that the fundamental development had been of financial derivatives and securities as new forms of money: this created growth, "fragile growth, of course, but growth".

---

* Alan Greenspan, in evidence to the Committee On Oversight And Government Reform, US House Of Representatives, 23 October 2008. https://www.gpo.gov/fdsys/pkg/CHRG-110hhrg55764/html/CHRG-110hhrg55764.htm

Michel Husson looked at trends which he had long discussed: capitalist investment failing to rise while profits rose, and the inherently "chaotic" character of the regulation of the world economy as it approximated a "pure" capitalism.

CHAPTER 1

The Long Trends of Profit (March 2008)

Discussion with Fred Moseley

The rate of profit is the key barometer of a capitalist economy, and more specifically it is the main determinant of business investment.

The rate of investment is in turn a key determinant of the overall growth of the economy. So, the first main reason why the rate of profit is so significant is its impact on investment spending.

Secondly, the relative proportion of profits and debt payment is a key indicator of the financial health of corporations. If the ratio of profit to debt obligations is low, then the corporations have greater vulnerability to bankruptcy.

Both on the investment side and on the financial side, profit rates are of crucial importance.

There has not been a complete recovery of the rate of profit in recent years. I don't want to overstate it. There are different measures of profit rates, but according to my estimates, which are for the total business sector of the economy, by 2006 the rate of profit was within 10% of its earlier post-war peak.

Mid-2006 was the peak of this current profit cycle. The profit share and profit rate have declined a bit in the last year or so, and the trajectory seems to be down right now.

But there was a substantial recovery in the rate of profit. The rate of profit had declined roughly 50% from the peak of the sixties to the trough of the 80s. At least half of that previous decline – I would say, more than half of that previous decline – was reversed. Today profits are, by almost any measure, a lot better than they were in the 70s and 80s.

Bear in mind also a couple of additional considerations. One is that these estimates are for the domestic US economy. They do not include foreign profits; and foreign profits are an increasing share of total US corporate profits. 30 or 40 years they were less than 10%, today they are 30%. None of that gets counted in the official US government estimates of profit rates.

Some people argue that including those foreign profits is appropriate in terms of gauging the financial strength of corporations, but if you are talking about the impact of profits on investment in the USA, then perhaps profits

* Previously published in *Solidarity* 129, 20 March 2008 and online at http://www.workersliberty.org/story/2008/03/19/marxists-capitalist-crisis-1-fred-moseley-long-trends-profit.

made in the rest of the world do not have much impact on US investment spending.

Another additional consideration is that these estimates of profits also do not include the salaries of top executives, which are going through the roof, and could more appropriately be considered as part of profits rather than wages.

In sum, I would argue that there has been a substantial recovery of profit rates. Maybe not complete, and we may disagree a few percentage points on the extent, but a substantial recovery.

Another indication with respect to the financial aspect of profits is a substantial reduction in debt obligations in relationship to profits. Those ratios are well down from their peaks, both due to higher profits and also to lower debt, for some corporations, and lower interest rates. So there is less danger of corporate bankruptcy today than ten or twenty years ago.

Those ratios are for the economy as a whole. If you look at the distribution of debt ratios, there is a pretty fat tail at the high debt ratio end. There are a number of corporations, ten per cent maybe, which have very high debt loads, in part because of the junk-bond-financed acquisitions. And particularly in danger of bankruptcy are the home builders, the construction industry. I'm not saying there won't be bankruptcies. But it doesn't seem to be a very widespread threat yet.

Another reason why the threat of corporate bankruptcy might be more serious than it looks is that debt may be underestimated. As we learned from Enron, there are all sorts of accounting tricks to keep debt off the books. We'll find out pretty soon who's holding the debt. As Warren Buffet says, when the tide goes out, you see who's swimming naked. The financial sector is in much greater danger than the non-financial sector.

But accepting that there has been a substantial recovery in the rate of profit, how did this happen? What were the main factors contributing to it? I would argue that it's basically been the holding down of wages. The average real wage in the US economy is almost the same as it was in the early 1970s. For the average worker, there has been little or no increase in the real wage. This is in striking contrast to the early post-war period, up through the 70s, when the average real wage in the US economy approximately doubled. That ended in the 70s with an all-out attempt to restore profitability, mainly at the expense of workers.

While real wages were being held constant, productivity increases continued every year – at a somewhat slower rate during the productivity slowdown of the 70s and 80s, somewhat faster since then, but they continued.

In Marxist terms, that reduced necessary labour time and increased surplus labour time, and therefore increased the rate of surplus value. Over the three decades we're talking about, the rate of surplus value has approximately doubled, from about 1.5 to around 3. Again, that is in striking contrast to the earlier post-war period, when the rate of surplus value increased a little bit, but not much. That sharp increase in the rate of surplus value has been the main reason why the rate of profit has increased substantially.

It could be interpreted as contrary to what Marx expected: he expected that once the rate of profit had declined, it would take the devaluation of capital and widespread bankruptcies and so forth to restore it. What Marx didn't consider was the scenario we've lived in over the last decades of enough government management and government intervention to put a floor under the economy; but even so it's taken a very long time to restore the rate of profit.

A puzzle here is that what appears to be a substantial recovery in the rate of profit does not seem to have led to a strong revival of investment. The connection between profit rates and investment seems to have been weakened. I haven't myself done a lot of work on this, but it seems like businesses are paying out a greater share of their profits as dividends, and using a greater share of profits to buy back their stock. Instead of investing in the expansion of the business, they are enriching themselves. There's a lot of talk about stock options, and managers who have substantial stock options running the company in a way to maximise the stock price. So, you have a bigger proportion of surplus value going to capitalist consumption rather than investment.

A slower rate of investment spending has meant a slower rate of growth, compared to earlier periods, and that the growth of the economy has become more and more dependent on consumer spending – in part the luxury consumption of capitalists. But it's hard for workers to increase their consumption with stagnant wages. There have been different ways round that. The first was to have more family members working, and longer hours. But more recently the big one is the expansion of consumer debt – an explosion of consumer debt. Now that debt has to be paid, and we have a debt crisis on our hands.

The numbers would suggest that the corporations should be more resilient in face of the crises in the financial sector. However, the housing sector and the construction industry will certainly not be resilient. The debt ratios could be understated, due to Enron-type tricks. And there is that "fat tail" of heavily indebted corporations.

The aggregate official numbers which show a healthier financial situation might be at least somewhat exaggerated. And the financial crisis is shaping up every day to look more and more serious.

The banks have responded by greatly restricting lending. If there are corporations out there that are heavily dependent on banks to refinance debt, there could be substantial effects. The shock that they're going to experience is certainly shaping up to be more serious than what occurred 20 years ago [in the Savings and Loans crisis]. Maybe the sounder financial figures for corporations will not be enough.

As regards estimating profit, the main difference between my estimates and Robert Brenner's, for example, is that mine are for the total economy and his are for the non-financial sector only. The recovery of profits in the non-financial sector is less than for the total economy. Even for the non-financial sector, I'd say it has been substantial – but not as close to full recovery as for the total economy.

Which measure is more relevant and important? An argument could be made that in terms of investment spending the non-financial sector profit rate is the more crucial determinant. I wouldn't argue too strongly for the preferability of the total-economy measure. And part of the financial profits may turn out to be fictitious – paper profits based on anticipated revenue from financial assets a lot of which are now having to be written down. The recovery of financial profits in the boom time could turn out to have been grossly overestimated. But even if we accept Robert Brenner's estimates – and I think foreign profits and executive salaries are important corrections to those – there has still been a substantial recovery of profit rates. As yet no large revival of investment spending, so the economy has become more dependent on consumer spending.

Why are there unequal profit rates in the financial and non-financial sectors? Part of it may also be that the financial profits are partly paper profits, as just mentioned. It's surprising that financial sector profits should rise as a share of the whole, for a couple of reasons. One is that interest rates are low. You would think that would contribute to a smaller financial share. Secondly, if you look at the figures for debt for non-financial corporations, with less debt there should be lower debt payments from the non-financial to the financial sector. Financial profits have been more and more coming from the consumer sector – from credit cards and from mortgages and so on. That expansion has now turned into sharp contraction, and financial profits will follow accordingly.

In terms of the long decline in the rate of profit, before the recent recovery, my emphasis has been on Marx's distinction between productive labour and unproductive labour. Productive labour is labour which produces value and surplus-value. According to Marxist theory, that is a fairly broad category, but it does not include two main types of unproductive labour – labour involved in various sales and circulation and exchange activities, including finance, and management or boss labour.

The relative proportions of unproductive labour and productive labour changed dramatically in the US economy in the early post-war period, up to the 70s. The ratio of unproductive to productive approximately doubled over that period; and, from the perspective of Marxist theory, that means a smaller share of the surplus value produced is left over for profits. An increasing share of the surplus value produced by productive labour has to go to pay the wages and other costs of unproductive labour.

When we talk about the rate of profit, in my estimates or in Brenner's estimates, this is always a net figure, only part of the total surplus value produced by productive labour. The doubling of the relative proportion of unproductive labour to productive labour had a negative impact on the rate of profit and was, best I can tell, the main cause of the substantial decline in the rate of profit in that period. The composition of capital also increased and also contributed, in part, to the long-term decline in the rate of profit, but the increase in unproductive labour seems to have been a more significant cause.

What has happened since then? The ratio of unproductive to productive labour has continued to increase, but at a much slower rate than earlier, and so that factor has had less of a negative impact on the rate of profit. The small continuing negative impact has been more than overcome by the very strong increases in the rate of surplus value.

The financial sector, in the US anyway, is still only a small percentage of the economy. It has increased. How is that consistent with the overall proportion of unproductive labour levelling off? Most of the levelling off has been in the supervisory element of unproductive labour, which is the majority of it. The financial sector is catching up now, but on the supervisory side, downsizing and eliminating layers of middle management have been a big factor.

Also, on the circulation side, the computer has greatly reduced circulation labour. Computer technology has perhaps been the main reason for the slowing down of the increase of unproductive labour, both in circulation and in supervision. You need fewer supervisors when you have computers. You could almost argue that the computer technology was developed to solve the problem of expanding unproductive labour.

In the end, I would say that the current crisis is more of a Minsky crisis than a Marx crisis. The main cause of the current crisis is not insufficient surplus labour in production, but rather excessive risk-taking by financial capitalists in search of higher returns, which was based on the erroneous assumption that housing prices would continue to rise forever.

The solution to this crisis has more to do with wiping out a large portion of the accumulated debt of households (and the corresponding assets of financial institutions) rather than the devaluation of production capital and the reduction of wages (although these latter will also happen to some extent). But that is a topic for another discussion.

CHAPTER 2

A New Sort of Financial Crisis (April 2008)

Discussion with Costas Lapavitsas

It has gradually become clear that one of the key features of the last thirty years is increasing autonomy of finance. Many things have happened in the world economy since 1973–4, which was basically the end of the long boom, but one thing that is clear is that the financial system has become proportionately much larger and increasingly autonomous from real accumulation – production and circulation of value and surplus value.

The reasons for this are many and varied. There are reasons of technological innovation. There are reasons of institutional and political transformation – the deregulation and liberalisation of finance which has been instigated by a number of governments. There are also reasons, more fundamental perhaps, which have to do with big capital, the large enterprises, becoming progressively less dependent on banks for credit to finance investment. And so the financial system has begun to target the personal income of private individuals – workers and broader strata of the population – as a source of profit. This is a new departure in capitalism. I'd call it direct exploitation – profit being extracted directly from personal income and not through the process of production. Financial institutions increasingly make their profits from private individuals by lending for housing, for consumer credit, and so on.

The US Federal Reserve's own figures show that the proportion of personal income paid out in debt servicing went up from 15.6% in 1983 to 19.3% in June 2007. A fifth of personal income is used to service debt. The figures in Britain are comparable. And remember, in the United States, financial profits are now a third of total profits. Money incomes that people receive as wages or salaries or whatever, are increasingly transformed into loanable money capital, and out of that, banks and other financial institutions make profits. The process has created new layers of the capitalist class, feeding off those profits – new power centres, new centres of influence over policy.

Financial institutions also make increasing profits by drawing fee income, that is, by mediating in financial markets – not lending and borrowing, but facilitating the lending and borrowing of others. This is an activity that

* Previously published in *Solidarity* 130, 10 April 2008 and online at http://www.workersliberty.org/story/2008/04/14/marxists-capitalist-crisis-2-costas-lapavitsas-new-sort-financial-crisis.

banks have engaged in since the beginning of capitalism, but the size and importance of it now are quite new in the history of capitalism. Altogether, interest income derived by banks out of profits made by industrial businesses has become proportionately smaller, though it remains fundamental. On the other hand, interest income drawn from wages and other personal income, as well as income from fees, have become progressively more important for banks.

These are key structural changes. As a result, there has been tremendous instability in the financial system and the economy as a whole. As banks and other financial institutions have made this turn in drawing their profits, they have created gigantic and novel forms of instability which implicate broad layers of ordinary people. The instability has to do with the methods through which the transformation of finance has taken place. To make the turn, banks and other financial institutions have to rely on technological advances. The reason is obvious – to make loans to large numbers of individuals, banks must have the ability to process large amounts of individual data.

Until recently, they were not able to do that. But with developments in computers and telecommunications, they have acquired this capability. Banks have started to use computationally intensive techniques and statistical methods in order to assess risk and to judge to whom they should lend. Bank lending has become more of an arm's-length process. People are turned into units which the banks can treat in a uniform way. Instead of going to see your bank manager to ask for a loan, you tick a few boxes on an application form downloaded from the Internet. The bank adds other information it might have about you and then makes its decision by assigning a credit score to you. This, of course, raises problems of democratic control of information, but the point here is that the bank has lost personal contact with the borrower. The judgement they make of the borrower as a risk depends on a numerical assessment of data provided at a distance.

Moreover, since the banks and financial institutions have also moved into making money from fees – and not just from lending – they take these mortgage debts, package them into new securities, and sell them in open financial markets. Thus, the mortgage debt that people used to owe to a bank for 20 or 30 years is now packaged by the banks to offload onto others. The banks create composite or derivative types of debt on the basis of the original mortgage.

It is worth stressing the change that has taken place by looking more closely at the process of mortgage securitisation. In the past, a bank would grant a mortgage by the bank manager talking to the borrower and deciding whether the borrower was a good prospect. The bank had a direct interest in working out whether the borrower was likely to repay regularly because otherwise it would lose its money. Nowadays it is not like that. The borrower ticks the boxes; if the credit score clears a threshold, the bank would give the money; and next week the bank would package the mortgage into new securities and sell it, essentially providing others with a right to the stream of debt payments from the mortgage. After that it is not ostensibly the bank's concern whether the borrower repays normally, or not. All that relies on someone else, other than the bank, vouching for the process by better examining the creditworthiness of the new securities. That was done by a credit ratings organisation, such as Standard and Poor's, or Fitch. But the credit ratings organisations are also remote from the borrower. They are also paid by the bank that creates the new securities, and so have a conflict of interest.

Finally, another institution, an insurer, would come along and guarantee the new securities. That again happens at a considerable distance from the original borrower. None of the capitalist enterprises involved in this mechanism has a solid interest in assessing the long-term reliability of the person who obtained the original mortgage. Each just wants to collect its fee, or sell its securities, and go on to generate new business of the same type.

If there is "cheap money" in the system in the first place, that is, if the central bank has made money available at low interest rates, then this mechanism is a secure way of making profits for banks and others. But, depending on how problematic the original mortgages were, risks are accumulating, and nobody knows where they are concentrated. In the USA, subprime mortgages were advanced to very poor people without real prospects of repaying regularly, especially if interest rates rose. As they defaulted on their mortgages, banks and others were left holding new securities that were not worth very much at all. That is ultimately why Bear Stearns, a huge bank, failed in March 2008. These problems were not clear until recently because this is the first time we have seen a financial system of this type emerge on this scale. At the time, economists and others were saying that it was a secure and stable way of doing things because the risk was spread out among a large number of people. Now we know that is far from the case.

The difference in responses to the crisis between the US Federal Reserve and the European Central Banks is based on a difference of outlook which has existed for a very long time. It has to do with how those institutions were set up. The ECB is far more focused on price stability, whereas the Fed also sees itself as looking after the economy as a whole. The Fed is also different from the ECB in the sense that the Fed produces world money and operates in the most important economy in the world. Its outlook is shaped by different concerns from the ECB's.

At the moment, my judgement is that the Fed is so worried about the state of the American financial system that it is prepared to do whatever it takes to rescue it. Hence the huge amounts of money that it has made available to JP Morgan rapidly to take over the failed Bear Stearns. Hence also the rapid lowering of interest rates. The ECB takes a different line. It seems to think that the European financial system is in less danger. In short, the Americans are less concerned about what is happening to the dollar and the international position of US capital, and even the domestic economy as a whole, than they are about rescuing the financial system.

Are they right? At the moment, there is evidence that inflation is picking up. For the first time for many years, inflation might become a serious problem because of oil prices and food prices. If that inflation problem materialises, then the Fed is going to regret what it is doing at the moment. Moreover, the Fed has been overseeing a substantial, but quite orderly, decline of the dollar. The decision-makers in the United States seem to want the dollar to fall in order to remedy the US trade deficit. Is there a risk of that decline accelerating out of control? It is very hard to say, but it might. If the financial system were to receive an even bigger jolt than it has so far, the decline of the dollar might accelerate out of control. That might happen, for instance, if some large financial institutions went under and holders of dollars across the world became very worried that US finance were collapsing.

There are some ruling-class commentators in the *Financial Times* and elsewhere who have argued that the Fed's measures might work, but at the cost of creating further problems for the future as they would be rescuing irresponsible banks. These comments are based on reality but most of those who make them are in an impossible position.

It is true that if interest rates are brought down, and if the Fed and other central banks pump money into the system, they are running the risk of creating another crisis down the road. The logical way of avoiding this would be to impose strong and pervasive controls on finance.

But the same people are completely against serious control and regulation of the financial system. They are in favour of liberalised finance. They believe that somehow the financial system, when it operates freely, improves the performance of the economy and everybody's incomes. On this basis, it is impossible to take a consistent position. My own view is that the Fed is reacting to very pressing requirements at the moment. It has to intervene to rescue the system. The risks are very great of a generalised crisis, and a few wrong moves by the Fed might lead to it. Whether as a result another crisis will happen down the road, in five or ten years' time, is another matter that requires profound structural reform of finance.

Yes, people like Martin Wolf are rather embarrassed by the operation of a minimally-regulated financial system which means that when things are going well, you pocket the loot; when they go bad, you go to the government and ask to be bailed out. Can the left put alternative ideas into play on the question of regulating the financial system? I think so. The ideas that are coming out of the orthodoxy and the capitalist class are terribly pedestrian. It's the same old stuff that we have been hearing for more than two decades but appearing in technically different ways. In short, free markets and minimal regulation.

It is very important for the left to put across ideas of control. There is no reason, for instance, why the financial institutions cannot be controlled in terms of the assets they are required to hold and the proportions in which they hold them. At the moment, all the regulation is in terms of the capital they are required to have – Basel 1 and Basel 2.[1] The financial institutions have become very good at bypassing those regulations and using them to their own advantage. At the moment, they can all meet the Basel 2 requirements, which presumably makes them safer, but at the same time several of them are at great risk, as we now know.

We should demand that regulation be imposed on where financial institutions lend and how. We should also demand that financial transactions are controlled and taxed. Financial institutions should not be able to trade any way they like, continually churning money over time and time again in order to generate fees.

More broadly and radically, we should insist that the mobilisation of money out of ordinary people's incomes should become detached from securitisation and other speculative practices of the financial system. Houses, pensions, health, basic consumption should not be sources of profit for finance.

There should be public mechanisms that provide ordinary people with pensions in secure and controlled ways. There is no reason why the housing problems of society should be dealt with through the financial system. In London, for example, bringing housing well and truly into the realm of finance has meant that house prices have increased by a factor of about five in the last 20 years while personal incomes have increased by a factor of two. That divergence is related, in large part, to the grip that the financial system has acquired on housing. We should demand good quality social housing, while detaching housing from the financial system.

---

1 An international agreement of 2004 – "Basel 2", superseding "Basel 1" of 1988 – set a "capital adequacy framework" for banks. Under Basel 1, capital (primarily, shareholders' equity) must be at least 8% of the bank's risk-weighted assets. Under Basel 2 it was proposed that large banks with technically sophisticated ways of measuring risk keep a lower percentage.

Since the 70s it has been a commonplace view, among Marxists and others, that the USA is in relative decline. But maybe it's not. In all the big international forums of capital, the USA is still the dominant voice.

The United States has declined in terms of measures to do with production. But if you look at finance, there is no relative decline. The leading financial institutions of the world are US institutions. US banks dominate financial markets, and US ways of managing finance are very influential across the world. Financial systems across the world increasingly imitate the ways of the US financial system.

The dollar remains the closest the world has to world money, and it is produced by the United States.

At the same time, the US is structurally weak because it runs a huge trade deficit. But it has managed to turn even the deficit into a source of strength. The countries that make the trade surpluses end up holding the dollar as reserves of world money. If the dollar were to collapse these countries would make significant losses.

In short, in the realm of finance, the US remains very powerful, but its power is precariously based. That, in a sense, is the key problem of present-day capitalism. Note though that the current crisis has not yet brought the international aspect of finance strongly into play. But as the USA continues to be wracked by instability, the crisis could well become truly international.

What about the rise of the BRICs – big fast-growing economics like Brazil, Russia, India, and China?

This is a development of the first importance. The centre of gravity of productive capital is shifting east – to Japan for a long time now, to China and East Asia, and to a certain extent to India, though that is not comparable to China. The implications in the sphere of finance are not as straightforward as the shift of productive power would indicate. The financial mechanisms are dominated by the United States, and world money is dominated by the United States.

A lot of the fast-growing economies trade in dollars and pay in dollars. Their key exchange rate is against the dollar. Consequently, they have an interest in maintaining stability of the dollar, and they accumulate dollar reserves. In the last ten years, many developing capitalist countries have accumulated vast reserves of dollars. This imposes a huge cost on very poor people, since it represents a transfer of capital to the United States that could have been used to sustain investment and production in their domestic economies. But it also gives to the countries that have the reserves some protection from the storms which are breaking in the world economy at the moment. The crisis which has broken out in the richer countries might not affect them as immediately as it would have done previously. How long this factor of protection will operate, nobody can tell. Already, for example, US financial institutions are moving into Mexico and similar countries in order to trade mortgage-backed securities there. This might reproduce the same effects there as in the USA, or there may be a knock-on effect if the US financial system suffers a more serious collapse.

The rate of profit is generally reckoned to be the key factor in crises, and generally we expect to see some decline in the rate of profit in the run-in to crises. Do the fairly high rates of profit in production currently mean that production is insulated against this financial crisis?

That takes us back to the autonomy of finance. The financial system is now more autonomous and draws more of its profits out of personal income rather than from the surplus value created by productive capitalists. Nonetheless, Marxist theory is of great use in analysing these phenomena. Marx differentiates between, on the one hand, financial crises which are continuations of a crisis in production, to do with profitability and the ability to sell, and on the other, crises which are generated within the realm of finance. The latter might or might not affect real accumulation in severe ways.

In other words, there has always been some autonomy of finance, and the world of finance has always created crises out of its own operations. In the last thirty years, the scope for this has become greater, and it now involves vast numbers of ordinary people, through mortgages, consumer credit and pensions. This makes financial storms more worrying and damaging for the working class and the majority of the population. By impacting on ordinary people, the financial crisis could well impact on real accumulation as it might lead to cutting down on consumption. In short, there are complex ways in which financial bubbles and crises could affect the real economy. Novel developments have taken place in contemporary capitalism and the standard guidance of Marxism needs to be reconsidered, while maintaining its core principles.

CHAPTER 3

The Crisis Depends on the Fightback (April 2008)

Discussion with Leo Panitch

I don't think that US hegemony has waned, and I don't think it's about to wane in the very near future, despite the current financial crisis. In my view, the better term for the US role in the world is Empire. That captures in my mind the way in which the American state plays a role of coordination and oversight and crisis-managing for global capitalism, in the absence of a global state.

It managed to do that in my hemisphere, on this side of the Atlantic, by penetrating other, independent states, in South America and North America, before the Second World War. Its capital penetrated those states and encouraged the restructuring of those states in a way that was consistent with fostering trade and the protection of the property rights of US capitalists, or in fact of foreign capitalists in general.

That became generalised after the Second World War, not so much with the Third World as with Europe and Japan, which became increasingly Canadianised. European and Japanese capital, in different ways, were penetrated by American capitalists. Conditions for that were established politically. That penetration was very deep, and it was done in collaboration with the ruling classes of those countries. This was imperialism by invitation. The ruling classes saw the American state as the safest guarantor of capital's rights, especially in the countries where the labour movement was strong.

From the 30s on, European capital had poured into the United States, even during the New Deal. So this has been a collaborative type of hegemony or Empire. When Europe and Japan were put back on their feet after the Second World War, and became competitive in terms of trade with the United States, the notion arose that meant American hegemony was fading. It was a very common view, but fundamentally misleading. It failed to understand that the Europeans and Japanese wanted the Americans to play a more active role in managing the global economy, not a lesser role. To the extent that they were unhappy with American policy, it was mainly for that reason.

That has continued through the era of neoliberalism. There have been moments where in very economistic ways, based on the size of the trade deficit or the penetration of foreign direct investment into the United States, people

* Previously published in *Solidarity* 131, 24 April 2008.

have predicted US decline as imminent. It has proved to be wrong in every case. The American state is still seen as the most important protector of global capital. Many people think that the deficit means that the US economy is a basket case; but, through the technological revolution we've just lived through, in information technology and so on, it has managed to maintain its dynamism as a capitalist power.

The deficit has reflected the fact that the United States has been the market for so much of what is produced in the world today. It has not reflected a decline in American exports, which over the last 15 or 20 years have increased more than any of the other G7 country.

To read off from the size of the trade deficit a problem in terms of American hegemony, I think, is not to understand the role that the United States, and New York as a financial centre, and American banks in London, play in terms of the glue of international capitalism. No-one is doing a favour to the United States by putting short-term capital into New York, or holding onto dollars. They are purchasing dollars and Treasury Bills because they remain the most stable store of value in a highly volatile capitalist world.

The volatile nature of international finance, in which free trade in currencies is a large factor, makes this a highly volatile set-up, and one that is prone to financial crises. Notably, not many financial crises have been dollar crises in the way that we saw sterling crises from the 1950s to the 1970s, when sterling was still a central currency. (London is still a big financial centre; but now it is essentially one of the great centres of American dollar finance).

What's been quite remarkable, at least since the 1979 Volcker shock, has been the extent to which, for all of the size of the deficit and the free floating of the dollar, there hasn't been a massive run on the dollar. Even in recent days, we've seen a rather managed decline of the dollar, and a decline which is functional to reducing the size of the US trade deficit. When the dollar got inordinately high, after the very high interest rates that established enormous confidence in the US Treasury Bill and the dollar, you then had the meetings around the Plaza Accord which coordinated a readjustment. People are constantly observing the level of the dollar, given the role it plays in the international capitalist economy. But what's astonishing is the extent to which the dollar has not suffered.

So it's like Keynes's comment that if you owe the bank £100, you have a problem, but if you owe the bank a million, the bank has a problem? The capitalists of the rest of the world have to keep the dollar up because so much of their interests are tied up with it.

Absolutely. And that reflects the degree of integration.

Marxists tend to discuss crises in terms of a decline in the rate of profit. But, by most accounts, over the last several years, profits have recovered quite considerably. Are we going to see a crisis without a prior fall in the rate of profit, or what?

Our position – my position and that of my comrade and co-author Sam Gindin – has been that the profit squeeze of the late 60s and the 70s was resolved by the defeat of labour, and to some extent the defeat of the Third World national-liberation radicalism that had produced a rise in commodity prices (though we may be seeing another surge of commodity prices now). With the restructuring that was brought about in the 1980s in the banking system and in industry, in the United States but also in Europe and elsewhere, the basis was established for profit rates to recover as they have done, especially in the last decade.

That account involves a very different interpretation of the cause of the profit crisis of the 1960s and 70s than is offered by Bob Brenner. It suggests an explanation of the profit crisis much more similar to the "wage squeeze" explanation that was offered way back in the 1970s by Andrew Glyn and Bob Sutcliffe.

We think you have to have a broader understanding of the factors squeezing profits than just wage militancy, though that was very important in some countries, in Britain and to some extent in the United States. There was a much more general range of pressures on capital that were expressed by the civil rights movement, the women's movement, the radicalisation of the students, all of which produced the fiscal crisis of the state and not as much room, for a period, for the state to cut back on corporate taxes.

Put all that together with the wage militancy of the working class, and we think that had a lot to do with the profit crisis – of course in the context of the renewed competition which made it difficult for any individual firm to raise prices.

We think that was resolved by breaking the back not only of the wage militancy but also of the tendency of the social movements to win extensions in the welfare state – by introducing neoliberalism. Brenner thinks the crisis was largely one of competition between national capitals, and that there has been a problem ever since in terms of not enough firms exiting. They're making some profits, not as high as they used to, but they stay in business. In our view, by contrast, we have been living through one of the most dynamic periods in the whole history of capitalism. It has been enormously exploitative, and has created enormous insecurity around the world, including in the heart of the Empire itself, but its dynamism has been related to its ability to be exploitative and create insecurity. It isn't only a matter of increased exploitation of the industrial working class, or of the low-paid service sector; it's a matter of getting the middle class, the petty bourgeoisie, the professionals, to work for corporations enormous hours.

The recovery of profits that we have seen has been substantial and real, and not, as Bob Brenner usually explains it, a matter of ad hoc ways of getting out of a continuing structural crisis. In my view, it doesn't make sense as a Marxist to speak of a crisis that lasts for forty or more years. Does all that rule out another serious profit crisis? No, it does not do so, by any means. We need to keep looking, even if not in orthodox terms of the "tendency of the rate of profit to fall", for the possibility of a serious profit crisis. How serious a profit crisis will be depends, I think, on how much the rate of exploitation can be raised again – that is, on how much working-class resistance there is to the type of restructuring that allows capital to get out of it. That is why so much hinges on how we interpret all these things in terms of working-class renewal and working-class strategy.

Capitalism is crisis-prone above all in the financial sector, but it remains crisis-prone in a deeper sense in the productive sector. How serious these crises are depends, in the end, on class relations. The most serious crises of capitalism are those in which it is difficult to increase the rate of exploitation. That is why the crisis of the 1970s was so protracted, because it was difficult to increase the rate of exploitation then, given the strength of militancy of rank-and-file labour.

Has the credit system become more crisis-prone?

The system has become larger, more complex, in some ways more efficient, and also more crisis-prone. The size and complexity of it are directly related to the neoliberal re-regulation which has allowed a lot more competition in the financial sector than was allowed in the New Deal type of legislation. The expanded credit system has been quite functional to the growth of global capitalism. When so much capital and trade is flowing round the world with free-floating currencies, you need a highly complex system of financial trading in order to be able to adjust the enormous risks involved in the marginal changes in currencies and interest rates, etc. This goes all the way back to the situation the farmer faced in the 1870s, and still faces today. When a wheat farmer in western Canada puts seed in the soil, in the spring, he doesn't know what the price of a Canadian dollar is going to be in October, when he will be selling the grain. One of the ways of dealing with that is by developing co-operatives, but the most fundamental way of dealing with it, going all the way back to the 1870s, when the Chicago Mercantile Exchange was established, is through a large, complex set of financial intermediations. That farmer would go into his little local bank and begin to hedge the price he might be able to sell the wheat when he was signing a contract in April to deliver it in October; and that would go through fifteen intermediaries before it would get to the Chicago Mercantile Exchange, where there would be a trade in wheat futures. The same was true in almost every other agricultural product. Today we see that all around the world in "derivatives". They play that role in the management of risk. It's no accident that, with the help of Milton Friedman, when Bretton Woods broke down in 1971, the market in derivatives around currencies was established at the Chicago Mercantile Exchange. The system has become larger, much more complex. The derivatives now cover not only real products, but financial instruments of all kinds. There are a gazillion players in this market, and they are all speculating.

But, as Dick Bryan argues (Bryan and Rafferty 2005) this may be the most important development in capitalism since the joint-stock company in terms of its ability to smooth out the enormous risk that's involved in this complicated and diverse global capitalism.

At the same time the system is more crisis-prone. It is more crisis-prone because it does involve speculation. It is enormously complex, and the people trading in it are operating on the basis of highly complex algebra that most of us don't understand and very few of them fully do. It's not clear, to anyone in the system, who holds a given piece of paper at a given time. Also, neoliberal regulation is mainly self-regulation. The banks are regulated through Basel and the Bank of International Settlements and the national or regional central banks; but they are regulated in a way that requires them to be self-regulating, that is, to keep a certain amount of capital adequacy on their books; and they are able to get around the regulation quite easily. What happened with the subprime mortgage market is that, going back to 1988, American investment banks began setting up in London the "structured investment vehicles" that allowed them to get around the capital adequacy standards that had been set up in Basel 1. They set up off-book accounts that allowed them to trade in risky products such as the subprime mortgage derivatives.

On top of it all, most national banking systems are not deep. I once heard Volcker speak at the Board of Trade in Toronto. He had just come back from Argentina. This was before the Argentine crisis. He had asked the head of the Argentine central bank what the total capitalisation of their banking system was. Before coming to Toronto he had stopped in Philadelphia, at a bankers' dinner there, and asked the second-largest bank in Philadelphia, a regional bank, what its capitalisation was. It was larger than all of Argentina's!

So he came to Toronto and said: "Look, this is impossible. What's going to have to happen is that Western banks are going to have to buy these banking systems". The former head of the Bank of Canada got up – and this guy is a pure monetarist – and said: "Well, that is all well and good, but most countries don't want their banking systems to be owned by foreigners". So there are contradictions, as well as efficiencies and functionalities, in this highly volatile, global financial capitalism.

The central banks and the finance ministries – and the Federal Reserve as a proto-world-bank, and the Treasury, though it has played this role less under Bush than it did under Clinton – have managed to keep the capitalist system going; they have managed to fire-fight; the crises have been contained, from moment of chaos to moment of chaos. One never knows whether they can keep on doing this. Their main function in terms of regulation is to know enough about the players in the financial market that they can manage crises. We may be seeing, out of this crisis, a turn towards increasing mandatory regulation, which will also be coordinated. I still think the system would be mostly self-regulated. It would be like Sarbanes-Oxley, where the boards of directors are required to sign off on accounting papers and become legally liable.

But maybe global capitalism doesn't have to continue to be neoliberal in the sense we have known it. I wrote an article ten years ago called "The Social Democratisation of Globalisation", and I think that is possible out of the current crisis. How far it will go, and whether it means anything in terms of shifting the balance of class forces – that really depends on whether the working classes, broadly defined, manage to act to shift the balance of class forces from below. But I do think it's possible that out of this crisis there will be more directive oversight on the part of capitalist states and the American state, even if the crisis drags on, as it may do, for a couple of years, with a shake-out in the banking system that produces further concentration in it.

The Federal Reserve and the European Central Bank have followed sharply different policies in the current crisis. International coordination doesn't seem to be working very well.

Yes and no. Going back to the beginning of this particular crisis, last August, there was immediately coordination between the US Treasury and Federal Reserve in terms of throwing liquidity into the markets, and the European banks threw most of it in. Some of the banks hit mostly heavily by the crisis with the subprime derivatives were ironically the quasi-public Landesbanks in Germany, and the European Central Bank, really acting for the Bundesbank, oversaw the remedial measures.

Interestingly, most of what they pumped in then immediately made its way to London, to the interbank market. There was coordination then. Then there was coordination around the liquidity thrown in in December. So on that level there been quite a lot of cooperation, and the European Central Bank has played a central role.

On the question of inflation, however – on the question of whether lowering interest rates is the way to go – you're right. It partly reflects the fact that the Bundesbank – and the European Central Bank has carried the same tradition forward – has always been, from the time Bretton Woods began, much more monetarist than any other central bank, much more concerned about inflation.

The New York Fed has been much more pragmatic about that. And it has had the room to be, because of the world confidence in the Treasury Bill and in the weakness of the left in the United States – there is much more confidence in the guarantee that the American state offers against default. Also, the United States is more populist. The Fed does not have the de facto independence from the political system that the European Central Bank has.

The different approaches are also, I would guess, a reflection of different policy judgements. There's a sense that the lowering of the interest rate is not enough, in itself, to make the financial system ready to be lending, and you see this in the fact that long-term interest rates are not declining. People have been saying that the Fed is pushing against a string, and that may be the case to some extent.

There is one way in which I think the Fed has acted as world central bank in a way that the ECB never does – so you see the hierarchy of imperial apparatuses here. When there were the beginnings of a stock market crash, in Asia and spreading to Europe, in January or early February, the Fed met on a Monday night and then on Tuesday morning announced the big interest rate reduction. The Fed felt it had to send that signal of a drastic reduction in interest rates, not so much for what it would accomplish, but for its symbolic effect in terms of reassuring the stock markets. The stock market has traditionally taken the view that a reduction in interest rates means that people shift from bonds to stocks, though I'm not sure how much that continues to operate today. In any case, the signal from the Fed did have an effect. There's a special role which the Fed plays which the European Central Bank does not play vis-a-vis global stock markets.

Some financial crises in recent decades have had relatively little knock-on effect on trade and production. Do you think that one factor in this is that the financial sphere is feeding much more off consumer credit? And then could we see this financial crisis, rather bigger than previous ones, feeding into a crisis in trade and production initially through a reduction in consumer spending rather than in investment spending?

So far, the indication is that it's not impossible in Europe, or in North America, or least of all in the Third World, to be raising funds for investment. If the derivatives play the central role they do, as Dick Bryan explains, in hedging risk, there is a question whether the financial crisis will affect trade in the long run. People tend to overlook the extent to which, even though real wages have not increased, or not increased much, since the 70s, living standards for workers in the advanced capitalist world have gone up. They've gone up primarily through those workers becoming integrated into finance.

They've gone up to the extent to which those workers have become indebted and the financial system has been willing to integrate them through the enormous growth in the credit card market and in mortgages. That is also reflected to a certain extent in the fact that workers' savings have been picked up through pension funds and institutional investment so that workers tend to think of themselves, astonishingly, as investors whose net wealth will increase as they get older. That all went so far, and then it fell apart, because it penetrated, not only in the credit card market but also in the mortgage market, to that portion of the American working class which has always been the Achilles heel of the integration of American workers into the American dream, and that is the African-American working class. You don't understand it at first when you walk around Washington Heights in New York and you see unemployed young black men wearing $200 sneakers. They're doing it on credit. It seems hard to believe that capital extended the types of loans it did to African-Americans in Cleveland to buy sub-standard housing stock with the promise that it, too, would increase in value; but it did that.

The question now is whether the ability of advanced capitalism to integrate workers through the credit market has run up against its limits, and what are the implications if it has. What are the implications in terms of economic crisis, and what are the implications in terms of workers not taking it any more. One wishes one would see much more radical protest than we have seen so far around the housing crisis in the United States. You hear enough about it in terms of politicians talking about people being affected as victims, but you don't yet see much mobilisation. That's not to say there won't be.

There is speculation in the *Wall Street Journal* today that the market is waiting for the American state to buy up all this bad debt – whether directly through the Fed, or through a special agency – in other words, to socialise it. The *Wall Street Journal* quotes one analyst from a private investment firm saying that he is not predicting that this will be done, but he is saying that it is what the market is looking for.

The operation would be like the British government has done with Northern Rock, but on a massively bigger scale. The bad debt even in the United States is probably in the hundreds of billions of dollars, let alone the total around the world. It's conceivable that might happen, and then the consumer's ability to get into the credit system would be replenished. But that hasn't happened yet, and I don't want to predict it necessarily will. It's not impossible that this crisis will be dealt with by Band-Aid measures, and it could lead to a significant shake-out whereby regional banks in the United States would close, intermediaries would go bankrupt, a piece of Citibank might be sold off...

I remember the late Harry Magdoff saying to me, in his apartment, after the stock market crash in 1987, when the question was to what extent were the banks implicated by their loans to the stockbrokers: "Well, so they'll nationalise a couple of banks!" In this context we have to understand nationalisation in an entirely different way than one might have understood it as a left-wing social democrat in England in 1945.

It's socialism for the rich!

Exactly. In the first place for the rich. But not only for the rich...

Even the perspective of a massive bail-out implies that the edges of the consumer credit system are pulled back in. Northern Rock is not writing ultra-easy mortgages any more.

Yes. And they're very worried about it. They're very worried about the fact that the financial system is reluctant to lend.

On the other hand, Martin Wolf in the Financial Times says essentially that what the Federal Reserve is doing might work, but he sort of hopes it doesn't, because there are fundamental structural problems with the very low level of savings in the USA, and if the Federal Reserve's measures allow things to stagger on a bit further, they are just paving the way for a bigger crisis down the road.

Yes. Wolf's a very smart guy. There's a more reactionary variant of the same argument coming from the *Wall Street Journal*. You hear the argument that if the Fed had not lowered interest rates in 2001 after the "new economy" bubble and 9/11, you wouldn't have had the housing bubble. But what are they saying? That they'd prefer to have this crisis then?

They're saying that they'd prefer to have a smaller crisis now that forces the resolution of unsustainable imbalances, before those imbalances become bigger.

But the fact is that agencies like the Fed are going to try to prevent crises – or, if not to prevent them, to stop them being catapulted into global capitalist crises. That is their nature. Ben Bernanke, the head of the Federal Reserve, wrote his PhD thesis on how the Fed and the Treasury could have prevented the Great Depression by supplying liquidity to the banking system instead of playing the orthodox banker role and requiring that the books be balanced. As I read all the inclination in the American state, and I think for the most part in Europe, that is the role that the central banks will try to play.

Also, I don't see that the result of a bigger crisis would be that Americans started saving again. I don't see that people would have the capacity to save. On the contrary, you'd see a rundown of savings of wealth. The greatest imbalance that people worry about is the US trade deficit. But that is being dealt with, so far, by this relatively managed decline of the dollar. There may be inflationary consequences; but the deficit was up at 7%, and it has fallen to 5% of GDP. Moreover, we need to remember that the world is not doing America a favour, as accountants seem to think, by covering the deficit with short-term capital inflows. People are buying Treasury Bills today because in this highly unstable world they are the closest things to gold that pays some interest rate. People are also buying gold and commodities and so on, and that reflects the volatility, but in so far as they are buying bonds, and they are, they are buying Treasury Bills. In Gindin's and my view, only the United States, by virtue of the asymmetrical nature of power in today's capitalism, can sustain such a deficit for a long time. But it can, because of the role that the dollar and the US Treasury Bill play in the world economy.

It's a bit like London, as a financial centre, and its "trade deficit" vis-a-vis the UK. It's a bit like New York, and its deficit vis-a-vis North America. Without thinking at all that national borders have been done away with, I think we need to look at the American deficit in the light of the special role of the dollar, which I don't think the euro is about to displace.

What about the effect of the decline of the dollar, and the resulting squeeze on US imports and rise in US exports, on China and the other big new exporting countries?

I don't have a crystal ball. The people who talked about "decoupling" are wrong. There is no "decoupling" that China can yet do from Western markets, above all from the American market. In that sense, to speak of a realignment of forces in global capitalism, as Giovanni Arrighi does, is misleading. We are seeing an increasing integration of global capitalism. China's role in global capitalism is much enhanced. But realignment is not the right word, if it is understood as Chinese capital displacing American capital, or Chinese power displacing American power.

But the decline of the dollar could have inflationary effects in those countries whose currencies remain pegged to the dollar.

If the measures that have been introduced in China to alleviate some of the discontent of the working class, whereby they've offered some labour-standards protections and some requirements for representation by the party-run Chinese unions, or the promised reform of the health system, were to come through, and you were to get inflationary pressures, you might get considerable class conflict, and that might spill over into regional conflict inside China. The uneven development in China is astonishing, and people in the regions not undergoing rapid capitalist development are highly dependent on remittances from workers in the cities.

The repercussions could be very real. But the different new exporting powers are all very different. Brazil and Russia are doing very well out of the high price of commodities, which represents a cost to China and India. I find it very difficult to gaze in a crystal ball here, given the enormously different social formations we are talking about, or to make any hard predictions.

CHAPTER 4

An Era of Rampant Inequality (May 2008)

Discussion with Simon Mohun

It's important to put the present difficulties into some sort of historical context. The early 1970s marked the end of what is often called the "Golden Age" of capitalism, the era of post-World-War-II expansion. From the end of that expansion (usually dated from 1973) we had a period of five to seven years of class struggle which was a stalemate. In that sense, there was the possibility of a substantial shift to the left. The rate of profit was collapsing, and matters were getting increasingly difficult for capital; labour was quite well organised, and was resisting moves by capital to resolve the crisis in a direction favourable to capital.

But it didn't happen – instead there was a substantial shift to the right, from about 1979–80. It was symbolised by Paul Volcker's raising of US interest rates in 1979; the election of Reagan in 1980, and his attack on the air traffic controllers' union; by the election of Thatcher in Britain in 1979 (and her subsequent labour market "reforms"); and by Mitterrand being forced into a policy U-turn in the early 1980s. All round the metropolitan capitalist world, there was a major shift in the balance of forces towards capital and away from labour. Since about 1982, the rate of profit has recovered.

This is still the era we are living in. Symbolised by the terms "globalisation", and "financialisation", it is an era of the dominance of pro-market ideologies on a world scale. Capital is very mobile; trade unions are very weak; and there is a convergence of policies by the major political parties. There have been huge increases in pay at the top of the distribution, while in the US for example, for about 83% of employees, real wages per hour were stagnant from about 1978 to 1997. The working class has taken a hammering in almost all metropolitan countries in the last 20 or 25 years in terms of labour organisation, income, and so on.

So it's a bit hard to speak of "crisis". This is a word of course almost devoid of meaning, because of its over-use on the left. But clearly something is currently going on! The issue is how to understand it. It is not a problem of rising wages squeezing profits. It is not a problem of technical progress somehow driving down the rate of profit. It is not a problem to do with the exhaustion

* Previously published in *Solidarity* 132, 14 May 2008.

of profitable lines of business. It is not a problem of capital running out of exploitable inputs. So in classical Marxist terms, the traditional explanations don't work. All we are left with is something a bit vague to do with the "anarchy of the market".

There are some interesting parallels between the present situation and the late 1920s, to do with consumer debt, buying on margin [borrowing to buy stocks and bonds and hoping to make money on rises or falls in price], and a credit crisis spreading into the rest of the economy. It's worth remembering that a cyclical downturn (recession) was transformed into the Great Depression by the three waves of US banking collapses after 1930, and that is just not going to happen today. The current Chair of the Fed [the US central bank] is Bernanke, who, as an academic economist, made his reputation in the study of the Great Depression. Bernanke, the Fed and the US Treasury are not going to allow those bank failures to happen today, even if they have to (in effect) nationalise all the bad debt. The failure of Bear Stearns in the US was contained, and the markets correctly took that as a signal that no matter what the pain, the financial system will not be allowed to implode. Similarly, in the UK: Northern Rock was effectively nationalised, and the Bank of England currently stands ready to allow the banks to swap their unmarketable mortgage debt for marketable government debt (even if not quite at 1 to 1) for up to three years. And similarly in Europe.

In sum, the activities of the major central banks are going to ensure that the system does not run out of liquidity. The quid pro quo of course will be a much more interventionist approach by financial authorities in the USA and around the world to regulating finance and investment banks. It is clear that the way in which that housing debt was securitised [bundled into pieces of paper giving titles to income, and traded on financial markets] is going to be much more heavily regulated in future. There will be a lot of pain in financial houses in the City and on Wall Street, but I think most people will say "serve them right"; and the interesting question for the future is the extent to which the financial institutions will be made to bear responsibility for the mayhem they have created.

Do we have a problem of liquidity, or is it a problem of solvency? [I.e. is it a crisis of people and firms not being able to get hard cash in time to cover the payments they have to make, or of them not having enough assets, liquid or illiquid, to cover their liabilities?] The central banks are determined to make sure a crisis of liquidity is resolved, by just pumping liquidity into the market, but will allow any institution that turns out to be insolvent to go bust. We'll have to see if that works. There are clearly risks, but my guess is that the underlying economy is stronger than a lot of the doom-sayers in the press claim. So, there will be some pain, particularly in the financial sector, and all the signs are that there will be a recession in the "real" economy, although probably not a very severe or long-lasting one.

I could be wrong. It's quite possible that the banks are still hiding things, and there are nasty surprises still in store. At present, because the banks are reluctant to lend to each other, the [high] interest rates that the banks are charging have become "decoupled" from [lower] official interest rates. Financial markets will be volatile for some time, until all the bad debt is out in the open. When markets correct, they generally overshoot, so that bubbles and then crashes in the prices of assets are not uncommon. The US housing bubble has been pricked, and the UK's housing bubble (more severe relatively than in the US) looks like it's following suit. Obviously as housing prices fall, some will suffer, and undoubtedly pain in consumer credit markets will spread to firms' production and investment plans. Nevertheless, the crisis does not look that dramatically severe to me.

I think there are three things we should be particularly concerned about. First, the growth in inequality. In the USA – I haven't explored this for other countries, because the data is much harder to get hold of – the rise in the rate of profit [profits as a rate of return on capital deployed] has not been reflected in an equivalent rise in the profit share [profits as a percentage of total income]. The rate of profit would have risen higher, with a rise in the profit share too, were it not that a lot of what might be called profit income was diverted into the pockets of the already wealthy. The share of productive labour [in the Marxist sense, i.e. of labour producing surplus value] in total labour in the USA remained roughly constant in the last two decades of the 20th century. The share of unproductive wages has dramatically increased, and that is largely driven by increased pay in legal services, finance, insurance and real estate, and business services. This increased pay is not because proportionally more hours have been worked, but because such unproductive labour has been paid a great deal more. Inequality of income has increased dramatically in the US, and especially at the top end of the income distribution. The same is true of the UK. These inequalities have corrosive effects on society. Fortunately, some of this is (ever so slowly) coming to be recognised (witness the fuss Labour backbenchers are currently making over the abolition of the 10p income tax band – the same MPs who cheered the reduction of the standard rate from 22p to 20p at the same time).

Second, there are major changes taking place in the structure of the world economy, consequent upon the rise of China, and to a lesser extent India and Brazil (and perhaps Russia if we confine attention to energy markets). The US economy remains the most powerful economy in the world, and one of the most resilient economies in the world; and it will remain that way for some time to come. But relatively speaking, the US economy is in decline. The dollar is not as powerful as it was in international markets. The euro is looking like a much stronger currency. Increasingly, those who run the treasury departments of central banks, particularly in the Far East, are looking very hard at their dollar portfolios, and asking whether they are a sensible long-run home for their assets. The dollar is significantly weaker as a world currency than it used to be. But this a slow process. A catastrophic slide of the dollar does not seem likely to me. It is always possible, but it would be so disruptive and so much against every individual country's short-term interest, that it is unlikely to happen.

But there are other effects that look more difficult. One is energy and its continuing price rises. The other is food in world markets and its price rises. These prices seem to be being driven by demand (especially in East and South Asia) at the same time as there are supply difficulties. These price rises are potentially calamitous for the world's poor, and it remains to be seen whether the supply situation will improve. They are also more generally inflationary. In the USA, for the Fed, more inflation might not be such a bad thing; it could bring down real house prices with a smaller fall in nominal prices. That's one reason why the Fed is more relaxed about inflation: it sees it as a way of easing some of the price adjustments that would otherwise be more painful.

Third, Marxists have not done very well in understanding the huge change in the balance of power within capital, which is often summed up in terms like financialisation. Since the early 1980s the resurgence of capital has also been a rise of finance, and that is to do with globalisation and the new facilities to shift large amounts of money around electronically. However, it would not be quite right to talk of this as a successful struggle of finance capital versus industrial capital. They are much more intertwined than that picture would suggest. There's been a celebration of markets, of money-making, of individualism, of greed, and so on, which is associated with a significant change in the way in which capital presents itself.

But the nature of capital has changed, with finance becoming much more preponderant. And the way in which this has happened is not through the extraction of income for financial interests via interest rates. Of course that still exists. But finance capital now mainly works through the extraction of very large fees for providing consultancy advice for services like mergers and acquisitions. I think theory is behind the game in this regard. And it is for this reason that the theoretical parameters of the current situation (the "crisis") are not well understood, which is where we began.

CHAPTER 5

The Imbalances are Unsustainable (June 2008)

Discussion with Trevor Evans

After the 1929 crash the United States government introduced very tight controls of the financial system. From 1933 to the early 70s the financial sector was very tightly regulated. By the 1970s the banks were looking for ways to get round the controls. There was a political shift in the late 70s, after Ford became President of the US, and from 1980 onwards there was a process of liberalisation. The most first important change was in 1980, when the legal upper limit on interest rates was abolished. There was a series of laws, under Reagan and Clinton, up to the 1999 law which completely abolished the remainder of the regulations which had been introduced in 1933.

This process of liberalisation of the financial sector created the basis on which all sorts of innovations could develop, and resulted in a huge expansion in the size of the financial sector relative to industrial and commercial capital. The whole pattern of capitalist accumulation has become much more centrally driven by finance than it was before 1980. The United States, since the 1980s, has been looking for new ways of promoting accumulation in the US and maintaining its international position.

The 1980s began with very high interest rates of about 20%. That resulted in a major recession which dealt a massive blow to working-class organisation in the United States and, indeed, around the world, as the high interest rates led to the Latin American debt crisis and the re-subordination of Third World countries. During the 1980s there was a huge wave of mergers and takeovers in the United States, comparable with the wave at the end of the 19th century – a massive restructuring of the US corporate sector, made possible by new forms of financial instrument, particularly junk bonds. It was followed by a process of rationalisation, with the least competitive units being closed, and constant pressure to force real wages down and re-establish a higher rate of profit for the first time since the big crises in the 1970s.

The banks then ran out of money at the end of the 1980s, and the Federal Reserve responded by lowering interest rates and pumping money into the economy to prevent the over-lent banks from running into problems. Lower

---

* Previously published in *Solidarity* 134, 26 June 2008.

interest rates led to a weaker dollar. That helped US exports, and laid the basis for a slow recovery in the early 1990s. The so-called IT boom followed in the second half of the 90s. You had a period when high profits, rising share prices, and very strong investment in fixed capital fuelled each other. Again, the process was very, very dependent on an expansion of credit. The huge investments in IT, particularly in the new global fibre-optic networks, were financed by credit. In addition, firms were borrowing to buy back their own shares in order to push up share prices and make themselves less vulnerable to takeovers.

The bubble burst at the beginning of 2000, and that is where we get to the beginning of the current story. The collapse of share prices from the spring of 2000 onwards was comparable to the crash in 1929. Why didn't we get a string of bank crashes and a depression? The Federal Reserve had learned to intervene very rapidly. It cut interest rates sharply, from 6.5% in January 2001 to a low of 1% two years later. That generated a massive expansion of credit. Anyone following the financial sector was sure that this was breeding trouble. Most people did not at first look at the subprime mortgage sector, but rather at the new wave of leveraged buyouts, in some ways a repeat of the 1980s, now led by so-called "private equity" firms, but essentially, again, financing takeovers by issuing debt. That looked like the most vulnerable point.

There was also the extraordinary growth of derivatives, particularly credit derivatives [bits of financial paper which "derive" from other bits – representing, for example, "future" assets, or "bets" or "hedges" on whether certain financial prices will go up or down]. That was probably the biggest time-bomb of all sitting in the system. And then there was the mortgage growth. The US system makes it relatively easy to refinance your house mortgage, so households took out new mortgages to pay off their old mortgages and draw an extra amount to finance consumption. That extra consumption from borrowing drove the expansion from 2001–2 to 2007. Business investment was very weak, because businesses had so over-invested in the late 90s.

As a result of financial liberalisation, it was possible for banks and other lenders to grant mortgages to low-income households who in the past would not have qualified. And it was attractive – they could charge much higher interest rates. They would send people out to working-class neighbourhoods to offer very attractive initial rates and convince people that they could get credit to buy a house more cheaply than they could rent. At a time when house prices were rising, and the borrowers could remortgage a couple of years later on an increased price for their house, that seemed like a good deal. The crisis which broke in August 2007 was the end of the third of the waves of expansion, since the early 1980s, which have been closely linked to the process of financial liberalisation. The housing credits were mainly then sold on, by grouping large numbers of mortgages as bonds that could be traded. Those bonds were in turn transformed into other bonds which could get more attractive ratings. It appeared that the big banks were selling the bonds on, but what became clear last summer was that many of them were also holding some of the new bonds themselves, not on their own books, but in off-balance-sheet vehicles to get round all the international rules on capital requirements [i.e. rules which say that banks must have a certain stash of cash, of their own, to underpin their operations].

Once everybody realised that this was going on, the banks took fright at lending to each other. In the second week of August, the inter-bank money market dried up. Banks were no longer willing to trust each other, because nobody knew who had huge liabilities which they had kept secret.

The expansion since 2001–2 has seen all sorts of financial instruments expanding on a huge scale. When the crisis broke, for example, many banks were left holding loans for leveraged buyouts which they had planned to sell on. Interest rates being low since 2001–2 meant that financial institutions could borrow cheaply, but on the other hand the financial return on their lending was quite low. That was why they were so interested in forms of lending which involved leverage, where the borrower uses a relatively small amount of his own capital and borrows the rest in order to buy up a firm. You had private equity firms which would borrow ten times as much as they would put up themselves for a purchase. The hedge funds [whose business is, essentially, betting in the financial markets with borrowed money] would borrow up to thirty times their own capital.

When the central bank sets a low interest rate, the financial sector goes searching for leverage. That means that if things go well, they get high returns; the moment things go wrong, the leverage goes into reverse, and they make huge losses. The Fed has now pushed its interest rate very low. That will relieve the pressure on some of the financial institutions under stress. But the traditional channels by which central bank monetary policy operate are running into problems. In the advanced capitalist countries, the main way that monetary policy operates is that the central bank buys bonds and thus provides central bank money to the inter-bank money market. Usually the central bank has a target for the interest rate in the inter-bank money market, and then banks in turn charge an interest rate which is a mark-up on that inter-bank rate for their outside lending. Since last August the inter-bank money market interest rate has been very substantially above the central bank interest rate. When the central bank pumps money in, it can keep the overnight interest rate at about the level it was, but one-month borrowing and three-month borrowing rates are significantly – in terms of the money markets: 0.5% or 0.75% – above the target of the central bank. The traditional transmission mechanism of central bank monetary policy is not working because the banks don't trust each other.

Clearly the Fed is helping financial institutions which are faced with liquidity problems [i.e. which have sufficient assets, but not sufficient ready cash]. Commercial banks have direct resort to the money markets, or they can borrow [from the central bank] on the lender-of-last-resort facility. But Bear Stearns was an investment bank [i.e. dealing only in the financial-investment markets, not in deposits from or loans to the general public or for commercial purposes]. It did not have access to the lender-of-last-resort facility. So the Fed had to engineer the takeover of Bear Stearns by J P Morgan Chase, which is a universal bank, i.e. commercial bank and investment bank. Lowering the official interest rate has guarded against further financial institutions going bankrupt. But in truth they are continually displacing the problem.

When the first post-1980 expansion ran into trouble at the end of the 1980s, and the Fed responded by pushing money in, it prevented a deep recession in 1991, and laid the basis for the next expansion – and the bubble at the end. By pushing money into the system in 2001, the Fed prevented another deep recession, at the cost of yet a further build-up of credit bubbles. They can't keep on doing that forever. The scale of the collapse being staved off becomes bigger each time. Whether they will stave off collapse this time, I don't know. Some commentators are suggesting that the worst of the financial crisis may be over, and it's possible. But these complex bonds are distributed around a huge number of people, and financial crisis could flare up again. In any case, pushing the extra money in means that the financial institutions are now more indebted. There is more overhang. If the Fed establishes the basis for a new expansion next year, it is going to start with even higher levels of debt, of higher financial liabilities, than the last one.

In past writings, you have emphasised that Marxist theories of capitalist crises do not see them as just financial. A crisis happens through the interaction of financial disturbances and basic movements in profits. But recently profit rates have been high. The rate of profit in Britain in 2007 quarter three was the highest since the statistical series started in 1965. Does that dispel the risk of the financial crisis having a big impact in trade and production?

Profit rates have been recovering in the advanced capitalist countries since the early 1980s. There have been intermittent downturns, but broadly speaking profitability was re-established in the major transformation of the 1980s. Each period of expansion has to find some way of realising the surplus value [i.e. of selling the commodities which exploited labour has produced].

The vulnerability of the most recent expansion, 2002–7, was that it was exceptionally dependent on consumer spending.

Profit rates in the US were also up to their best values since the 1960s. But, particularly in the US, it now looks as if we are faced with a recession not just from the financial crisis, but from that very rapid growth of consumer spending coming to an end. That recession is going to feed back, in the course of this year, into a financial system which already has its own big internal difficulties. US profit rates peaked in 2006. There is already a slight downturn. As consumer spending falls – investment spending was already weak, and strongly driven by investment in housing – we will probably see the coming-together of problems arising from the financial sector and of others which come from business profits falling because of slacker consumer spending.

Martin Wolf, in the Financial Times of 1 May 2008, writes that: "The ratio of household liabilities to disposable income [in the UK] jumped from 105 per cent at the end of 1996 to 164 per cent at the end of 2006... Such a rise cannot be repeated". There has to be a correction; and in the US, too, though the figure there is slightly lower, 138 per cent. Do you agree?

On this occasion, I would agree with Martin Wolf! We never know beforehand how far the elastic can be stretched. Marx wrote that the credit system is notoriously elastic. But the expansion of household debt cannot go on indefinitely. It means the level of debt service is constantly rising; a higher share of households' disposable income goes out in interest and capital repayments.

What do you expect to happen to inflation?

The Fed's policy seems to be based on thinking that somewhat higher inflation is not a big problem, and may even help ease the credit crisis. The Federal Reserve in the US has a different attitude on this from the European Central Bank. The Fed does not have an explicit inflation target. Once inflation gets to about 4%, they start reacting, but anything under 4% does not worry them. The European Central Bank has an extraordinary fetish that any inflation above 2% is unacceptable – it's a continuation of the policy of the [German] Bundesbank – and hence, since the introduction of the euro in 1999, it has been following a monetary policy that is unnecessarily restrictive. In 2002 and 2003 the concern was about the US or Europe falling into experiencing deflation and the sort of problems that Japan had faced in the 1990s. Now it is different, with higher inflation, driven principally by primary commodity prices, energy and foodstuffs.

A recession in the US and Europe will ease those primary commodity prices, since primary commodity prices have followed the business cycle in the developed capitalist countries quite closely. But there are long-term structural issues here: there are limits to the quantity of oil available, and there is pressure on land for growing food. The era of very low inflation we have had over the past 10 or 15 years, driven above all by falling prices of manufactured exports from Asia, seems to be over. Prices have begun to rise fairly fast in China now. The inflation is concentrated in food prices, but that feeds through to wages. In the export manufacturing areas along the southern coast, wages are rising.

The other dimension to understanding commodity prices is the policy of the IMF and the World Bank since the early 1980s. Primary commodity prices were relatively high in the 1970s. In the early 1980s the IMF and the World Bank turned to so-called structural adjustment programs, forcing developing countries to open up their economies and re-specialise on the basis of comparative advantage [producing whatever export commodities their relative costs indicate as most advantageous]. The supply of primary commodities increased quite strongly from the late 1980s. But that phase is also over.

The US had a major change of policy, starting in the early 70s under Nixon. Until then it had been concerned with building up a strong capitalist bloc in the world [in competition with the bloc led by the USSR], and it had been willing to countenance countries like Germany and Japan having undervalued exchange rates to promote their exports. In the early 70s that changed. And since the 1980s we have seen the US pursuing a series of short-term moves – not a long-term strategy, because it doesn't have one – to maintain its position in the world. Part of that is the role of the dollar in the world economy, which enables the US to run its repeated current-account deficits. This has involved the US continually having to reassert the power it has in financial markets, in economics, and of course militarily. It is going to be increasingly difficult for it to do that.

It is still the biggest and strongest economy in the world. It has a representation in most key sectors of production. It has a huge trade deficit; its exports are rising, but it has a huge trade deficit which it must finance, in effect, by borrowing from the rest of the world. But, as with households in Britain, the US cannot indefinitely continue to accumulate international indebtedness. I did say that ten years ago, too, and here we are today, but it really cannot go on forever.

One of the things we are seeing now is an adjustment of the relative strength of the dollar in the world economy. The US will be looking for ways to reassert itself, and that makes it quite dangerous. We hope that the rulers of the US have learned from the fiasco in Iraq, but we can't be sure. The US has been enjoying a standard of living above its capacity to produce for 25 years. The overwhelming bulk of that increased consumption has gone to the top 20%, and a big part of it to the top one per cent. But those people are never satisfied. They want more and more. They want to ensure they have continued access to energy and they can continue to run the current account deficits. I think it's going to be difficult. Over the last two or three years, China has shifted from a dollar standard [for its currency] to a basket of currencies. Russia has done the same. One or two of the smaller countries in the Middle East are shifting towards a basket of currencies, although Saudi Arabia still links its currency to the dollar. The willingness of countries to use the dollar as reserve currency is beginning to shift, too. Many countries face a difficult dilemma at present. Countries like China have large reserves already held in dollars, and anything they do which weakens the dollar is going to hurt them. But – so far as we can tell: they don't publish figures – new current account surpluses are not being invested solely in dollars, but more widely dispersed.

Clearly, New York is the financial centre of the world. In a sense, when we talk about international capital markets, we are really talking about the international extensions of the US capital market. There aren't markets hanging above the Pacific or the Atlantic. But the importance of that is declining. The euro area capital market is now in some respects comparable in size to the US capital market. It is much more fragmented; but it is slowly becoming more integrated. There is now more investment in euro instruments than there was before, although it is still much smaller than the trade in dollar instruments.

The overwhelming majority of capital flows in the world are between Europe and the United States. The Asian countries and China are investing their surpluses in dollars. That's predominantly a one-way flow, whereas the capital markets between Europe and the US are deep, deep, deep [i.e., because of their large flows in many directions, they can generally accommodate large transactions without jerky movements in prices]. As the euro capital markets develop, that gives firms more opportunities for diversifying their holdings. Of course, there is a risk that the current crisis could spiral into a catastrophic decline of the dollar. The IMF's World Economic Outlook of 18 months ago was focused on scenarios for the collapse of the dollar, and all the factors the IMF identified in that report as creating a danger of what they called a disorderly devaluation of the dollar are still present. The last time that happened was in the first week of October 1979, when Paul Volcker [then chair of the Fed] famously had to leave the IMF meeting in Belgrade, fly back to New York, and raise interest rates very dramatically, leading to a three-year recession in the whole world.

If it happened, it would probably happen very quickly. It only needs one thing, possibly even a rumour, to set off a chain of selling, and the markets can move very quickly. The US central bank would have to react instantly, and it would do so in conjunction with the other central banks. Much as they are deeply disturbed by the way the US manages its monetary policy, in a situation like that the other central banks would have no choice but to instantly collaborate with the US. The emergency action would mean raising interest rates in the US. But in the present situation that is complicated, because it would exacerbate the credit crisis.

The growth in the last five years or so of the BRICs [Brazil, Russia, India, China, etc.] has been quite closely linked to the expansion in the US. China, although its domestic market is growing, is dependent on exports of manufactured goods. Although Brazil has a very impressive industrial sector, it has been above all exports of primary commodities – partly to the US, but also to China – which have driven recent growth. The BRICs will continue to grow. But the rate at which they have been growing in the last five years has been linked to the consumer spending boom in the US, so they will all be to some extent affected by a downturn in the US.

The situation in China is extraordinary. There is a completely depoliticised government which is concerned at all costs to keep consumption rising for those sectors of the population that have been incorporated into the new economy – the urban population and in particular the new middle class. At the same time the government is trying to do something about the terrible situation in the countryside and about the disastrous environmental situation.

There are huge imbalances. The government is trying to deal with the rising wages in the coastal regions by encouraging new investment inland and in particular to the west, where wages are much lower. But the central state does not have much control over investment. China still does not have properly functioning market-based mechanisms, but the planning mechanisms, in so for as they now exist at all, are at a regional level, and each province wants to have its own car factory and its own steel factory. There has been huge over-investment in fixed capital.

Share prices in China have been rising to absolutely absurd levels, too. There will be a political problem when the middle class who have put their money into shares suddenly discover that it's gone. If the government continues shifting towards a market-based financial system, there will be a financial crisis at some time, and that will hit living standards and pose a big threat to the legitimacy of the regime.

CHAPTER 6

The Inventiveness of Capital (July 2008)

Discussion with Dick Bryan

Much of the current discussion of global finance focuses on massive growth in credit. We get stories about the huge growth in fictitious capital, about speculation, and about how money and finance have grown out of proportion to the "real" economy. But there is more to finance than the credit system – recall that this is how Marx depicted money all of 150 years ago.

If the current financial situation were just a story of big financial growth it would be of no great consequence. We would find, and we are finding, that the credit bubble will burst, there will be losses (amounting to personal hardship), but no systemic challenge. The really significant change of the last 20 years is not growth of the credit system. It is the fact that money has increasingly taken the form of financial derivatives and securities. In other words, money has in a sense moved into the sphere of commodified risk. It has invited us to consider the possibility that we may need to change our understanding of what money is in modern capitalism. In the current financial crisis, for instance, it is securitised debt, not debt itself, that has been at the heart of the problem. This is important, not incidental, because to understand money and finance, we now need to go via derivatives and securities, as much as via "the over-expansion of credit", "speculation" and "hot money". The latter are really just cheap, moralistic jibes.

To get to what this means, we need some historical context. The state used to oversee the stability of the money system. The state linked the present to the future. It controlled interest rates. It controlled exchange rates. It controlled agricultural prices. As the state withdraws from doing these things, people, and financial markets, face a lot of risks and uncertainties. As the state has withdrawn, the market has come in. The market is now linking the present to the future, and this is done in a competitive and contestable way that doesn't produce stable prices. For some this is a signal that capitalism is in trouble because it can't trade at fundamental values, with stable money. But this is only one possible interpretation.

The contestability of prices may also be understood as adding a new competitive dimension to capitalist accumulation. Indeed, a whole new range of

---

* Previously published in *Solidarity* 135, 10 July 2008.

products have emerged to compensate, as it were, for the absence of state guarantees. They are products that specialise in price contestability. Things like futures and options and swaps are the market's alternative to what the state used to do. So we find that financial derivatives, relating to interest rates and exchange rates evolve to provide insurance against financial contingencies (including the risk of financial failure: credit derivatives). What's more, when we see these financial futures, options and swaps trading exposures to interest rates and exchange rates, they themselves start to look very much like money. More precisely, they start to blur the distinction between what is money and what is capital.

This explanation could go further, too. The state used to oversee lending practices for housing. Now it doesn't. Instead, we see subprime and securitised debt as the market takes over the risks of home lending. Debts become commodified in highly liquid markets – and they start to play a money-like role. But these are a very different sort of money from the way we usually think about money as cash and bank deposits. And the notion of "credit" doesn't capture what is important here.

Costas Lapavitsas (Lapavitsas 2006) responds to your idea by writing: "The commensurating function [of derivatives] is nothing more than the carapace of the commodity form placed over hedging and speculative strategies involving several underlying financial assets. Derivatives have no obvious hoarding and paying functions in the world market, and they are certainly not 'the anchor of the global financial system'. In so far as such an anchor exists today, that is the US dollar..."

Indeed, Costas is quite hostile to this interpretation. But we need to clarify what is misunderstanding and what is disagreement. Costas wants to draw all money back to "credit", as if this is the ultimate descriptor of capitalist money, and anything not looking like credit is ipso facto precluded as money.

Even within a functionalist definition, derivatives do play a money function. They are a store of value in volatile markets. They aren't like a bank vault, though, because they store very large amounts of money for very short periods. Take for instance a futures contract on wheat: it is an alternative to storing wheat in a silo. It is in a very immediate sense a store of value. Financial derivatives on say exchange rates are no different in this specific sense: they preserve value. They reflect the money uses of capital, where a store of value means not preserving something, but benchmarking its value to competitive processes. They store across time (when interest rates change unpredictably) and they store across currencies (when exchange rates change unpredictably). The problem, I think, is that when, like Costas, you start with functionalist definitions of money (money as means of exchange, store of value, unit of account, etc.), then financial volatility, such as we are currently seeing, is posed as a threat to the functionality of money, and hence as some sort of "crisis". And it leads simply to arguments that we need better regulation, so that the functionality of money can be safely restored.

This is a view that has respectable support within and outside of Marxism. And one need not disagree with the benefits of such regulation. But Marxists must surely have more to say about the changing nature of money itself. Perhaps here also is the problem that money is posed as only a product of the state, so the state is the only one that can fix it up.

But as a Marxist, I start from a different position – not from the premise that all money emanates from the state; rather that there can be no presumption that the financial system "should" be stable or in some sort of proportion to production, or any of these "balance" sorts of premises. Hence, I think we have to start by saying that financial instability is not itself an issue of crisis. The left seems so keen to call everything volatile a crisis!

If you start from the presumption that money embodies contradictions, and they can play out as volatility, different questions arise from those of how to regulate to restore stability. The first question is to frame the contradiction, and how it plays out. The next issue to ask is how does capital itself deal with volatility, and one answer, I think, is that it uses financial derivatives. This is the sense in which derivatives are a monetary anchor. The US dollar wins the popularity contest as the world's most used currency, but when the value of the dollar itself is not anchored (such as to gold under Bretton Woods) and it is of uncertain value (as it is right now), it cannot be called an anchor. Anchoring has to be about the commensuration of value, not popularity, and in that process, the critical issue is not "can everything be converted to US dollars?" (for that is trivial), but how do we deal with discrepancies when there is no single stable measure of equivalence. The answer I give is that non-equivalence has itself been turned into a commodity to be bought and sold. By creating financial derivatives, capital has made it profitable to solve its own problems of non-equivalence!

Those are the sorts of questions we need to pose. The current so-called subprime crisis will pass. It will play itself out. The regulations may or may not change. But the changes to finance through derivatives and securitisation are here to stay. We will always have derivatives and securitisation within capitalism. They may be recent innovations, but they describe an essentially capitalist way of calculating the relative values of different parts of capital and different forms of money.

Notice also, that the way I've framed this issue, we don't have a disjuncture between money and the "real" economy. Derivatives and securities are part-money and part-capital, so we don't need to frame these spheres as separate. So the analytically-impoverished observation that finance has grown out of proportion to the "real" economy – as if there are correct proportions, and as if there is a clear dichotomy (following Friedman and the monetarists!) – does not arise. As an aside: who would have imagined 20 years ago that the mortgage-backed securities would have the liquidity of Treasury bonds, or that, as their liquidity dried up, central banks would be exchanging mortgage-backed securities (of indeterminate value) for cash. It's a sign that the world of capital and the world of money just can't be separated.

Having said that, liquidity always brings its own particular disturbances because where assets are easy to buy and sell, rumour and perceptions can drive trading decisions. Perceptions can always turn down. There can always be some flow-through from financial aggregates into trade and investment. Keynes got this right, though it is a particular politics that says that the state should take over and manage, and that the outcome is a remedy. The possibility of that Keynesian remedy was contingent on a whole set of conditions that were only in place for a relatively brief period. It's time to look more closely at the conditions that characterise our age.

I don't see the current disturbances as a fundamental crisis. Company profit rates are high. In general, companies aren't exposed to significant debt. Investment levels are high. The world economy is booming. But we have found that risk has been underpriced in the last few years. The pricing of risk is being recalculated. Companies that want to borrow now have to pay more to borrow, and that's probably as it should be. In the foreseeable future, capital will be funding investment increasingly out of retained earnings and share issues. Leveraged buyouts (private equity deals) will be fewer. What's happening is a not an unreasonable adjustment. But it's an adjustment with collateral damage. The odd bank will go broke. Individuals lose their houses. Bad things happen. And there is an important class dimension here, as many of the costs are borne by an organisationally weakened working class, where risks are being transferred onto individuals and households.

You say that we should not overestimate the role of the dollar in the world economy. Would you also say that the role of the US state in the world economy more generally is overestimated? You have said that the state is withdrawing from many economic functions. Does this mean that the international markets are becoming much more important than the formal international institutions in which the US is still hegemonic?

At the World Economic Forum in January, George Soros announced the end of the dollar era. Soros has made many correct calls – indeed he has just published a book crowing about his recent successes in volatile financial markets. But this one was a big call, and there is no immediate answer. He may have won shorting the dollar, but I'm not sure what alternative money unit he's gone long on. The US dollar is far and away the world's most used currency. The Bank for International Settlements data show that the dollar is on one side of 86 percent of financial transactions. The Euro is on one side of less than 40 percent (think of 100 transactions – with 200 "sides" to those transactions). It is anyone's guess whether there will be diversification away from the dollar and indeed also from the euro.

But on the specific role of the US state and its role in managing global finance, I think US hegemony should not be so closely tied to an idea of the elevated status of the dollar. The City of London is the predominant world financial market for currencies, but it doesn't rely on the predominance of the pound. I can imagine a world in which the dollar is a much less important currency, but it wouldn't necessarily preclude US institutions being hegemonic within the global financial system. But I think we need to disentangle a few issues here. One is the global authority of US institutions. I don't feel an expert on this, but I always find Panitch and Gindin persuasive.

Another is an evaluation of the strength of the US economy itself, and whether there is evidence of an economic decline that might itself precipitate a loss of US hegemony. In this context we often see cited the huge US current account deficit, and the idea that the US economy has something unsustainable about it. It is argued that this is the Achilles' heel of the US economy, and undermines its global standing.

I think concerns about the deficit are out of place. The Federal Reserve recently put out a document which I think is absolutely right. It says that the US makes up about 30% of world capital formation. About 30% of mobile international investment is going to the US. If you were a financial adviser, you would describe this investment spread as a balanced portfolio (there's that word again). It so happens that when the rest of the world puts 30% of its mobile assets in the US, that materialises as a huge current account deficit for the US economy. Put another way, the question is why so many people and organisations want to put their assets in the US; not why those actions generate a net deficit.

There are two different logics at play. One is the logic of individual investment and competition between investment alternatives – where will people put their assets? how will capital perform? – and the other is the national logic – how does it look on national balance of payments data. As Marxists, we should be saying that it is the former logic that really drives development. We should look at what impels capital to locate where it does. The national aggregations which show that the capital flows lead to a huge current account deficit, or to a huge debt position for the US economy, should be very much a secondary consideration. It remains important only because a lot of people think it is important. Its importance has no profound material basis.

And internationally, US companies are highly profitable. It is worth remembering that the US produces two sorts of balance of payments data – the conventional one, based on geography, which measures activity of the territorial space; the other based on ownership, which compares the performance of US (owned) companies (at home and abroad) with foreign companies (within the US and outside). We may have reservations about how ownership is measured, but it shows consistently that while the US space is in deficit, US companies globally are in surplus. If we are talking about US global hegemony, this latter fact would seem important.

A lot of central banks are buying US Treasury bonds and, because of the decline in the dollar, losing quite heavily on them...

Coming out of the subprime crisis, we can expect to see, and do see, in the financial markets more caution and conservatism. What does conservatism mean here? It could mean treating the US dollar as a safe haven. That has been the conservative position for the last 50 years. Another version of conservatism is to hedge against the dollar and acquire a diversified portfolio. You don't just hold US assets; you hold euros, Australian dollars, renminbi... You spread your assets around a range of currencies (and different forms of assets) because each individual one will go up and down.

The battle is going to be about which of these conservative positions is dominant. One possibility here is that we will find that the hedge funds and the pension funds are likely to go for the diversified portfolios, and the big banks are more likely to go for the US dollar. The fact that the banks have a bias towards the dollar is in itself a sign of continuing US hegemony. These banks are big institutions. They look to the US economy as their engine-room. They have a lot of investment in the US economy. It is a world they understand. There is something conservative about big banks, and they "grew up with" the US dollar. Hedge funds and pension funds on the other hand, looking for rates of return, will want to spread their assets to give constant returns to their investors. There are different financial cultures in the different institutions. I would not play it up too much; and it's not a clear dichotomy. But there are different tendencies that are worth considering as we look in the crystal ball.

Then the question becomes: are we going to see, as some people argue, a "re-intermediation" of finance? that is, more and more transactions and asset management going through the big banks? In that case, there will be more likelihood of people buying US Treasury bonds and relying on the integrity of the US dollar. Or are we going to see continued disintermediation, because the big banks are seen as high-cost, cumbersome, and so on, and more money going through hedge funds and pension funds and more diversified portfolios? I think that is too hard to call at this stage.

Costas Lapavitsas has stressed the degree to which finance has come to feed more off consumer revenues than off loans to business...

Yes, I think this is an important point. One of the corollaries of that is that capital is having a second dip at surplus value. You put a worker on a loan and part of their wages come back to capital in the form of interest payments. But the process should be seen as broader than just the second dip at surplus value. It's not just about interest payments coming out of wages. In the last 20 years or so we have seen labour being treated like capital, the household being treated like a small business. History has asked households to take on a lot of financial decision-making. One aspect here is servicing the mortgage, but more than that. It requires households to decide whether to have a 20 year or 30 year mortgage, and at fixed or floating rate; how to balance the car loan with the credit card etc. These are complex financial calculations that require taking positions about an unknowable future. It comes back to the issue of the state withdrawing from guaranteeing the future. And it's not just decisions about interest-payments. It's about deciding whether or not and how to "invest" in a range of things. Education is no longer sufficiently provided by the state, so it has to be a personal investment. How much do I invest? Where do I borrow, etc.? For my telephone and electricity, which provider will I use?; which contract will I sign? Which superannuation fund or pension fund do I join; what risk profile do I want it to adopt? The list is long, and you don't really have the choice of not playing. So being working-class now means engaging in competitively-driven risk calculation and management.

Also, because the interest payments are contracted before the wage is earned – if you don't work that week, you still have to make the interest payments – you lock workers in socially and culturally to the capitalist production system. Workers don't want to go on strike. They can't afford it. They have the interest obligations they have to meet.

But on the other hand, workers today have easier access to credit. If they don't get paid for a while, they can let their credit card bill mount up. And they can put off mortgage payments for a month or two...

Perhaps, although there is a lot of evidence of low income people being "maxed out" on credit – the multiple credit card problem, of borrowing to repay debts. The evidence shows that the best predictor of working-class financial insolvency is not so much low income, but irregular income; in particular, a period out of work. That's when a difficult but viable debt-servicing becomes non-viable, leading to re-financing on worse and worse terms, etc. And the reality is that to strike itself makes income irregular. But let me put this matter more broadly as a class issue, not just an income issue. The IMF has, perhaps surprisingly, described households as the global financial system's depositories of risk of last resort. Households absorb all sorts of risks to underwrite capital, the most important being flexibility in employment contracts. In terms of risk analysis, capital has devices to hedge its risk. I've talked about them earlier. For workers, labour power cannot be hedged – it can't be securitised, because it cannot be separated from the worker him/herself. For capital, financial insolvency means the company goes under, but limited liability means that personal assets go untouched. Investors in Bear Stearns lost their investments, but they did not have to put their wealth into covering the company's losses. But for labour, where labour power cannot be separated from the worker, insolvency means personal insolvency. In the subprime crisis, insolvent mortgagees have not just lost their investments; they have lost their homes.

Some other aspects of families can be hedged – through things like insurance on health, car and home, through going to the dentist for checkups. But the evidence is showing that poor families are bailing out of these sorts of forms of risk management – they need current income to keep the family going and repay the debts. So the risks households are exposed to mount and mount. Sickness, a car crash, a toothache can lead to insolvency. And not because of poverty per se, but because of financial over-commitment. These are the ways in which households are the risk-absorbers of last resort.

Can we discern the limits and contradictions of what you see as this new expansionary regime of capitalism?

I don't know that it has any contradictions that are different from the fundamental contradictions of any capitalist economy – between production for use and production for profit. We are seeing a system of accumulation that is getting bigger and bigger, and in a sense also more and more efficient. Capital is increasingly able to turn things into commodities. It can increasingly break down its own bundles of assets into the constituent assets, price each of them separately, and maximise the efficiency with which it uses each asset.

We are seeing a huge intensification of accumulation, and critical to it is the intensification of the performance of capital. In a sense that is a newly discovered phenomenon of the last 15 to 20 years. It is tempting to predict that it can't keep on accelerating at the rate of that recent period. But we have seen an amazing period of growth in the last 20 years. We know, historically, growth always goes in cycles. It will slow down at some time. Where the slowing is going to come from, I don't know. What staggers me is the inventiveness of capital in finding more and more things to turn into commodities. Perhaps the next wave is the environment – polluting rights are being turn into commodities, and creating a hugely profitable industry. That bubble might burst, just as the dot.com bubble burst, but the inventiveness of capital will continue.

The growth is fragile growth, of course, and it is bound up with accusations of speculation and the like, but it is growth, and it is what capitalism is about. But I think what finance shows us is actually how powerful labour potentially is. In part this shows through the capacity of low income mortgage borrowers to bring down some big financial institutions. Alternatively, the global pool of superannuation funds – labour's capital – shows how critical labour is to the funding of investment. The broad political task is to move this beyond labour as capital (failed capital, in the case of the sub-prime market) and frame it as the financial form of labour's capacity to mobilise and transform the world of capital for itself.

CHAPTER 7

A Systemic Crisis, both Global and Long-Lasting (July 2008)

Discussion with Michel Husson

How do you assess the changes in the financial system over the last 25 years? How should we assess the current crisis in the light of those changes of the financial system, and how should we assess those changes in the light of the crisis?

The transformations of the financial system should be analysed on the basis of two fundamental tendencies which have been operating since the beginning of the 1980s. The first is the tendency of the rate of exploitation to rise: almost everywhere in the world, the proportion of the wealth produced which comes back to the wage-workers has decreased, and the emerging economies are no exception here. Even the IMF and the European Commission are now registering this fact. This decrease of the wage-share has allowed a spectacular recovery of the average rate of profit from the mid-1980s. But, and this is the second tendency, the rate of accumulation has continued to fluctuate around a level lower than that before the crisis. In other words, the drain on wages has not been used to invest more.

The "Schmidt theorem" stated by the German Chancellor Helmut Schmidt at the beginning of the 80s – the profits of today are the investments of tomorrow and the jobs of the day after tomorrow – has not operated. The growing mass of surplus value which has not been accumulated has mainly been distributed in the form of financial revenues, and that is where the source of the process of financialisation is to be found. The difference between the rate of profit and the rate of investment is a good indicator of the degree of financialisation. We can also see that the rise of unemployment and casualisation goes together with the growth of the financial sphere. There too, the reason is simple: finance has succeeded in grabbing the greater part of gains from increased productivity, to the disadvantage of the wage-workers, by keeping wages down and by not reducing sufficiently, or even by increasing, work hours. The relations between productive capital and financial capital have thus been profoundly modified, and the demands of super-profitability come to bear, through a feedback effect, on the conditions of exploitation.

---

* Previously published in *Solidarity* 136, 24 July 2008.

For all that, we should not take a "financialist" view of contemporary capitalism, one which would see an autonomous tendency to financialisation plaguing the normal functioning of "good" industrial capitalism. That would be artificially to separate off the role of finance and the class struggle over value-added. We must articulate the analysis of the phenomena correctly: when the rate of profit rises thanks to a wage slowdown, without recreating the conditions for profitable accumulation, finance takes up a functional role in reproduction by providing market outlets alternative to the economic demand from wage earners.

This approach is confirmed by taking into account globalisation. In the progressive constitution of a world market, finance plays a role of abolishing, as far as can be done, the marking-off from each other of spaces of valorisation. The great strength of finance capital is that it ignores geographical or sectoral frontiers, because it has gained the means of moving very rapidly from one economic zone to another or from one sector to another: capital movements can now be deployed on a considerably expanded scale. The function of finance here is to sharpen the laws of competition by making the displacements of capital more fluid.

Paraphrasing what Marx said about labour, we could say that globalised finance is the process of concrete abstraction which subjects each individual capital to a law of value whose field of operation expands ceaselessly. The principal feature of contemporary capitalism is thus not an opposition between financial capital and productive capital, but the hyper-competition between capitals generated by financialisation.

Marxists habitually consider the rate of profit to be a key index of the health of capitalism. But, on some estimates, the increase in the rate of exploitation has brought about a substantial recovery of the rate of profit since the 1980s. Do you agree with this assessment?

The analysis of the current crisis should indeed start with a study of the development of the rate of profit. After the generalised recessions of 1974–5 and 1980–82, a new phase opened in the functioning of capitalism, one which one could for convenience call neoliberal. The beginning of the 1980s was a real turning point. A fundamental tendency towards increasing the rate of exploitation was unleashed, and that has led to a continuous rise in the rate of profit. For a Marxist used to thinking about the tendency of the rate of profit to fall, this about-turn may be disconcerting. One can of course evade this difficulty by trying to show that if the rate of profit is correctly measured, then it will after all have a tendency to fall. But such efforts are not theoretically well-founded, and, though I do not have the time to discuss this in detail here,

I believe that the traditional argument about a falling tendency of the rate of profit is erroneous.

It is more enlightening to focus on the fundamental characteristic of the neoliberal phase, more or less unprecedented in the history of capitalism: the recovery of the rate of profit has not led to a simultaneous rise of the rate of accumulation. The rate of accumulation, taking an average over the various fluctuations, and excepting the "new economy" episode in the USA, has remained at a relatively low level. If we analyse this starting from the Marxist schemas of reproduction, we see a problem of realisation, since neither wage-earners' economic demand, nor accumulated surplus-value, are rising at the same rate as the social product. The solution to this problem is based on the recycling of the non-accumulated surplus-value through the financialisation of the economy.

This quick sketch thus leads us back to two essential points. First, that financialisation is not an autonomous factor, but the logical complement of the reduction of the wage-share and of the scarcity of sufficiently profitable openings for investment. Second, that the increase in social inequalities (within each country, and between zones of the world economy) is an essential trait of contemporary capitalism.

Financial crises sometimes lead to crises in production and trade, but not always. The current financial crisis comes at a time when rates of profit are generally high. Do you think that it will nevertheless lead to a serious crisis in production and trade, and how?

The current crisis is not just a financial crisis, because it puts into question the mode of growth in the USA and the configuration of the world economy. In the USA, growth was based on a push from consumption, sustained by a continuous decline in the savings rate of households. It was in a way growth on credit, which presupposed an inflow of capital from the rest of the world to finance the trade deficit which resulted from the lack of domestic savings. Add to that the budget deficit, explained in large part by the costs of intervention in Iraq. That model of growth is thus based on a double imbalance, internal and external. Finance plays an essential role in managing both imbalances. Internally, it is finance which has made possible the growth of debt, especially on the mortgage market. Externally, finance has the function of maintaining the balance of payments. The current crisis puts that regime of accumulation into question. Household debt is now blocked, and capital inflows are no longer guaranteed. Consequently, the financial crisis will probably led to a recession in the USA, or at least to a long-lasting slowdown of growth. Will that slowdown be transmitted to the rest of the world economy? There is talk these days about "decoupling", meaning that the growth of the emerging economies could keep up world demand sufficiently that the impact of the US slowdown will be limited. But that does not take into account the interweaving of the world economy, which also involves the relations between Europe and the USA and between China and the rest of Asia. Dependence on exports to the USA cannot be measured simply by the percentage which they make up in the total exports of China. That would be to underestimate the criss-cross relations between China and other countries of Asia.

In Europe, too, economic growth will slow down, for three reasons: the very high rate of exchange of the Euro in relation to the dollar; prices of imported primary materials; and government economic policies unfavourable to growth and employment. Finally, the crisis may possibly encourage more internally-centred economic growth in China, reducing its contribution to world trade.

The financial sector feeds more and more on individual incomes rather than on business transactions. What are the implications of this fact for the impact of the crisis on working-class households?

The big question is, which social layers will bear the costs of the crisis? The answer differs in the different zones of the world economy. We can sketch the main outlines. In the USA, obviously the mortgage crisis is plunging a large number of households into poverty. In numerous developing countries, the rise of food prices has already sharply increased the number of people affected by malnutrition or even famine. They are paying the price for neoliberal agricultural policies which have focused on exports and destroyed traditional agriculture. In Europe, the restrictive monetary policy of the European Central Bank aims to make wage-earners' purchasing power bear the impact of the rise in primary-product prices.

The implacable code of capitalism insists that it be the working people who thus have to pick up the pieces for the vagaries of the system. To absorb the losses, it will be necessary to clean up the economy on the backs of the working class, by braking growth, by raising interest rates, and by using the current world-economy disturbances as a pretext once again to push down the wages of the majority. According to the latest report of the ILO [International Labour Organisation], the financial turmoil could lead to a five-million increase in the number of unemployed in the world in 2008, a year "full of contrasts and uncertainties", as the ILO director general prudently puts it. If these tendencies sharpen, they can only worsen the recessionary effects of the crisis by curbing demand. Conversely, this fact shows that the outcome of the crisis is an eminently social question.

Everywhere in the world, a transition to a less chaotic mode of growth would necessitate a different, more egalitarian, distribution of income, which would allow a reduction of the flows of liquid assets which are at the root of the recurrent financial crisis, a reduction of the intensity of international trade (and thus, by the way, of carbon dioxide emissions), and a better response to social needs. The case of the USA is almost caricatural in its extraordinary degree of inequality in the distribution of income. Over the last 15 years, only the top 10 or 20% of the population have profited from the economic growth, and they have thrown themselves into a frenzy of consumption. To establish a stabilised mode of growth, a radical redistribution of income is necessary. There too, we come up against the social question.

How do you see the current situation of capitalism? Is it still stuck in a "global turbulence" originating in the 1970s? Or has it developed a new model of generalised expansion?

In terms of Ernest Mandel's theory of long waves, we face an ambivalent configuration. On the one hand, we could say capitalism has been successful, since it has re-established a high rate of profit, and the current phase could thus be characterised as one of expansion. But if we take the rate of accumulation ("the law and the Prophets" of capital, according to Marx) as criterion, we could on the contrary say that capitalism is stuck in a phase of recession and diminished dynamism. Add to that two economic elements: the specific instability created by the weight of finance, with a countless series of crises, and the fundamental imbalance which the trade deficit of the USA introduces into the current configuration of the world economy.

This fundamental imbalance is the symptom of a systemic crisis which is also without precedent in the history of capitalism, and is situated at a more profound level, putting into question the essential mainsprings of this mode of production. The source of this crisis is the growing gap which exists between the social needs of humanity and the capitalist mode of satisfying those needs. Social demand goes for commodities which are not susceptible of being produced with the maximum of profit. The gap grows in two main dimensions.

The first, in the developed countries, is the displacement of demand from manufactured goods (in the production of which productivity is high) towards services with which smaller productivity gains, and thus smaller perspectives of profit, are associated. No new economic outlet has taken up on a sufficient scale the role which the car industry played in the preceding, "Fordist", phase.

The second dimension is geo-economic, and results from globalisation. Globalisation tends to create a world market, or in other words an expanded space of valorisation. The lower levels of productivity of the less advanced sectors are directly confronted with profitability demands set according to the performance of the most competitive countries or businesses. A "crowding-out" effect results, so that a certain number of lines of production and thus of social needs which they could satisfy are no longer admissible because of the criteria of hyper-profitability which they face. In these conditions, the reproduction of the system goes through a double movement: extension of the domain of commodities, and refusal to respond to non-profitable needs.

Contemporary capitalism is thus a "pure capitalism", in the sense that it has brought together the conditions which it itself demands for an optimal functioning from its point of view. Rather than an improvement in social welfare, pure and perfect competition, free from regulations, rigidities and other distortions, brings to light a total absence of legitimacy, since social regression is explicitly the main desideratum for the success of the system.

Since the 1970s at least, the prevalent view among Marxists has been that the USA is in the process of losing its hegemonic position. Do you think that the USA's hegemony is really in decline? Or will be in the near future? If it is, will this decline generate imbalances and crises in the system?

The hegemony of the USA has had this paradoxical feature, that it has rested, for two decades, on the import and not on the export of capital, contrary to all the classic definitions of imperialism. No other country would have been able to run such a trade deficit without incurring a currency crisis; and it is indeed its position as the dominant power which has allowed the USA, recently, to let the dollar's exchange-rate decline. We could talk about an "imperial decline of the dollar" in the sense that, in that recent period, the strength of the USA has been measured by the weakness of its currency. Besides the fact that the dollar functioned as world money, there were in this situation some more objective determinations: the stability of the financial investments offered, notably Treasury bonds, and relatively good financial performance.

But the permanent inflow of capital could also be explained, from the middle of the 1990s, by the acceleration of productivity gains in the USA. This phenomenon seemed to mark the reaffirmation of the supremacy of the USA in the productive sphere itself, as a dynamic site of innovation and thus of profitability. It was at the foundation of the "new economy" and the stock market boom which accompanied it. That is why the question of knowing whether the productivity leap constituted the material base of a new phase of expansion, or a high-tech cycle, is absolutely decisive.

In the first case, the foundations of US hegemony would be renewed on the basis of an objective productive advance. In hindsight, the facts now seem to confirm the thesis of a high-tech cycle. Hourly labour productivity in the USA has in fact slowed down in recent years, and has slipped back to a rate of growth below 2%, comparable to the rate during the three decades preceding the "new economy". Thus the "new economy" appears as an interlude, provisionally reviving the rhythm of the phase of expansion which ended in 1967.

Do you think that the talk in recent years of the rise of the "BRIC" countries (Brazil, Russia, India, China), and perhaps also of other countries such as South Korea, Mexico, or South Africa, is just superficial journalism? Or that it reflects a real change in the capitalist relation of forces on a world scale?

The rise of the emerging economies manifestly represents a major inflection in the configuration of the world economy. We can pick it out objectively in the relative rates of growth of the different regions of the world. But the most spectacular change is in the inversion of capital flows, or in other words, the fact that the emerging economies have become net creditors. The recent bailing-out of the banks of the richest countries by the sovereign wealth funds of countries of the South is the most spectacular manifestation.

We could talk here of a "boomerang effect" of globalisation which puts into question the classical notion of imperialism, not to speak of the mainstream theories. Of course, there are still immense zones of "classical" dependency. This new configuration generates uncertainties as to its medium-term sustainability. In fact it is based on the trade surpluses achieved by the emerging economies, swollen for some of them by the rise of primary-product prices. The main counterpart of those surpluses is found in the trade deficit of the USA, which needs a regular inflow of capital.

But with the recession and the fall in interest rates, and the continual depreciation of the dollar, there is less motive for capital to place itself in the USA. Today, it is the central banks of the emerging economies that finance the US deficit, and that is a matter of a purely political choice which has no reason to be sustained for ever. Objectively, the central banks would do better to hold their assets in euros rather than dollars, or at least in a better balanced mix of the two.

If we now look at the productive aspect, the counterpart of the surpluses of the emerging economies is found in an extraversion in their economies which implies a holding-down of internal demand and, for the majority of the population, an advance in purchasing power much lower than the growth in the economy. This schema is not sustainable, and it is inevitably going to lead to social struggles which may open onto a more internally-centred mode of growth, a bit like in South Korea, and thus a reduction of surpluses. But that is a mid-term perspective which is not an immediate solution to the crisis. That is why the world economy has entered, for an indeterminate time to come, a period of deepening of trade wars and of inter-capitalist contradictions, full of threats.

Do you think that the current economic disturbances will develop in such a way as to generate crises in the "BRIC" countries? How do you assess the probability that the enormous inflow of capital to the USA from Asia and the oil-exporting countries will dry up, and that a disastrous decline of the dollar will result? In the course of the current disturbances? Or in the coming years?

The dollar has already hit a historic minimum, and, since its fate today depends on the attitude of the central banks of the countries in trade surplus, it can hardly go lower. Thus no further depreciation of the dollar, to adjust the USA's balance of payments, can be counted on. A dose of recession will doubtless be necessary, but also, above all, a serious slowdown of growth. From this point of view, the main result of the subprime crisis is surely to have put a definitive end to the mode of growth in the USA established in the Reagan era.

Moreover, rather than just engaging in an exercise in forecasting, it is more stimulating to reflect about the coordinates of a more balanced configuration of the world economy. The way to deflate the sphere of globalised exchanges and to reduce global imbalances is basically the same everywhere: namely, to re-focus economic activity on internal demand, or in other words on the satisfaction of social needs.

But that path implies a radical calling into question of the current tendencies of today's "pure capitalism", and even a recession will not be enough to set such a reorientation in motion. Spontaneous reactions in defence of the social interests of capitalism will push in the contrary direction, because it is difficult for the possessing classes to forgo the large and disproportionate sums that they extort from the wage-earners of the whole world. Suppose that this year produces a very uneven slowing-down of the world economy, and it does not transform itself into a generalised recession. Even in that case, 2008 will demonstrate how unsustainable the fragile balance of the world economy is, and how it is now on the brink of breakdown.

As we have seen, the USA will have difficulty in continuing to make the rest of the world finance its profound trade deficit, or in hoping to reduce it by an endless slide of the dollar, without that setting off new tensions with China and Europe. The structural dysfunctionalities of the European Union will also be exposed in all their clarity. And the mode of the growth of the emerging economies, totally reliant on exports, will also show its limits.

Thus 2008 will allow us to understand the social content of the current configuration of the world economy: its imbalances are based on the profoundly inegalitarian character of the social arrangements which underlie it. Over and above the obvious differences which exist between the USA, China, and Europe, these three great poles have a fundamental trait in common, which is the regular reduction of the share of wealth produced which goes back to those who produce it. It is that tendency which creates the super-indebtedness and the deficit in the USA, unemployment in Europe, and the export priority and over-accumulation in China.

The other lesson that we can draw from this story is that the legitimacy of capitalism today is profoundly weakened. The successes which it marks up are directly proportional to the social regression which it manages to impose, without compensation or counterpart. Even if the relation of forces is in its favour, one thing at least should be clear: projects aiming to regulate, discipline, or humanise such a system are in the current context tantamount to pure utopia, in the bad sense of the term.

PART 2

After September 2008

∵

INTRODUCTION TO PART 2

"This sucker could go down"*

Michel Husson estimated that the governments' anti-crisis measures, introduced in haste after the Lehman Brothers collapse in September 2008, could avoid "a crisis like that of the 1930s", but not a longer depression. In that depression, there would be "a race between the rise of orientations of a nationalist or protectionist type, and the rise of social struggles". Costas Lapavitsas reckoned that to restore growth the governments would have to "restrain the strength of the financial interest", but they could not and would not do that fast.

Andrew Kliman saw the crisis as rooted in the failure of the usual destruction-of-capital mechanism for restoring profits after slumps to operate in recent decades. The crisis, he thought, was now so huge that "a lot more government control" in economics was likely. Leo Panitch reckoned that what he had written about as a "social-democratisation of globalisation" was likely, though without much democracy or "social" element for the majority.

Fred Moseley saw the root of the crash in an overhang of debt, which the governments' measures were not fixing. Simon Mohun, observing that the crisis was bigger than he first thought, foresaw "a move to a much more state-managed economy", maybe in "an unpleasant corporatist form".

Robert Brenner, rather like Andrew Kliman, saw the background as "a persistent tendency to overcapacity" caused by profit-squeezes not bringing the level of scrapping required for a big revival. Governments had tried to cope with the problem by expanding credit, but that had reached its limits. He feared "a return of far-right politics of protectionism, militarism, anti-immigration, nationalism".

Dick Bryan criticised responses limited to wishing for markets to be "more efficient, more transparent, more ethical".

---

* George W Bush, 24 September 2008, quoted in for example Blinder 2013, p. 177.

CHAPTER 8

The Crisis of Neoliberal Capitalism (December 2008)

Discussion with Michel Husson

Do you think that the recent nationalisations and big bail-outs signify a major change in the configuration of capitalism? What sort of new regime could result from the crisis?

The nationalisations are only pseudo-nationalisations. They are partial, provisional, and almost unconditional. They are aimed at re-establishing the profitability of the banking system and furnishing it with the instruments for restructuring. If it was really a matter of reconfiguring capitalism, these injections of public money should have been the occasion for imposing tighter rules of functioning on the banks. The speeches about the need for regulation and the struggle against tax havens are only distractions. The most probable outcome is that the liquidity handed out today will just feed the next bubble. The public intervention nevertheless constitutes a confession which puts into question one of the foundations of neoliberalism, namely the optimality of private finance. But it is not enough in itself to set in motion a transition to a new regime.

The old regime was based on the reduction of the wage-share, compensated for by households becoming over-indebted, plus, in the case of the United States, the financing of growth by the rest of the world. The two pillars of that model are now in question: households can no longer hold up market demand by expanding their debt, and so the recession has become a classic crisis of overproduction and difficulty in "realising" surplus-value. And the deficit financing of the United States has become uncertain, all the more so because the surpluses of the emerging economies are going to tend to shrink.

The governments are trying to put into practice what their economists have learned, as regards stabilisation policies, from the study of the 1930s and of the depression in Japan in the 1990s. What are the limits and capacities of these policies?

The reflationary measures are inadequate in so far as they cannot lead to a re-establishment of a more equitable distribution between wages and profits.

* Previously published in *Solidarity* 146, 12 February 2009.

That is the essential condition for the establishment of, or rather for a return to, a model of the Keynesian-Fordist type. But it would presuppose a challenge to the inequalities which have increased in recent decades, to different degrees, in the United States, in Europe, and even in China. The stabilisation policies are thus going to allow the system to avoid a crisis like that of the 1930s, but they do not involve measures capable of avoiding a depression analogous to that which Japan suffered throughout the 1990s.

The subprime crisis in the United States, although sizeable, involved much smaller sums than those in play in the crisis today. How is that a relatively small disturbance produced such huge consequences?

The spread of the subprime crisis to the whole financial system is a revelation of the degree of integration of the world economy and of the financial system. The hypothesis of "decoupling", put forward at the start of the crisis, according to which Europe and China would be safe from the effects of the crisis and so would allow the world to avoid a generalised crisis, rapidly misfired.

In recent months, it has been governments, not only banks, in trouble. The reserves of the IMF are relatively small, and the biggest funds are held by the governments, the central banks, and the sovereign wealth funds of East Asia and the Gulf states. Do you think that this crisis could bring an important shift in the balance of forces at a world level?

The crisis is far from over, and the degree of coordination among the capitalist authorities (governments, banks, IMF, sovereign wealth funds, European institutions, etc.) is advancing under the pressure of the emergency. But it is not enough to make us envisage the establishment of a new Bretton Woods. The most probable scenario on the months to come is, on the contrary, the sharpening of the contradictions. Despite the globalisation of production, inter-state contradictions are going to take on a new sharpness, with each state trying to pass the costs of the crisis onto others. The United States is going to try to impose a new reduction of the exchange-rate of the dollar, which is necessary to rebalance their trade deficit.

In Europe, each country is very differently positioned in relation to the crisis, depending on the relative weight of finance, of the property market and the car industry, and its mode of insertion into the world market. A truly coordinated economic policy is thus beyond reach, all the more so because the European Union has voluntarily deprived itself of the institutions which could allow it to be pursued, in particular a sufficient federal European budget. The countries of the South, especially Latin America and Asia, will tend to re-focus themselves on their internal and regional markets, on the model of the import substitution policies pursued in Latin America after the crisis of the 1930s.

Inside each country, the capital-labour contradiction will be deepened. There are few things in the plans for rescue or reflation which favour wage-workers, and meanwhile businesses will seize the opportunity of the crisis to re-establish their conditions of profitability. Finally, public budgets will be weighed down by the sums squandered in hand-outs to banks and businesses, and so social budgets will be cut again. The political conjuncture of the months and years to come will doubtless be characterised by a race between the rise of orientations of a nationalist or protectionist type, and the rise of social struggles.

CHAPTER 9

The Debacle of Financialised Capitalism (January 2009)

Discussion with Costas Lapavitsas

What sort of new shape of capitalism do you think might emerge from the shake-out of this crisis?

First of all, we have to see how capitalism looked before the crisis. My own view, as I argued previously, is that capitalism has been financialised. Finance has penetrated every aspect of economic and social life, and turned towards extracting profit from individual income. It has also substituted itself for the public provision of various services, and now mediates them – housing, pensions, health, education... It has done a very bad job of it, not only in terms of the everyday inequalities and inefficiencies, but also in terms of the gigantic crisis that has now manifested itself and its disastrous effect on the lives of many, many people.

Is that trend going to be reversed? At the moment, I don't see any serious thought being put into reversing it from the top. There are plenty of steps taken and noises made as regards macroeconomic policy. Monetary policy has lost influence compared to its previous status, and fiscal policy has been adopted. But in terms of restructuring finance, in terms of altering the relation between the productive sector and the financial sector, in terms of reorganising the capitalist economy as a whole, I see no serious proposals or serious thought from the mainstream. From those who make policy, it's not clear where they're going to go. Part of the reason, of course, is the residual strength of the financial system. It's enormous. So despite all the talk from Obama, for example, that he is going to change everything, his economic team comprises people who were there in the Clinton era and who are beholden to Wall Street. Any big change will take time to materialise.

Leo Panitch talks about the possibility of a "social-democratisation of globalisation", and Simon Mohun says that we could see something more like the regime of 1945–73...

---

* Previously published online at www.workersliberty.org/node/11912, 26 January 2009.

I am far more sceptical about that. In the medium-term – give it a few years – I do expect changes to happen – possibly in that direction, in that we will see direct intervention by the state across the economy. Whether that can be called social-democratic or not, we need to discuss, but it's possible. In the short-term, we are seeing increasing intervention by the state, but it is not leading towards that medium-term possibility yet. The governments are not willing to touch the financial system at present. They are not willing to intervene there, or, when they do intervene, they are not willing to draw the conclusions of their own interventions.

But they do have a problem. Expansionary fiscal policy, as they want to pursue it, and not touching the financial system, are not particularly compatible aims. At the same time, they will have to do something about the financial system at some point if they want to sustain this expansionary fiscal policy. They will have to confront the problem of the enormous growth of finance and the enormous power of finance. It will probably take them some time to realise that. When they come to confront the problem, it is not clear how they will go about it.

How do you think the present financial system undermines fiscal policy? More generally, the economists are dragging everything they can out of the lessons of the 1930s and of the Japanese depression of the 1990s to look for ideas. What critical assessment can we make of the ideas for stabilisation that they are coming up with?

They are not exactly squeezing out all the lessons of the thirties. Actually they have been very careful. In the 1930s, for example, a clean separation of investment banking activity and commercial banking activity was imposed in the US. There has been none of that now. It is true that they have brought interest rates down, but even that they have done by putting enormous amounts of liquidity in. They haven't done it by putting formal controls on interest rates and the way finance lends. They are allowing, for the moment, a market determination of those things. So it's not true that they have done everything that they did in the thirties. They are very careful not to step on the toes of the financial system.

They have been using the lessons of the 1930s, as far as they understand them, to promote expansionary fiscal policy. But that will mean state debt, and it may also mean printing money. It is not easy for the US or the UK state to borrow now, and not because they are over-borrowed – actually their debt is quite low. There are no domestic savings for them to borrow from, because of the policies they have been following for the last 15 to 20 years, so they have to borrow abroad. That is not easy, certainly not for the UK. It is easier for the US, but even in the US there are serious problems in relying on Arab money, or Russian money, or Chinese money, for expansionary fiscal policy.

Finance will not like the increase in debt, and they will not like the increase in money supply that may be necessary to support fiscal policy. Finance will act as a brake on these things. Finance will also act as a brake in the sense that while the state will be spending and expanding fiscal policy, finance will actually be reining in demand, because banks are over-extended and they need to adjust their balance-sheets. Finance is also a problem in the sense that individual people are hugely over-extended with debt. That debt is like a ball and chain on people. For many decades, we have been told that debt is good. Now people are going to discover that debt is not good. Finance will be acting as a pressure on individuals, extracting income, stopping the economy from expanding. The governments will have to do something about it. They will have to restrain the strength of the financial interest. But it will take them a time to see that they have to do it. And it will not be easy, because the financial interest is still very strong.

We talked before about the fact that many of the securities being traded had their prices worked out by mathematical formulas. Some writers have suggested that the calculations were faulty, in the sense that they disregarded highly improbable turns of events, while in fact, given the scale of the markets, those highly improbable things were going to happen.

There is definitely something true in that argument. It has to do with the ideology of risk management, and the practice of risk management adopted by the financial institutions in recent years, whereby financial institutions seem to have become less capable of assessing creditworthiness. They used to assess creditworthiness in a relational way, by accumulating knowledge, by knowing the debtor and finding out about the debtor's business and prospects. In recent years that has largely be replaced by mathematical and quantitative handling of risk based on assumptions about probability distributions which drew on past events and correlations between variables.

The assumption made by the people who built these models is that extraordinary events happen very, very rarely, so they could afford to disregard them. But capitalism generates the extraordinary quite regularly! And lo and behold, it has happened. On top of that there has been a question of problematic practice in the financial markets, not just because they made the wrong assumptions about what might happen, but also in terms of how these large capitalist institutions work internally. They may seem to be buccaneering enterprises, but in fact they are very large bureaucracies, stodgy, multi-layered. People were passing estimates from desk to desk without doing any serious work, as long as the right boxes were ticked. The end result was disaster, because problems were accumulating that nobody knew about, or that everybody turned a blind eye to. It is yet another example of the inefficiency of modern capitalism. It likes to pretend that it is very competitive, very efficient, but even in the competitive environment of those large financial institutions, internally they were very inefficient.

The total outstanding notional value of financial derivatives in the world is over $600 trillion – $100,000 for every person in the world. There are different ways of counting the total, but however you count it, it is an enormous amount. And a lot of it must be the same underlying assets repackaged again and again. So, isn't it a case of some problems being invisible because of the scale and speed of the markets?

I was thinking more of how the mechanics of risk management operate within the large investment banks. It's important, because these banks are supposed to be the social institutions that assess risk in a market economy, but in fact they don't do it very well. I'm not sure that the size as such is a problem. The nominal sums are misleading. It is an example of Marx's "fictitious capital". But those who run the big business were losing sight of who owns what, where, and in that sense the system became less easy to read, more opaque, as it became more and more multi-layered.

Looking back on it, the mortgage crisis in the USA seems very small compared to the repercussions. How can we explain that this relatively small disturbance – on the scale of world capitalism – had such huge repercussions?

This is not a crisis in the normal mould, and Marxists would do well to appreciate that, in order to say useful things about it. The mortgage market is sizeable, but obviously, it is not on a par with what has happened in recent months. It is securitisation that has done that – the fact that on the back of a fairly moderate amount of debt from poor people in the United States an enormous structure of other debt had been developed, owned by financial institutions across the world. That is not all. The money markets are frozen. The way the crisis unfolded, and the way the authorities have mishandled it, allowed the money markets to freeze completely. Lehman Brothers was a critical moment. Any capitalist financial system pivots on the money market. If the money market – that is, the market in which banks exchange reserves among themselves and facilitate their other transactions – doesn't work, then everything is frozen. That is what magnified the effect of the disturbances and made them spread across the world.

On top of that, large numbers of working people in key developed countries are over-indebted. They have been hit very badly, and can't spend at the same level. The combined effect of the money markets freezing, and therefore credit freezing, and ordinary people suffering loss of buying-power, has catapulted the productive sector into a major crisis.

The money market is important, not only because a freeze there means that banks do not lend to other banks, but also because it makes it more difficult for industrial corporations to issue short-term debt to obtain cash to pay wages and so on. Working capital for big business has been very hard to procure, and as a result they have cut back output and employment. So, you get unemployment rising.

In recent years, the New York financial markets, operating with cash put in from all across the world, have acted as a sort of lender of last resort to the world. Is there a prospect that they won't be able to do that anymore? That we will have a world without a lender of last resort, and so a severe disruption of the world system and also a rebalancing of it so that New York will no longer be central?

There has been a period of US hegemony, including in finance. The major financial institutions are either US-owned or multilateral institutions which are US-backed. US hegemony in the political sphere has been matched by US hegemony in the financial sphere, and the US has been one of the main drivers of the financialisation of world capitalism. But in the last 20 years, that has been done while the US has been suffering from structural balance-of-trade deficits. It has been done on the basis of other people giving the US money to borrow. In the 1990s, that tended to be the Japanese and the Europeans. In the last decade, the Japanese have remained significant suppliers of finance, but in the last four or five years it has been more the emerging capitalist economies in Asia. Some very, very poor countries have been sending funds to the US.

So the US has been absorbing funds from across the world. The US has a unique advantage, because it issues the money that is best available approximation to world money, the dollar. It can impose a sort of tribute on the rest of the world because of imperial power. The rest of the world, in a sense, sends money over to enable it to use the dollar. Can this be maintained? Will things change? In the medium term, I think they will. This is a major shock to the United States. The crisis is to do with US-centric methods of financial capitalism, and the crisis is very severe in the US specifically. In the medium term, I expect US hegemony, in the sphere of finance and perhaps more broadly, to suffer.

But I stress: in the medium term. In the short term, it is different. The dollar has become stronger, for a variety of reasons, but its use as a last resort has something to do with it. And one of the main providers of funds globally, to allow smaller capitalist countries to keep ticking over, has been the Federal Reserve. They have provided, of course, enormous amounts of money to capitalist firms in the US, but they have also created new and unprecedented facilities for Brazil, Mexico, Singapore, and South Korea, as well as allowing other central banks across the world access to dollars. The Federal Reserve has emerged as a major player globally in the stabilisation effort. It is not as if the US is on its last legs, and Sarkozy and others are making all the running. That is not what's happening. But in the medium term the omens are not good for US hegemony.

How might a world with reduced US hegemony look? If the dollar is not the world money, what will be?

That, in a sense, is the major problem of capitalism today. Marxists had better appreciate that and start discussing it. Domestic financial systems and monetary arrangements are always problematic for the capitalist classes, but over the years they have developed institutions and practices to handle the problems – not always successfully, and with contradictions, but they have mechanisms in place. On the global level, it is different. The history of the last thirty-odd years, since gold was finally detached from the dollar and stopped functioning as a world money, has been one of tremendous unrest, volatility, instability. And that in turn has boosted financialisation.

The options for finding a reliable world money to replace the dollar are very limited. At that level the contradictions are very hard to reconcile. Maybe they are impossible to reconcile with a capitalist organisation of production. It is possible that without the dollar as world money, then, as far as the eye can see, the world economy, if it continues on a capitalist basis, will subsist on the basis of global instability, with unstable exchange rates and unstable flows... maybe bilateral arrangements, maybe a number of competing world moneys.

What might a limited decline of US financial hegemony look like, then?

A rise in the power of China, in the first instance – and a more confident role for Chinese capitalism, if it doesn't itself implode. China possesses enormous financial reserves. It might invest them in other parts of the world. We might see multinational Chinese corporations emerging. And then, gradually, if China manages to find some modus vivendi, there might be some Asia-centred monetary system emerging. But the problems are enormous in that respect, mainly political problems.

Do you think that the monetary policies followed by the governments in the last few months are likely to lead to high inflation after the period of low inflation, or deflation, which seems likely in the coming months since we know that oil prices and basic commodity prices have gone down already? The central banks have done all the things which they said absolutely must not be done for fear of causing inflation.

It's quite incredible what the central banks have done. I have recently looked again at the balance sheet of the Federal Reserve. Bank deposits with the Federal Reserve, "high-powered money", the basis of the money supply, are now about a trillion and a half dollars, up from about $800 billion in the space of just a few months. The Federal Reserve has increased the supply of money to the banks phenomenally, by buying from the banks financial assets which it would not have dreamed of buying just six months ago.

But the banks have been sitting on the money. At the moment, monetary policy does not work, for reasons that Marxists have long known about. Keynesians call it the liquidity trap – not exactly the same, but a related idea: that there comes a moment in a crisis at which money is the only way to hold value. So we have financial institutions hoarding the money that the central banks are providing to them. Potentially this could lead to inflation. But I doubt it, because of the severity of the crisis and because of the previous experience of Japan. The Japanese central bank did the same thing – it bought all kinds of assets and expanded the money available to banks. It never led to inflation. In fact, prices maintained a downward slope.

The reason was, again, hoarding. In Japan, people and institutions have been hoarding money, and they have been doing it because of their predicament. Over-borrowing, uncertainty about the future, uncertainty about jobs, make people and institutions more conservative. That is what I think will happen. No-one knows for sure, but at the moment it looks like falling prices rather than inflation. It looks like a major shock to prices, because capitalist operations cannot borrow, consumers cannot borrow, no-one is spending. Given the over-extendedness of borrowing consumers, that is not likely to change soon. People are hugely over-borrowed in this country, to the extent of 160% of disposable income. It is similar in the United States. In other words, monetary policy has shot its bolt. The ruling class has begun to realise that and turn to fiscal policy. Fiscal policy opens up all kinds of possibilities for the left. Fiscal policy has been the great unmentionable for many years past, because financial interests do not want it.

Fiscal policy allows the left to argue on a different basis about what needs doing in the economy, and which way it should be directed – should it be tax cuts, or targeted state spending, and so on? It takes us back to a terrain which is far better suited to the interests and the desires of the left. It also presents the possibility of arguing for socialism. Fiscal policy is where the governments are heading to, but the financial system will keep dragging it back. The left should then be arguing for true socialisation of the financial system. Private finance has failed, and failed abysmally.

CHAPTER 10

The Level of Debt is Astronomical (December 2008)

Discussion with Andrew Kliman

Do you think a markedly new regime of capitalism is going to emerge out of this crisis?

I don't think we can assume that capitalism will emerge from this crisis. Things are still very dicey. There is an acute lack of confidence. There are acute problems with the availability of credit. The Fed, the Treasury, and so forth have been able time and again to stop the panic from breaking out into more severe panic, but only temporarily, and the underlying problems are getting worse.

Much of what is happening is unprecedented. The future will largely be shaped by the exigencies that emerge in the crisis. The authorities will do whatever it takes to save the system, but what that means will depend on particular circumstances. For instance, we all knew that the Treasury Secretary, Hank Paulson, is not an advocate of nationalisation, but that is what it took to stave off collapse thus far. I think we are going to see similar things down the line.

That said, I expect that for a while we are not going to see anybody attempting to return to the free market or so-called neoliberal policies. In the 1970s, with the high inflation and the economic crisis, there was a consensus that Keynesianism was no longer the way to structure the economy. It seems that a similar consensus is now emerging that they should not be going back to neoliberal policies.

I think they are going to keep the economies open to foreign trade and investment, try to develop export-oriented economies, and so on. But they are also going to try to prevent crises recurring, by means of new regulatory measures. I don't think that will succeed, and I think they're aware that it won't succeed, but they will try.

Regulation is not mostly an ideological issue. It's mostly a pragmatic issue of what is needed to keep capitalism afloat. It's not conceivable that the government can say it's guaranteeing private loans or whatever, but at the same time

* Previously published online at www.workersliberty.org/node/11807, 12 January 2009.

allow banks and other corporations to go ahead and take whatever risks they want.

It will be very interesting to see if they try to outlaw certain kinds of financial products, certain kinds of derivatives, and certain kinds of behaviour, for example what they call naked short-selling. Those are fairly minor matters in the end. We will have a lot more government ownership, a lot more government regulation, a lot more implicit or explicit government control. Coming out of the crisis – if they do manage to come out of it – we are going to see a lot more nationalisation and a lot more government control over financial institutions and activities that they don't nationalise.

Also, Wall Street is basically a thing of the past. Three of the five firms that dominated Wall Street are gone, and the remaining two, Goldman Sachs and Morgan Stanley, have turned themselves into bank holding companies, that is, companies that own commercial banks and so fall under existing banking regulation. We already have a system extremely different from what we had just a few months ago.

Beyond that, our ability to forecast the future is so meagre at this point. Everything is in great flux. You can't even say that there are specific camps within the ruling class in terms of what they're trying to do. They're all just trying to get through the crisis as best they can.

Sure. But it's useful to get a view of possibilities. Is one possibility that we get a lot more regulation of financial markets, but that goes along with neoliberalism as regards labour-market policies, contracting-out, the end of welfare, and so on?

That is a likelihood if they do manage to get through the crisis. Our notion of the New Deal and regulated capitalism comes from the 1930s, when regulation came at the same time as a social safety net. But there's nothing about a regulated capitalism or state ownership that automatically means you're going to get progressive policies. In the 1930s you had more closed economies, especially in the USA. Today, in order to keep remain competitive in many industries, each country's ruling class will continue to need to keep labour costs down and promote labour flexibility. Economic stabilisation has traditionally been understood as a combination of regulation and Keynesian pump-priming. I don't think that automatic association is correct any more. I doubt whether the tactics used by the governments so far are really going to work. "Quantitative easing" [measures for the government to try to pump more credit into the economy even when official interest rates are reduced to zero or near-zero] did not really work in Japan. They supposedly ended quantitative easing there in 2006 because the deflation was over, but the deflation actually didn't end until the latter part of 2007. Of course, it may be that the quantitative easing prevented even worse deflation.

The deflation in Japan in the 1990s and the early part of this decade was not very drastic. The governments are worried about much worse deflation now. Today's problems are continuations of trends over the last 30-odd years. You have had debt crises, papered over by more debt, and then more severe debt crises. At the point where things are now, you'd have to throw in a lot of dollars over a long period of time to change the perception in financial markets that assets are overvalued and that prices will come down. Financial assets are not worth what they were originally, but no-one knows what they are worth now. It is hard to prop up the system when such information, which is necessary for capitalism to function, has been distorted so much. The Federal Reserve is creating dollars at an amazing rate – injecting liquidity into the system in a way that is the equivalent of printing dollars on a phenomenal scale. But to stabilise the economy will require much more than solving short-term liquidity problems.

House prices in the US have collapsed. They could go down a lot more. One recent projection is that the total decline will be 40%. If job losses continue at the rate we've seen recently, then surely the house price collapse will continue. That is because the crisis in the real economy will lead to further pressure in the financial markets, which in turn will react back on jobs and incomes in a spiralling fashion.

If the crisis in the real economy, in jobs and production and incomes, continues and accelerates, it is going to react back strongly on home prices, which are at the core of the crisis. Each problem is going to feed back on the others. That is already starting to happen. I can't make a prediction as to how far things are going to fall. But there is a danger of a collapse of prices and jobs well beyond the government's ability to manage.

In recent decades, New York has acted as a sort of lender of last resort for the world economy, lending other people's money. It may be that the global financial markets centred in New York can no longer keep the credit going at that level. What are the implications for the balance of power in the world system?

I tend to think that these matters are effects of power rather than causes of power. The supremacy of the dollar is due to the supremacy of the United States, and that supremacy largely boils down to the United States being the sole military superpower. That is not likely to change. The economic crisis shows very strikingly something that is always the case: capitalists like stability. For their system to function, there has to be a certain stability. And I think capitalists around the world look to the United States to provide that. But once again, it's very hard to say. The authorities are no longer in control. The exigencies of the crisis are in the driver's seat. Assuming they get through this, we're more likely to see the relative economic power of the United States increase than decrease.

The entire world economy is being propped up by the guarantees of the United States government to lenders. Other governments are also making guarantees, but those of the US are crucial, because the US is where the losses are biggest. So now, when the US government is committing itself to trillions of dollars in guarantees, they are nevertheless having to pay almost no interest when they borrow. It's a very perverse situation. The US government is at greater risk, but relatively speaking, in a situation of higher risk everywhere, US government securities become a much better bet in investors' eyes. Buying Treasury debt is so much safer than anything else. The capitalists care about a stable, secure environment, and any stability there is, is coming from the might of the US government.

On the other hand, the obligations of the US government are huge. It could come to pass that the financial markets look at all this and say that the US government is overextended – that it won't pay back, or it will pay back with dollars grossly devalued by high inflation or a falling exchange rate – then we could see the loss of US supremacy very, very quickly. Still, what is holding the system together at present is the guarantees of the US government. Up to this point, the US government has done more and more and more, and it has quelled the panics, more or less. It's hard to say whether it can continue doing that. But I don't see how capitalism can emerge from this crisis without the US continuing as hegemon.

You linked the US's hegemony in the world financial system to its military superpower. How do you see that link working?

The capitalist world has to have a regime which exercises power, or the threat of power, sufficient to maintain the stability of the system. If you don't have that, you have blocs vying for power, and you have World War I, or the Cold War. Right now, the military might of the US, its ability to intervene on behalf of property rights, is fundamental to keeping things together.

But neither the Afghanistan war nor the Iraq war helps global capitalist property rights in any clear way...

That's right. The motives behind these particular wars are rather different. But underneath it all, the system requires the stability that comes from military might, and there's a fundamental question of whether the system is going to make it through this crisis. George W Bush said that he had to sign the $700 billion bail-out bill because otherwise "this sucker could go down". It's an amazing statement from a sitting President. The key issue here is fear and lack of confidence. The system has come close to panic. The guarantees of the US government have been very important. Then you have to ask, why do the guarantees of the US government matter in a way that the guarantees of, say, the government of Iceland do not matter? The US has a certain hegemonic status. The source of the hegemonic status is not the US having the strongest economy. It is the biggest economy in the world because the US is a big country, but in terms of GDP per person or similar measures, it is not significantly ahead of other powers. The US is not an especially great technological leader. Productivity is no longer significantly greater in the US than in other developed countries. So why does the US remain the undisputed world power, in the sense that people and institutions are willing to hold dollars, denominate their debt in dollars, and so forth? I believe that it is to do with the military supremacy of the United States. Military power can often be tacit. It does not need to be exercised because people know it is there.

The subprime mortgage crisis is very big for the people who are losing their houses, but in terms of the world economy the sums involved are small. How is it that such a relatively small financial disturbance triggers this enormous collapse?

I don't think it was ever a subprime crisis as such. It was a house-price bubble that burst. Its impact came most severely and first among subprime mortgages, but the source of the problem was the collapse in house prices. The reason why the crisis is so much bigger than it seemed, say, a year ago, is that there has been a continuing fall in house prices. The fall has accelerated; the great bulk of the fall has come during the past year. The latest data indicate a fall to date of 22%. Now a much larger part of the mortgage market than just subprime is involved. Then there is securitisation of the mortgages. The banks pool mortgages, and the investors buy paper which gives them a share of the whole pool of mortgages. The risk gets spread throughout the financial system.

Twenty years ago, we had in this country a Savings and Loan [equivalent of building societies] crisis. It was a crisis confined to one sector. Now we have the crisis spreading throughout the US economy and across the globe, engulfing institutions that are very far removed from mortgage lending. Even more important is the degree of leverage, of debt, in the system. Wall Street institutions were able to acquire, say, $100 of assets by borrowing $97 while only having $3 of actual assets to back it up. The commercial banks had leverage of about 10 to 1: for each $10 of assets, they could purchase another $90 using borrowed funds.

When house prices were going up, a lot of debt was being created. When the process goes into reverse, what is lost is not only income from mortgage payments; the debt build-up also goes into reverse. We see firms re-capitalising – in other words, banks and other institutions are taking the money that's coming in and shoring up their cushion against losses. They're doing this because what they regarded as assets that they owned are no longer worth as much as they thought, or they may not be sellable at all. This is a main reason why there's a big drop in lending.

The leverage in the system created a lot more obligations over and above the obligations to repay mortgages. So the bursting of the bubble has caused a deleveraging and a shrinkage much in excess of what you would expect just by looking at the amount of mortgages unpaid. Also, there are a lot of fancy derivatives now. Derivative prices are very tricky. They are all based on guesses as to future cash flows. In a profound crisis like the one we have seen, what derivatives are worth becomes very much up in the air. That greatly increases firms' aversion to taking risks. It was always a misnomer to call it a subprime lending crisis. It was an asset bubble that burst.

How is all this connected to the fundamental mechanics of capitalism?

My view is a classic view that comes from Karl Marx – the way the capitalist system gets out of crisis is fundamentally by a destruction of capital – partly physical destruction of machines and so on that are left to lie idle, but mostly a collapse of the value of assets, a destruction of "capital" that is fictitious, overvalued, phoney. When the asset values go down, that is a spur to a new boom, because if the new owners buy the assets at say one-tenth of what they cost before, then their rate of return on capital is ten times as great. In the Great Depression and World War II there was a massive destruction of value, which laid the basis for the ensuing boom. After 1973 we had a new crisis, but this time the system did not experience the destruction of value seen in the Great Depression of the 1930s and after. There were mechanisms which prevented the system from fully collapsing the way it did in the Great Depression – but the prevention of collapse also prevented a real new boom.

What we've seen since 1973 is the management of a system which has not fully recovered. Between 1950 and 1973, GDP per head went up by an average of 2.9 per cent a year, world-wide. From 1974 to the early part of this decade, the rate was 1.6%, or if you exclude China 1.1%. That is because there has not been a major purging of value from the system. Governments and banks have been throwing debt into the system to prevent that from happening. That has also meant an entire history of debt crises and burst bubbles over the period since 1973. There was the Third World debt crisis of the early 1980s; the Savings and Loan crisis of the early 1990s; the currency crisis of 1997–8 that began in East Asia and spread to Russia and Latin America 1997–8; the bursting of the "dot-com" bubble at the start of this decade; and others.

My belief is that the authorities have been trying to prop up the economy by artificial stimulation when there are not the conditions for it to trigger sustained growth. They can paper over bad debt by issuing further debt. This process can go on, even up to today. But the level of debt is becoming just too astronomical. You have to wonder whether we are going to reach the point that the financial markets are going to say that they no longer have confidence in the US government.

CHAPTER 11

The Chain Broke at the Weakest Link (December 2008)

Discussion with Leo Panitch

Last time we talked, you said that out of this crisis we will see more directive oversight by capitalist states, and we might even see something you called "the social-democratisation of globalisation". Do you see things going that way? And what will it look like?

With all the calls for regulation; with states buying shares in banks, not taking any directive control over them, but using moral suasion the way Brown has been doing to get them to reduce interest rates as the Bank of England reduces interest rates; with the kind of fiscal stimulus programs that all the governments are committed to – the British and the Americans, interestingly, more than the Germans – I think you are getting a "social-democratisation of globalisation". Bear in mind that my view of "social-democratisation" is that it is in no sense the old type of reformist, gradual socialism. It is "social-democratisation" in the sense of what the Labour Party has become under Blair and Brown.

So this is not social democracy as in the 1940s, 50s, and 60s?

No. I never had a very positive view of that in any case. That orientation was more about corporatist arrangements with labour. I don't see much of that going on. I see that it's unlikely that Obama will press for the labour legislation that US unions have been calling for. That would be more like an old-style social-democratisation.

The governments are trying to put into practice everything that economists can suggest to them, in the way of stabilisation policies, that they have learned from the study of the 1930s and from the depression in Japan in the 1990s. How would you assess the possibilities, the limits, and the defects of these as stabilisation policies?

We have seen massive drops of liquidity into the banking systems. We have seen it being decided that the problem is solvency, not liquidity, and

* Previously published in *Solidarity* 145, 29 January 2009.

the governments putting public capital into the banks, so that the banks will have enough trust in each other's solvency to lend to each other. None of this is solving the crisis. This indicates that the banks may not be able to go back to lending at their previous rates. The decades-long process of banking and financial-system securitisation, where lending has been done on the basis of slicing and dicing and repackaging loans so as to turn them into securities to be traded internationally, was a fundamental basis for the dynamism of financial capitalism and globalisation in the last twenty years or more. That system of securitisation is now weak everywhere, even in corporate financing, and not only in the financing of mortgages and consumer debts. It has largely imploded. That is in large part why the banks have not been lending – they have been restructured to depend on doing lending through that securitisation.

That indicates that the crisis is really very severe. In terms of what is to be done about it, it raises – and we should be raising, as socialists – the obvious question of converting the banks into a public utility. In a complex society, you can't have banking for the masses without having state guarantees of deposits. The system has been kept going on the basis of central banks acting as lenders of last resort. The case for the banks being brought into public ownership properly needs to be put on the agenda, much more vociferously than the left is putting it on the agenda.

I do not mean, as in Britain, just giving public capital to the banks and saying please operate on commercial lines, a move involving no executive powers whatsoever. I mean taking the banks properly into public ownership and changing the function of the banks, as Mitterrand did not do in France in the 1980s, so that the criteria on which they invest are redefined as social purposes, to be democratically determined.

Looking back on it, the subprime mortgage crisis seems to involve tiny sums, compared to the fall-out now. How did that subprime crisis – sizeable, but small compared to what is in play now – produce such huge repercussions?

The subprime crisis was comparatively small, but subprime mortgages were packaged with other mortgages and then the securities were sold on. People were buying general mortgage-backed securities based on a mixture of mortgages. When the defaults started in the subprime sector, it became difficult to sell, or to sell on, any mortgage-backed securities. It had the effect of making the banks more reluctant to lend for new mortgages, and that helped burst the house-price bubble. Then the loans made more generally on the basis that house prices would continue to rise were called into question. You got a vicious circle in the whole housing and mortgage sector.

Once you had this loss of confidence, and inability to value securities – you didn't know how to value those securities anymore, because you couldn't sell them; the formulas on which the valuations of those mortgage-backed securities fell down – then a whole set of questions came onto the books in respect to other sorts of securities and how those might be valued. Here there is an element of confidence and psychology. However much we as Marxists see that as not primary, it is an element. The banks knew damn well how over-leveraged they all were. They began to wonder whether even the people they lend overnight to – the other banks – were solvent. They became reluctant to lend.

And so the disturbance moved beyond the original source of the problem. Insofar as the risk was spread so widely – and that was the point, credit was cheap because risk was spread so widely – it pulled in vast sectors in other countries and across the world. You could say that the crisis was triggered by the subprime crash. There is a certain racist element to the story, insofar as the growth of subprime mortgages was the attempt to incorporate the black working class through finance into the American dream. When that weakest link in the chain of financial capitalism went, then – unlike when Lenin used the metaphor of the weakest link for Russia in the chain of world capitalism – it began to undo the whole chain.

A few months ago you said that you thought US hegemony had not waned, and would not wane in the very near future. I agreed with that then. But you compared that US hegemony with the sort of hegemony that a financial centre like New York or London has in its national economy. It used to be the case that the global financial markets, centred in New York, centred round the dollar, were where any large capitalist anywhere in the world could go for credit. Isn't that ceasing to be true? Aren't governments and firms looking elsewhere for credit? Aren't we seeing the beginning of that process of US hegemony waning?

I don't think so. I'm not sure where else people would go for credit. And in fact capital has flowed to the dollar and to the US Treasury Bill. That is puzzling unless you understand that the US state is the state of global capital. Despite everything that has happened, global capital still looks on the US as the safest haven and the ultimate guarantor. And the US government has behaved that way. The decisions to nationalise Fannie Mae and Freddie Mac and AIG were taken very much with an eye to the US's responsibility to honour its commitments to China and Japan and Germany and Britain – above all to China, because the Chinese had bought a lot of Fannie Mae and Freddie Mac securities.

The American state is absolutely central. It is no accident that the G20 meeting took place in Washington. Everyone sees that whatever resolution there is to this crisis will have to be undertaken under the aegis of the American state, and everyone is hoping that Obama will be able to provide the kind of leadership – for capitalists – that will accomplish that. So I think the American state is still very much at the centre of global capitalism. The material underpinnings of that hegemony have rested in part on New York as a financial centre. So, it's a good question, what happens to that hegemony if New York seizes up as a financial centre? But I just don't see what could conceivably replace it. Certainly, nothing in Asia could replace New York as a financial centre. People can start arguing that the Chinese state has financial clout, but we see how much the Chinese economy has been affected by this crisis originating in the US economy.

It will certainly be an enormous challenge for the Americans to hold it all together. But it is only the Americans that can hold it all together; and all the world's capital, more than ever, is looking to the Americans to hold it all together.

But if the US government does it very imperfectly...

Yes, but I don't see any grounds for serious inter-imperial rivalry unless there are fundamental changes in the balance of class forces and state structures in other parts of the world, so that countries move in a national-socialist, fascist direction which would break down globalisation, or there is the kind of change in class relations that would put socialist options on the agenda, which would mean disarticulating from capitalist globalisation and attempting to re-articulate on the basis of new international socialist strategies. On the basis of the class configurations that exist in the regions outside North America, I don't see either of those things happening soon.

The question remains of whether the Americans will pull it off. If they don't, will that produce social and political disruptions that would lead to something else? Maybe. But on the basis of the current configurations, with the types of capitalist classes and state bureaucracies that are oriented to maintaining the relationships that have developed over the last 30 years under global capitalism, I don't think we can speak seriously of inter-imperialist rivalry.[1]

---

1 Leo Panitch suggested the scenario of "the social-democratisation of globalisation" in an article in the US magazine *Monthly Review*, 50/5, October 1998. The article was a discussion of the World Bank's World Development Report for 1997, *The State In A Changing World*. In the fresh days of neoliberalism, it was all for "rolling back the frontiers of the State", as Margaret Thatcher put it in 1980. But now, Panitch noted, "the World Bank advocates a large role for the state in correcting and protecting markets", and worries about countries "overshooting the mark" in the direction of the "minimalist state". This is social-democratisation, however, in

the sense of 1990s European social-democracy – which led 14 out of 15 EU governments at the time of Panitch's writing – or the Clinton Democratic Party in the USA. It is for: 1. "privatisation in general... especially the 'hiving off' of utilities and social insurance"; 2. "liberal trade, capital markets, and investment regimes"; 3. market provision of welfare, albeit with a safety-net for the poorest: "even in the areas of urban hospitals, clinics, universities, and transport... the report takes the view that markets and private spending can meet most needs, except for those of the very poorest..."; 4. "the regressive shift in taxation from corporate and personal income taxes, and trade taxes, towards consumption-based taxes like VAT"; 5. central bank independence, geared to restraining inflation. It is distinguished from the most gung-ho neoliberalism in wanting: 1. "not... a minimal state, but rather an efficient capitalist state"; 2. strong regulation of the financial sector, not for "channelling credit in preferred directions" but for "safeguarding the health of the financial system".

CHAPTER 12

The Bondholders and the Taxpayers (December 2008)

Discussion with Fred Moseley

Do you think that the recent extensive measures of nationalisation and bailing-out, and talk by governments of increased regulation of the financial sector, mark a serious change in the shape of capitalist development? What sort of new regimes might emerge from the crisis?

I think we should nationalise the banks, and really and truly nationalise them, not the pseudo-nationalisations that most governments have done so far, which are really not much more than bail-outs of the stockholders and especially the bondholders of the banks. Most importantly, these government bail-outs make it possible that the debt of the banks to their creditors will be paid in full; i.e. the creditors will be "made whole". In the event of future losses, which are likely to be very significant, the government bail-out money will be used to pay off the bondholders. So the government bail-out of the banks is really a bail-out of the banks' bondholders, paid for by taxpayers.

Under current policies in the US, the total sum of money transferred from taxpayers to the banks' bondholders could be as much as one trillion dollars (some estimates are higher than that), which is about $4,000 for each man, woman, and child in the United States. $16,000 for a family of four. From taxpayers to the bondholders. The financial elite wheeled and dealed and made lots of money during the recent boom, but their excessive wheeling and dealing caused the current crisis, and now taxpayers are supposed to bail them out and pay for their losses? What is wrong with this picture? "Socialism for the rich", as some have described it. And economic injustice for the rest of us. This is truly outrageous and should be stopped immediately.

Once it has been recognised that that the government will always bail out large banks ("too big to fail"), then it follows as a matter of logic and economic justice that these financial institutions have to be nationalised. Otherwise, the implicit bail-out promise is a license to take lots of risks and make lots of money in good times, and then let the taxpayers pay for the losses in the bad times.

* Previously published in *Solidarity* 144, 15 January 2009.

So the bail-outs of the banks today sow the seeds for future crises, which will require more bail-outs, again at the expense of taxpayers, etc.

The only way to avoid this legal robbery of taxpayers is to nationalise the banks. If taxpayers are going to pay for the losses, then they should also receive the profits. Ironically, the justification of private profit is that capitalists take risks and could suffer losses. But if the losses are not suffered by the capitalists, but instead by the taxpayers, then this justification for private profit is no longer valid.

Instead of bail-outs, governments should fully nationalise any bank that needs to be rescued, i.e. fully take over and run the bank's operations, and replace the current management and board of directors with government banking officials (with no "golden parachutes" for the displaced executives). And, most crucially, nationalisation should not guarantee the debt of the bank to its bondholders. The value of the banks' debt must be written down to be commensurate with the current value of the banks' assets, as in normal bankruptcy proceedings.

The extent of the write-down (or "haircut" as it is called) would vary from bank to bank, but in many cases would be very large. Bankruptcy judges would decide the size of the write-downs, as they normally do. Bondholders would also have the option to swap their debt for equity in the new government banks (as is often the case in bankruptcy proceedings). The nationalisation of banks is not a "pie in the sky" demand that we have to struggle for 20 years to get on the national agenda. "What to do with the banks?" is already very much on the national agenda in the US and UK and probably elsewhere. It is immanently possible. It is the most reasonable and most equitable solution to the current financial crisis. Governments are being forced by the severity of the crisis, and contrary to their free-market ideology, to move in this direction. The government pseudo-nationalisation opens the door for real nationalisation.

I was in Argentina recently, just after the pension funds had been nationalised, and there was a cartoon in one of the daily newspapers, in which a government official says: "We are just following Yanqui imperialism!" Similarly, we should be following pseudo Yanqui nationalisation with real nationalisation for the people. Nationalised banks is not socialism, to be sure. But it could be an important step toward socialism. The goal of the banking system would be to serve the interests of the people, rather than to maximise profits for a few shareholders. That is a fundamental socialist principle that could eventually be applied more broadly to the economy as a whole.

The governments are trying to put into practice what their economists have learned, as regards stabilisation policies, from study of the 1930s and of the depression in Japan in the 1990s. What are the limits and defects of these stabilisation policies?

The most obvious and serious defect of the current bail-out policies is that they are unjust and unfair – they are a massive transfer of income from the poor and middle classes to the rich, as discussed above. Beyond that, these bail-outs do not solve the fundamental problem in the economy right now, which is too much debt in relation to income, especially for households. To solve this problem the debt must be reduced to a more sustainable level. The government bail-outs of the bondholders do the opposite – they pay off the too-big debt at the expense of taxpayers. So household debt would stay at their current unsustainable levels, and there would be more debt crises in the future. If instead the debt levels were written down to more sustainable levels, then there would be fewer debt crises in the years ahead.

Also, these bail-outs have not been successful in achieving one of their main objectives – an increase of bank lending to businesses and households, which would help stabilise the economy and lessen the severity of the current recession. At the present time, banks do not want to increase their lending, in spite of the government bail-out. They have suffered enormous losses over the last year, and they fear that more enormous losses are still to come in the months ahead. So banks prefer instead to hoard capital as a cushion against future losses.

Mervyn King of the Bank of England even threatened recently that, if UK banks did not increase their lending, they might be nationalised! I say, Mervyn, go ahead! Follow through on your threat! Nationalisation is clearly the better solution. Instead of giving money to the banks and begging them to lend, the government should nationalise the banks and lend directly to businesses and households, and in that way contribute more effectively to a general economic recovery.

The subprime mortgage crisis in the USA, though sizeable in its own terms, initially involved small sums compared to those in play now. Why has such a relatively small disturbance had such big repercussions?

Because debt levels in the US economy and around the world are at such high levels. High levels of debt make the economy more vulnerable to a downturn; the higher the debt, the bigger the eventual downturn will be. Debt has to be repaid out of income, so debt cannot continue to increase faster than income indefinitely. In the US, the ratio of household debt to household disposable income increased from 40% in 1950, to 60% in 1980, and then accelerated to 100% in 2000, and to 140% in 2007. So debt has increased more than twice as fast as income since 1980. In the UK, the household debt to income ratio is even higher: 220%! Some of us have been saying for a long time that these unprecedented levels of household debt were not sustainable, and would eventually lead to a more serious crisis in the future, and that is exactly what is happening.

With the development of the crisis in recent months, now governments as well as banks or mortgage or insurance companies are in trouble. The IMF's resources are small compared to the sums involved. The bigger stashes are in the hands of the central banks, governments, and sovereign wealth funds of east Asia and the Gulf. Do you think that the unfolding of this crisis could mark a shift in the balance of financial and economic power on a world scale?

One possible consequence of the Fed's wildly expansionary monetary policy in recent months could be fears of higher rates of inflation in the future and a flight from the dollar. If that happened, and the dollar lost its status as the world's reserve currency, then the balance of international financial and economic power would change drastically, probably in the direction of Europe and China. Actually, this flight from the dollar may have started in December 2008, triggered by the Fed lowering its target interest rate to 0% (!) and announcing that it would now purchase unlimited amounts of almost any kind of securities, including mortgage based securities and credit card backed securities. As a result, the dollar has fallen sharply. Clearly, the dominance of the US free-market style of capitalism has taken a serious blow, and will no longer be regarded around the world as the ideal to which all other countries aspire or are pushed. Emerging countries are also likely to demand and receive more participation in governing the world economy. We have already seen the beginning of this shift. When President Bush called the international meeting in November to deal with the global crisis, he invited the G20, not the G7.

CHAPTER 13

The Neoliberal Model is Bust (January 2009)

Discussion with Simon Mohun

You've argued that out of this crisis we may see capitalism move to a set-up more like 1945–73. However, though there is a lot of talk about regulation, it's all about regulation of the sort designed to stop banks taking unsustainable risks, rather than direction of investment, planning the development of a national industrial base, and so on. Governments are nationalising banks, but still privatising utilities and services.

I wanted to point to the idea that the neoliberal model is clearly bust. People don't believe any more in leaving everything to the free reign of markets. It is not at all clear how this will play out in terms of government policies. At present the policies seem to be focused on providing state guarantees to institutions which are insolvent. (In parenthesis: these interventions always appear to be too little and too late. And of course, they will always appear as too little and too late until the economy turns around). The government does have a view that more regulation is required; and is proceeding with such regulation as if the world has not really changed. Northern Rock appears to be being given a more dynamic loans policy which it has to pursue, and the government stake in other nationalised banks is being increased; but these banks are being governed by a "hands-off" structure in which personnel are drawn from the people who got us into this mess in the first place.

However, I cannot see how the neoliberal world order will be re-established. That means that all sorts of questions and spaces for political action are opened up in a way that has not been the case for 30 years. Therefore, it is quite possible that we will see a move to a much more state-managed economy, with much more emphasis on consensus as to how the economy should be run. This could take an unpleasant corporatist form. It could take some sort of traditional social-democratic form. It could look like the German social market economy. It does not look likely at present that it will take a Scandinavian-type social-democratic form, because neither this government, nor any likely future government, wants to do anything serious about the huge inequalities that have arisen in society in the last thirty years. The future is unpredictable.

* Previously published online at www.workersliberty.org/node/12523, 4 June 2009.

It is all up for grabs. And it really all depends on the pressures the left is able to put on to… towards – well, at the moment, fairly minimal social-democratic goals, like greater equality and greater equality of opportunity.

Are you postulating as a likely outcome, also, the return of exchange controls, fixed exchange rates, and so on, as between 1945 and the 1970s?

Yes and no. No, in the sense that there appears to be little pressure at the moment for curbing international capital mobility. At the same time, I think it is quite likely that Britain will be forced to join the euro, and there you have several economies with a fixed exchange rate between them. It's quite likely that there will be a move towards creating large blocs of countries with fixed exchange rates between them. What will happen, then, to relations between the euro and the dollar, for example, is another question. I have no idea.

The Financial Times reports that you can deduce from market movements that financiers reckon on a 30% probability of one or another country currently in the euro being forced to abandon it. And currencies previously pegged to the dollar, like the Chinese renminbi, have drifted further away from it.

In trying to think about the future, we have to use the distinction popularised by Donald Rumsfeld, between known unknowables and unknown unknowables. Economists tend to say that this is the distinction between risk and uncertainty. Risk we can try to quantify by using probabilistic methods, uncertainty we can't. Will a country leave the euro? I have no idea whether that is a (quantifiable) risk or an (unquantifiable) uncertainty, and I don't believe anyone else does. But if a country should decide to leave the euro, then my guess is that there would be a unsustainable run on its currency. Because of that, I don't think that any country will leave the euro. Will the dollar collapse at some point? Everyone thought that because of the structural weaknesses in the US economy, the dollar would be weak now. Rather surprisingly, it has proved to be strong, as wealth-holders have flooded into dollar assets, particularly US Treasury bonds, as safer assets in a period of turmoil.

There is a view that this cannot go on for ever, and at some point, the dollar will weaken and even collapse. Weakening is not a significant problem; collapse certainly is. If that happens, it's impossible to know what the consequences will be, but they will be very nasty, because the US is still a quarter of world GDP. Relatedly, another big unknown is the Sino-US relationship. Rebalancing the world economy requires much more Chinese domestic consumption (and in order that Chinese consumers save less, there will have to be better social security, medical insurance, pension provision, etc.) and much more domestic US saving. These are very big changes which will need time to be implemented. What all this means for the dollar-renminbi relationship remains to be played out.

Do you see anyone in government circles beginning to propose the sort of reshaping of capitalism which you think likely?

No. But it may be that one lever to get changed policies in place will be the environment question. One of the things needed is, not an extension of the carbon trading which we have at present, but a big carbon tax. Apparently one of the issues which has paralysed the Government up until now is the feeling that it cannot afford politically to impose a tax increase. One of the ways to tackle the growing inequalities would be big taxes, especially income taxes, on the rich, and tax cuts at the lower ends of the distribution. That appears to be politically impossible to propose, despite the popular venom against bankers' bonuses. It may be that a carbon tax is the way to get acceptance that serious tax changes are needed to promote a more equal society. However, the Government has, quite incredibly, just approved a third runway for Heathrow.

When we talked last year, you were expecting the crisis to be relatively small. That made sense if you looked at the scale of the US subprime mortgage liabilities – large in absolute terms, tiny in relation to the financial system as a whole. With hindsight, what can we identify as the elements which led to a relatively small disturbance triggering this huge crisis?

That is a difficult question. I have to hold my hands up and say I was wrong. It is clearly a much deeper crisis than I thought a year ago, or even six months ago. The world economy fell off a cliff when Lehman Brothers was allowed to go bust; but I still haven't seen a good explanation other than seizing up of credit markets, and I still don't really know why aggregate demand fell so quickly.

I've seen some work on the US economy, looking at the situation of the people who were lent the subprime mortgages. Why did they default? There is a story going round which says "it's the fault of all of us. We were all too greedy. We all borrowed too much". In the USA, a big proportion of earners had been very stretched for a long while. The political process of deregulation and liberalisation, together with stagnant real wages, has led to costs like education, child-care, and health-care taking larger proportions of essentially fixed household budgets.

It could just be that so many people were stretched that rather small changes in asset prices were sufficient to trigger major collapses in household budgets. There is no firm evidence for this, but it is an interesting line for research, especially for us on the left. There is a culture of "blame the victim", and maybe the victim wasn't to blame. It is not clear to me that the crisis is anything other than an indication of how dependent the modern economy is on flows of credit. I always knew that theoretically, but to be confronted with it empirically is something of a shock.

When we talked earlier, you thought that the price rises for oil, wheat, and so on [the "Brent crude" oil price rose from $51 to early 2007 to $145 in late summer 2008] were rooted in fairly long-term supply-and-demand factors. Since then we have seen those prices fall sharply ["Brent crude" oil down to $38 in late December 2008; it recovered, then fell again from early 2012].

I still think I'm right about that. It is clear that large speculative positions were taken in some of those commodities [i.e. people bought large advance contracts on them, expecting price rises; and that buying, in turn, pushed the prices up]. These commodities are fairly limited in supply. When demand drops, prices can fall precipitously [because supply cannot quickly be reduced to match]. But the world economy will in due course recover. The big oil companies have spent very little in the last 20 or 30 years on exploration and on adding new refining capacity. I would expect the oil price to rise very fast once recovery starts, and I would expect the same with other commodities too.

When the oil price was going up, many writers said that the rise was chiefly driven by speculation. I thought at the time that the price rise was too large and too well-established for that to be true. But maybe I was wrong.

I'm sure that there was a speculative bubble. Trying to pick exactly what of the price rises was due to speculative activity and what to more long-term trends is almost impossible. A lot of oil-price speculators will have got hammered by the price falls. Attempts to corner the market in commodities with a limited supply are tempting, but almost invariably unsuccessful. The last one I know is the Hunt brothers' attempt to corner the silver market in 1980. It looked as if it was going to work, but then failed spectacularly. [The silver price went from $5 an ounce in early 1979 to a peak of $54 in early 1980, then collapsed back to $10.80 in March 1980. The Hunt brothers were bankrupted and convicted on charges of manipulating the market].

There are two reasons why prices move: "economic fundamentals" and "market noise". There will always be market noise, and within that there is a short-term tendency that if prices are rising they are more likely to go on rising; if prices are falling, they are more likely to go on falling. In the long run the opposite is the case: long periods of price rises tend to be followed by long periods of price fall. It is very difficult to predict the "market noise", so the only realistic approach is to step back and focus on the "economic fundamentals".

The oil market is an unstable market. There will be speculative swings, but they will be around a trend line built on "economic fundamentals", and that trend line is upwards.

You have said that financialisation involved a big change in the balance of power within capital, but also that it is wrong to see that as a struggle of finance capital versus industrial capital. So – a big change in the balance of power between whom and whom?

A change in the balance of power between those whose positions rested on liberalisation and the rule of free markets and minimal government intervention, and those who would prefer to operate in a more managed, "corporatist" world, like, say, steel companies. Many, many industrial companies have substantial financial portfolios, so I still think it's wrong to see a simple split of interests between the financial world and the industrial world.

Would one sector be the more globally-oriented corporations, who might even prefer a more managed environment but know that there is no mechanism for getting it on a world scale, and the other firms focused on domestic markets?

Possibly. But I think the left has to be very careful about lining up with small business against big business. Politically, that would not be very astute.

Of course. Do you think that the balance of power is shifting back, towards sectors of capital more interested in economic management by governments?

It is too early to tell. There is a widespread recognition that free markets have been shown not to work well. What happens as a consequence of that recognition is still open. We don't know.

The world of laissez-faire and the Gold Standard was pretty much shot as soon as the First World War happened. Yet a big shift in government orientations [to Keynesian policies] did not come for a long time after that. Do you see a similar delay as likely now?

The problem with looking backwards like that is that it is difficult to disentangle the intertwining of economics and politics. In the British case, for example, the period between the two World Wars was one of a consistently rising rate of profit. The way I see the pattern, moves to establish a new international order happen towards the top of a period of rising profit rates. The mechanisms used to establish the new order will probably be different in every case. It is true that the Gold Standard was effectively destroyed by the First World War. It staggered on, limply, until 1931, when it completely disintegrated, but it was not replaced by anything until the late 1940s. Why did it take so long?

There was the Second World War. There were all sorts of particular historical conjunctures. If we look at the period from 1980 to 2000 as a recovery of the rate of profit, then in terms of historical parallels it is time for some sort of major change in global capitalist arrangements. But it's clearly not going to happen in the same way.

In capitalist development over the long term, we tend to get free-market, neoliberal periods which coincide with broad, long-run, rises in the rate of profit; and more "managed" periods which coincide with long-run falls in the rate of profit. That has happened in the past. Whether it is an immutable pattern of capitalist development is difficult to say. The future is unknowable, and is partly down to us and our political activity.

CHAPTER 14

The Economy in a World of Trouble (April 2009)

Robert Brenner interviewed by Seongjin Jeong

Most media and analysts label the current crisis as a "financial crisis." Do you agree with this characterisation?

It's understandable that analysts of the crisis have made the meltdown in banking and the securities markets their point of departure. But the difficulty is that they have not gone any deeper. From Treasury Secretary Henry Paulson and Fed Chair Ben Bernanke on down, they argue that the crisis can be explained simply in terms of problems in the financial sector. At the same time, they assert that the underlying real economy is strong, the so-called fundamentals in good shape. This could not be more misleading. The basic source of today's crisis is the declining vitality of the advanced economies since 1973, and, especially, since 2000. Economic performance in the United States, western Europe, and Japan has steadily deteriorated, business cycle by business cycle in terms of every standard macroeconomic indicator – GDP, investment, real wages and so forth. Most telling, the business cycle that just ended, from 2001 through 2007, was – by far – the weakest of the post-war period, and this despite the greatest government-sponsored economic stimulus in US peacetime history.

How would you explain the long-term weakening of the real economy since 1973, what you call in your work "the long downturn"?

What mainly accounts for it is a deep, and lasting, decline of the rate of return on capital investment since the end of the 1960s. The failure of the rate of profit to recover is all the more remarkable in view of the huge drop-off in the growth of real wages over the period. The main cause, though not the only cause, of the decline in the rate of profit has been a persistent tendency to overcapacity in global manufacturing industries. What happened was that one after another new manufacturing power entered the world market – Germany and Japan, the northeast Asian Newly Industrializing Countries (NICS), the

* This interview conducted by Seongjin Jeong for the Korean daily newspaper *Hankyoreh* was published in Korea on 22 January 2009 and is reproduced here (with permission) in the slightly edited version printed in *Against The Current*, March-April 2009 (https://www.solidarity-us.org/site/node/2071).

South East Asian Tigers, and, finally the Chinese Leviathan. These later-developing economies produced the same goods that were already being produced by the earlier developers, only cheaper. The result was too much supply compared to demand in one industry after another, and this forced down prices and in that way profits. The corporations that experienced the squeeze on their profits, moreover, did not meekly leave their industries; they tried to hold their place by falling back on their capacity for innovation and speeding up investment in new technologies. But of course this only made overcapacity worse.

Due to the fall in their rate of return, capitalists were getting smaller surpluses from their investments. They therefore had no choice but to slow down the growth of plant and equipment and employment. At the same time, in order to restore profitability, they held down employees' pay, while governments reduced the growth of social expenditures. But the consequence of all these cutbacks in spending has been a long-term problem of aggregate demand. The persistent weakness of aggregate demand has been the immediate source of the economy's long-term weakness.

The crisis was actually triggered by the bursting of the historic housing bubble, which had been expanding for a full decade. What is your view of its significance?

The housing bubble needs to be understood in relation to the succession of asset price bubbles that the economy has experienced since the middle 1990s, and especially the role of the US Federal Reserve in nurturing those bubbles. Since the start of the long downturn, state economic authorities have tried to cope with the problem of insufficient demand by encouraging the increase of borrowing, both public and private. At first they turned to state budget deficits, and in this way they did avoid really deep recessions. But as time went on, governments could get ever less growth from the same amount of borrowing. In effect, in order to stave off the sort of profound crises that historically have plagued the capitalist system, they had to accept a slide toward stagnation. During the early 1990s, governments in the United States and Europe, led by the Clinton administration, famously tried to break their addiction to debt by moving together toward balanced budgets. The idea was to let the free market govern the economy. But because profitability had still not recovered, the reduction in deficits delivered a big shock to demand, and helped bring about the recessions and slow growth between 1991 and 1995.

To get the economy expanding again, US authorities ended up adopting an approach that had been pioneered by Japan during the later 1980s. By keeping interest rates low, the Federal Reserve made it easy to borrow so as to encourage investment in financial assets. As asset prices soared, corporations and households experienced huge increases in their wealth, at least on paper. They were therefore able to borrow on a titanic scale, vastly increase their investment and consumption, and in that way drive the economy.

So, private deficits replaced public ones. What might be called "asset price Keynesianism" replaced traditional Keynesianism. We have therefore witnessed for the last dozen years or so the extraordinary spectacle of a world economy in which the continuation of capital accumulation has come literally to depend upon historic waves of speculation, carefully nurtured and rationalized by state policy makers – and regulators! – first the historic stock market bubble of the later 1990s, then the housing and credit market bubbles from the early 2000s.

You were prophetic in forecasting the current crisis as well as the 2001 recession. What is your outlook for the global economy? Will it worsen, or will it recover before the end of 2009? Do you expect that the current crisis will be as severe as the Great Depression?

The current crisis is more serious than the worst previous recession of the post-war period, between 1979 and 1982, and could conceivably come to rival the Great Depression, though there is no way of really knowing. Economic forecasters have underestimated how bad it is because they have overestimated the strength of the real economy and failed to take into account the extent of its dependence upon a build-up of debt that relied on asset price bubbles. In the United States, during the recent business cycle of the years 2001-2007, GDP growth was by far the slowest of the post-war epoch. There was no increase in private sector employment. The increase in plant and equipment was about a third off the previous post-war low. Real wages were basically flat. There was no increase in median family income for the first time since WWII. Economic growth was driven entirely by personal consumption and residential investment, made possible by easy credit and rising house prices.

Economic performance was this weak, despite the enormous stimulus from the housing bubble and the Bush administration's huge federal deficits. Housing by itself accounted for almost one-third of the growth of GDP and close to half of the increase in employment in the years 2001-2005. It was therefore to be expected that when the housing bubble burst, consumption and residential investment would fall, and the economy would plunge.

Many assert that the current crisis is a typical financial crisis, not a "Marxian" one of overproduction and falling profit, arguing that the financial speculation-bubble-bust has played the central role in this crisis. How would you respond?

I don't think it's helpful to counterpose in that way the real and financial aspects of the crisis. As I emphasized, it is a Marxian crisis in that it finds its roots in a long-term fall and failure to recover the rate of profit, which is the fundamental source of the extended slowdown of capital accumulation right into the present. In 2001, the rate of profit for US non-financial corporations was the lowest of the post-war period, except for 1980. Corporations therefore had no choice but to hold back on investment and employment, further darkening the business climate.

This is what accounts for the ultra-slow growth during the business cycle that just ended. Nevertheless, to understand the current collapse, you have to demonstrate the connection between the weakness of the real economy and the financial meltdown. The main link is the economy's ever-increasing dependence on borrowing to keep it turning over, and the government's ever greater reliance on asset price run-ups to allow that borrowing to continue. The basic condition for the housing and credit market bubbles was the perpetuation of low costs of borrowing. The weakness of the world economy, especially after the crises of 1997-1998 and 2001-2002, plus East Asian governments' huge purchases of dollars to keep their currencies down and US consumption growing, made for unusually low long-term interest rates. At the same time, the US Fed kept short-term interest rates lower than at any time since the 1950s. Because they could borrow so cheaply, banks were willing to extend loans to speculators, whose investments drove the price of assets of every type ever higher and the return on lending (interest rates on bonds) ever lower.

Symptomatically, housing prices soared and the yield in real terms on US Treasury bonds plunged. But because yields fell ever lower, institutions the world over that depended on returns from lending had an ever more difficult time making sufficient profits. Pension funds and insurance companies were particularly hard hit, but hedge funds and investment banks were also affected.

These institutions were therefore all too ready to make massive investments in securities backed by highly dubious sub-prime mortgages, because of the unusually high returns they offered, ignoring their unusually high risk. In fact, they could not get enough of them. Their purchases of mortgage-backed securities allowed mortgage originators to keep lending to ever less qualified borrowers. The housing bubble reached historic proportions, and the economic expansion was allowed to continue.

Of course, this could not go on for very long. When housing prices fell, the real economy went into recession and the financial sector experienced a meltdown, because both had depended for their dynamism on the housing bubble. Today, the recession is making the meltdown worse because it is exacerbating the housing crisis. The meltdown is intensifying the recession because it is making access to credit so difficult. It is the mutually reinforcing interaction between the crises in the real economy and financial sector that has made the downward slide so intractable for policymakers, and the potential for catastrophe so evident.

Even if one grants that post-war capitalism entered a period of long downturn in the 1970s, it seems undeniable that the neoliberal capitalist offensive has prevented the worsening of the downswing since the 1980s.

If you mean by neoliberalism the turn to finance and deregulation, I do not see how it helped the economy. But if you mean the stepped-up assault by employers and governments on workers' wages, working conditions, and the welfare state, there can be little doubt that it prevented the fall in the rate of profit from getting worse. Even so, the employers' offensive did not wait until the so-called neoliberal era of the 1980s. It began in the wake of the fall of profitability, starting in the early 1970s, along with Keynesianism. Moreover, it did not result in a recovery of the rate of profit, and only further exacerbated the problem of aggregate demand. The weakening of aggregate demand ultimately impelled economic authorities to turn to more powerful and dangerous forms of economic stimulus, the "asset price Keynesianism" that led to the current disaster.

Some have argued that a new paradigm of "financialisation" or "finance-led capitalism" has sustained a so-called "Capital Resurgent" (Gerard Duménil) between the 1980s and the present. What do you think of such a thesis?

The idea of a finance-led capitalism is a contradiction in terms, because, speaking generally – there are significant exceptions, like consumer lending – sustained financial profit-making depends on sustained profit-making in the real economy. To respond to the fall in the rate of profit in the real economy, some governments, led by the United States, encouraged a turn to finance by deregulating the financial sector. But because the real economy continued to languish, the main result of deregulation was to intensify competition in the financial sector, which made profit making more difficult and encouraged ever greater speculation and risk taking.

Leading executives in investment banks and hedge funds were able to make fabulous fortunes, because their salaries depended on short-run profits. They were able to secure temporarily high returns by expanding their firms' assets/lending and increasing risk. But this way of doing business, sooner or later, came at the expense of the executives own corporations' long-term financial health, most spectacularly leading to the fall of Wall Street's leading investment banks.

Every so-called financial expansion since the 1970s very quickly ended in a disastrous financial crisis and required a massive bail-out by the state. This was true of the third-world lending boom of the 1970s and early 1980s; the savings and loan run-up, the leveraged buyout mania, and the commercial real estate bubble of the 1980s; the stock market bubble of the second half of the 1990s; and of course the housing and credit market bubbles of the 2000s. The financial sector appeared dynamic only because governments were prepared to go to any lengths to support it.

Keynesianism or statism seems poised to return as the new Zeitgeist. What is your general assessment of resurgent Keynesianism or statism? Can it help to resolve, or at least, alleviate the current crisis?

Governments today really have no choice but to turn to Keynesianism and the state to try to save the economy. After all, the free market has shown itself totally incapable of preventing or coping with economic catastrophe, let alone securing stability and growth. That's why the world's political elites, who only yesterday were celebrating deregulated financial markets, are suddenly now all Keynesians. But there is reason to doubt that Keynesianism, in the sense of huge government deficits and easy credit to pump up demand, can have the impact that many expect. After all, during the past seven years, thanks to the borrowing and spending encouraged by the Federal Reserve's housing bubble and the Bush administration's budget deficits, we witnessed in effect probably the greatest Keynesian economic stimulus in peacetime history. Yet we got the weakest business cycle in the post-war epoch.

Today the challenge is much greater. As the housing bubble collapses and credit becomes harder to come by, households are cutting back on the consumption and residential investment. As a consequence, corporations are experiencing falling profits. They are therefore cutting back on wages and laying off workers at a rapid pace, detonating a downward spiral of declining demand and declining profitability.

Households had long counted on rising house prices to enable them to borrow more and to do their saving for them. But now, because of the build-up of debt, they will have to reduce borrowing and increase saving at the very time that the economy most needs them to consume. We can expect that much of the money that the government places in the hands of households will be saved, not spent. Since Keynesianism could barely move the economy during the expansion, what can we expect from it in the worst recession since the 1930s?

To have a significant effect on the economy, the Obama administration will likely have to contemplate a huge wave of direct or indirect government investment, in effect a form of state capitalism. To actually accomplish this however would require overcoming enormous political and economic obstacles. The US political culture is enormously hostile to state enterprise. At the same time, the level of expenditure and state indebtedness that would be required could threaten the dollar. Until now, East Asian governments have been happy to fund US external and government deficits, in order to sustain US consumption and their own exports. But with the crisis overtaking even China, these governments may lose the capacity to finance US deficits, especially as they grow to unprecedented size. The truly terrifying prospect of a run on the dollar looms in the background.

What is your general assessment of the victory of Obama in the last [2008] Presidential election? Many regard Obama as a F.D.R. of the 21st century who will bring a "new New Deal." Do you think the anti-capitalist progressives can give critical support to some of his policies?

The triumph of Obama in the election is to be welcomed. A victory for McCain would have been a victory for the Republican Party and given an enormous boost to the most reactionary forces on the US political scene. It would have been seen as an endorsement of the Bush administration's hyper-militarism and imperialism, as well as its explicit agenda of eliminating what is left of unions, the welfare state, and environmental protection. That said, Obama is, like Roosevelt, a centrist Democrat who cannot be expected on his own to do much to defend the interests of the vast majority of working people, who will be subjected to an accelerating assault from corporations trying to make up for their collapsing profits by reducing employment, compensation, and so forth.

Obama backed the titanic bail-out of the financial sector, which represents perhaps the greatest robbery of the US taxpayer in American history, especially as it came with no strings attached for the banks. He also supported the bail-out of the auto industry, even though it is conditional on massive cuts in the compensation of auto workers. The bottom line is that, like Roosevelt, Obama can be expected to take decisive action in defence of working people only if he is pushed by way of organised direct action from below. The Roosevelt administration passed the main progressive legislation of the New Deal, including the Wagner Act and the Social Security, only after it was pressured to do so by a great wave of mass strikes. We can expect the same from Obama.

According to Rosa Luxemburg and recently David Harvey, capitalism overcomes its tendency to crisis by way of geographical expansion. According to Harvey, this is often facilitated by massive state investments in infrastructure, to back up private capital investment, often foreign direct investment. Do you think that capitalism can find an exit from the current crisis, in Harvey's terminology, by way of a "temporal-spatial" fix?

This is a complex issue. I think, first of all, it's true and critically important to say that geographical expansion has been essential to every great wave of capital accumulation. You might say that growth of the size of the labour force and growth of the system's geographical space are the essentials for capitalist growth. The post-war boom is a good example, spectacular expansions of capital into the US south and southwest and into war-torn western Europe and Japan.

Investment by US corporations played a critical role, not only in United States but in western Europe in this epoch. Without question, this expansion of the labour force and the capitalist geographical arena was indispensable for the high profit rates that made the post-war boom so dynamic. From a Marxist standpoint, this was a classical wave of capital accumulation and, necessarily, entailed both sucking in huge masses of labour from outside the system, especially from the pre-capitalist countryside in Germany and Japan, and the incorporation or re-incorporation of additional geographical space on a huge scale.

Nevertheless, I think that by and large the pattern of the long downturn, since the late 1960s and early 1970s, has been different. It is true that capital responded to falling profitability by further expansion outward, seeking to combine advanced techniques with cheap labour. East Asia is of course the fundamental case, and unquestionably represents a world-historical moment, a fundamental transformation, for capitalism. Yet even though expansion into East Asia represented a response to falling profitability, it has not, I think, constituted a satisfactory solution. At the end of the day, the new manufacturing production that emerged so spectacularly in East Asia is to a great extent duplicating the manufacturing production already taking place elsewhere, though more cheaply. On a system-wide scale, it's exacerbating not resolving the problem of overcapacity. In other words, globalisation has been a response to falling profitability, but because its new industries are basically not complementary for the world division of labour, but redundant, you have had a continuation of the problem of profitability.

To actually resolve the problem of profitability that has so long plagued the system – slowing capital accumulation and calling forth ever greater levels of borrowing to sustain stability – the system requires the crisis that has so long been postponed. Because the problem is overcapacity, massively exacerbated by the build-up of debt, what is still required, as in the classical vision, is a shakeout from the system of high-cost low-profit firms, the subsequent cheapening of means of production, and the reduction of the price of labour.

It's by way of crisis that capitalism historically has restored the rate of profit and established the necessary conditions for more dynamic capital accumulation. During the post-war period, crisis has been warded off, but the cost has been a failure to revive profitability, leading to worsening stagnation. The current crisis is about that shakeout that never happened.

So you think that only the crisis can resolve the crisis? That's a classical Marxian answer.

I think that that is probably the case. The analogy would be this. At first, in the early 1930s, the New Deal and Keynesianism were ineffective. In fact, through the length of the 1930s, there was a failure to establish the conditions for a new boom, as was demonstrated when the economy fell back into the deep recession of 1937-1938. But eventually, as a result of the long crisis in the 30s, you shook out the high-cost, low-profit means of production, creating the basic conditions for high rates of profit.

By the end of the 1930s, you could say that the potential rate of profit was high and all that was missing was a shock to demand. That demand was provided of course by the massive spending on armaments for World War II. So during the war, you got high rates of profit and those high rates of profit provided the necessary condition for the post-war boom. But I don't think that Keynesian deficits could have worked even if they had been tried in 1933, because you needed, in Marxian terms, a system-cleansing crisis first.

Do you think that the current crisis will lead to a challenge to US hegemony? World-system theorists, like Immanuel Wallerstein, who was also interviewed for this newspaper Hankyoreh, *are arguing that the hegemony of US imperialism is declining.*

This is again a very complex question. Perhaps I am mistaken, but I think that many of those who believe that there has been a decline in US hegemony basically view it as mainly an expression of US geopolitical power, and in the end, force. From this standpoint, it's mainly US dominance that makes for leadership, it's US power over and against other countries that keeps the United States on top. I don't see US hegemony that way. I see the elites of the world, especially the elites of the capitalist core broadly conceived, as being very happy with US hegemony because what it means for them is that the United States assumes the role and the cost of world policemen. This is true, I think, of the elites even of most poor countries today. What's the goal of the US world policeman? Not to attack other countries – mainly, it's to keep social order, to create stable conditions for global capital accumulation. Its main purpose is to wipe out any popular challenges to capitalism, to support the existing structures of class relations.

For most of the post-war period, there were nationalist-statist challenges, especially from below, to the free rein of capital. They unquestionably were met by the most brutal US force, the most naked expressions of US domination. Although within the core of the system there was US hegemony [meaning general consensus, enforced by the threat of military power only in the final analysis – ed.], outside of it there was dominance by violence.

But with the fall of the Soviet Union, China and Vietnam taking the capitalist road, and the defeat of national liberation movements in places like southern Africa and Central America, resistance to capital in the developing world was very much weakened, at least for the time being. So today, the governments and elites not only of western and eastern Europe, Japan and Korea, but also Brazil, India and China – most anyplace you can name – would prefer the continuation of US hegemony.

US hegemony will not fall because of the rise of another power capable of contending for world domination. Above all, China prefers US hegemony. The United States is not planning to attack China and, until now, has kept its market wide open to Chinese exports. With the US world policeman ensuring ever freer trade and capital movements, China has been allowed to compete in terms of cost of production, on an equal playing field, and this has been incredibly beneficial to China – it couldn't be better.

Can US hegemony continue in the current crisis? This is a much harder question. But I think that, in the first instance, the answer is yes. The world's elites want more than anything to sustain the current globalising order, and the United States is key to that. None of the world's elites are trying to exploit the crisis, or the United States' enormous economic problems, to challenge its hegemony. China keeps saying, "we're not going to continue to pay for the US to continue its profligate ways," referring to the way that China covered record-breaking US current account deficits during the past decade and to the titanic US budget deficits now being created. Do you think China has now cut the United States off? Not at all. China is still pouring in as much money as it can to try to keep the US economy going, so that China can keep developing the way it did. Of course, what is desired is not always possible. The depth of the Chinese crisis may be so great that it can no longer afford to finance US deficits – or the ballooning of those deficits and printing of money by the Federal Reserve could lead to the collapse of the dollar, detonating true catastrophe.

If those things happened, there would have to be a construction of a new order. But under conditions of deep crisis that would be extremely difficult. Indeed, under such conditions, the United States as well as other states could easily turn to economic protection, nationalism and even war. I think, as of this moment, that the elites of the world still are trying to avoid this – they are not ready for it. What they want is to keep markets open, keep trade open.

They understand that the last time states resorted to protection to solve the problem was at the time of the Great Depression, and this made the depression way worse, because in effect when some states started to protect, everybody moved to protection, and the world market closed down. Next, of course, came militarism and war. The closing of world markets would obviously be disastrous today, so elites and governments are doing their very best to prevent a protectionist, statist, nationalist, militarist outcome. But politics is not just an expression of what the elites want, and what elites want changes over time. Elites are, moreover, generally divided and politics has autonomy. So, for example, it can hardly be ruled out that, if the crisis gets very bad – which at this point would not be a big surprise – you could see a return of far-right politics of protectionism, militarism, anti-immigration, nationalism.

This sort of politics not only could have broad popular appeal. Growing sections of business might find it the only way out, as they see their markets collapse, see the system in depression, see a need for protection from competition and state subsidies of demand by way of military spending. This was, of course, the response that prevailed in much of Europe and Japan during the crisis of the interwar period. Today, the right is on its heels, because of the failures of the Bush administration and because of the crisis. But, if the Obama administration is unable to counter the economic collapse, the right could easily come back... especially because the Democrats are really offering no ideological alternative.

You spoke about a potential crisis in China. What do you think of the current state of the Chinese economy?

I think the Chinese crisis is going to be a lot worse than people expected, for two main reasons. The first is that the American crisis, and the global crisis more generally, is much more serious than people expected, and in the last analysis the fate of the Chinese economy is inextricably dependent on the fate of the US and global economy. This is not only because China has depended to such a great extent on exports to the US market. Most of the rest of the world is also so dependent on the United States, and that especially includes Europe. If I'm not mistaken, Europe recently became China's biggest export market. But, as the crisis originating in the United States brings down Europe, Europe's market for Chinese goods will also contract. So the situation for China is much worse than what people expected, because the economic crisis is much worse than people expected.

Secondly, in people's enthusiasm for what has been China's truly spectacular economic growth, they have ignored the role of bubbles in driving the Chinese economy. China has grown, basically by way of exports, and particularly a growing trade surplus with the United States. Because of this surplus, the Chinese government has had to take political steps to keep the Chinese currency down and Chinese manufacturing competitive. Specifically, it has bought up dollar-denominated assets on a titanic scale by printing massive amounts of the renminbi, the Chinese currency. But the result has been to inject huge amounts of money into the Chinese economy, making for ever easier credit over a long period.

On the one hand, enterprises and local governments have used this easy credit to finance massive investment. But this has made for ever greater overcapacity. On the other hand, they have used the easy credit to buy land, houses, shares and other sorts of financial assets. But this has made for massive asset price bubbles, which have played a part, as in the United States, in allowing for more borrowing and spending.

As the Chinese bubbles bust, the depth of the overcapacity will be made clear. As the Chinese bubbles bust, you will also have, as across much of the rest of the world, a huge hit to consumer demand and disruptive financial crisis. So, the bottom line is that the Chinese crisis is very serious, and could make the global crisis much more severe.

So you think the capitalist logic of overproduction is also applied to China?

Yes, just as in Korea and much of East Asia later in the 90s. It's not that dissimilar. The only thing that hasn't happened yet is the kind of revaluation of the currency that really killed the Korean manufacturing expansion. The Chinese government is doing everything to avoid that.

Then you do not agree with characterizing Chinese society as a kind of non-capitalist market economy.

Not at all.

So you think China is currently capitalist?

I think it's fully capitalist. You might say that China had a market non-capitalist economy maybe through the 80s, when they had very impressive growth by means of the town and village enterprises (TVEs). They were publicly owned, owned by local governments, but operated on a market basis. That economic form, you might say, initiated the transition to capitalism. So perhaps up to maybe the early 90s it was still a kind of non-capitalist market society, especially because there was still such a big industrial sector owned and planned by the central state. But from that point on there was a transition to capitalism, which has certainly by now been completed.

What do you think of the severity of the coming Korean economic crisis? Do you think it could be more severe than the IMF crisis of 1997-1998? In order to cope with the coming crisis, the Lee Myung-bak government is now reviving Park Chung-hee style state-led investment for the construction of huge social infrastructure, especially Korean peninsula's "Great Canal", while copying Obama's green growth policies. However, Lee Myung-bak's government still tries to stick to the neoliberal deregulation policies of the post-1997 crisis period, especially by turning to the US-Korea free trade agreement. You might call this a hybrid approach, combining what seems to be an anachronistic return to a Park Chung-hee style state-led method of development with contemporary neoliberalism. Will it be effective in combating or alleviating the coming crisis?

I'm doubtful that it will be effective. This is not necessarily either because it represents a throwback to Park's state-led organised capitalism or because it embraces neoliberalism. It is because, whatever its internal form, it continues to depend on globalisation at a time when the global crisis is bringing about an extraordinary contraction of the world market. We were just talking about China, and I was arguing that China is likely to be in serious trouble. But China has low wages, potentially a huge domestic market, so over time it conceivably could have a better shot than Korea of confronting the crisis, though I'm far from sure about this.

Korea, I think, will be hard hit. It was hard hit in 1997-1998, but saved by the US stock market bubble and the resulting growth of US borrowing, spending and imports. But, when the Wall Street stock market bubble burst in 2000-2002, Korea went into what promised to be an even more serious crisis than 1997 globalisation-1998. Nevertheless, the US housing bubble came to the rescue of Korea during the recent period; now the second US bubble has collapsed, and there's no third bubble to get Korea out of the current crisis. It's not necessarily because Korea is doing the wrong thing. It's because I don't think there's going to be an easy way out for any part of what has become a truly global, interdependent capitalist system.

So what you are saying is that external environment is far worse than ever before.

That's the main point.

What then are the urgent tasks of progressives in Korea? Korean progressives are very critical of Lee Myung-bak, because Lee is very reactionary. They usually support the growth of the welfare-state and redistribution of income as an alternative to Lee's project of investing in Canal construction, of big social overhead capital. This is the hot issue in Korean society today. Korean progressives point out that although Lee Myung-bak talks about green growth, his construction project would destroy whole environments. Do you agree with them?

We should oppose such ecologically-disastrous projects.

Do you think that building a Swedish-type welfare state would be the reasonable strategy for Korean progressives in the midst of the economic crisis?

I think the most important thing Korean progressives could do would be to re-strengthen the organisations of Korean labour. Only by rebuilding the Korean working-class movement could the left build the power that it needs to win whatever demands it's advocating. The only way that working people can really develop their power is through building new organisations in the course of struggle, and it's only in the course of struggle that they are likely to come to a progressive politics, or indeed decide what a progressive politics actually should be at this moment.

I think the best way to forge a left political response today is to help the people most affected to gain the organisation and power to decide what's collectively in their interest. So, rather than try to figure out now, from above in a technocratic way, what's the best answer, the key for the left is to catalyse the reconstitution of the power of working people.

The Korean labour movement has obviously been weakened a great deal since the crisis of 1997-1998. At minimum, the priority for progressives is to do what they can to improve the environment for labour organising, for re-strengthening the unions right now. That goes not only for Korea, but everywhere around the world. That's the key objective. Without the revival of working-class power, the left will quickly find that most issues of government policy are truly academic. I mean if the left is to affect state policy, there must be a change, a big change, in the balance of class power.

Do you expect that there will be an opening for progressives in a world with the recent failures of neoliberalism?

The defeat of neoliberalism is definitely creating major opportunities that the left did not have before. Neoliberalism never much appealed to large parts of the population. Working people never identified with free markets, free finance and all that. But I think that large sections of the population were convinced of TINA, "There Is No Alternative." But now the crisis has revealed the total bankruptcy of the neoliberal mode of economic organisation, and you can already see the change very powerfully manifested in the opposition by American working people to the bail-outs for the banks and financial sector. People are saying today is that "We are told that saving the financial institutions, the financial markets, is the key to restoring the economy, prosperity. But we don't believe it. We don't want any more of our money going to these people who are just robbing us."

There is an ideological vacuum, consequently there is an opening for left ideas. The problem is that there is very little organisation of working people, let alone any political expression. One can say there is a big opportunity created by the change in the political environment, or the ideological climate, but by itself that will not provide a progressive outcome. So once again, the top priority for progressives – for any left activists – to be active is in trying to revive the organisations of working people. Without the recreation of working-class power, little progressive change will be possible, and the only way to recreate that power is through mobilisation for direct action. Only through working people taking collective mass action will they be able to create the organisation and the power necessary to provide the social basis for a transformation of their own consciousness, for political radicalisation.

CHAPTER 15

The Underlying Contradictions of Capitalist Finance (June 2009)

Discussion with Dick Bryan

In your book Capitalism with Derivatives, *you say that derivatives are a new form of money. In this crisis we have seen a flight from derivatives into cash. Doesn't that mean that the derivatives were not in fact money?*

It's not that derivatives are money in the sense that they are like state money, or that they have replaced more conventional forms of money. My argument is that derivatives are breaking down the distinction between what is money and what is capital. It is important to go back a step here. In all sorts of monetary conventions – from orthodox economics to most Marxism – there is a clearly delineated (though poorly defined) category of "money". And in most conventional analysis, there is an association of money with the state: indeed, in the tradition of Keynes, there is an understanding that money is "state money", as opposed to "commodity money" such as gold. State money is bits of paper, or entries in a balance sheet that are themselves valueless, but trust in state guarantees gives them effective value; commodity money is valued in itself.

But there are not just two absolute forms of money: there is a spectrum of moneys. There is (generally) safe, low-return money, which is state money in the form of cash or money in the bank. There are also highly liquid assets which are serving money functions, but they are not state money. They are derivative forms of money. Let me give you an illustration. A local government has $100,000 spare cash. What will it do with it? Will it put it in the bank? Will it buy government bonds? Maybe it buys some mortgage-backed securities instead. In this case, mortgage-backed securities are being treated as a way to store value – as a direct alternative to putting money in the bank. And – wrongly it turned out – this local government authority believed these securities were as safe as bank deposits. There is definitely a money dimension here.

On the other hand, other organisations – like investment banks – were treating mortgage backed securities as capital – as an alternative to money. So the "moneyness" of mortgage-backed securities depends on who is using them, and for what reason. The point is that there is no single, or universal,

---

* Previously published online at www.workersliberty.org/node/12683, 30 June 2009.

differentiation of what is money and what is capital. And that's the point in the current financial crisis. It first manifested as a crisis of stores of value (that asset values "disappeared") and in that sense, it has not just been a "financial crisis" pertaining to financial institutions and their solvency, but also a "money crisis", pertaining to what is used in financial markets as money. But in the crisis, the value of these assets crashed and their moneyness disappeared – that's what's meant by a liquidity crisis. It seems to me very significant that the first intervention of the governments and central banks was not about shoring up financial institutions directly, it was to say to financiers: bring in your mortgage-backed securities and we will convert them into state money.

It's a signal to me that these securities were indeed being treated like money, in the sense that when their moneyness suddenly disappeared, the state sought to convert them into another money form. The initial response to the crisis of governments and central banks was not to say, as the stock markets fell, bring in your shares and we'll convert them to cash. Nor did they say to banks, bring in the titles to your properties and we'll lend to you against your physical assets. They said, bring in your securities, and we'll convert them to cash. It is, to repeat, a signal that the initial liquidity crisis, when securities markets crashed, was about a crisis of money.

These mortgage-backed securities turned out not to be functional money. But we are not functionalists, and we should not be caught adhering to the conventional, functionalist definitions of money. The dash for cash, for me, means that there was a shift from high-risk, high-return liquid assets to low-risk, low-return liquid assets – from mortgage-backed securities back into state money – and the state wanted to oversee it.

In your book, Capitalism with derivatives, *there's really no discussion of securitisation...*

Yes, and I regret that. I think it is that the derivativeness of securities is less emphatic than is the case with more obvious derivative products like options and futures, and the object of the book was to explain derivatives. If I were writing the book again, I would have no difficulty feeding issues of securitisation into the text. But I don't think it would change the substance of the text. The securitisation story is directly compatible with the way I've been talking about derivatives for a few years. What Mike Rafferty and I missed in telling the story is that the pointy end of derivatives, which was going to become so conspicuous, was around the securitisation process. We didn't manage that, but our story is securitisation-compatible.

Securities are a form of derivative: indeed, it is the derivative characteristic of a security that is critical, and I think a lot of people don't get that. With mortgage-backed securities, what got sold into the market is not the mortgages, but claims on the income stream from the mortgages. And what is critical about derivatives is that they are financial exposures to an asset without ownership of the underlying asset. With an oil future, you own exposure to the price of oil, but without owning any oil itself. So it is with mortgage-backed securities: you own exposure to the performance of a bundle of mortgages, but without owning the mortgages themselves. And that separation is critical, for the mortgages themselves are illiquid, they last for 20 or 30 years, but the securities on the mortgages were highly liquid: they could be repackaged with other sorts of securities, turned into fancy products, and on-sold and re-sold. Further, the derivative dimension – the difference between ownership of the asset and ownership of an exposure to the performance of the asset – was precisely what made sub-prime lending so profitable, as long as it lasted. The financial markets could separate out the performance of mortgages from the performance of house prices. They could sell the former, but retain the latter.

That is the reason that mortgage originators could keep lending to people who would buy houses that were expected to increase in value, even though they would almost certainly not repay loans: it was possible to hold the exposure to the prices of houses and sell off the exposure to the repayment of mortgages. It was a smart strategy for capital as long as house prices didn't fall!

You talk about derivatives markets going "beneath the veil" of the corporation, enabling the corporation to assess the profitability of different assets within the corporation. Isn't securitisation quite central here? And isn't it also the case that securitisation in this sphere is not very far advanced? Corporations aren't selling securities based on the performance of individual operations within their enterprise.

I agree it is not hugely advanced in terms of securities markets trading of exposures to particular assets within corporations and it is somewhat tentative to identify a trend towards the pricing of particular assets or particular exposures within the corporation, rather than of the corporation itself. In principle, they could. But the critical question here is, how do we think about slicing the corporation down into its constituent elements? We could look at the asset sheet of a corporation, read the list of its assets, and ask whether derivatives permit the pricing of individual sites or individual bits of machinery. They are not the sort of things that are being securitised. But then think about the corporation as a set of risks, rather than a set of assets. It has exposures to exchange rates, exposures to interest rates, exposures to property prices. You're not thinking about the corporation in a physical form. You're thinking about it in a framework of risks. These risks will be aggregated across particular sites.

Here we're analysing the performance of the corporation not by sector, or by region, or by site, but by forms of risk.

Perhaps readers will know of Mike Lewis' book *Moneyball* – I believe it is being made into a film – about how derivative traders were used to evaluate the risks of a baseball team, and to price ball players in terms of the cheapest way of covering a set of risks. That captures the flavour of what I'm talking about. There is a bit of overstatement there, and baseball teams aren't standard corporations. This is still an emerging form of market. I can foresee that derivatives markets are going to start to price many, many more forms of risk. But at this stage, I think these are still ways in which corporations are evaluating themselves and their own performance, and it is from these calculations that the pressures come to labour to increase its performance: because within the corporation, all assets' performances are increasingly being measured relative to each other.

You argue that recent decades have seen not so much deregulation, as a shift to regulation by global market mechanisms in place of states. How would you assess the current talk about new and tighter government regulation?

What I was describing is what a lot of people would call neoliberalism, although some of them, Leo Panitch and Sam Gindin for example, would explain that neoliberalism is not about the decline or absence of the state; it is about the state doing certain things on behalf of capital. It is a class agenda, not a free-market versus regulated-market agenda. Nonetheless, until very recently there was a belief in "self-regulation" – in the state withdrawing from responsibility for the determination of market prices. All those models and textbooks have been torn up. All the textbooks about monetary theory have to be completely rewritten. Intellectually this is a watershed. The free-market visions of how the world works have been shown to be unsustainable. What concerns me is that the response from those in power will be to re-write new textbooks and central banking manuals that are scarcely different from the old ones – just with extra emphasis on transparency, information, and greater prudence.

But perhaps more concerning is that there is a wish on the left to go back to the 1960s and 1970s, to an era when everything was run by the state – an uncritical swing back to an era which itself was unsustainable, albeit for different reasons. The big project now is to get people to think about these issues differently, in a way that is not just about saying we've had too much de-regulation and now we need more regulation. What gets left out here are the underlying contradictions of capitalist finance and I think critical here is the breaking down of the difference between money and capital.

Simon Mohun has raised the same scenario as you, of a shift back to the approach of the 1960s. But he saw it not as a worry, but as something hopeful. He says it will open up a debate about what governments do economically, into which the left can intervene, rather than just being told that the market decides and that is that.

In Treasuries and central banks, the intellectual culture has been so uncritical of the regulatory changes that I think there is likely to be no-one around who can think outside the square. The discourse that most people think within is just less regulation or more regulation. The debates over the coming years are largely going to be around aspiring to regulations that will make markets more efficient and more accountable. As a Marxist, I'm not opposed to markets being more efficient or more accountable. It's not a matter of being innately opposed to the regulatory agenda.

But is that debate going to open up an agenda for the left? Open up a space where new initiatives can develop?

For a liberal, social-democratic left, this is the stuff of life. But is the new regulation in fact likely to take nasty corporatist forms? I'd put my money on that, rather than the development of a space where a Marxist left could get a hearing. What's gone wrong in the markets is partly about regulation, a loss of order and morality in markets. Those things are now being widely criticised. But there is another element here, about the nature of money. What concerns me in left and liberal debate is the strand that says that if we can make markets more efficient, more transparent, more ethical, then markets will not be volatile. That seems to be a basic premise, and it's basically wrong.

Money is itself the expression of a social relation. The concept of value is contested. The concept of equivalence is contested. We see that most starkly in exchange rates. What is one currency is worth in terms of another? There is no real answer. The neo-classical economists want to talk about fundamental value, but we know that doesn't work. And it's not just at the level of exchange rates. Within a currency, equivalence is a contested concept. As Marxists, we should be pointing that out – that there is social conflict expressed in the money form. Any suggestion that once we have better regulation, money will become harmonious as a social unit, and then we can enter into debates about good or bad monetary policy, misses the point that money is always contestable. It has never been objective.

We have played out little social myths to construct money as objective. We had gold. We had Bretton Woods. We have "fundamental value" provided by neo-classical economists. They were all trying to tell us that money is an objective measure, and what we have to learn is that money is not an objective measure. Money is capitalist money, and it is money within capitalism. We have to keep pushing the politics of that.

And central to that politics is new ways of resistance to the way in which the finance system, for all its fancy trading of risks, has systematically shifted risks onto labour – until, that is, labour (in the form of house buyers) itself financially imploded, and the risks were suddenly thrown back onto capital. But, of course, it was then passed on to the state, which in turn will pass it back onto labour, but at a slower pace than was done by financial risk shifting, and in ways where labour's implosion will not be at the cost of capital.

The point here is to analyse what's happened so as to clearly identify the risk-shifting process and the best points of resistance to it; not to join the search for a clever set of state regulations which will somehow tame finance and place it at the service of production.

Independent of whatever theoretical schemes government economists may propose, do you see such measures now being taken as extensive nationalisations, bail-outs, and so on, as adding up to a serious change in the shape of capitalism?

The longer-term meaning of all this in terms of the shape of capitalist development – that's something on which I just wouldn't want to make a call. The state has always fudged on the issue of "moral hazard" – of the extent to which the state should intervene to mop up for capital when capital stuffs up, and whether such mopping-up puts bad incentives into the market. In all the financial sector reforms, and not just in the financial sector, there has always been a fudge about the question of whether there will be bail-outs. We've found something out. We've found that the state will always bail out big capital, in particular big banks. The role of finance cannot go back to what it was. It would be laughable. The regulatory regimes around finance just cannot be the same. At the moment, no-one is talking in big terms because policy circles are too much taken up with crisis management.

What becomes most interesting in this – and I can't think through it, really – is, how much of a watershed is this in the concept of markets, and how the states regulate markets? The moral hazard issue, historically framed as a dilemma, is now solved. What does that say about the virtue of profitability and entrepreneurship – those moral virtues of the market, let people enjoy success because they also face the threat of failure? If that threat of failure is now going to be qualified, what is the constraint of the upside? If we are to have the carrot of profit, but not the stick of loss, how is that going to play out in wider social circles? That question does open up the space for Marxists to have something very useful to say in popular debate.

PART 3

After 2009

• •
•

INTRODUCTION TO PART 3

The Endless Bail-out

The governments' anti-crisis measures of late 2008 and 2009 got the slump to bottom out by late 2009. But stagnation and further troubles, especially sovereign-debt crises for European states, followed. The ruling classes had no answer but to pump more money into the banks, via ultra-low interest rates and then "Quantitative Easing", and to squeeze the working classes further by austerity and "labour market reform". In 2010 governments swung back, mostly, towards neoliberal orthodoxy.

Barry Finger argued that the backdrop was a chronic tendency of the rate of profit to fall. Leo Panitch argued for the left to push for public ownership of the banks and increased social provision: otherwise we were probably "facing the destruction of public sector trade unionism". Michel Husson also took up that call for the public ownership of high finance. He analysed the Eurozone crisis, rejected calls to quit the euro or for "de-globalisation", and called for social, rather than "national", answers.

Daniela Gabor analysed the options for Europe on the eve of the Greek election of June 2012 in which Syriza almost gained the government office which it would eventually win in January 2015. The crisis, she said, showed that central banking was "a very political activity".

CHAPTER 16

The Falling Rate of Profit (July 2011)

Barry Finger

Socialists have been at loggerheads concerning the immediate relevance of the falling rate of profit as an explanatory backdrop to the current crisis. At the extremes are those, such as Andrew Kliman, who have argued that rates of profit in the American economy have fallen since the late 1960s and have never fully rebounded and Michel Husson and Gérard Duménil and Dominique Lévy who have argued that neoliberal policies have so raised the rate of exploitation to have, in effect, neutralized or undermined this as an underlying cause of the current crisis. I have no intention of intervening directly in the issues raised in that debate. While I come down squarely in Andrew Kliman's corner as far as the immediate issue is one of using "historical" cost measurements, I question how both sides of the debate handle other uses of National Income and Product Accounts. But on the matter in immediate dispute, the costs that enter into commodities as consumed constant capital are based on an average of historically given prices, of capital goods of various pricing vintages. To employ "replacement" prices as Husson does (and as the NIPA does), blurs how new technology gradually permeates each sector; reducing cost prices by displacing stepwise the existing processes. New average cost-prices are, so to speak, constantly coming into being, which is why the historical approach better captures a snapshot of that blended process at any moment in time. "Replacement prices" tips the entire calculation replacing average cost prices with that associated with the most recent vintage of embodied technology.

Where I differ, however, is in their treatment of exploitation. Both sides of the debate fail to properly distinguish between productive and unproductive labour in the private sector economy. Of course, this is easier conceptually than practically. The Bureau of Labour Statistics, for instance, distinguishes these categories with respect of manufacturing, mining and construction, broadly defined. And it does so in a manner compatible with Marxist conceptions. But the vast majority of labour power throughout the economy is now no longer expended directly to expand value, but rather takes part in the ancillary

* Previously published online at www.workersliberty.org/node/17123, 19 July 2011.

processes essential to the reproduction of the system as a whole. The entire capital applied in this way, included the flow of wages consumed in trade and finance (as well as in many services), generally constitute additional costs added to the price of the final product. Such wages are not variable capital for purposes of determining the rate of exploitation. As such the wage share of GDP understates the degree of exploitation and its change over time and tells us nothing about its trajectory. The wages of unproductive workers in the private sector must be considered a special form of circulating constant capital. This is not to argue that unproductive labour power is not exploited. It is important to remember that such work is paid only for that fractional part of the working day needed for its reproduction. It does not, however, transmit new value to output and its wages must be made good from the final sales price.

Insofar as neither side in this debate attempts to integrate wages, both productive and unproductive, into their measurements of the rate of profit, both ends of the debate miss a vital element in the so-called transition to a "service" based economy. For, all other things remaining equal, a rising ratio of non-productive to productive labour will always decrease the rate of profit, just as would say an increased consumption of fuel or raw materials, and can also under certain conditions transform what would appear to be an increase in the rate of profit into a falling rate of profit.

Even if profits grow faster than the value of tangible assets (buildings, machines, etc., including the value of the physical capital invested in non-productive sectors of the economy), they might still grow slower than the sum of tangible assets plus the stock of unproductive wages. Thus we have come to expect a fall in the rate of profit to be associated with a rise in the value composition of capital in productive sectors that exceeds any associated rise in the rate of exploitation. But we might also find a fall in the rate of profit despite a rise in the rate of exploitation that actually exceeds that of the value composition of productive capital – as long as the total growth in non-productive expenses is sufficiently robust.

Each side of the debate, from the vantage point of the analysis advanced here, are prone to underestimate both the rise in the rate of exploitation and the increase in the total constant capital. Still a capital accumulating upon a relatively, if not absolutely, narrowed base of productive labour power, and applying ever more of its accumulated labour-time to trade, finance and insurance might reasonably be expected to experience secular difficulties in capital self-expansion. Yet the statistical findings often appear less than resoundingly supportive of this proposition.

At least in Marxist circles. Nevertheless, if we were to consult US government statistics, the following results can be obtained for the average rate of profit for domestic non-financial corporations: 1960–9: 11.1 percent; 1970–9: 8.3 percent; 1980–9: 7.4 percent; 1990–9: 8.3 percent; 2000–9: 6.6 percent. This is calculated on net profits after taxes divided by the net stock of physical assets plus inventories valued at current prices. These results therefore suffer from all the frailties discussed above, but nevertheless demonstrate a rather clear downward trend. And if we eliminate the decade of the 1960s – arguably an anomaly in the historical patterns of capitalism, the material seems much less compelling.

That said, the omission of the entire financial sector still gives a distorted picture of the entire period. For during that time, the financial sector came to claim almost 40% of total profits at its pre-collapse peak. And many, if not most, large firms specializing in production also germinated financial offshoots to finance purchases of their products. Conversely many financial institutions acquired holdings in manufacturing and other commodity generating sectors. Official statistics are at pains to disentangle these mixed enterprises and isolate only non-financial activities. Yet the problem remains. Marxists are not clear how the rate of profit should be calculated for a sector whose product consists of claims to future surplus value. Most of the capital here never interacts directly with productive labour. It also seems pointless to calculate a rate of return based on the value of physical structures – buildings, office equipment, computers and software – when such balance sheets are composed basically of liquid and near liquid assets.

And yet this is key. Capital is a social relationship in which value takes the general form of money in the process of self-expansion. Marx derived the falling rate of profit directly from the contradictory nature of value-creation, by the need to constantly raise productivity by investing in capital augmenting technological improvements. These raise the value composition of capital and diminish the labour power base upon which new value is generated. But the process of social reproduction requires ever more specialisation. This means spinning off ever more distinct sectors needed to harvest idle balances and keep them actively engaged so that capital is not needlessly tied up in inventories build-ups or non-interest bearing demand deposits. But this also multiplies the claims on future profits. And, insofar as the manipulation of monetary instruments enlarges claims without directly expanding productive capacity, the tendency to produce assets in excess of profits should only compound the problems identified by Marx in the generation of value.

It is therefore not surprising that the world of finance, which specialises in activating what would otherwise remain as dormant capital, has generated proper general measurements for rates of profit. These are perfectly applicable to both the financial and non-financial sectors and come far closer to expressing a more integrated gauge of capital's ability to propagate earnings than comparisons with "physical stocks" of capital and inventory. The most general form of this measurement of profitability is the rate of return on assets (ROA). This involves examining the balance sheet of corporations and comparing profits (sometimes calculated before deductions are made for interest and taxes) also called, somewhat confusingly, net income, with the total amount of fixed and current assets (measured at historical prices) at the corporation's command. Fixed assets consist of structures, equipment and machinery which are depreciable. Current assets are cash accounts and instruments, including inventories, which can be converted into cash at short notice, within a business's fiscal year.

When profitability is examined from this vantage point a much clearer picture emerges of the underlying fragility of the American economy. This has been done by the authors of the so-called "Shift Index" produced by Deloitte LLP and has received broad attention in the business press including the *Harvard Business Review*. This comprehensive review which includes all corporate sectors found that "US companies' return on assets (ROA) have progressively dropped 75 percent from their 1965 levels despite rising labour productivity", a doubling of labour productivity to be more precise. That is, for all the efficiencies gained in managing capital, in squeezing labour, in becoming leaner and stripped down – of massively raising the rate of exploitation – firms are experiencing ever lower returns to their balance sheets. The Shift Index explains this decline rather lamely by heightened competition among firms. But we might better consider this "heightened competition" more a result of a falling rate of profit than its cause.

A graph from the report (Hagel 2013), reproduced below (Figure 16.1), presents a stark overall view of the perilous decline in total corporate profitability.

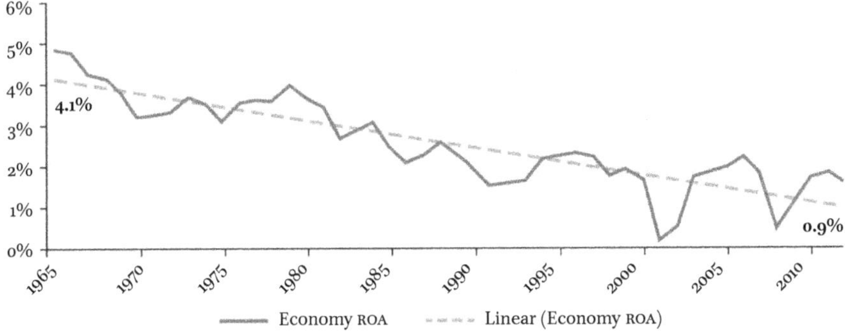

FIGURE 16.1 *Economy-wide Return on Invested Capital (ROIC), USA, 1965–2012*
SOURCE: COMPUSTAT, DELOITTE ANALYSIS

Note that the decline in absolute terms demonstrates that corporate returns have been hovering through the past decade in a range that is just barely positive. This contrasts starkly with the picture usually painted of in Marxist studies based of robust profits (and growing profitability) just prior to the economic meltdown.

We also see these results in disaggregated form. Deloitte also reports a declining rate of return on assets in the technology sector. This sector, it should be noted, exhibited some of the most robust gains in labour productivity, at almost three times the growth in the economy as a whole, yet could not escape the general trend. A disaggregated review of the banking and securities industries actually demonstrates a very slight improvement in trend-line banking performance until the last decade, but was otherwise incapable of making much of an impact on the larger economic performance.

A word by way of a conclusion. Most capitalist crises of significance are crises of profit shortfalls. It is true that there are crises of proportional dislocations caused say by weather or natural resource limitations. But these are rather short lasting due to the adaptability of modern capitalism. The larger problem resides in the very nature of value creation from which all the various claims on surplus labour arise. The American economy has grown in recent decades in spurts associated with financial bubbles and punctuated by their deflation despite continuous improvements throughout the economy in labour productivity. Capital has simply been unable to accumulate faster than the decline in profitability. This is the forty-year backdrop to the Great Recession.

Yet Marxists are paradoxically among the last to grasp what is painfully apparent to the business community and reflected in its literature.

CHAPTER 17

The Banks' Crisis and the Left's Crisis (August 2011)

Leo Panitch

A common response of the left to the financial crisis that broke out in the USA in 2007–08 was often a kind of Michael Moore-type populist one: Why are you bailing the banks out? Let them go under. This kind of response was, of course, utterly irresponsible, with no thought given to what would happen to the savings of workers, let alone to the pay checks deposited into their bank accounts, or even to the fact that what was at stake was the roofs over their heads.

On the other hand, the even more common response was all about asserting state responsibility: This crisis is the result of the government not having done its duty: governments are supposed to regulate capital, and they didn't do so. But this response was in fact fundamentally misleading. The United States has the most regulated financial system in the world by far if you measure it in terms of the number of statutes on the books, the number of pages of administrative regulation, the amount of time and effort and staff that is engaged in the supervision of the financial system. But that system is organised in such a way as to facilitate the financialisation of capitalism, not only in the US itself, but in fact around the world. Without this, the globalisation of capitalism in recent decades would not have been possible.

It was indicative of the left's sorry lack of ambition in the crisis that its calls for salary limits on Wall Street executives and transaction taxes on the financial sector were far more common than demands for turning the banks into public utilities. It was, of all people, the mainstream LSE economist Willem Buiter (the former member of the Bank of England's monetary policy committee, appointed in November 2009 by Citibank as its chief economist) who in his *Financial Times* blog on September 17, 2008 a few days after Lehman Brothers' collapse endorsed the "long-standing argument that there is no real case for private ownership of deposit-taking banking institutions, because these cannot exist safely without a deposit guarantee and/or lender of last resort facilities, that are ultimately underwritten by the taxpayer." And he went further: "The argument that financial intermediation cannot be entrusted to the private sector can now be extended to include the new, transactions-oriented,

* This article originally appeared in e-bulletin no. 536 of the Canadian group Socialist Project (http://www.socialistproject.ca/bullet/536.php).

capital-markets-based forms of financial capitalism... From financialisation of the economy to the socialisation of finance. A small step for the lawyers, a huge step for mankind."

This sounds a little bit, if you've ever read the Communist Manifesto, like the call that Marx made – among his list of ten reforms – for the centralisation of credit in the hands of the state – which just goes to show that in a crisis you don't have to be a Marxist to have radical ideas if you have any sort of ambition or self-confidence. Most Marxists don't have that ambition and self-confidence today. But you do have to be a Marxist to understand that this is not going to happen by bringing some lawyers into a room and signing a few documents. What Buiter was putting forward was the technocratic notion of how reform happens. But fundamental change can only really happen through a massive class struggle, which would involve a massive transformation of the state itself.

Even in terms of calls for better regulation, with a working class that is not mobilised to put pressure on, you can't expect this state to simply follow policy guidelines that come from technocrats, progressive liberals or social democrats. So we at least ought to be using our opportunity to do more than offer left technocratic advice to a policy machine; we ought to be trying to educate people on how capitalist finance really works, why it doesn't for them and why what we need instead is a publicly owned banking system that is part of a system of democratic economic planning, in which what's invested and where it's invested and how it's invested is democratically decided.

The sort of bank nationalisations undertaken in the wake of the fallout from the Lehman's collapse – with the lead of Gordon Brown's New Labour government in the UK being quickly followed by Bush's Republican administration in the US – essentially involved socialising the banks' losses while guaranteeing that the nationalised banks would operate on a commercial basis at arm's length from any government direction or control. All they asked was that these nationalised banks seek to maximise the taxpayers returns on their "investment." As sagely put in the 2010 *Socialist Register* essay on "Opportunity lost: mystification, elite politics and financial reform in the UK," this really represented "not the nationalisation of the banks, but the privatisation of the Treasury as a new kind of fund manager." The most important reason for taking the banks into the public sector and turning them into a public utility is that you would remove thereby the institutional foundation of the most powerful section of the capitalist classes in this phase of capitalism. That's the main reason for nationalising the banks in terms of changing the balance of class forces in a fundamental way.

A second socialist reason for nationalising the banks would be to transform the uses to which finance is put. Let's take an example. Where I come from in Canada, the backbone of the southern Ontario economy, apart from banking, is the automobile industry. With the layoffs that occurred and the plants that have been closed (this has been going on for three decades, but it was heightened during this crisis very severely) you are not just losing physical capital. You're losing the skills of tool and die makers. A banking system that was turned into a public utility would be centrally involved in transforming the uses to which credit is put, so those skills could be put to building wind turbines, so they could be used to develop the kind of equipment we need to harness solar energy cheaply rather than expensively.

We cannot even begin to think seriously about solving the ecological crisis that coincides with this economic crisis without the left returning to an ambitious notion of economic planning. It's inconceivable. It can't be done. We've run away from this for half a century because of command planning of the Stalinist type, with all of its horrific effects – its inefficiencies, but even more its authoritarianism. But we can't avoid any longer coming back to the need for planning. The allocation of credit is at the core of economic planning for the conversion of industry. When we on the left call for capital controls, we can't just think about that in the sense of capital controls that would limit how quickly capital moves in and out of the country. We need capital controls because without them we can't have the democratic control of investment. It's not just capital controls at the border that matter; what matters all the more for socialists is control over capital to the end of directing, in a democratic fashion, what gets invested, where it gets invested, how it gets invested.

Now, people often say that socialists in the last 20 or 30 years have not laid out a programmatic vision. I don't think that's true. As the *Socialist Register* 2000 volume on Necessary and Unnecessary Utopias showed, there were more writings on what a future socialism would look like in the last two decades of the 20th century than probably ever before. But the detailed pictures of a socialist order they painted – whether involving some combination of plan and market or participatory economic planning – have been exceedingly sketchy on two crucial things. One is immediate demands and reforms. And the other is how the hell would we get there. What are the vehicles? What are the agencies? How are the vehicles connected to building the agencies? It is certainly very true that, whatever the vehicle or the agency, you are never going to mobilise people simply on the basis of the need to nationalise the banks for economic planning, when they know that can't come for decades, given the lack of political forces to introduce it. People need to be mobilised by immediate demands, as they were by the demands for trade union rights, a reduced workweek, a public educational system, a welfare state, etc.

Some 15 years ago, when the FMLN in El Salvador after the settlement of the civil war turned itself from a guerrilla army into a political party, I was one of the people invited to help them set up a party school. And I had a conversation there with Facundo Guardado, who had been subcommandante on the San Salvador Volcano, and who later ran for president under the FMLN banner. He said to me, everybody thinks that the long term is the next election which, since this was in 1995, would have been in 1999 there. He said: they're completely wrong – in fact, that's the short term. What we have to hope is that by 1999 we will be strong enough, have a strong enough base, to be able to make a decent showing in the next election. The medium term is 2010, when we have to hope that we will have a broad enough representation and a deep enough development of our members' capacities that we actually could have an influence on the direction of the country. The long term is 2020, when we will be able to get elected as a government that can actually do something, that can transform the state. Angela Zamora, who as the head of party's educational program was hosting me, sat there and listened to this and suddenly said, in that case I'm leaving the party. I can't go back to the people who I've been leading in struggle for 15 years and tell them they have to wait for 2020 for immediate reforms. It's impossible. I can't do it.

So, one needs to figure out how to combine a clear, ambitious sense of immediate demands with this longer-term vision. But in the current crisis the Left's immediate demand could and should have centred around bringing the banks into public ownership. The case for this could have been made in terms of the need for a massive program for public housing. After the Great Society program in the 1960s left-wing Democrats, rather than calling for more public housing to rebuild America's cities, instead called for the banks to lend money to poor black communities – in other words, for the problem to be solved by letting black people, who had been largely excluded from the banking system, into it. It was similar to liberal feminism's demand that women should be able to get credit cards, which they were largely not allowed to do by the banks until the 1970s. Well, you should be careful what you hope for. One of the effects of winning those demands was a channelling of those communities more deeply into the structures of finance, the most dynamic sector of neoliberal capitalism. Clinton carried those reforms much further in the 1990s, appealing to the Democratic Party constituency (Clinton was known as "the black President" for this) on the basis of we're going to let you succeed at the capitalist housing game. And then Bush, of course, let every crook that he could find into the mortgage business.

Of course, there's no reason why black people or women shouldn't want the same rights as everybody else – why shouldn't they look forward to their homes appreciating in market value? But you need to understand the dynamics and contradictions that are involved in trying to win reforms for people through integrating them more deeply into capitalist credit relations. And the results are now clear.

We should be also demanding universal public pensions, as the private pension plans won by trade unions now are coming unravelled for both public sector and private sector workers. And that would contribute to strengthening the working class, because it would eliminate the kind of competition amongst workers that employers have played on with their private pensions. Indeed, increasingly we see that even the unions in largest corporations today as well as unions of public employees cannot sustain their members' pension plans.

We should also be calling for free public transit – to be available like public libraries, public education and public health care. All of this involves trying to take a crucial portion of what we need for our livelihood, our basic needs, and decommodify them as far as possible within capitalism. People respond positively to such demands even in North America. The trouble with them, however, is that there's not that much room for manoeuvre left for reform in today's capitalism, because in order to have a major program of public housing, in order to have free public transit, you very quickly run up against where are the funds going to come from? It's possible to argue, given how cheap public bonds are today, that you can go to the bond market, but that also means that you become subject to the kinds of pressures from bondholders that is requiring the Greek and the Portuguese and the Spanish states to do what they're doing to their public sector in order to guarantee that they won't eventually default on those bonds. So you come back fairly quickly to the need to at least begin a process of socialisation through taking the banks into the public sector.

We need to try to see this moment of crisis from the perspective of what openings it could create. The limitations of a purely defensive response to the crisis lie in not taking advantage of the opportunity that the crisis creates. Despite the "Another World Is Possible" rhetoric, the left has been more oriented to attempting to hold on to things than to taking things in a new direction. Whether the struggle has been to prevent water privatisation, or whether it's been to protest at G7 and G20 meetings, however militant the action, it's often primarily defensive in the demands that are articulated.

This is, oddly enough, one of the limits of a perspective that says you can change the world without taking power, without engaging on the terrain of the state, without transforming the structures of the state. What is on the agenda is mainly to prevent the state doing certain things and what is off the agenda is to change the state in such a way that ensures that when new progressive reforms are won they lead on to further structural reforms. We need to appreciate the reasons for the anti-statism that is so on the Left today; the suspicion of talking in terms of building new parties or transforming the state is understandable. But we need to go beyond protest, or we will be trapped forever in organising the next demo.

And as this current crisis is transferred down to the regional and local levels, which every central state will try to do, we will run up against the limits of what can be secured in struggles at those levels. We have to learn how defensive and localized struggles can be linked up, and how they can be transformed so they are directed into a struggle for state power. Otherwise, all the protests will run up even more quickly against the kind of limits of the immediate reforms that don't lead on to more fundamental ones.

This is enormously important because we probably are facing the destruction of public sector trade unionism unless there's a shift in the balance of forces in the context of this crisis. Capitalism can only go on so long with the private sector being as limited in its unionisation, its density being so low, in terms of collective bargaining rights and recognition, and the public sector being almost universally unionised. It can't continue. Part of the onslaught on state expenditure that is taking place now is to destroy public sector trade unionism. The ability of public sector unions to resist in this crisis is being very severely tested. That's how serious this is.

Speaking more generally, it is increasingly clear that trade unions, as they evolved through the 20th century, not only in the advanced capitalist countries, also in most of the countries of the South, are no longer capable of being more than defensive. They are not able to win new gains, and they are not able to organise in ways that develop the capacities of their members. The challenge now is to build a trade unionism that is actually a class organisation, one that goes beyond organising people by the workplace alone and organises people in relation to the many facets of their lives touched by this crisis.

CHAPTER 18

Nationalise the Banks! (September 2011)

Michel Husson

The crisis has taught us a lesson: "neoliberal Europe" was a badly-conceived thing, which has become more and more rickety over the years and appears to be incapable of standing up to the "stress test" of crisis. Right now, there are only two ways out: either everyone is going to take their marbles home and quit; or the whole edifice will have to be rebuilt, from top to bottom. But sticking plasters are being stuck over sticking plasters. How things turn out in Greece will serve as a barometer for this whole stop-starting process: everyone knows that Greece won't be able to pay its debts, but everyone is acting as if it could succeed in its impossible task, by means of bail-out plans and inadequate loan extensions, and break its economy in order to pay back its debt.

The other side of the problem is obviously the exposure of European banks to the risk of a Greek default, although it was they who pushed the country into debt. If Portugal, Ireland and Greece defaulted, the loss would be 100 billion euros, but if Italy and Spain followed (for two thirds of their debt), the loss would reach 800 billion euros, which is more than is held by the European Financial Stability Fund (250 billion euros today and 440 billion euros in the future). That the next President of the European Central Bank (ECB) is Mario Draghi, the ex-chief of the European arm of Goldman Sachs, which helped Greece cook its books, is just another element of the comedy that we are watching unfold.

When the crisis broke, states came to the rescue of the banks. But they didn't match this aid with any kind of re-thinking of the way finance works. To take one example, "naked Credit Default Swaps" [in which the buyer does not own the underlying debt – you don't own the thing on which you are buying insurance] were not banned, and they allow one today to speculate on public debt which the buyer does not even own. The bill for the crisis has passed from the private sector to the public sector, and states are looking now to pass the bill on to the taxpayer, with all the sense of fairness and equity that you'd expect.

* First appeared in French as "À contre-courant/ Nationaliser les banques", *Politis*, http://www.politis.fr/articles/2011/09/a-contre-courant-nationaliser-les-banques-15214/. First published in English in *Solidarity* 218, 28 September 2011, http://www.workersliberty.org/story/2011/09/28/nationalise-banks. Translation by Edward Maltby.

The debts weren't cleared – they were just passed on: that is what explains the persistence of the crisis.

Things are even more tangled up by the fact that state budgets are inextricably linked with banks' balances, with a total absence of transparency. It is not even certain that the banks know exactly where they are at themselves. One thing, however, is clear: that the "stress tests" which were supposed to evaluate the resilience of banks were either "laughable" or "pathetic", to use the words of [French senior civil servant] Jacques Attali. All this explains [IMF chief] Christine Lagarde's recent pronouncement about the "urgent" need to recapitalise a certain number of European banks. But the banks do not want to hear this and prefer to moan about the too-restrictive (for their profits, that is) rules of [the new package of banking rules requiring banks to have greater holdings backing up their investments] "Basel III".

The only rational means of untangling the skein of debts would be to nationalise the banks, to take everything back to square one, once and for all, and to organise the inevitable default of the most exposed countries. The distributions of dividends would be forbidden, and a citizens' audit would make it possible to target illegitimate debts. This nationalisation could be permanent (the radical option) or it could be temporary (the moderate option) like in Sweden in the 1990s.

Ultra-left fantasy? No, just objective analysis. It is striking that two economists, authors of a book [Augustin Landier and David Thesmar, *Le grand méchant marché*] which defends the virtues of the market against a "French fantasy" make the same argument: "recapitalisations must take place under states' hands, and in certain cases temporary nationalisations". That liberals see that the logic of the banks cuts against "the public interest" and are calling for "coercion" should give pause for thought. From this point of view, the spinelessness of the left is dreadful. When they are not bowing down before the financial markets, like Papandreou or Zapatero, they are competing to make austerity. [Leading French Socialist Party member François] Hollande: "We have to balance our public accounts from 2013… I am not saying that in order to give in to any sort of pressure from the markets or the ratings agencies". [Other leading French Socialist Party member Martine] Aubry: "3% in 2013, as it is the rule today". Finance is trembling!

CHAPTER 19

The Endless Bail-out of Europe (November 2011)

Michel Husson

The decision by Greek prime minister Georges Papandreou to put the Euro-summit agreement to a referendum marks a new step in the European crisis. To understand the causes and what is at stake in this crisis, we must first situate it in the broad sweep of events. It is not just a sovereign debt crisis. It is also, and more fundamentally, a crisis of the European construction. Today it is obvious that neoliberal-style Europe was botched. The single currency was supposed to serve as a wage-control instrument, since it became impossible for governments to devalue. But that constraint was in part evaded circumvented by over-indebtedness, boosted by low real interest rates and growing external deficits.

For a decade, 1995–2005, the countries of Europe's "South" (Spain, France, Greece, Ireland, Italy, Portugal) had growth rates almost one per cent higher than the countries of the "North" (Germany, Austria, Belgium, Finland, Netherlands).

That could not last, and the situation reversed from 2006. Since the crisis, and except in 2009, the growth of the countries of the "South" has been clearly lower than that of the "North". The crisis has thus exposed the incoherences of the European model and deepened the divergence between the trajectories of the different countries. (See figure 19.1)

The growth of public debts itself has three causes: the mechanical effect of the recession, the costs of bailing out the banks, and also the poisoned fruit of the policies carried through for many years of reducing the taxes paid by business and the richest households. The brutal shift to budgetary austerity thus sets a vicious circle going: by cutting expenditure, they slow down economic activity, and that cuts tax receipts and so the deficit is not cut.

A priori there were several possible scenarios. The austerity scenario meant getting into a long period of social regression to bring down the debt bit by bit at the expense of the living standards of the majority of the population. But it was known that a certain number of countries, in the first place Greece, could

* First published in French as "note hussonet n°41, 2 novembre 2011" on http://hussonet.free.fr. First published in English in *Solidarity* 224, 9 November 2011. http://www.workersliberty.org/files/224.pdf. Translation by Edward Maltby.

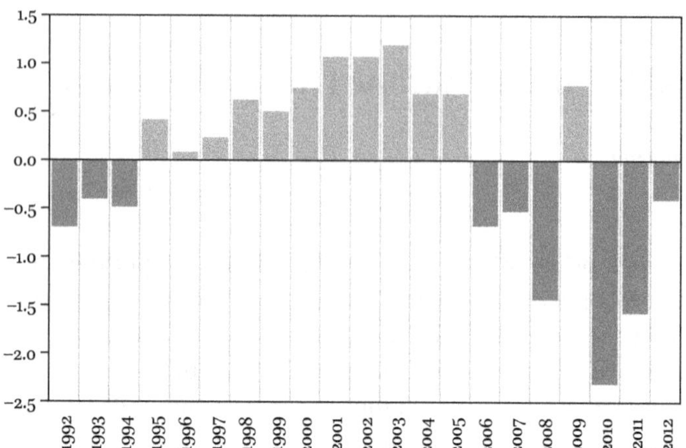

FIGURE 19.1 *Growth gap between countries of the South and the North of Europe. South: Spain, France, Greece, Ireland, Italy, Portugal. North: Germany, Austria, Belgium, Finland, Netherlands*
SOURCE: EUROSTAT, HTTP://EC.EUROPA.EU/EUROSTAT/TGM/TABLE.DO?TAB=TABLE&PLUGIN=1&LANGUAGE=EN&PCODE=TEC00115.

not meet their debt payments. Thus, the risk of contagion to other countries, leading to a scenario of the breakup of the Eurozone.

The scenario of federalisation would have meant taking responsibility for the totality of the European debts in a pooled way by various methods of which the main one is the monetarisation of the European debts by the European Central Bank. That is in fact the only way to avoid exposing the financing of the states to speculation on the financial markets.

Finally, the radical scenario would, since the sovereign debts are in large part held by the European banks, mean nationalising those banks and organising default for the most exposed countries.

For almost two years the governments of Europe have been feeling their way between several pitfalls. The first is what economists called moral hazard: looking after a Greek default could be a signal encouraging other countries to evade austerity measures. The cost of the default would fall back on the "virtuous" countries, especially Germany, and the financial markets would put the debt of numerous other countries under the rule of speculation. But a break-up of the Eurozone is also seen as a major risk, including by Germany, which through such a break up would lose its advantages in world competition.

The 27 October 2011 agreement was, like the previous ones, a provisional and cobbled-together solution which confirmed Germany's refusal to accept a change in the statutes of the European Central Bank which would allow it directly to finance states. The Greek debt was theoretically cut by half, but at the cost of a veritable placing under supervision, sharpened austerity, and a massive program of privatisation.

Technically, the weak points of this agreement, which was probably still-born, were obvious. The debt cutback is voluntary, as the text of the agreement explains:[1] "We invite Greece, private investors and all parties concerned to develop a voluntary bond exchange with a nominal discount of 50%". Indeed, they wanted to avoid declaring a Greek default which would unleash the diabolical mechanism of the CDS (Credit Default Swaps), whose owners would then come to demand their dues. To avoid contagion for other countries, appeal was made to the European Financial Stability Facility. This fund, created in May 2010, had been endowed with 440 billion euros, but after the bail-out plans for Greece, Ireland, and Portugal, it had only about 200 to 250 billion left. For it to serve as a firewall, it had to be able theoretically to command 1000 billion euros. But the states do not want to pay, and this sum was to be got by the same methods which led to the financial crisis: leveraging and a "Special Purpose Vehicle", with an appeal to the emerging powers and especially to China.

The banks were also to be recapitalised, but not too soon, so that they should not be obliged to cut back their profits and their dividend distributions. As one of the negotiators of the agreement puts it: "You don't have to be paranoid to be terrified" (see: "The euro deal: no big bazooka", *The Economist*, 29 October 2011[2]). The most terrifying thing, however, is the drive of the ruling classes to make the peoples of Europe pay the cost of the crisis.

Quitting the euro is presented as a miracle solution. It would allow the country involved, Greece for example, to devalue and re-establish its competitiveness. This claim is based on the observation that the European construction was flawed from the start in so far as it did not take account of the divergent trajectories of the different countries of the Eurozone. The serious response would be to introduce mechanisms of harmonisation: a large European budget, a unified system of taxation of capital, funds for social harmonisation, a European minimum wage. That solution may seem out of range. Quitting the euro is not however a better solution: to think that would be to put the cart before the horse and to make a strategic error. The debt would indeed be increased in proportion to the devaluation rate, and the new currency would be exposed, without defence, to speculative attacks. Those pressures would then serve to justify an even harsher austerity policy.

1 http://gesd.free.fr/esummit.pdf.

2 http://gesd.free.fr/nobigbaz.pdf.

In France, the supporters of "deglobalisation" do not all advocate quitting the euro, but their preoccupations are similar. Since they make free trade the source of all our ills, they mainly propose fiscal protectionism, or in other words taxes on imports. There too, the aim is to re-establish competitiveness. It is hard to see how such measures could, as if by magic, re-establish a fairer distribution of income: it is not a border tax that will make the profiteers give up their privileges. In any case, competitiveness depends on many other factors besides commodity prices.

And, above all, this approach would mean getting into a doubly perverse logic. First into the logic of competition: but a country can improve its situation by better competitiveness only by taking market share (and thus jobs) from neighbouring countries. And then into the logic of productivism, which sees no way to create jobs other than more economic growth.

The preconditions for a way out are to establish a balance of forces favourable to the working class and to wipe out at least a portion of the debt. A feasible strategy is thus composed of unilateral measures which clash with the rules of neoliberal Europe but which would aim at the extension of progressive measures across Europe.[3]

The technical responses exist and are based on this coherent triangle:

1. Monetarisation of the debts by the European Central Bank;
2. Nationalisation of the banks;
3. Cancellation of the illegitimate portion of the debts.

This combination of measures would allow for settling the crisis by way of making those who profited from the frenzies of financialised capitalism pay.

But the issues at stake are above all social, and the situation is in the last analysis simple to sum up: thanks to deregulation, financialisation, etc., a small minority grabs the wealth produced, as the rise of inequality shows. It goes further: that minority organises economic and social life in line with its interests, and has the power to decide social priorities and deprive the peoples of any say in their fate. That minority will not give up those privileges without a powerful social intervention which must combine a global point of view with local or sectoral initiatives.

In any case, capitalism is in an impasse: the neoliberal model can no longer function, and return to capitalism of the "golden age" of 1945–75 is impossible. A progressive solution must therefore involve a radical questioning of

---

3 See "Exit or voice? A European strategy of rupture", *Socialist Register* 2012, http://hussonet.free.fr/sreg122.pdf.

this system: the redistribution of wealth is the immediate point of leverage, but the approach must include a total inversion of the capitalist logic. We must make the satisfaction of social needs the decisive priority, and from that work out what are the necessary and useful jobs, and prioritise non-market public services and the development of free time above the search for profit and individual consumption. Those are, besides, basic preconditions if we want to meet aims for the reduction of greenhouse-gas emissions. Since such a project puts the very logic of capitalism in question, a very broad alliance is necessary, between the social movements defined in the broad sense.

CHAPTER 20

Europe: The Bankers vs the People (June 2012)

Discussion with Daniela Gabor

If a left government is formed in Greece after 17 June 2012, and it repudiates the memorandum, the Troika is likely to cut off the bail-out funds. Would a Greek government run out of cash?

Greece has had a big budget deficit. The Greek economists I talk to say that if Greece stays on the austerity plan, then it will have a primary surplus [a budget surplus if you don't count its debt payments] by the end of 2012. However, a government which did not continue the austerity policies would probably increase wages and so on, and that would reverse the trend. The government would have to find money to finance the deficit. Governments can finance deficits in a variety of ways, but two are to borrow on global financial markets and to get the central bank to print money. Greece has difficulty raising money on financial markets, and it has difficulties getting money from the European Central Bank, so probably it would have to get out of the euro and print its own separate money in order to have some leeway on financing the deficit.

How would the European Central Bank prevent the Greek government creating extra credit for itself at the Greek central bank?

Money is created in the Eurozone by banks going to the European Central Bank, providing collateral [financial assets pledged to guarantee their credit], and getting cash in return. Since the crisis the national central banks have been allowed to do something called Emergency Liquidity Assistance. Traditionally, when there is a crisis which affects the banking sector, and a crisis of confidence, then the central banks lend against lower-quality collateral in order to stabilise the system. When, recently, the ECB said that four Greek banks could no longer get liquidity [cash] from the ECB, the Greek central bank was allowed to accept from those banks lower-quality collateral that could not be used directly with the ECB, and so inject liquidity into the Greek economy – the ECB's governing council only needs to approve ELA access above a certain threshold, partly because the national central bank assumes all the credit risk associated with ELA liquidity injections.

---

* Previously published in *Solidarity* 249, 13 June 2012.

Little of the liquidity in the system today is actually notes and coins. Mostly it's accounting transactions like that. But at some point, the ECB would have to take a political decision to intervene against the Greek central bank creating more credit for the Greek government?

The ECB makes lots of political decisions anyway. Central banking is a very political activity. The ECB can tell the Greek central bank that it cannot create any more Emergency Liquidity Assistance liquidity. For me, every day that the European Central Bank refuses to intervene in sovereign bond markets in order to stabilise them, it makes an explicitly political decision. This is because a central bank's mandate in crisis is to improve funding conditions for banks. The Eurozone efforts towards financial integration have led to this paradoxical outcome where banks' ability to fund themselves on financial markets depends on the quality of collateral they can produce – and in a crisis, that collateral is only made of sovereign bonds. Yet not all sovereign bonds are the same – where a government has increased deficits, be it because it resorted to fiscal stimulus during a crisis, or because it had to bail out banks, its debt (sovereign bonds) becomes less attractive (it requires higher haircuts) to use as collateral. So European banks will start dumping the debt of a sovereign that appears under threat and move to the highest quality sovereign (i.e. Germany) to ensure that in the event of a Eurozone break-up, they have the kind of collateral that would be most acceptable.

The only institution that can prevent this downward spiral is a central bank – its ability to print money allows it, in theory, to make credible commitments that it will preserve the role of a government bond as marketable collateral. Yet the ECB, with the institutional and political constraints it operates under, refuses to assume this role. This refusal is political.

Instead, the LTROs [cheap three-year loans to commercial banks] that the ECB resorts to every time there appears to be an impending collapse of the Eurozone implicitly rely on private European banks to preserve the role of sovereign bonds as marketable collateral (i.e. to preserve their value). But banks are reluctant to demand government bonds if confronted with the possibility that austerity will not work (and we know it rarely does). This is why the February 2012 LTRO only had very temporary effects on the Spanish sovereign bond market.

Then what if the Greek central bank says sorry, but we need to create this liquidity anyway?

I think that is far-fetched. I don't think the Greek central bank can extend liquidity to Greek banks without ECB approval above the allowed (ELA) threshold. Anything like that would mean moving towards a system of parallel currencies where you would have Greek euros created by the Greek central bank, and an exchange-rate between those Greek euros and ECB euros. I think the ECB would say that the new euros issued without its explicit approval could not be legal tender.

Greeks are being told that if they elect a left government, then the bail-out funds will be cut off, and the next day everything will fall into a black hole. Could the experience of the Irish bank strike in 1970 be relevant here? All the banks were shut by a strike for six months, no-one could get cash from their bank, and yet the economy continued reasonably normally, with people using cheques and IOUs.

Some people discuss a system of parallel currencies. You keep the euro for bank deposits and for foreign transactions, and you introduce some form of IOUs that will cover other transactions. This "Greek euro" will start depreciating. It's another way of achieving an internal devaluation. It's not clear to me that the Greek government would want that. But Goldman Sachs thinks it's possible, and Deutsche Bank too. But if a left government is elected in Greece, it will immediately have to impose capital controls, and suspend convertibility between cash and bank deposits.

And the left government would nationalise the banks.

That's another way of solving the problem. Nationalising the banks might be useful. It raises questions about the Greek banks' subsidiaries in Eastern Europe; but never mind, I don't think the Greeks will really care about financial investors at that point. It will probably mean that Greece will not have access to financial markets for quite a while.

The European Union leaders say that they have a firewall in place, so Greece can default and drop out of the euro, and they can make sure that everywhere else is all right.

It could be true, depending on what the ECB decides to do. The perceptions of liquidity in different markets are very important. I can't see how a firewall can stabilise government bond markets without ECB intervention. If you tell banks that you don't know what is going to happen to the value of the collateral they have on their books – sovereign bonds – then the banks will try to get rid of any bonds that are not German.

Unless the ECB completely changes track and says that now, with Greece out, it will commit to stabilising government bond markets by buying large amounts of government bonds, the firewall can't work. The order of magnitude is too big. I really doubt there will be such a dramatic change, but who knows what a Greek default would trigger. It's a very unpleasant scenario for Greece, to have to go away in order that the ECB policies should finally change.

Of course the ECB does not only have external pressures. It also has internal disagreements on the course it takes. The central bankers of the Eurozone sit on the ECB council, and we know that the German central bank is much more concerned about compliance with austerity than anything else.

The costs to German capital of "contagion" following a Greek exit would be enormous ...

Germany has benefited from the troubles in the sovereign bond markets of the peripheral countries. If you have discrimination in collateral markets [i.e. some financial assets are accepted as collateral to be exchanged for cash, but some aren't] then you will have a flight to the safest instrument, so Germany is benefiting [i.e. the German government can borrow very cheaply]. The German government can now sell bonds almost at negative interest rates. But the German banks have cross-border exposures, and I can't see how a collapse of the Eurozone would not affect German manufacturing and German exports.

You see a continued spiral of governments having difficulty in bond markets, and banks having difficulty because the quality of their collateral (the government bonds they hold) is worsening?

Yes. Spain is going that way. Spain is much more significant in terms of cross-border holdings of sovereign bonds than Greece is. Greece's situation is a worry in the first place because of the social implications, but also because of the precedent it sets. As regards the EU leaders, I think they care not much about the Greek people, but more about what it shows about how the EU deals with unexpected situations.

85% of the people in Greece say they want to stay in the Eurozone. They want the EU to cancel the imposed cuts, and they say that doing that would be better from the point of the view of the whole Eurozone too.

Syriza seems to be betting that the European politicians will be so concerned about the consequences of a Greek exit that they will allow a change of direction. It's a gamble. If Syriza is elected, it will have to keep up its anti-austerity policies and at the same recognise that the Greek people do not want to be pushed out of the euro. But if Greece leaves the Eurozone, one of the benefits is that it will have an independent central bank that is able to redesign the banking system and provide support to its government. The difficulty will be to contain the inflation that may accompany the devaluation, particularly since I don't see how, immediately, Greece is going to have a big increase in export competitiveness.

There is no likely equivalent for Greece to the soybean export boom which boosted Argentina after it defaulted on its debt in 2001.

Greece is definitely not Argentina. Apart from the soybeans, Argentina has a much more significant industrial base than Greece has. But Greece will be confronted with some of the problems Argentina faced in its crisis – how to prevent capital flight, how to devalue and whether to follow the deeply unpopular Argentinian restrictions on withdrawal of bank deposits (i.e. the convertibility between bank deposits and cash). Even though the Greeks don't want to abandon the euro, both macroeconomics and the politics of a left-wing government tell us that it makes little sense to keep the euro outside the Eurozone – why would Greece not want to have its own independent central bank and remove some of the restrictions on economic policy it had inside the Eurozone? Even outside the Eurozone, Greece would have the same dilemmas as inside it, so long as it decides to keep the euro.

I don't see how political pressure will change the way the ECB deals with the Greek central bank. It may make the European Union leaders relax some of the austerity demands, but that's all. I think the EU leaders hoped they would not be confronted with a Greek government saying it does not want austerity but it wants to stay inside the Eurozone. That is the worst of both worlds for EU politicians. They have to make an explicit decision to kick Greece out, or to move away from austerity, with all the implications about their fiscal compact and their constitutionally-enshrined rules for primary surpluses. It's a huge headache. But I can't see how, if Greece stops payments on its debt, the ECB will respond by relaxing the rules on what the Greek central bank will do.

PART 4

After 2010

∴

INTRODUCTION TO PART 4

Neoliberalism Resurgent

Leo Panitch, Andrew Kliman, and Simon Mohun, all in different ways, had argued that the crisis had discredited neoliberalism, or at least the orthodox neoliberalism which had developed since the 1980s. Pushes towards a different, more state-regulated, economic order were likely. Maybe the left could at least inflect them.

Hugo Radice, in a discussion just before the Greek election of June 2012 which Syriza came close to winning, thought that the EU had no choice but to ease debt-servicing constraints and boost public investment, but tempered his optimism with the observation that labour movements lacked political ambition.

Paul Hampton and I, in 2013, tried to sum up how the world had been reshaped under neoliberalism since the 1980s. We analysed neoliberalism as a well-embedded *world* regime, thus resistant to less-than-drastic political impulses in individual countries. And so, neoliberalism had survived the shock of 2008, with some mutations, but in some respects intensified. Barry Finger criticised our account, contesting in particular our rejection of the idea of a tendency of the rate of profit to fall.

Three years later Andrew Gamble discussed again why neoliberalism had been so resilient. He also saw big changes as likely if Trump should become US president: "the whole carefully-constructed web of relationships and dependencies by which the US has run the international system could be blown away".

CHAPTER 21

No Choice but to Change (June 2012)

Discussion with Hugo Radice

What concessions do you think are likely from the EU on "growth strategies"?

Some left-wing economists, for example the Euro Memorandum group, have been calling for a growth strategy throughout the crisis. Until recently most media, academic and business economists believed that a strategy of cutting public deficits would automatically lead to a resumption of private-sector growth. But by the end of 2011, not only were commentators like Martin Wolf of the *Financial Times* calling for more public investment, but also the financial markets started to be as afraid of economic stagnation as they are of the level of government debts. Only the German government seemed oblivious to the threat of a slide back into recession.

Now, I don't think the Germans have much choice but to change their position, because pretty much everybody else is calling for growth strategies. Mechanisms have been identified, particularly the European Investment Bank as a source for infrastructure investment. Further elements of a growth strategy would require more radical measures, for example the issuing of Eurobonds, which would mean the Eurozone taking collective responsibility for each individual country's borrowing. That is likely to take much longer. The Project Bond Initiative announced by the EU on 22 May is tiny by comparison with the scale of the crisis. The more important idea in circulation is that of stretching out the terms of deficit reduction – giving Greece and Spain, for example, more time to meet the conditions attached to their bail-outs. Even if the European Investment Bank does get moving, even if the EU budget were deployed, that will take time to implement.

If a left government is elected in Greece and repudiates the memorandum, what do you think will happen?

The assumption in Brussels, Frankfurt and the financial markets is that repudiation of the bail-out conditions would automatically lead to a debt default. In the past when countries have defaulted on their debt, like Argentina in 2001–2, most investors had already covered their backs, and given the small size of Greek debt compared to the whole EU economy, it may be that the immediate losses could be absorbed without much difficulty. Given that

* Previously published in *Solidarity* 249, 13 June 2012.

Greece is three per cent of the EU, and the total amount of money involved in the Greek crisis is peanuts compared to the resources of the whole Eurozone, it would be a simple matter for Germany alone to stump up the cash to resolve Greece's crisis.

However, if Syriza does win the Greek election, and it cancels the austerity plan and stops debt payments, there will in any case be a great deal of disruption in day-to-day financial transactions between Greece and the rest of the EU. There would have to be some sort of emergency arrangements, and something like the summit after the Lehman Brothers collapse in September 2008. This explains why there has been so much pressure, both on the softer elements in Syriza to make it back down, and on the whole Greek electorate, with dire warnings. The Greek ruling-class strategy is to ensure that New Democracy comes first in the poll, by whatever means they can do that, and then ND forms a coalition with Pasok and the Democratic Left.

For the Eurozone as a whole, the consequences of a forced break-up of the Eurozone are anyway far too dangerous for the ruling classes for them to allow it for lack of transferring a few billion more euros. The ECB made a high profile decision in December, when Mario Draghi decided to provide unlimited three-year loans available to all the banks in the Eurozone; the banks borrowed €500 billion, and a further €500 billion in February. This averted a looming liquidity crisis in the banks, which were then able to help fund government deficits, especially in Spain and Italy, but in May the imminent collapse of the Spanish bank Bankia signalled that the period of respite was over. However, the ECB funding of the banks shows that it is able to make the sort of high-profile political decision it would have to make if Greece elects a left government.

In addition, the ECB acts as a clearing-house for intra-Eurozone trade – this is the so-called Target 2 system – and Germany is in credit in that system to the tune of €700 billion, while Greece and Spain are debtors. One way of easing things for Greece would be to postpone settlement of those balances.

The word credit is derived from the Latin credo, I believe. If you believe it's all going to get sorted out in the end, then there are really no limits to the extension of credit. But we have to go back a bit to summer 2011. One of the main things that caused the crisis to deepen in the second half of 2011 was the withdrawal, in effect, of American investors from European markets. A lot of the liquidity provided to European banks until then was coming from America, especially from money-market funds, who could make more money by purchasing European bonds with higher yields than US Treasuries. In the summer of last year, US investors became seriously worried and began to pull their money out. That was a major reason why the European banks then faced deteriorating credit conditions up to the point of the ECB rescue in December.

There is talk of the EU having a "firewall" sufficient to block "contagion" if Greece is suspended, expelled, or exits from the euro. Is that so?

I'm not sure that the claimed EU "firewall" would work, because once Greece is forced out, the whole mystique of the Eurozone is broken. In that case, it is very hard to imagine any sum of money being sufficient to reassure the financial markets, unless there is a very clear and agreed plan to ensure that the euro's credibility problem is resolved once and for all. This requires fiscal solidarity between Eurozone member states, and that in turn needs a complete political change of heart in which Eurozone governments and political elites agree to move away from competing with each other and using the old nationalist arguments to blackmail their working classes. Without that, I think the euro is finished.

The fiscal pact as designed by the Germans in December lacks any legitimacy because it needs to be underpinned by some sense of solidarity, and up until now it isn't. In contrast, in the USA the federal government has a whole range of mechanisms which redistribute the fiscal burden among the 50 states. There is a fundamental flaw in the December pact. It is based on the notion of the structural deficit, and a rule that the structural deficit must be limited to 0.5% of GDP. But the structural deficit cannot be measured. The idea of making legally binding an indicator which can't be objectively measured is farcical.

Among the big bosses in Europe, the bosses of the major corporations, there must be an awareness that if the Eurozone starts unravelling, they will face huge upheavals. Europe is too integrated to pull apart now. I think they will keep muddling through, and concessions will be made to Greece to keep it in the Eurozone. The mystery is why they are taking so long to deliver the concessions that are clearly needed.

There will have to be a substantive fiscal pact and an agreement to shift a substantial part of budget decision-making to the European level. That then raises the question of the balance between the apparently democratic structures of the European Parliament, and the intergovernmental structures and the Commission. There would have to be a major reworking of the European treaties.

What should the left elsewhere in Europe say?

What do the social-democratic forces of Europe do? After 30 years of retreat before neoliberalism, this will be the moment of truth. There is a possibility, particularly if the SPD wins in Germany, of moving towards a Social Europe Mark Two, but maybe I'm being wildly optimistic. Trade union movements have remained essentially trapped within a national Keynesian framework in each country. There are contacts between national unions and federations, through the European TUC and its sectoral bodies, but the links are very much on a bread and butter level, sharing experiences about the evolution of collective bargaining and so on. It would take a huge change in the nature of trade unionism across Europe, and in this country more than most, for trade unions to be willing to re-enter the political arena, after having abandoned it for most of the last 20 or 30 years.

CHAPTER 22

The World of Neoliberalism (October 2013)

Paul Hampton and Martin Thomas

1. We have argued that since 1945, global capitalism has experienced an epoch of the "imperialism of free trade", in which it has been successively restructured into an aggregate of politically independent states which are authentically bourgeois (rather than being states dominated by pre-capitalist factions, or colonies) and which accept and internalise the discipline of the world market.

2. The step-by-step ending of the old era of colonial imperialism, and the vast expansion to new areas of industrial production for the world market, bring shifting sub-hierarchies; but they do not mean a "flat" or even development. Global capitalism remains highly uneven, and keystoned and policed by the US superpower.

3. This regime, overseeing the combined and uneven development of capitalism across the globe, survived the economic crises of the 1970s, mutating into neoliberalism. Then in the 1990s it expanded to incorporate the former Stalinist states and to include at a higher level many centres which had developed manufacturing industry for the world market at a substantial scale since the 1960s. It has thus far survived the economic downturn that began in 2007. The "imperialism of free trade", despite many contradictions, is likely to dominate for the foreseeable future.

4. The "imperialism of free trade" – or "Empire of Capital", as Ellen Wood has called it; or "Global Capitalism", as Leo Panitch and Sam Gindin call it – differs from earlier periods of capitalism. It is broadly a world of capitalist states, which act to make the conditions for capital accumulation. It is a world where multinational corporations produce and trade across borders, aided by international institutional structures (IMF, World Bank, WTO) designed to facilitate these global production chains. In the neoliberal era, since the 1980s, it is increasingly a world in which capitalist states set their policy by the priority of making their territory a safe and workable area for global capital to invest in, rather than that of constructing a more-or-less integrated national industrial base.

* Previously published in *Solidarity* 298, 2 October 2013.

5. This regime is also the imperialism of finance. Money capital, bank capital, credit and speculation are necessary moments in circuits of capital. Capitalism is inconceivable without them. Financial capital plays a dominant economic role, pooling and distributing the social surplus, creating credit in advance of production, disciplining wayward firms and determining channels for new investment. The relative weight and speed of global financial markets has increased enormously since the 1980s, and that trend continues.
6. The "imperialism of free trade" is superintended by the US hyperpower, which has overwhelming military superiority and uses military force to police global capitalism. It is what Marx called "the dull compulsion of economic relations", reinforced by states and especially the US state, rather than resort to military occupation and colonisation, which largely shapes the international economy. Bourgeois society, organising its fundamental processes of exploitation through more-or-less free market relations rather than the relations of personal subordination characteristic of serfdom or slavery, nevertheless requires much larger police forces than those older societies: in the same way the "imperialism of free trade" is accompanied by the growth of big armies acting as global police, and especially the US armed forces. In the Cold War era, the US frequently used military might to topple regimes it thought to be too friendly to the USSR or likely to "go Communist". It sustained dictators like Somoza or Batista, Trujillo or Pinochet or the Shah of Iran, the type it deemed to be "a son of a bitch, but our son of a bitch". Even then, it did not seek colonial rule. In an era when even the poorest countries had gained substantial urban populations and where national awareness was widespread, the USA considered colonial rule archaic and counterproductive. The USA's economic strength would, with much less strict political conditions than required for colonial rule, give it enough clout; and if the USA sought colonial rule, that would help the USSR gain support from and control over anti-colonial movements.

Since the early 1990s, the USA has generally preferred to sustain bourgeois democracies (of a sort, and on condition, of course, that they accept the rules of the world market, which generally they do out of the self-interest of the local bourgeoisie). The USA maintained that preference even while deploying large military actions (Kuwait 1991, Kosova 1999, Afghanistan from 2001, Iraq 2003–11). Since George W Bush agreed, in 2008, to full US military withdrawal from Iraq, the US has been more cautious about military action. It retains a very large military machine, and the readiness to use if it sees its interests threatened seriously and in a way which military action can fix. The global capitalist economy does not have, and is not likely to have, a proper system of bourgeois-democratic global law. We cannot and do not endorse the "liberal interventionist" illusion (Euston Manifesto, etc.) that the US military will be, or might if nudged be, an agency of a bourgeois-democratic international rule of law, even to the extent that a bourgeois police force can administer a rule of law in a bourgeois democracy like Britain.

We must distinguish the usual real role of big-power military action in the world today both from those "liberal interventionist" illusions and from the illusion that the action is just a re-run, or the beginning of a re-run, of old-style colonial conquest.

7. US hegemony persists, despite its setbacks due to the Iraq fiasco. Since the early 1980s, US economic growth, manufacturing productivity and volume of exports have been higher than other G8 countries. The US continues to dominate R&D spending and maintains its share of global high-tech production, e.g. aerospace, pharmaceuticals, computers and office machinery, communication equipment and scientific instruments.

8. American-based corporations continue to invest huge flows of capital abroad and employ 10 million workers overseas. The US also receives large inflows of capital, which are channelled into domestic consumption and investment. Its capacity to capture global savings reflects the structural strength of its imperial form of rule. The US trade deficit is not evidence of its weakness. During the recent crisis, capitalists have continued to purchase dollars and US Treasury Bills because they remain the most stable store of value in a volatile capitalist world.

9. Capitalist globalisation consists of spreading capitalist social relations and world-market imperatives into every corner of social life and to all parts of the world. Over the last half century, close linkages have been established between the American state and the other Western states. The internationalisation of capital is now based on foreign direct investment and multinational corporations. American capital now exists as a material social force inside most other social formations, with a consequent impact on social relations, property rights and employment relations. Capitalist states compete primarily by trying to make their territorial spaces attractive as sites of accumulation for foreign as well as domestic bourgeoisies.

10. While China may perhaps emerge eventually as a pole of inter-imperial power, it is currently far from reaching that status. Contradictions and tensions persist between and within states across the globe, but China currently enjoys a symbiotic relationship with the American state. Although certain elements within the US are concerned to maintain its current unipolar power and prevent the emergence of future imperial adversaries, this is not evidence that such contenders already exist.

11. The combined and uneven capitalist development in recent decades has generated rapid economic growth in parts of the South. New centres of capital

accumulation have developed, and in certain cases, sub-imperialist states vying for regional predominance have emerged. Whilst many states (particularly in Africa) remain mired in poverty, the rapid spatial extension of capitalist social relations of production and the spread of waged labour have characterised the modern epoch of capitalism.

12. An essential corollary of capitalist globalisation is the massive growth of the world proletariat. The international working class has at least doubled in size in the last 30 years. The working class in East Asia increased nine-fold— from about 100 million to 900 million workers. China's employed working class tripled, growing from 120 million to 350 million. By the turn of the century, China had more than twice as many manufacturing workers as the world's largest industrial nations combined. The large size of the "semi-proletariat" in many countries—people engaged in a fluctuating combination of casual waged work, petty trade, etc.—makes it difficult to draw precise boundaries, but we have probably passed the tipping point at which more of the world's direct producers do waged work than do peasant agriculture. Far from the working class disappearing, globally its social weight has never been greater.

13. The run-up to the 2007–8 crisis was a period of capitalist exuberance. The onset of crisis was not rooted in any sharp profit decline or collapse of investment. In 2006–07, profits were at peak, productivity continued to increase substantially in manufacturing (with wages lagging behind) and low-cost production chains continued to spread. With some important exceptions (notably in the car industry), American corporations went into the crisis in generally solid financial shape in terms of profits, debt and cash flow.

14. The crisis was rooted in the dynamics of finance. Before it broke, the market in titles to future surplus-value inflated. It expanded particularly fast in the last period because of the growth since the 1980s of an increasing variety and depth of global financial markets. Bad debts which were fairly small on the scale of the whole system produced considerable turmoil in the global system, because no one seemed to know where the bad debt was, or which apparently sound debt might in fact depend on bad debt. What had appeared to be calculable risk of financial mishap, which could be offset and managed, was revealed to be incalculable uncertainty (so-called "Knightian uncertainty").

15. There are some signs of recovery, although the revival may be weak. It may predictably make for another crisis on similar lines before too long. But often capital "lives with" that: there is no automatic, or even reliably vigorous, mechanism to make capitalist classes seek, identify, and implement more serious problem-solving or even problem-displacement. The crisis has reaffirmed the centrality of states (particularly the American state) in the global capitalist economy, while multiplying the difficulties of managing it.

16. No major state has seen the crisis as an opportunity to challenge or undermine the American state. Rather, the integration of global capitalism has meant that there has been extensive international coordination across states in the provision of liquidity to financial system, in fiscal stimulus, the avoidance of tariff wars and in establishing new regulatory regimes for finance.
17. Neoliberalism should be understood as a particular form of class rule and state power, which emerged in the late 1970s, although on foundations laid after the Second World War. It intensifies competitive imperatives for both firms and workers; increases social inequality and luxury consumption by the rich; increases insecurity for working-class people; increases dependence on the market in daily life and reinforces the dominant hierarchies of the world market, with the US at its apex. The ruling-class hegemony which Gramsci wrote of is today organised as much through market transaction mechanisms, shaping people to see life as "an investment", as through parties, media, schooling, etc.
18. Predictions of the demise of neoliberalism at the outset of this crisis in 2007–08 have proven to be false. Some neoliberal dogmas have been discredited, but mainstream neoliberalism never excluded Keynesian measures, and the political-economic conditions that gave rise to the basic parameters of neoliberalism have not been exhausted or undone by this crisis. There is currently no move to a new regime. At the peak of the financial crisis, governments nationalised, bailed out, and ran budget deficits, on a huge scale. That shows that economic life today cannot operate without social regulation; but the regulation remained "socialism for the rich". Governments remain intent on having such crisis measures serve a new neoliberal push, rather than having them become the start of a new departure.

We underline, in our explanations, the proof given of the irrationalities of the capitalist market – the wisdom and efficiency of which had been so lavishly praised since the early 1980s – and we argue for a workers' government to replace the "socialism for the rich" by "socialism by and for the working class".
19. The program of the [2010–5 Tory and Lib-Dem] coalition government in Britain – more marketisation, more cuts in welfare, more privatisation, harsher pressure on organised labour, in short, more neoliberalism – is not an anomaly. The German government is driving a sharply neoliberal course across Europe. The US administration is more cautious about rapidly reducing budget deficits than the European governments, but remains firmly within a neoliberal framework.
20. Many on the left proceed like generals who, overtaken by events, make elaborate plans to fight the last war. The spectre of the 1970s and even the 1920s still hang over much of the left. Many socialists still regard imperialism in

terms of (a garbled version of) the analysis Lenin made during the First World War. They repeat a cannibalised "Leninist", actually Stalinist account of imperialism. On this view, the world is still divided principally between a few large imperialist states and others that are little better than semi-colonies.

21. Lenin's 1916 analysis of imperialism, which synthesised the best of Second International geopolitics, was a more-or-less adequate assessment of the First World War conjuncture. However in many respects it was flawed even for its time: its conflation of finance capital with, alternately, the merger of bank and industrial capital, or, in contrast, purely speculative or rentier; the derivation of the drive of capital to export abroad from a supposed "glut" or absence of investment opportunities in the home country.

And the commonly-accepted version of Lenin has much worse problems than his original analysis. Since Lenin's 1916 pamphlet contains essentially no discussion of the economic effects of imperialism in subordinate countries (because that was not Lenin's focus in that particular text), scattered phrases and offhand polemical swipes from Lenin have been reconstructed to theorise imperialism as a simple process of plunder rather than a species of capitalist development.

The end result is to conflate "imperialism" with "whatever advanced capitalist states do internationally" and, in turn, with simple plunder. There is, of course, no lack of real evidence that simple plunder is part of the routine international activity of advanced capitalist states: the question is whether that is all there is to it, and whether plunder is a feature uniquely of *advanced* capitalist states rather than of all capitalist states. In the cod-Leninist discourse, "imperialism" (meaning advanced capitalism) is opposed not so much because it is capitalist as because it is advanced.

22. Kautsky's article on ultra-imperialism, which we republished in 2001 when it had long been out of print, read in 1914 as a rationalisation of the SPD's support for its own government and an evasion of the tasks of the day in favour of speculative hopes about better conditions emerging, of their own accord, in future. However Lenin never denied the possibility of interdependence and cooperation among the powerful states. Kautsky's scheme of a fixed division between "industrial" and "agrarian" territories was of course false. His idea that the big capitalist states would ally stably on a more-or-less equal basis was false too: the "ultra-imperialist" features of the current era rely on the role of the US as superpower. Yet a century on, after further capitalist development and state formation, and in the absence of socialist revolutions internationally to overthrow capitalism, some aspects of Kautsky's picture are visible in the current mode of bourgeois rule and the global relations.

23. Many left analysts claimed that the crisis proves the US empire is in decline. They argue by analogy with Britain as the declining hegemon in the late

19th century, that the US is driven to war and occupation by its loss of power, prestige and position, e.g. in Afghanistan, Iraq and Syria. But this ignores the continuing centrality of the American state in global capitalism and its role in policing capitalist relations i.e. a more specifically capitalist form of imperialism, rather than the colonial imperialism of earlier epochs. The Iraq fiasco was produced by overconfidence of a US ruling class drunk on success (collapse of the USSR 1991, Kuwait 1991, Kosova 1999, and, so they wrongly thought in 2003, Afghanistan 2001). It was not a desperate resort of a ruling class scared of eclipse by rivals. To posit a terminal decline in US imperial power is to attempt to accomplish in theory what remains to be done in political struggle.

24. Yet many analysts argue that relations between the developed states of the "North" are characterised by the declining power of the hegemon (the US) and consequently rivalry leading ultimately to war. Every sign of disagreement between the big powers and the US is treated as the prelude to the anticipated repetition of earlier historical patterns and the mechanical, reasoning-by-analogy replication of previous inter-imperialist rivalry.

25. For others on the left, relations with other states of the "Third World" are governed by dependency and impeded capitalist (under)development. Such an assessment underestimates the development of the working class and the potential for an organised labour movement. It implies a nationalist alliance with the domestic bourgeoisie rather than the struggle for independent working class political representation.

26. There is a common assumption in Marxist discussion that crises – or, at least, serious crises, "Marxist" crises – are preceded, initiated, set off, by falls in the average rate of profit. But in fact they are not – or not always. In the recent discussions, few economists have based themselves on the old Marxological "tendency of the rate of profit to fall", but that tendency has been much referred to on the activist left, and it casts a very large shadow on all discussions of the relation between profit rates and crisis.

27. The argument is that as capital expands, the ratio of constant capital (machinery and materials) to variable capital (laid out on living workers) rises. Profit is produced only by living labour. Therefore, even as the absolute mass of profit increases, its ratio to the total stock of capital required to produce it, the profit-rate, tends to fall. However, theoretically, Marx identified numerous counter-tendencies, arising from the same processes that give rise to the downward tendency. We cannot assume a "law of the tendency of the rate of profit to fall". A long-lasting tendency for the rate of profit to fall cannot be substantiated at the general level of argumentation by Marx in *Capital*. The rate of profit may tend downwards over a long-ish period. However, the rate of profit can also rise over long periods, as it did between the mid-1980s and 2006–7. Whatever the

trends, a downward tendency cannot provide a sufficient explanation for all capitalist crises, including the latest downturn.

28. Many on the left argue that the crisis of the 1970s was never resolved. They say that a decline in profitability which led to that crisis had continued. (To make the statistics fit this thesis is difficult, but, given the complexities of exactly defining profit rates, not impossible). Or they say that ruinous over-competition which triggered that crisis has continued because of inadequate scrapping of industrial overcapacity and constant growth of new industrial capacity in new areas. Thus stagnation: what appeared to be growth was only superficial flurries thanks to spatial-temporal fixes, asset-bubbles and other ad-hoc measures.

This is no adequate explanation for the neoliberal resurgence of bourgeois power and of profitability from the mid-1980s. Nor does it yield an adequate prognosis of the current crisis and the prospects for revived working class struggle in the near future. If capitalist income as measured by the capitalists rises, that is a capitalist expansion whatever refiguring may be done to try to show that strict Marxist definitions could deflate the statistics. If growth was not as fast in Europe, Japan, and the USA as it was in the 1950s-60s "Golden Age", it has been faster elsewhere (in East Asia, for example); and anyway, growth does not have to be at "Golden Age" pace to be growth. If the growth was, on a certain level, a matter of contrivances and unstable flurries – when is capitalist growth ever anything else?

29. To depict the last forty years as a constant crisis of global capitalism is also to slur over the specificity and the drama of the actual crisis which opened in 2007–8. It looks like leading into a stretch of depression rather than any quick recovery. The Tory government's current ballyhoo about economic recovery in Britain glosses over the fact that capitalist business investment continues to shrink. The instabilities which set off the 2007–8 crisis are still in the system, and are likely to set off similar crises in future. The political repercussions of the economic crisis are as yet very far from being fully played out, and in substantial part depend not only on the general mechanisms but also on the character and energy of the working-class response. We shall see. Our focus should be on fighting through the contradictions within capitalist development, and helping the increased economic weight of the working class find political expression, not on hoping for capitalism to bring itself down through (illusory) permanent crisis.

CHAPTER 23

An Alternative View on the World of Neoliberalism (January 2014)

Barry Finger

Paul Hampton and Martin Thomas have presented an analytically rich background document on "The World of Neoliberalism." I am in fundamental agreement with the politics of the argument. But where the argument fails me is in this. In its emphasis on the novelty and specificity of the current crisis, Hampton and Thomas dismiss any attempt to place this crisis in a larger historical context as futile. They are at pains to dismiss the tendency for the rate of profit to fall, which marks them in agreement with the preponderant opinion of academic Marxists, but at odds with business economists such as those from Deloitte, who, as I have previously argued, have clearly demonstrated in their "Shift Index" that the rate of profit (in the US) has fallen since the mid 1960s. These conclusions have been discussed in such ruling class sanctuaries as the *Harvard Business Review* and *Forbes*. This divergence – this inversion – itself should be a cause for note, if not concern.

And of course, Hampton and Thomas argue consistently. Once the tendency for the rate of profit to fall is found wanting, there is no other general dynamic of capital accumulation through which the current crisis can be contextualized. "Underconsumptionism" is a dead end. It argues, at least in its Marxist forms, that accumulation requires additional sources of demand outside the framework of the capitalistically generated market place. Rosa Luxemburg, for instance, famously argued that capitalism needed a third (external) market of consumers who are not producers of value to offset values for which there are no (internal) consumers. And "disproportionality", rarely today cited as an alternative, is so general – so all-applicable – as to be functionally meaningless.

Yet the underconsumptionist argument had one great merit. It situated imperialism at the very centre of capitalist accumulation. Militarism, war and colonialism were seen as essential to keeping national capitalist economies afloat in part by providing a state generated third market for armaments but,

---

* Previously published at http://www.workersliberty.org/story/2013/10/02/world-neo-liberalism#comment-31438, 1 January 2014.

more vitally, by defending and expanding captive markets at the expense of global competitors.

The problem with Hampton and Thomas' analysis, I fear, is that it fails to identify any alternative explanation that links the politics of imperialism with the economics of accumulation. It suggests, instead (am I misreading this?), an imperialism that is a contest of force, in part, between established and rising capitalist powers. It is true that they talk about the "imperialism of free trade" and "global production chains." But if what is meant by these are the amounts extracted directly through profit and interest repatriation from overseas investment, such numbers are relatively paltry. American corporate profits extracted from the rest of the world (and that prominently includes the other advanced capitalist economies) amounted to $430 billion in 2012, less than a third of the profit total ostensibly generated domestically. The proposed defence budget in the same year, prior to the sequester, was $671 billion. If we presume that this is required to police the "imperialism of free trade", it is hardly a cost-effective trade-off.

But perhaps Hampton and Thomas mean that the US, as the imperial hegemon, bears the burden of policing the global south for the benefit of the developed economies as a whole. In which case, the extraction of profits and interest flowing from south to north should be the crucial determinant and relevant comparison. Very well. But where has the case been made that most of the profits and interest redistributed among the advanced economies originate in the South rather than within the developed nations themselves? In fact, that proposition, should it be asserted, could probably not be sustained.

Why even dignify the essential economic relationship of the advanced to the developing capitalist economies with the grandiloquent term of imperialism, if the direct extraction of value is so apparently marginal, even dispensable, to the wellbeing of the capitalist metropolises? More important, what is there to capitalism that requires imperialism? I can't really find an answer to this in Hampton and Thomas' piece. Underconsumptionism is not a problem even worth raising; profitability is not a problem worth considering. What unanswered need is addressed by imperialism?

Before that can be answered, we need to take a step back. Hampton and Thomas concede that capitalism did suffer from a crisis of profitability prior to the current neoliberal phase that originated in the 1980s. But they, assert, the subsequent opening of the former Stalinist economies to capitalism and the offshoring and outsourcing of production combined with the massive growth of the third world proletariat turned that crisis around, arresting and reversing the fall in the rate of profit that climaxed – according to them – in the crises of the 1970s.

Again, if not by the massive infusion of profits from Eastern Europe and the third world, then how? Perhaps (in part) by suppressing the wage demands of the western working classes threatened by third world competition, thereby massively jacking up the metropolitan rate of exploitation? And then (also in part) by unequal exchange based on global wage disparities that allow the capitalist Triad to diminish the costs of imported inputs and thereby increase the spread between cost and revenue.

Hampton and Thomas do not discuss the latter proposition. And while neither do they expressly discuss wage suppression, such a conclusion might not be too far a leap, nevertheless. But had they made they made either of these propositions explicit it would bring the argument full circle. It reintroduces the question of functionality. Imperialism serves primarily as a bulwark against the resurgence of a falling rate of profit. It restores that tendency to the centre of our consideration, compelling us to ask what forces within capitalism arise to periodically fend off the very dynamic that Hampton and Thomas deny the existence of.

Even so, has imperialism reversed, or even eliminated, the falling rate of profit as a factor in the current crisis? I would argue – no. There is, I believe, a prior inherent shortcoming on how we conceptualize the rate of profit, once the stripped down framework of *Capital* is extended to encompass movements in a modern – corporate dominated – capitalist economy over time. Marx's purpose was not to demonstrate that there is a tendency for the rate of profit to decline. This proposition was accepted by all classical economists. Even Keynes argued that there was a long term tendency for the "marginal efficiency of investment" to diminish. What Marx attempted to demonstrate was how this tendency is rooted in the process of commodity production itself – in the very warp and woof of capitalism, a demonstration that bedevilled classical economists. But Marxists have tried to shoehorn our arguments, both pro and con, about the consistency and empirical relevancy of this proposition, within the all too restrictive framework of Marx's discussion. Corporations do not measure their rate of profit against capital invested in structures and equipment. They own a spectrum of assets that generate income streams, among which are not only tangible means of production, but also a variety of financial assets such as consumer and corporate loans, CDs, Treasury bills and so on. All these pool together to comprise corporate profits. In practice it is very difficult on a macro level to map the stream of income associated with each individual class of assets. It is therefore difficult to isolate that stream solely associated with productive investment from all the other sources of income, such that asset A is associated with income stream a, B with b, etc. Of course, for individual corporations who need to periodically rebalance their assets this knowledge is crucial to maintain profitability. But the point is this. Corporate profitability measures the sum of all these income streams with respect to the entirety of its assets, including cash on hand, which, in the absence of deflation, yields no appreciable return.

And that is precisely what most Marxists have failed to do. Much of the literature is focused on taking the sum of corporate income streams and comparing its growth against the increase in tangible assets. This invariably invites a degree of randomness. It neglects the fact that consumer loans, and instalment credit, imposed on workers, constitutes a second stream of exploitation that takes place outside the production process. The extraction of interest on consumer debt converts paid labour time into unpaid labour time. It is a reversion to a form of absolute surplus value extraction. Similarly, state taxation of wages (net of the flow-back as extra-market wage supplements) to pay banks also constitutes a reduction in paid labour. To the extent that capital holds public bonds and securitised debt, it retains for itself a supplementary source of surplus-value that it counts as income. And it is the rise of this secondary source of surplus value that gives heft and sweep to the so-called financialisation of capitalism. It means that capitalism is increasingly focused on bypassing production as a means of supplementing surplus value.

The increasing emphasis on detour, at the expense of productive investment, suggests how deep the crisis of manufacturing profitability had been. Yet the financial sphere, by multiplying claims on surplus value, without expanding the productive base, pumps up one avenue of surplus value while suppressing what might otherwise be translated into an increase in relative surplus value. And in either case it, like all other means for the extraction of surplus value, faces natural and cultural limits.

So if, on the other hand, we were to more accurately measure the movement of income streams with the totality of assets that are associated with such streams, we would generate an entirely different picture of how the rate of profit moves over time. This I have tried to do by plotting corporate profits before taxes against corporate assets valued at historical cost for the non-financial sector of the American economy. This yields the results shown in Figure 23.1.[1]

This pattern seems to be compatible with Henryk Grossmann's formulation of a secular decline in profitability expressed through cyclical movements in asset (capital) accumulation and destruction. And it is a remarkably tight fit over a protracted period of time, roughly the entire post-war epoch.

1 Series https://fred.stlouisfed.org/series/A464RC1Q027SBEA divided by https://fred.stlouisfed.org/series/TABSNNCB, source: FRED Economic Data, Federal Reserve Bank of St Louis, https://fred.stlouisfed.org/.

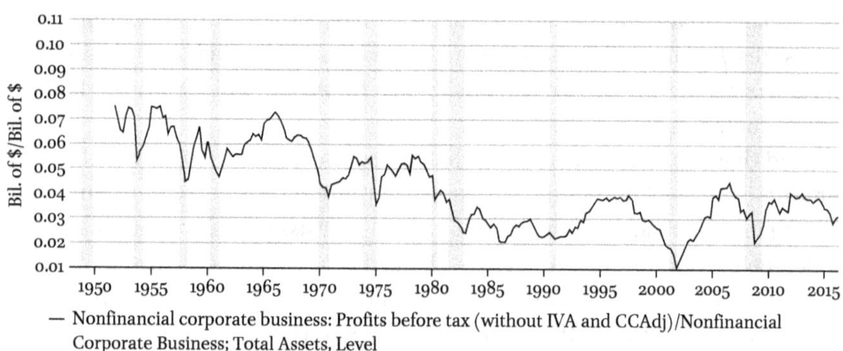

FIGURE 23.1 *Corporate profits before taxes against corporate assets valued at historical cost for the non-financial sector of the US economy, 1940–2012*

What it does not do is verify Marx's argument per se. And in this Hampton and Thomas are dead right. It certainly may not be the case that the fall in the rate of profit during any of these cycles – or for the period as a whole – can be explained solely by the rise in the organic composition of capital invested in the sphere of commodity production in relation to the stream of surplus-value extracted exclusively through production. But why is that essential? To prove our "orthodox" Marxist bona fides? Capitalism is not simply a mode of production, but a mode of social reproduction. It develops primarily by expelling labour from the process of production, while multiplying the claims on surplus value through the accumulation of capital – not just means of production, but commercial capital, banking capital, speculative capital. It is this contradictory tension that it is at pains to suppress. The system holds together as long as it can expand the mass of profits. When the countervailing forces of imperialism – of wage suppression and unequal exchange – of innovation and rationalisation of the production process no longer suffice to that end, crises are needed as a last resort to restart the clock by eliminating excess claims on surplus-value. If we are going to understand neoliberalism, why not start here?

CHAPTER 24

The Resilience of Neoliberalism (June 2016)

Discussion with Andrew Gamble

You say, "neoliberal ideas have become more hegemonic to a much greater extent than other consensus ideologies". There is a paradox here. This is true at the level of government, and mainstream opposition, policies. But in circles which discuss economic theories, this is much less true. Most economic theorists criticise Osborne's austerity. This contrasts with the 1930s, where heterodox theories were more marginal, but governments attempted experiments more readily.

I think that is correct. It is a strange feature of this crisis, as opposed to the last one. I think you can explain it partly in terms of the way that ideological discourse has shrunk, but there are also a lot of material factors: the strength of the labour movement across the capitalist democracies is much weaker than it was. I think several decades of financialisation and individualisation have changed the nature of politics. It may not be permanent but that's what it feels like at the moment. So the difficulty of organising collective resistance to what's been going on appears much harder.

Also, I am very struck by how in the 1930s, most of the utopians were on the left. Today, there are very few left utopians; the utopians now are on the right – the fantasists of the libertarian right. There is a lack of ambition on the left about imagining different futures, a much more defensive approach. Although there are anti-capitalist movements, they are nothing like the anti-capitalist movements of the 1930s, that is clear.

One of the striking things of the current crisis is that although lots of incumbent governments have been toppled, they have tended to be replaced by another mainstream party. Until Syriza broke through in Greece, there hasn't been an example in Europe of a party opposed to the mainstream winning office. The test would be if something like the Front National won power, or a similar party. Le Pen does have a lot of anti-globalisation rhetoric, but whether that would translate into an alternative economic policy does remain to be seen. Like UKIP, they have made gestures towards protectionism, but have nothing like a properly worked-out plan. If they were to withstand the enormous forces of international markets which would be brought to bear on them, they would

* Previously published at https://senseofgfc.wordpress.com/2016/06/19/questions-to-andrew-gamble/, 19 June 2016.

need a strategy for resisting it. So, it is a puzzle. It is very much an identity politics that they are proclaiming. One of the disturbing things from a left point of view about Europe at present is the way that sections of the working class are much more attracted by an identity politics than they are by a class politics. Identity politics, for many workers, seems to trump class arguments. And for any sort of left politics, that is deeply debilitating.

The intellectual classes have gone to the left on a whole set of issues, whether it be climate change or the question of poverty and inequality. But at the same time, these intellectual strata have become more detached from the national public. So, the old way in which labour movements used to work, and the way in which intellectuals were integrated with political movements, has been fraying badly. The hollowing-out of political parties which has taken place in the neoliberal era means that parties no longer provide a bridge. So, the intellectual strata, in the old phrase, the "free-floating intelligentsia", have become more free-floating. They are fierce critics, they have journals and so on, but they haven't had much impact, however, on neoliberal orthodoxy, and they also haven't managed to connect very successfully with the mass of citizens. The French Socialist Party seem to have really quite a small base in the working class now. The Socialist Party seems to represent rather different strata within French society. And many of the social layers which used to form the base of the Communist Party have gone to the National Front.

The old big, encompassing coalitions that the Left used to have are much harder to assemble. We've seen that trend across Europe. One shouldn't exaggerate it, but it is a trend. The left is weaker as a mobilising agent. You see that in the EU referendum campaign. Although Labour is relatively united on the question of whether Britain should remain a member of the EU, for lots of good economic and class reasons, that message is not getting through. It has been rejected by a lot of the traditional working-class base of the party. The Corbyn leadership is as much a part of that divide now as the Blairites were. That does seem to be a very strong trend in our politics. That old glue of the intellectual strata within the old labour movements seems to be gone, and this seems to reflect the decline of the labour movements as a political and industrial force.

Syriza had lots of intellectuals and a big working-class base. But you have seen a move in Syriza from being a confident, buoyant movement, into just being a neoliberal administrator. How does that work?

I suppose in the end, they weren't brave enough. There was a part of the party that wanted to go all the way. But then they reached a point where they had to capitulate, or call the bluff and say, "we're coming out of the Euro, and we'll take the consequences". The consequences for Greece of doing that could have been so serious that they blinked at the prospect. Although Syriza won the referendum, they then immediately capitulated.

We just don't know what would have happened. I can see it both ways: that if they had decided to do call the bluff, and if the Greek economy had then collapsed into a very desperate siege economy, with a drachma which was worth almost nothing on the international exchanges, the government might have collapsed, and the opportunity for Golden Dawn or other very radical parties, or even for the military, could well have resulted. The majority of the Syriza leadership judged that they were not prepared to take those risks, and they capitulated. But that was a huge setback for an alternative to neoliberalism. It means that resistance of small countries on the periphery is not likely to succeed. So change has to take place in the core, in Germany and other core countries of the Eurozone; but that looks a very long way away.

The Syriza experience is a very dispiriting one. The leadership did back down. I think it is difficult to say that they were wrong to back down, because presumably they weighed up the consequences very carefully. Presumably they thought the EU would offer them a better deal and it didn't; but the result of calling the EU's bluff could have been horrendous, not just for Syriza but for the people they represent. We are left still with a very dysfunctional Eurozone and little challenge to the dominant politics in the EU. And with the exception of Spain, most of the challenges to that politics are coming from radical right-populist movements, rather than from the left.

I think there is a bit more to the Syriza experience, about what happened before they "blinked". By the time of the election in early 2015, they had pared their platform down to their Thessaloniki Platform, which really wasn't an anti-neoliberal platform, but one which just said "we will negotiate a better deal with the EU and redistribute the proceeds in welfare spending". In 2012, when it looked like Syriza might win, Tsipras went to Paris and Berlin, to address meetings called by the left. He was trying to build a movement across Europe. Inadequately, but trying nonetheless. In 2015, Syriza didn't do that: they sent Varoufakis around Europe to talk to the finance ministers, not to labour movement meetings. They had given up on building a movement across Europe.

If they had chosen differently, they might at least have forced some concessions from the Eurozone. There were plenty of people – not just the radical left – who were saying the program for Greece was unworkable. Immediately after Syriza's election, the German trade unions put out a statement to support the demands of the Greek government. Within weeks the SPD were vying with Schäuble to see who could take the harder line on Greece. Syriza quickly gave up on doing anything that could shift the balance of forces across Europe.

And later on they had "brinkmanship" options. They could have printed euros for use only in Greece. They could have put the onus on the European Central Bank to expel them, thereby making it possible to organise cross-Europe pressure on the ECB *to reverse the suspension of Greece. That would not have required a social revolution all across Europe. Had Syriza tried such things, they'd have a much better chance of taking their base with them through the immediate economic consequences of a break with the Eurozone. Of course suddenly declaring that they would leave the euro could not have taken their people along with them. To keep your "Plan B" secret from your base cuts off all such possibilities.*

The dominant faction around Tsipras was never really prepared to call the bluff of the EU in the sense of having a Plan B. That was also the calculation that the EU negotiators made, I think. The more general lesson is that if you are going to take on some of the most powerful institutions that govern the international neoliberal order, you've got to have a very serious plan for what you do and how you carry your supporters with you. Syriza made some steps on that road, but not nearly enough.

It's a classic example of power politics and how the weaker side will give in when it understands the nature of the force field into which it has entered. It often enters in without a serious intent, because it has not analysed the forces involved or the measures that might give it victory – often it just enters on a hope and a prayer. That is a story which is replicated many times, I'm afraid.

Your sketch four global scenarios in your book Crisis Without End? *They all more or less exclude the possibility of large variations from neoliberalism. What about the argument that it is becoming clear to ruling circles that this mode of management is not working, so there will be changes, however delayed?*

I agree that neoliberalism has a whole series of problems which are undermining it. There are all sorts of tensions and contradictions within the neoliberal model of the economy. These are very serious for the future, because the economy has not recovered since the crisis. Interest rates are at zero almost everywhere, and productivity, investment and growth are low. The sense of an impasse is strong. When you see an impasse, you think that something must break and there will be a change. But it is hard to foresee is what sort of change that might be; and an impasse can last a very long time.

The problems are serious. But, for the moment, the second wave, the Eurozone crisis, has been contained. Now we have this third wave, a crisis in the emerging economies. That has checked the growth of some of them, and sent others like Brazil into a serious tailspin. But the process has so far been managed. The question is whether something might blow the whole system to pieces again. A meltdown in China, with its colossal and growing debts, could precipitate a huge shock and further recession. And if another financial shock takes place, all the policy instruments to stabilise the financial system in the advanced capitalist countries have been used up. As HSBC has said, there are "no lifeboats left".

There could be another cataclysm. The difference with 2008 is that then the bulk of decision-makers and financial institutions thought that the whole thing could have a soft landing. This time there are much more widespread fears and analysis of what could go wrong. I don't know if there could be sufficient co-operation to forestall or manage it. The possibility that we are actually reaching the limits of managing these crises could indicate the possibility of another major shock. We don't really know this yet, and it may be that the pressures holding the problems down and managing the situation could continue for some considerable time.

In your book you stressed the power of the G20, and at the time that was reasonable. But now, you have this slump in Brazil and severe problems in China, in Russia, in South Africa. No-one is asking what the G20 will do about those things in the same way that they talked about what the G20 would do about the slump in the USA in 2008. Is the G20 still central?

The G20 is not central. It had a short time in the sun. Substantial effort was put into making it a major world forum for discussing international and financial issues. It did lead to greater co-ordination between central banks and so on, which has led to some changes in regulation. But in every other respect it has failed to develop as a serious forum for discussion, and we have gone back to hearing much more about the G7. It seems to me that the Americans were keen for a while, and now put much less effort into the G20. It has proved not to generate the kind of deals that people thought for a short while might have been possible after the big shock of the financial crash. The G20 is still there, it could be revived, but I do not think that the political will is strong in any G20 country to actually do that. There are parallels with the economic conference in 1933, where a lot of fine words were spoken but very little action resulted, and the world drifted towards trade blocs and protectionism.

In the G20's communiques at the peak of the crisis, the main commitment was not to raise trade barriers. And indeed there was no spiral into protectionism. Aside from that, what did the G20 do? There was some co-ordination between central banks. But in fact the Fed did a lot of that by itself, hoping that Congress wouldn't notice.

That's true of other central banks, too – they tended to operate under the radar. So there is co-operation between central banks which does not seem to have been much facilitated by the G20. And then there was the Toronto G20 summit in June 2010 which called in a much more definite way for the end of fiscal policy and balanced budgets. And from then on, really nothing.

In spite of early talk of about the 2008 crisis damaging the prestige of the US, it seems in fact that the system of US hegemony is kept going by a certain amount of dysfunction. If you have a crisis focused on the US, you need an international effort to sort it out, and that was the role of the G20, as an adjunct to US hegemony.

I think that's right. The US has been so used to setting the rules in the international market order for so long, that for a brief time, the shock of the financial crisis meant that the US started thinking seriously about creating new institutions, it took the G20 and gave it a new status, and it was thinking about ways of getting a more inclusive form of government.

But then the US lost interest for a variety of reasons. It has reverted to a much more traditional model, where the US wants to make as few concessions as possible to rival powers or blocs. Even the idea from the Obama administration that China and others would enjoy bigger voting rights in the IMF was vetoed by Congress. It is still stuck in the Senate. Since the US administration can't get such proposals through Congress, and Congress won't accept anything which it thinks is a dilution of US power in the world, the deadlocks there are really quite severe.

We're now back, really, to a world in which the US is still unilateral in its approach to the world. The US, while still dominant, is not as powerful as it once was: so it's quite a fractious relationship. It's being managed at the moment, but there could be much more serious conflicts ahead, and there are clearly a number of flashpoints, one of which is in the South China Sea. There are security issues, but they are fundamentally linked to economic issues as well and who decides the rules on freedom of the seas and movement of goods and so on. I suspect we are drifting into an era of conflict between the rival powers.

So in terms of your scenarios, we are in scenario number 1 for the near future, but that could move over into scenario 4. But look at Brazil now. The new government is dealing with a huge economic crisis, originating from the dysfunction of the US-centred world system. Its response is to go for more US-friendly policies. Economists say it is likely that Mercosur will be downgraded, in favour of more deals with the US. You have the same trend in Argentina now. The dysfunctions in the US-dominated system seem to be strengthening, rather than weakening, US domination.

The US has always been very adept at divide and rule. It has often succeeded at isolating its enemies. It has also benefited from other dysfunctional aspects of the system. It has always depended on external threats in order to mobilise its population for an internationalist policy, and military policy. The Cold War performed that function. Since the end of the Cold War, there has been something of a lull. But the rise of China in particular, and to a lesser extent the rise of radical Islamist movements in the Middle East, has provided the kind of external threat which has helped the US maintain domestic political support for its role in the international political and economic order.

One of the big uncertainties in all this is Trump. If Hillary Clinton wins the White House, then it's business as usual. US policy won't change very much. But if Donald Trump wins, that could be a huge shock to the way in which the international system works, if he only carries through a small proportion of some of the things he has said. It would rupture a whole part of the American political class. It is set to split Republicans perhaps even more than Democrats. He is not interested in NATO, he is not interested in defending Japan and Korea. The whole carefully-constructed web of relationships and dependencies by which the US has run the international system could be blown away. It is not surprising that Vladimir Putin is a fan of Trump.

On a deeper level, Trump's candidacy indicates is that there is a revival of that very strong sense of US primacy, and also of isolationism and a desire to disentangle from the kind of role that the US has played for the last 60–70 years. That has always been there in American politics, it was present at the birth of the post-war American empire, and it is interesting that it is re-entering the mainstream in the shape of Trump's candidacy.

Part of the US has always been quite unilateral, but it has always been accompanied by a measure of giving concessions and incorporating other countries and managing conflicts and divisions. Most obviously with Marshall Aid straight after the Second World War, but also to a lesser extent since. The US, with its array of international institutions, has always been pretty skilled at that sort of management. That makes it so difficult to crack. And that is why the new government in Brazil, instead of trying to pursue a more radical course and resist the United States, goes the other way. It flees to the "security" of having its policies endorsed by the United States. Whilst Trump might be blocked on much of his domestic agenda, he has a lot of power over things like trade deals. So there would be very big changes.

There is also the possibility that Trump would end up as a "fake-right", an American Ian Paisley.

He might just blink and sell out as soon as he got into the Oval Office. It is possible that most of the promises he has made, he would just not carry out. There is an unpredictability about him. The support base he has created is because of the more outlandish things he has said, like building a wall on the Mexican border. A lot of the American right are worried about Trump because they don't think they can control him. They may be able to control him. But some American conservatives are seriously worried about what a Trump presidency might mean. Some of the foreign policy right, neoconservatives and so forth, are just aghast at some of the things he has been saying and claiming that he will do. I rather suspect he won't actually win, the odds look quite strong against him winning. But who knows? American politics has become a very strange affair.

PART 5

After 2015

INTRODUCTION TO PART 5

Chaotic Regulation

By 2015, the continuing stagnation after 2009 was suggesting a new crash could come even before a sizeable recovery. China, which had powered through the 2008–9 crash by ordering a surge of state-financed investment, showed signs of slowdown and instability. The other so-called "BRICS" economies, other than India, were also in trouble.

Michel Husson investigated the statistics to show that returns on capital had not revived substantially, and investment rates generally remained low. Productivity gains were petering out. The "regulation" of the world economy was more "chaotic" than ever.

Fred Moseley thought debt overhang was still central, but now mostly private corporate debt in the so-called emerging economies. Andrew Kliman restated his thesis of declining profit rates and capitalistically-inadequate destruction of assets, and reckoned that a shift away from neoliberalism was already underway.

Dick Bryan said that the failure, despite predictions, to curb derivatives trading showed how fundamental they had become to the workings of the capitalist economy, reaching right down into individual working-class lives.

Hugo Radice, looking back, said that in 2012 he had "totally underestimated the determination of the Germans to force through their [neoliberal, budget-balancing] policies". Leo Panitch noted that the USA, in a partly hidden way, in an ugly way, had acted as the centre of global capitalism in the crisis: the more grievous the dysfunctions in the US-centred system, at least up to a point, the more the centrality of the USA was reinforced. He warned of the "enormous dangers of ... nationalist and racist movements on the right", though he thought globalised bourgeois interests would be a brake on them.

Simon Mohun, in 2016, still thought he had been right in 2008 to see the end of the neoliberal era; only, the transition would be protracted and complicated.

The concluding discussion with Alfredo Saad-Filho traces issues in how the crisis has played out in the South. He discussed the "ratcheting up, or forward, of neoliberalism" in Latin America, and why the "important gains" of Workers' Party government in Brazil had been so limited and eventually not sustainable.

CHAPTER 25

The Coming Crisis (October 2015)

Michel Husson

While the Eurozone is embarking on a very moderate period of recovery, alarmist predictions are multiplying about the overall trajectory of the world economy: "Chinese growth slows, world economy suffers", was, for example, a headline in *Le Monde* of 20 October 2015. "On the economic front, there is also reason to be concerned" says Christine Lagarde,[1] and Jacques Attali[2] announces that "the world is approaching a great economic catastrophe".

Let us begin with a brief overview: world growth is slowing, mainly in the emerging economies, with the exception of India. This tendency is self-reinforcing, with a fall in prices of raw materials, and it is being transmitted to the advanced countries. International trade is also slowing down, at the same rate as world GDP, as if productive globalisation had reached a ceiling. The Eurozone is registering a very timid and uneven recovery. The USA and the UK are doing relatively well, but growth is tending to slow in the former and appears artificial in the latter. In the "financial sphere", quantitative easing is feeding stock-market bubbles rather than productive investment, which is stagnating. And the mere prospect – held back so far – of a renewed rise in Fed interest rates hangs like the sword of Damocles and is destabilising the currencies and markets of many countries. In short, "Uncertainty, Complex Forces Weigh on Global Growth", to quote the IMF's formula in its latest survey.[3]

From this impressionistic picture, we can draw out three essential characteristics:

- The persistence of "the legacies of the global financial crisis";
- disturbances in the world economy;
- the prospect of "secular stagnation".

* First published in English as: Economie. Les coordonnées de la crise qui vient, *A l'encontre*, 23 October 2015, https://alencontre.org/economie/economie-les-coordonnees-de-la-crise-qui-vient.html First published in English in *Solidarity* 389, 13 January 2016, http://www.workersliberty.org/hussoncqv. Translated by Ed Maltby.

1 Christine Lagarde, "Managing the Transition to a Healthier Global Economy ", September 30, 2015, https://goo.gl/9XGphi.

2 Jacques Attali, "La crise, Acte 2", 17 août 2015, http://goo.gl/69Td7E.

3 IMF, Uncertainty, Complex Forces Weigh on Global Growth, *World Economic Outlook*, October 6, 2015, http://goo.gl/h8Onf9.

The Legacies of the Global Financial Crisis

Quantitative easing means a central bank buying securities. In this way, the bank creates money which, injected into the economy, is supposed to kick-start it. We can even concede that this worked for a time in the USA. Nevertheless, the new fact is that we have begun to see that this course of action has substantial collateral effects. The president of the Federal Bank of Dallas, Richard Fisher (a minority voice in the Fed), summarises his scepticism thus: "the money we have printed has not been as properly circulated as we had hoped. Too much of it has gone toward corrupting or, more appropriately stated, corrosive speculation".[4] In his speech, he went so far as to quote a verse by Jonathan Swift, from 1735: "Money, the life-blood of the nation/ Corrupts and stagnates in the veins,/ Unless a proper circulation/ Its motion and its heat maintains."

The inefficacy so far of monetary policy can be explained by various mechanisms or secondary effects which weigh upon the current conjuncture. To start with, this injection of money is blind and nothing guarantees that the liquidity will be used in a manner that is favourable to investment. On the contrary, it will feed speculation and provoke an increase in asset prices which will benefit only the richest and which will lead to the creation of a bubble.

Historically Low Interest Rates

Quantitative easing simultaneously leads to a reduction in interest rates. This could contribute to re-starting investment in housing and productive investment in general. A recovery in investment is in any case the key issue for an overall recovery. But that recovery has not taken place, because businesses are not investing, for lack of outlets and/or profit. They restore their margins, make money, increase mergers and acquisitions, pay out dividends, but their investment is flatlining.

Over the same period, the injection of money leads to an inflation in financial asset prices, but not to inflation in prices of current goods and services. Low interest rate and weak inflation together mean that real interest rates (discounting inflation) cannot become strongly negative. Nominal interest rates approach what American economists call the ZLB (zero lower

4 Richard Fisher, "Monetary Policy and the Maginot Line", July 16, 2014, http://goo.gl/Y3VbYP.

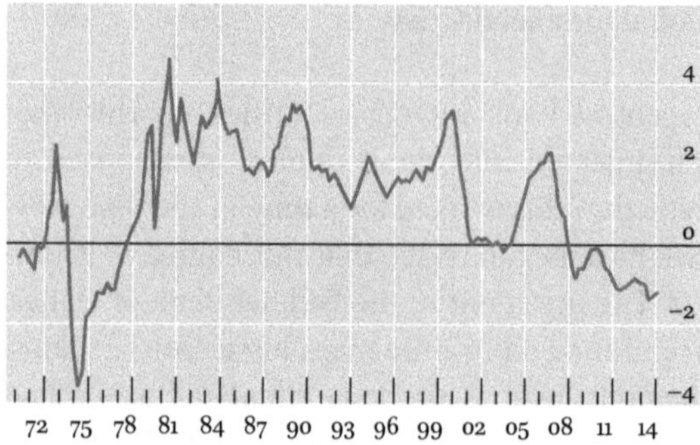

FIGURE 25.1
Central bank official interest rates. Germany, USA, Japan
SOURCE: BIS-BRI[5]

bound). This limit is, for some, like Lawrence Summers,[6] the result of secular stagnation, characterised by high rates of saving, aversion and a weak tendency to invest. To rescue the situation, negative real interest rates would be required to re-launch activity, and they are out of reach. This interpretation is dubious, because it misses out the most structural determinants of possible secular stagnation.[7] Nevertheless, Summers is right on one point when he expresses a fear that "If a recession were to occur, monetary policymakers would lack the tools to respond. There is essentially no room left for [monetary] easing…" The same worry was expressed by Claudio Borio,[8] the economist of the BIS (Bank for International Settlements, headquartered at Basel), when he presented his annual report: "Interest rates have been exceptionally low for an extraordinarily long time. They reflect the central banks' and market participants' response to the unusually weak post-crisis recovery, as if they are fumbling in the dark in search of new certainties." (See also fig 25.1). In other words, we have asked too much of monetary policy for relaunching growth.

Accumulation of Debt

The result is a huge accumulation of private and public debt. According to a study by the McKinsey Global Institute,[9] this debt represents almost 200,000

5 BIS, 85th Annual Report, June 2015, http://goo.gl/oAlIsE.

6 Lawrence Summers, "The global economy is in serious danger", *The Washington Post*, October 7, 2015, http://goo.gl/VQRIt9.

7 Michel Husson, "Stagnation séculaire: le capitalisme embourbé ?" *A l'encontre*, 5 Juin 2015, http://goo.gl/EsqZd3.

8 Claudio Borio, Media briefing on the BIS Annual Report 2015, 24 June 2015, http://goo.gl/WTLDX7.

9 McKinsey Global Institute, Debt and (not much) deleveraging, February 2015, http://goo.gl/vmrYoV.

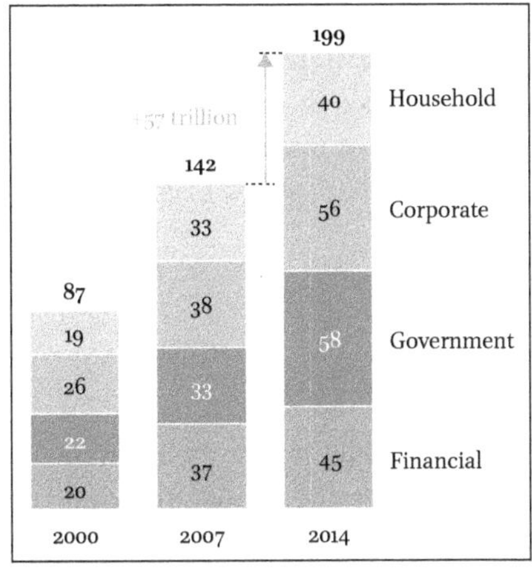

FIGURE 25.2
Global stock of debt
SOURCE: MCKINSEY GLOBAL INSTITUTE

billion dollars at the world level, or 286% of global GDP, up on 269% in 2007, before the crisis struck. The increase is particularly clear for state debt, but also for businesses (fig 25.2).

In particular, the debts of non-financial businesses in emerging economies have quadrupled between 2004 and 2014. The IMF asks itself whether one should worry,[10] and it tells businesses to prepare themselves for the effects of a worsening in financing conditions: "as advanced economies normalize monetary policy, emerging markets should prepare for an increase in corporate failures and, where needed, reform corporate insolvency regimes".

This panorama thus leads us to two scenarios which could unleash the next crisis. The first has been described by François Morin in his latest book.[11] His point of departure is the existence of financial bubbles in public debt, but also on the financial markets which have been doped up by very low interest rates. The trigger element could be the failure of a systemically important bank, with a chain reaction on other big banks.

The second scenario relates to the IMF's worries regarding emerging economies. The trigger here would be an increase in interest rates by the US Federal Reserve Bank and the hardening of conditions for financing business which the IMF refers to. It would lead to a bursting of bubbles, starting with the emerging economies, with repercussions for the rest of global finance.

10 IMF, *Global Financial Stability Report*, October 2015. Chapter 3: "Corporate leverage in emerging markets – a concern?" http://goo.gl/zpkcAF v.

11 François Morin, *L'hydre mondiale: l'oligopole bancaire*, Lux, 2015, https://goo.gl/3k5GW4; see also this video by the author: https://goo.gl/qGFdx8.

In summary, the risk factors focus around this contradiction: on the one hand, quantitative easing policies are not getting any traction on the real economy, are feeding bubbles and have set world finance on a course which cannot continue indefinitely. But an increase in interest rates would provoke an uncontrollable bursting of bubbles, in a context where states have almost no ammunition left to save the banks again.

In Defence of Fictitious Capital

Christine Lagarde is therefore right to speak of "sequels to the global financial crisis". More precisely, the overall picture is as follows: the period preceding the crisis was characterised by an enormous accumulation of fictitious capital, in other words, of drawing rights on future surplus value to be produced by the exploitation of wage labour. For capitalism to start anew on a healthy basis, it would have been necessary to destroy this fictitious capital (and surely also a part of the productive capital). There have been losses, but around the world policies were guided by an essential principle: preserve the fictitious capital and the drawing rights that it represents. That was done in two ways: on the one hand, by converting private debts into public debts and, through austerity measures, drawing on surplus value; on the other hand, by massive injections of liquidity. In the first instance, we can say that capitalism respected the law of value, because it tried to adjust the ratio of fictitious capital/surplus value by increasing surplus value. In the second instance, on the contrary, it tried to deny or subvert the law of value by acting on the numerator. At the most fundamental level, the next crisis could be interpreted as being a severe reassertion of the law of value.

Even if it gives priority to austerity via "structural reforms", capitalist Europe is turning, rather tardily, towards artificial solutions. There is quantitative easing à la Juncker, which is tottering just as much as in the USA. But there is better: the latest big idea of the European Commission is to launch an "Securitisation Initiative"[12] which will be a part of a broader "Capital Markets Union" project. Under the cover of regulation, the real objective is to restart securitisation markets, but this time "safely", to thus obtain "over €100bn of additional funding", or "half of pre-crisis levels".[13] It should be recalled that this objective was also that of the IMF in... October 2009, when it tried to "discern

12 European Commission, "Securitisation initiative", September 2015, http://goo.gl/Uurqih.

13 European Commission, "Capital Markets Union", flyer, September 2015, http://goo.gl/iv7q1z.

how securitisation can positively contribute to financial stability and sustainable economic growth."[14] Here is a striking example of systematic will to favour the rise of fictitious capital.

Before the crisis, the world economy was structured around a China-US axis, often called "Chinamerica".[15] This axis is starting to disintegrated, and without a doubt that is one of the key elements of the remodelling of the global economy.

The End of "Chinamerica"

The disintegration is symmetrical: on the one hand, the American model is departing from its pre-crisis operation – growth on credit – because of a renewed increase in the rate of saving and a reduced dependence on energy imports. These two factors reduce the motor role in the global economy which the USA had previously played. China is currently in a transition phase, fraught and difficult to be sure, towards a model centred on domestic demand. It is clearly moving away in any case from export-based growth: exports' portion of Chinese GDP went from 36% in 2006 to 26% today. The complementarity between the two biggest economies is declining and this move, with its collateral effects on emerging economies and Europe, is unbalancing the whole world economy.

This reorientation of the Chinese economy is manifested by a change in the structure of its external trade,[16] but also contributes to a slowdown in world trade. It is another subject of worry for economists, who puzzle about the causes and wonder if this is an ephemeral phenomenon or something more structural. All the evidence is that we are seeing a lasting change of trends[17] which corresponds to a slowdown in the splitting-up of value chains. The organisation of production across two different zones of the global economy characteristic of contemporary globalisation is reaching its limits, and, with it, the faster growth of global trade than of world GDP which it drove. This phenomenon is particularly marked with regard to China, but also the USA,

14 IMF, *Global Financial Stability Report*, October 2009. Chapter 2: "Restarting Securitization Markets: Policy Proposals and Pitfalls", http://goo.gl/PM1nPY.

15 Michel Husson, "Chine-USA. Les lendemains incertains de la crise", *Nouveaux Cahiers Socialistes* n°2, Montréal, septembre 2009, http://goo.gl/OQEB84; "Etats-Unis: la fin d'un modèle", *La Brèche* n°3, 2008, http://goo.gl/lNJqYl.

16 Michel Husson, "La fin de l'émergence du Sud ?" *A l'encontre*, 22 mars 2015, http://goo.gl/gCYkZY.

17 Sébastien Jean, "Le ralentissement du commerce mondial annonce un changement de tendance", *La lettre du Cepii* n° 356, Septembre 2015, http://goo.gl/YgLZ3G.

Korea and Japan, which confirms that the China-USA axis is in the process of coming apart.

Desynchronisation and Volatility

The instability of the global economy is also aggravated by desynchronisation between the USA and the Eurozone. A detailed study by the IMF[18] shows that these divergences have substantial collateral effects (spillovers). The authors show their worries by asking "whether liftoff in the US may not only strengthen the dollar vis-à-vis the euro, but also push interest rates up in the euro area, or whether QE in the euro area may not only weaken the euro, but also continue putting downward pressure on US yields".

The same document has an interesting insight into the emerging economies. Its authors distinguish two transmission channels. The "traditional" channel is that capital goes towards the zone which is enjoying renewed growth (the USA or the Eurozone), with a resulting appreciation in the value of the currency in the zone enjoying this influx of capital. But they identify another channel, the "risk-appetite channel": capital anticipates a recovery in the emerging economies driven by the recovery in the "centre" zone. This influx of capital into the emerging economies leads to an appreciation in the value of their currency. These analyses show that the functioning of the world economy is eluding regulation, and that the emerging economies are exposed to movements of capital which have destabilising effects, whether entering or leaving. The recent period has been characterised precisely by an increased volatility of those movements of capital.

The Exhaustion of Productivity Gains

Presenting the latest projections by the OECD, its chief economist Catherine Mann stressed that "the potential growth slowdown in advanced countries is an ongoing concern".[19] And Christine Lagarde, for the IMF, evoked the "new mediocre", in other words "the risk of low growth for a long time" which, according to her, "looms closer".

---

18 "Big Players Out of Synch: Spillovers Implications of US and Euro Area Shocks", IMF Working Paper, September 2015, http://goo.gl/Jdxawt.

19 Catherine Mann, "Puzzles and uncertainties", OECD Interim Economic Outlook, September 2015, http://goo.gl/Bx2GwM.

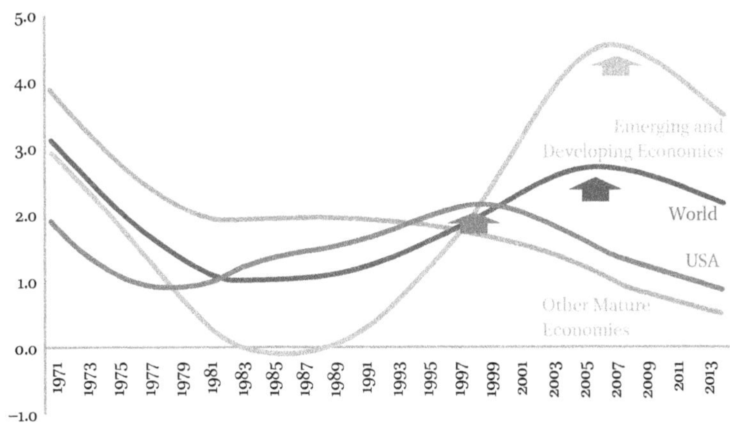

FIGURE 25.3 *Tendencies in growth of labour productivity*
SOURCE: THE CONFERENCE BOARD "PRODUCTIVITY BRIEF 2015", HTTP://GOO.GL/HHQKNB

Underlying this configuration, there is the exhaustion of gains in productivity. This tendency is not new, as it was set in motion in the developed countries from the start of the 1980s, with strong fluctuations in the case of the USA. But, in the end, the emerging economies took up the baton and the productivity gains they made could in large part be captured by the "old" capitalist countries. At the start of the crisis, the emerging economies kept up world growth. But the great dislocation in the world economy could have reached an inflection point: the most recent data from the Conference Board show that growth in hourly labour productivity has clearly fallen in the emerging economies since the start of the crisis (fig 25.3).

However, productivity, and more directly global factor productivity, is an essential element in the dynamic of the rate of profit. That rate has been restored in the major capitalist countries, in spite of the exhaustion of productivity.[20] This achievement was only made possibly by a whole series of initiatives: financialisation, growth in indebtedness, inequality, fall in wage share, etc. At the same time, the drying-up of profitable investment opportunities leads to a stagnation in productive investment rates.

20 Michel Husson, "Les limites du keynésianisme", *A l'encontre*, 15 Janvier 2015, http://goo.gl/KNwrjV.

The Rate of Profit in Disorder

There is no alternative for capitalism, other than getting the neoliberal model back on track, while trying to reduce destabilising factors. In this quest for a way out of the crisis, the key question is clearly the restoration of the rate of profit, which can only be achieved in the first instance by an increase in the rate of exploitation. However, a striking fact is the disparity of performances. Among the advanced countries, we can see differentiation in rates of profit, in the first place between the USA and the Eurozone, and then again within the latter (Figure 25.4). This phenomenon implies a sharpening of competition between multinationals, which would tend to lead to a general downturn in the rate of profit. This is, in any case, the finding announced by the McKinsey Institute[21] which foresees that global corporate profit should move from 9.8% of GDP in 2013 to 7.9% in 2025, more or less back to its 1980 level.

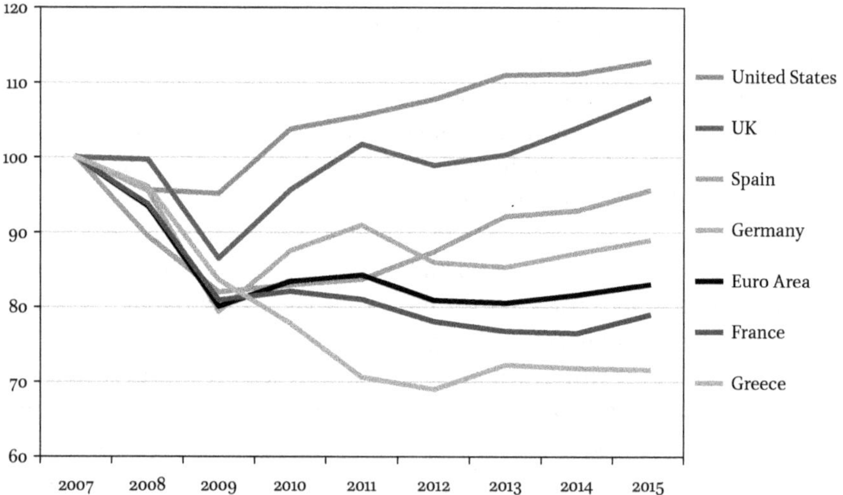

FIGURE 25.4 *Rate of profit, 2007–2015*
Note: Base 100 in 2007
SOURCE: AMECO, "NET RETURNS ON NET CAPITAL STOCK: TOTAL ECONOMY"

21 McKinsey Global Institute, *The new global competition for corporate profits*, September 2015, http://goo.gl/zyvgy9.

No Profit, No Recovery

This divergence can be illustrated by means of a more detailed analysis of the conjuncture within the Eurozone. The exercise has been undertaken recently by the European Commission:[22] it compares the timid current "recovery" with others. The results of this study are illustrated by Figures 25.5 and 25.6 which compares the cycle 2002–2015 with the previous (1986–1999). In the two cases, the reference year is the year preceding the lowest point (respectively 1992 and 2008). Two key variables in the dynamic of capitalism are examined: investment and wage share. The profile is comparable in terms of the phase in the cycle preceding the recession. But what happens next tells two very different stories.

After the 1993 recession, investment fell, but revived progressively and after six years regained its pre-crisis level. The wage share, which had risen slightly from its 1989 low point, returned to its inexorable downward tendency and fell by almost 4% of GDP between 1992 and 1999. It was a good way out of the crisis for capitalism, with an improvement in profitability and a recovery in accumulation.

But what has happened after the latest crisis is not a classic cycle. Wage share increased strongly in 2009, then fell, but now it has stabilised at 2% of GDP higher than its pre-crisis level. In other words, the return on capital has

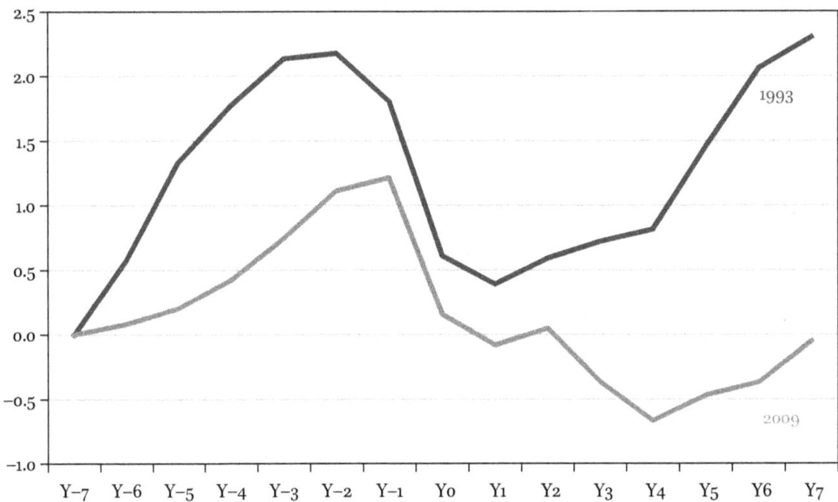

FIGURE 25.5 *Two episodes of recession in the Eurozone: Investment*

22 "The euro area recovery in perspective", European Commission, Quarterly Report on the Euro Area, n°3, 2015, http://goo.gl/uyggrk.

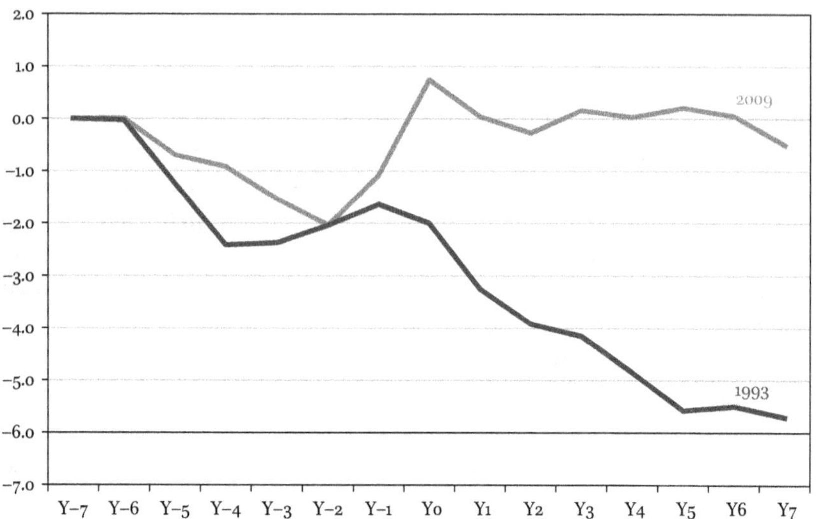

FIGURE 25.6 *Two episodes of recession in the Eurozone: Wage share*

not revived. And we see the effects on investment: it started to revive in 2011, following the pattern of the previous recession. Then the sharpening of austerity policies created a double dip in growth and investment fell again before starting to recover from 2014. Today it remains more than 1.5% of GDP lower than its pre-crisis level.

Financial Causes and Real Effects

Understanding how finance and production interact is an essential but difficult task. A recent study by BIS economists[23] sheds some light on this question by proposing a model which links "financial causes" to their "real consequences". The authors construct an index measuring the contribution of labour reallocation across sectors to aggregate productivity growth. Then they show that this index is significantly correlated (negatively) to financial booms. In other words, when credit grows faster than GDP, employment moves to sectors with lower productivity. They also show that the value of this index before the financial crisis determines the subsequent trajectory of productivity. And this mechanism is self-perpetuating, because the recourse to credit feeds what it

23 Claudio Borio et al., "Labour Reallocation and Productivity Dynamics: Financial Causes, Real Consequences", BIS, May 2015, http://goo.gl/my4uZN.

is supposed to compensate for, i.e. the slowdown in productivity. This modelling of links between productive efficiency and financial movements seems particularly pertinent to an analysis of the Eurozone.

The Coming Crisis?

One conclusion follows from this (too) swift review: the "great recession" has opened a period of "chaotic regulation" at the global level. A new crisis seems today to be more or less inevitable. It is difficult to tell where the point of rupture will be (stock exchange, bank, debt, exchange rate?), but this episode will in any case be evidence of deep structural contradictions. Global capitalism is currently subject to a fundamental tension. On the one hand, the crisis which opened in 2008 was dealt with according to two essential principles: don't clear the accounts (the "legacies"); reconstitute the pre-crisis neoliberal model, while seeking to control the most deleterious effects. In practice, this means guaranteeing the rights to draw on future surplus value acquired by the "1%" and the freedom of action of the banks and the multinationals. But the fundamental mainspring of capitalism's dynamism, that is, productivity gains, is currently heading towards exhaustion. This configuration leads to complex interactions between changes within the productive sphere and the manipulation of financial and monetary instruments. This is why, as in 2007–2008, the precise location of the trigger for the next crisis will not provide an adequate explanation of the deeper causes.

CHAPTER 26

Too Much Debt in Relation to Income (January 2016)

Discussion with Fred Moseley

Your article "From a profitability crisis..." [Moseley 2013] does not, if I understand it right, argue that the crisis around 2008 arose from low profit rates, but rather that the capitalist drive to redress profits led to an explosion of household debt which eventually proved unsustainable and triggered crisis. But isn't there evidence that increased household debt did not, on balance, increase consumer demand as it was reputed to do?

I am not familiar with this evidence. I think that during the bubble household debt mainly boosted buying houses and residential construction, which is counted in the national statistics as investment, rather than consumption. And intuitively I find it hard to believe that household debt did not increase consumer spending to some extent. There were lots of second mortgages that were used to purchase something. And even if the surge of household debt did not increase consumption that much, it certainly added to the fragility of the economy and when the debt bubble burst it was the major factor in bringing on the financial crisis and the Great Recession. The housing construction industry was the biggest bubble before the crisis and it declined the most during the crisis.

Increases in debt are always likely to create fragility, because they create streams of payment obligations before the revenues from which payments can be made. But is there in fact a definite ceiling above which household debt becomes unsustainable? What is it?

It is hard to be very precise about what the ceiling for household debt might be, especially since triple-digit household debt ratios are a new phenomenon. In the US, the ratio of household debt to household disposable income was about 40% in 1950, 80% in 1980, and 130% in 2007! For comparison, this ratio

* Previously published at: https://senseofgfc.wordpress.com/2016/02/17/fred-moseley-26-january-2016/, 17 February 2016.

was 30% in 1929. Some research has suggested that the sustainable ceiling for this household debt ratio might be around 100%. Since 2007, this household debt ratio has come down a bit – to around 115% – and is more sustainable now than in 2007, primarily because interest rates are so low. But this debt ratio is still very high and above the 100% "danger zone"; and if interest rates increase in the months ahead, then the household debt burden would be less sustainable.

What do you think are the main problems in the world economy today?

The main problem in the world economy today is the debt of "emerging market" economies, especially China, and also a number of other countries, especially in Latin America. The debt of emerging market economies has doubled since 2007! And this debt is primarily private corporate debt (instead of government debt as in the "third world debt crisis" of the 1980s), which makes defaults and bankruptcies more likely and the effects on the world economy more costly. And much of this debt is in dollars, made possible by the Fed's super-expansionary monetary policy. Which means that the ongoing devaluation of the currencies of emerging market will increase their debt burdens in their own currencies and will make bankruptcies all the more likely. Emerging market debt will be the sub-prime mortgages on the next crisis.

Are you predicting another crisis?

I think the current situation in the world economy is very precarious and becoming increasingly so. The last crisis was caused by too much debt in relation to income, but since the crisis overall debt has continued to increase faster than income. These trends cannot go on forever and probably cannot go on much longer. And this time around, there will not be much the Fed and other central banks can do, since interest rates are already near zero. At some point, it seems very likely that the whole big global debt bubble will burst and bring on an even worse and longer-lasting crisis.

In December 2009 you said: "the dominance of the US free-market style of capitalism has taken a serious blow, and will no longer be regarded around the world as the ideal to which all other countries aspire or are pushed". It seems the dominance has recovered from that blow. The Heritage Foundation, which promotes and measures adherence to that free-market style, reported in its 2015 Index of Economic Freedom "a third annual global increase... a 2.8-point overall improvement since the inception of the Index in 1995". Why has that neoliberal dominance proved so robust?

Yes, neoliberalism has rebounded, using the crisis to force more business friendly policies (e.g. Greece). There has been some resistance to neoliberalism and austerity, but unfortunately not enough. But neoliberalism hasn't solved the fundamental problem of unsustainable debt – in fact that problem is worse today than in 2007 – and its day of reckoning is nigh. We'll see if neoliberalism survives the next crisis.

CHAPTER 27

The Situation Has Long Been Unsustainable (January 2016)

Discussion with Andrew Kliman

In 2008 you described the crisis as the bursting of a debt bubble. So what made the build-up of debt unsustainable at that moment?

I think that the situation had become unsustainable long before. The Federal Reserve managed to kick the can down the road for several years. When the dotcom bubble of the 1990s burst in 2000, by 2001 the situation was pretty desperate in the judgement of the Fed – if you can read the Fed's actions and policy statements. That seems a bit of an overreaction, but they did a lot of stuff to kick the can down the road, to reinflate the economy, so to speak, to create new bubbles. For instance, from the middle of 2002 to the end of 2005, short-term inter-bank interest rates were negative in real terms. That means that banks were borrowing and paying back less than they had borrowed after inflation had been taken into account. That's an unusual situation, although we've seen that for the last seven years now. They're doing it again.

That easy-money situation and lax regulation led to the home price bubble, but there was also a new bubble in shares, in equities in the stock market, and in commercial real estate. They were all really frothy at that time. The situation eventually burst because these bubbles were more widespread, in more markets, and they were in a market that had a really big effect: the real-estate market. Through the securitisation of mortgage loans, the packaging them as mortgage-backed securities, this risk spread throughout the world and every sector.

So this ballooning of debt, risk and so on only needed some small disturbance somewhere to throw it off?

I share the view of those who think it was a kind of perfect storm. To have a downturn of that magnitude – and it would have been orders of magnitude worse if we had had a laissez-faire policy like the USA had when the Great Depression hit in 1929, so it was a very, very serious situation – in order to have a

* Previously published at: https://senseofgfc.wordpress.com/2016/02/17/andrew-kliman-january-2016/, 17 February 2016.

downturn of that magnitude, a number of things had to go wrong all at once, and they pretty much did. There were various things that could have prevented it. If, for instance, the credit-ratings agencies had not been so disastrously wrong in their risk assessments – the risk of losing money on your mortgage-backed securities and collateralised debt obligations and so on. What are, in retrospect, better assessments of the risk might have prevented the thing from blowing up so disastrously. A lot of things had to go wrong to produce a crash of that magnitude.

But that's not the issue of sustainability, really. You can have a situation that's not good, and you're limping along, like they had for several years before then. That shows that the situation isn't sustainable as well. So you can't really predict that there's going to be a massive meltdown, but there are warning signs that the state of the economy isn't healthy. That had been building up for a long time. That's not just my view, it's the whole strain of mainstream economic thinking that goes by the name of "secular stagnation" now – Larry Summers, Paul Krugman, Martin Wolf, there are people who kind of share this assessment out there.

The backdrop in this view is the long-term decline in the rate of profit. You say that there are background trends, endemic to capitalism, which cause this, but specifically that there had not been a major purging of value from the system, no real bust in the 1970s and 1980s. But there's a problem at first sight. If you look at the 1930s – River Rouge lays off lots of workers for long periods, but is never shut down. But you've had whole industries scrapped in a number of countries since the early 1980s – whole industrial areas just stripped. By what measure is that an inadequate purging of value?

What is adequate depends on the effect that it has in clearing out the deadwood, so to speak. That makes it seem tautological, but it really isn't, because there are things that destruction of capital-value does to restore the health of the economy. And that can be elucidated and discussed. When we talk about the destruction of capital value, we're not only talking about production and real values as opposed to fictitious values, or the valuation of assets. It's principally the valuation of assets that's at issue. For instance, if you look at the period 1929–1932 in the USA, the Dow Jones Index fell by 89%. So a security that was worth $100 at the peak was worth $11 at the low point. We didn't have anything of that magnitude. We didn't have a wave of bankruptcies and bad debt write-offs in the way it seems we had it in the Great Depression (although the data are not that clear for way back then).

For all you can say about the recent crisis – the financial crisis that triggered the Great Recession, all the banking problems – the US government came in with TARP and prevented the collapse of almost all of the banking system. That didn't happen in the 1930s. There was a big, big collapse of the banking system.

I'm looking at the graph for the Dow Jones. You're quite right: it goes down very rapidly after 1929. But by the mid-1930s, it has risen again – not quite to the 1929 level, but certainly to the late-1920s level. It remains about that for a while, and then goes up again until the early 1960s. So, if you have a fall in share prices which is then redressed within a couple of years, is that really a purging of value?

Yeah, I think it was. The period from 1929 to 1932 or 1933 was a massive shake-out of the US economy. It was extremely wrenching. What happened thereafter is a measure of how effective that destruction of capital-value was. There are reasons why the US economy and the world economy didn't fully recover after the Great Depression – other things are needed besides the destruction of capital-value – but the "liquidation" was massive, and massive enough that the stage was set for a recovery after 1934 or so.

Now, the other thing you mention is that the technological revolution seems to be a cause of the relative stagnation of the economy during the last several decades because of faster moral depreciation. But that runs directly counter to another narrative in economic thought, which says that booms are associated with waves of technical innovation and that slumps are associated with a slower rate of technical innovation. Would you say that high technical innovation is correlated with depressions?

No, I wouldn't say that; and I don't think what I'm saying "runs counter." What you call an association… you're absolutely right: booms are associated with a lot of adoption of new technology. But that begs the question of what's the cause and what's the effect. I think the cause is this: these new techniques have been designed, there are prototypes, everything is waiting to go, but when the economy is in a slump, you won't get a lot of investment or actual adoption of the new techniques. Then the economy goes into a new boom, and you get a lot of investment, but you're not just getting more investment in the same technology. You're getting the new technologies. So when the boom comes along, yeah: you get a wave of adoption of new techniques, and that eventually runs its course. And the boom eventually runs its course as well.

So you will, then, see this pattern of booms and rapid technological advance, and then a slowing of the boom, maybe downturns, and an end to the wave of technological advance. That's all true. What I don't think is true that technological advance creates a boom; I don't think the causation is ….

Booms are more likely to create technological advance than depressions.

Absolutely.

However, the technical advance in its turn, by increasing the rate of moral depreciation, is likely to cause depression. So the boom causes technical advance, which causes...

I wouldn't say it causes depressions. It tends to depress the rate of profit, and that tends to lead to slower growth, less investment, more instability, and then you need all kinds of financial factors and so forth to get a depression in addition to that. After the interview you conducted with me in 2008, I went and researched this question and I found that the increase in depreciation of US corporations was due to great investment in information technology. That led to a situation where between 1990 and 2009, on average 27% of potential after-tax profit was lost because of that rise in obsolescence or moral depreciation. That's a big effect. More than one quarter of all potential profit just vanished because... you've got software for three years, then it's not worth anything. You've got some computer hardware, it's not worth anything after 7 or 8 years, and after three years, more than half its value is gone. That had a big effect; depreciation is an expense. It's a deduction from profit.

That makes sense. Another thing you said back in 2008 was that for a while we were not going to see anybody attempting trying to return to the free market or so-called neoliberal policies. Discussing with you by email, I cited the global Index of Economic Freedom figure from the Heritage Foundation as showing an increase (i.e. more neoliberalism) in recent years. You said that for individual counties, the major countries, it shows the opposite trends. But for 2015, the general picture is not very much movement at all, Germany is up .4, the UK is up .9, the US is up .7 ...

From the previous year?

The previous year, yes. Since 1995, the general picture is not a lot of movement at all, but in Germany you see quite a clear rise; in the US you see a drop, on their criteria, in about in 2009–2010, and then it evens out again. And just descriptively, plainly it seems to me that there is more privatisation, more marketisation, more social cuts, and in the European Union since 2009–2010, you have the German government pushing these balanced-budget constitutional amendments (with all sorts of loopholes in them). In Britain, we've had Osborne's Fiscal Charter, which is, again, balanced-budget legislation. So in some ways neoliberalism has been sharpened, rather than retreated from.

First of all, I can't comment on your new discussion of the Heritage Foundation numbers. I have to look at them. As you mentioned, I did comment on your original discussion of the Heritage Foundation numbers for the Index of Economic Freedom. The headline number is a simple average of all of the 150 or so countries. That's not real relevant to my point that we're not going to have a return to free market or so-called neoliberal policies; I was talking about the advanced countries. The headline number is being influenced by really tiny economies.

I looked at the five biggest economies, the 10 biggest economies, the 15 biggest economies, in terms of GDP. I don't think the year-on-year figures are real helpful if we want to talk about trends. It seems to me more helpful to go back to 2007, before the Great Recession, and compare that to 2015. And what I found was, according to the Heritage Foundation, there was less economic freedom in 2015, compared to 2007, in four of the five largest economies, in eight of the top ten economies and in 11 of the top 15. And generally where you had any improvement, it was negligible, and where you had declines, it was pretty substantial. For instance, in the top 10 economies, there was improvement in Germany and Canada, and decline everywhere else. The improvement in Germany and Canada was 0.3 points in both cases. But in the US, there was a fall of 5.8 points; in the UK, 5.7 points. So just looking at the Heritage Index, which I don't think is exactly what we want to look at, my reading is that the general trend is away from free-market policies.

If you look at the broader issues ... I don't think that year-on-year figures are real helpful. As an economy improves, and there has been short-term improvement in these economies, that's what we should expect – a partial return to the status quo ante. In the depths of the crisis, you're going to see more regulation, more of a heavy hand of government – and that's what we saw – and then some freeing up. But I think it's got to be viewed as only partial in most of these cases.

The major exception is Germany. But if you look at the role of Germany in the Eurozone, especially vis-a-vis Greece, I think it would be a travesty to call those free-market policies. What you had is one national government with very strong influence over the whole Eurozone, basically saying, "here's the way it's going to be", and enforcing that on Greece. So here you have one national economy being totally controlled by a foreign government. What kind of free market is that?

I suppose one answer is, it is an imposed free market – the German government and its allies say to Greece "you've got to sell off your ports, and airports, and so on." It's imposed, but what they're doing is opening up more areas to freer operation of market forces. That it is forced tells you that the free market isn't freedom, and it is not something that happens naturally without governments doing anything.

I think that's an oxymoron, to have an "imposed free" market. That is probably the source of our disagreement. I think there is a tendency on the left to view any pro-capital policies as if they were free-market policies, and I think that's just not the case. So I think we have a very different understanding of "the free market" underlying this. I use the term in a more literal way than I think you're using it.

Well, how would you characterise the dominant direction of capitalist government economic policy in the period we're living through, which is still a period marked by the crash of 2008? It's a period of very limited recovery, even in the US and much more limited in Europe and in a lot of other parts of the world. It wasn't classically free-market even before. But if you can take "neoliberalism" just as a common-sense description of the policies before, how would you describe the policies now?

It obviously depends a lot on the specific country. Germany has pursued one policy at home and a different policy vis-a-vis the rest of the Eurozone. The UK has practiced austerity. In the United States, we haven't had austerity at all. We've had very wild expansionary fiscal and monetary policies. There's been a humongous increase in federal government debt, on the order of 105% since the end of 2007. You've had god-knows-how-many years of quantitative easing and ridiculously low interbank interest rates, the federal fund rate – it's been negative in real terms. So the banks are borrowing and paying back less than they borrowed. This has been going on year on year, and it's all been engineered by the Fed.

For instance, when I talk about these budget deficits and so on... there are these programs are supposed to be self-financing, like Social Security, and Medicare (the healthcare system for retirees). They've been running big deficits for years now. The funds that are coming in are not paying their way; the government is covering that. For a couple of years, 2011–12, they reduced the Social Security tax on people's earnings. Instead of 6.2% we paid 4.2%. Almost a third was forgiven and the government made that up. Lots of heavy intervention there, and not all of it can be said to be just for the benefit of the banks and so on. The government picked up a third of our social security tax.

So how would I characterise it? The things going on in the UK, Germany, the US are really different. It is hard to characterise the total picture. But I would say that in each case there are pragmatic considerations, conjunctural, contingent considerations, that are dictating policy, and the goals are to keep the system and in particular the national capital afloat and to try to make it as healthy as possible. These are definitely pro-capitalist policies, but they are not ideologically driven, as far as I can see, in terms of market vs. state. They seem to be all doing what you would expect given their particular situations... with the exception of the UK, where the degree of austerity, I think, is hard to understand. Either it was a profound miscalculation, or some ideological cranks just got control of things. It was clear ahead of time that it was going to have the disastrous effects that it had. Everybody knows that. You don't have to be a Keynesian economist, you barely have to be able to breathe, to know that was going to happen. So that one is very hard to explain.

Not only did they do it, they got away with it, they got re-elected, they are doing more of the same now, and on the way a lot of the critical voices actually went quiet. In 2010, Ed Balls, the then-Shadow Chancellor, was denouncing the whole policy straight off. A few years later he's saying, "well, we don't need as cuts as big as this, it is being done badly: but we do have to sort out the deficit". That represented a fairly wide consensus in a whole section of the capitalist class saying, "it is worth having further depression for the sake of the longer-term advantages in class relations, which follow from using the opportunity of this crisis to impose these social cuts, to marketise things further". What they've done to the health service is not "the free market", but they are introducing a great number of market forces into it. Like what they've done to the school system. Nearly half of all state schools in England are now directly funded from the government. So basically, their financial subsistence is dependent upon begging for funds for different things. So, it's not quite a market system, but it is drastically different to how it was where elected local authorities managed schools in their areas. It's not just cranks – they've built a ruling-class consensus around it.

Private versus state is one set of issues, but it is different from austerity. You can have a largely-privately-run but largely-state-financed educational system. And it can be rather expensive. And I don't think it's contrary to the interests of British capital to do what it's doing, because it's a relatively small economy and an open economy. It has to be competitive; it's not shielded from competitive forces to the degree that, say, the US economy is. The problem is that when you're in the doldrums, like the UK economy is, that is not the time to be implementing that kind of a policy, and everybody knows it. You want to stabilise the economy, do more along the lines of what the US is doing, even if in the end, you know you can't ultimately afford it and run an economy permanently on that basis. That is what seems to be so shockingly stupid about what they've done in the UK economy. It doesn't seem to me to be laying a foundation for the future.

You might want to say that they're trying to establish certain markers – make changes that aren't going to be rolled back, change the nature of the economy, have less regulation, less state, and so forth. The problem is that it's a very dangerous thing, if it's intentional. The economy could just collapse. I don't think it's going to collapse, but what happens if the UK has what they've had in Japan for 20–25 years? Is that good? I don't think that's in the interests of British capital, frankly.

Should we move onto the estimation of the rate of profit, and historical cost and replacement cost? Firstly, if you do it in replacement cost, that gives you a measure of proportionate self-expansion on an ongoing basis, as you replace things cumulatively, rather than a more static historical accounting as if capitalist enterprise were a one-off thing. Secondly, historical-cost accounting will mean that your reported rate of profit will always tend to decline when inflation slows down, whatever is happening in production. The third thing is: generally capitalist planners don't look at global rates of profit. They look at expected rates of profit on projects, which they calculate in terms of net present value, or internal rate of return, or some algorithm like that. When they do that, either they estimate future revenues in real terms, and assume no inflation because it's too complicated to take account of, or they deflate them by an assumed interest rate, an assumed rate of inflation. Either they assume replacement costs are the same as historic costs because it's too complicated to take account of shifts in prices, or they make a rule-of-thumb adjustment for that. Those are three several slightly different questions, all about the replacement cost versus historic cost measure.

I don't agree with your characterisation of what you get when you try to measure the rate of profit using replacement costs. First of all, the measurement of the capital stock, or fixed assets, at replacement cost is completely legitimate; it has many important uses. I have no beef with it. What we're dealing with here, however, is the rate of profit. It's not even mis-measuring or misestimating the rate of profit to look at profit as a percentage of what it would cost to replace all of your capital stock. That is just not a rate of profit. It's a misuse of the term "rate of profit". A rate of profit is a rate of return on investment. It's the profit you get out compared to an earlier sum of money that you advanced or invested.

I want to read something from Marx's *Capital*, volume 1 Chapter 4, page 251 of the Penguin edition. He's defining surplus-value. He says, "*more money is finally withdrawn from circulation than was thrown into it at the beginning...* This increment or excess over the original value I call surplus-value" [Kliman's emphasis]. He also calls it profit. It's not even a question of the rate of profit. Is that what you mean by "profit" – the amount you are getting out, compared to what you originally invested or advanced? That is the crucial issue. When you look at profit in comparison with what it would cost today to replace all of your fixed capital – that you have no intention of replacing, because it consists of a bunch of typewriters, and you're now using personal computers – it's just not a rate of profit.

On net present value and internal rate of return: yes, when companies invest, they are forward looking; they look at the cost of their capital today. But they look at their future returns. The so-called "replacement cost rate of profit" is not that at all. It's not a proxy for, and it's not at all identical with, net present value or internal rate of return calculations. Those calculations compare future returns, based on future prices, with the cost of the capital today. It's a comparison of future prices and the cost of capital today, based on today's prices. That's my conception of a rate of profit: returns based on prices of one time compared to investment based on prices of an earlier time.

What the so-called replacement-cost or current-cost "rate of profit" does is compare the profits based on prices of today, with the cost of capital based on prices of today. That just does not make any sense. For instance, we know that, measured in terms of speed or storage capacity, computer prices fall maybe 30–50% year on year. So imagine you've got a firm that makes computer stuff. They invest in computer stuff to make some computer stuff. It would be crazy for them to say, "we're buying this computer and it's worth 10,000 and we're going to make two computers in a year and they'll be 10,000 each. The price per computer will be constant at 10,000". That's nuts. You've got to say, "we're buying this for 10,000, and this will generate two computers, and maybe they're going to be worth 6,000 each, not 10,000 each". You always have to look at the prices of one time and the prices of another time. And that's what the replacement-cost calculation does not do, and it does not give you a measure of a return on an actual investment.

Now the issue of inflation that you've mentioned is a very important issue. In my book, *The Failure of Capitalist Production,* I did an adjustment for inflation; I computed an historical-cost rate of profit adjusted for inflation, using a conventional measure of inflation (I think it was the GDP price index) for the US. And it gives you a completely different result – completely different results – from the so-called "replacement-cost rate of profit". So the replacement-cost rate of profit is not a proxy for an inflation-adjusted rate of profit, either, for various technical reasons.

On the other hand, there are reasons why one might want to look at – and for certain purposes should look at, also or instead – a rate of profit that's not adjusted for inflation. For some questions, you adjust, for others, you don't. When you want to look at the indebtedness of companies, and most corporations are net debtors, they owe more than they own, inflation matters. Let's say you have $10.5 million debt payable this year, and without inflation, you have $10 million in profit. You can't cover your debt; you go bankrupt. But if there's

10% inflation, you get $11 million in profit, you can cover your debt; you can stay afloat for a while. Debts are denominated in nominal terms, so there is some value in looking at nominal rates of return.

Once you think about it like that, it makes perfect sense: the higher the prices you get, the more profit you get. You can call that inflation, but you're getting higher prices. Inflation is pumping up the prices, so it's pushing up the rate of profit. That is to be expected. All that means is: the rate of profit is not the only measure of the health of capital. You have to look at a total situation. You might want to look at a post-inflation rate of profit. For some purposes, you want to look at a pre-inflation, unadjusted rate of profit.

But you certainly don't want to take profit based on prices of today and compare it to the cost of your capital stock based on prices of today, because that's not any measure of the rate of profit. Nobuo Okishio was the founder of the Okishio Theorem, which supposedly disproved Marx's law of the tendential fall in the rate of profit. That theorem is based on this alleged rate of profit, the "replacement-cost rate of profit". In probably the last thing he wrote before he died, in the *Cambridge Journal of Economics*, Okishio admitted flat-out that the replacement-cost rate of profit is only an adequate measure of the rate of profit if prices don't change from the time you purchase your machinery to when your returns are coming in. So if prices remained constant, then it would be serviceable as a measure of the rate of profit. But if you're looking at something like the computer industry, where the prices are always falling, year after year, or pretty much anything else – prices change – it is not an adequate measure of the returns of one time compared to the investment of an earlier time.

If you take the net present value calculations, for pretty much any project, it's not just that you make a big investment in a lump now, and then it's just revenues. The streams that you're dealing with will include future expenditures as well as future revenues. You build up your project bit-by-bit, there are bits that have to be replaced before other bits have even been developed, and so on. Capitalists assess these things on an ongoing basis. It's not a matter of expenditures that all come at a certain point, and revenues all at a certain later point. You're right that a certain measure of inflation is very advantageous to capital, for all sorts of reasons. But still, generally, they either assume inflation will be very low, or they make some accounting for it. Considering the rate of profit as a guiding force in capitalist calculations, they're always looking at future costs, as well as future revenue.

I agree with you. For simplification, I was assuming an investment – a dose of investment today – and a stream of future returns. If you have a project where you need multiple doses of investment – if you're going to evaluate the expected profitability of that investment, yeah, you have to look at all the doses of investment and all of the returns. And for certain purposes, you're going to want to do that without adjusting for inflation; for certain purposes, you're going to want to put in your expected-inflation adjustment. So we're in agreement.

The important point is that this is totally antithetical to this so-called replacement-cost rate of profit, which would value each and every dose of investment, and each and every return, at the same set of prices, no matter when they occur, from now to infinity.

Your net present value or internal rate of return computations value returns based on the prices expected when those returns come in. They value all doses of investment – costs of equipment and so forth – at the prices, or expected prices, when those investments are made. That's the way to do it. And you can correct for inflation for certain purposes; for other purposes, you might not want to. So we're in agreement about that: that's the right way to do it for planning purposes.

None of that has the slightest affinity with – it's totally incompatible with – the so-called replacement-cost rate of profit, because it values every return, every sale, and every cost, every expenditure, every investment, at the same set of prices, such as the prices of today. If you look at what Duménil and Lévy do, and Michel Husson, Fred Moseley, and so forth, what they call a rate of profit is the profits that have come in, based on end-of-year prices, divided by what it would cost to replace the whole capital stock at the end of the year, based on these end-of-year prices. This is not what a return on investment is, which is future returns compared to past investments. So you could look at the returns today compared to the actual amounts invested in the past. That gives you the actually-realised rate of profit. Or for planning purposes, you could look at the costs today compared to the future revenues (and future costs), and that gives you a forward-looking, expected, rate of profit. You're always comparing expenditures at one time and returns at a later time. And that's the whole idea behind an investment.

So when these folks talk about the "rate of profit", they give us the impression that they're talking about a rate of return on investment. But in no way, shape, or form can you think of what they're doing as a rate of return on investment. And it would be equal to a rate of return on investment – it would be an adequate measure – only in the case (as Okishio conceded) in which prices never change.

Let's leave that now. The last question I wanted to ask was: if you step back from this, and look in more Marxist terms, do you think it is excluded that the cheapening in constant capital, and increases in the rate of exploitation, could offset increases in the composition of capital for long periods?

Which means that the rate of profit would tend to rise rather than fall?

Yeah, for longish periods. Is that possible?

In principle, it's not excluded at all. And I did some calculations, some estimates, when writing my book. Looking at the nominal-value composition of capital – which is the amount of money invested in the fixed capital divided by the wages of the workforce – that nominal-value composition was basically at the same level in 1999 as it was in 1958. So a lot of things can be done, at least at certain times, to offset the tendency of the rate of profit to fall. So it's a tendency. It's not something that has to happen, necessarily, in some sense of mathematical inevitability.

Right. So why is it that that tendency would tend to dominate in the long term? 1958 to 1999 is quite a substantial period.

Right. I think it's an empirical matter in the end whether the tendency dominates or not. If it does, then the rate of profit has a downward trend. If it doesn't, then the rate of profit does not have a downward trend. Why should one effect be stronger than another? I think that that's not answerable in general. But I think your question is based on a presupposition that I don't happen to share: that when Marx talks about the law of the tendential fall in the rate of profit, he's trying to prove some sort of inevitability. That's been a very common interpretation of what he was doing, but I think it's completely wrong. I and several people, a few years back, in 2013, wrote a response to a paper by Michael Heinrich that was in *Monthly Review*. The response was from myself, Alan Freeman, Nick Potts, Brendan Cooney, and Alexey Gusev. We argued, and I think it's incontrovertible when you look at Marx's text, that he didn't call it a law because he was trying to prove some inevitability. He was trying to explain why there is an empirical fact – or what he and the classical economists regarded as an empirical fact – that the rate of profit does tend to fall.

What Marx was saying – and he says this very explicitly near the start of Chapter 13, in Vol. 3 of *Capital* – is that these folks – Smith, Ricardo, the other ones – recognised that the rate of profit tends to fall, and they tortured themselves in unsuccessful attempts to explain it. But here, for the first time, I – Marx – am able to explain, successfully, this empirical fact.

And that's why he called it a law. Because he didn't just have the phenomenon that the rate of profit tends to fall, which was accepted by all of them as a fact. He now had theoretical principles: his value theory – combined with the bias of technical change under capitalism (to replace workers with machines) and ongoing accumulation. Those three things enable one to make sense of, to make intelligible, that tendency of the rate of profit to fall. So it's a law in the sense of a principle that makes something intelligible or explains it. I think that's why Marx called it a law.

I don't think that he claimed anywhere that it would be inevitable in a mathematical sense that the rate of profit had to fall over the long term. I think that's just a misreading. And oftentimes – not always, but oftentimes – it's a tendentious reading meant to make what he was arguing look very silly. On the other hand, you have a lot of fatalists out there who want a silly theory. They kind of favour that kind of reading of what Marx was doing with the law as well.

So I'm going to answer, always, that in principle it's contingent; I can't give you a theoretical reason why it has to be the case that the rise in the technical composition has to dominate over the counteracting factors. It doesn't have to be that way. If you believe the classical economists and Marx – and I think there is good reason to do so – and if you look at the statistics for, say, the US economy since World War II, you do have a downward trend in the rate of profit. And then you want to explain it. And I think Marx's theory does a damn good job of explaining it. But it can't predict inevitability.

Right. But really, you first have to establish the trend. The general theory doesn't tell you, for example, that you can be pretty sure that the rate of profit will decline over the next ten years.

Yeah, I would never want to say anything like that. No, I don't believe in inevitabilities or almost-inevitabilities, even, when it comes to economic matters. Shit happens.

CHAPTER 28

We Become a Hedge Fund of Our Own Lives (January 2016)

Discussion with Dick Bryan

In 2008 there was a lot of talk about derivatives being weapons of mass destruction and predictions that derivatives trading would be curbed. But that hasn't happened at all. Why not?

The simple answer would be: they capture something integral about the nature of capital. But the more concrete version of that answer is: the pricing and trading of risk in an era of highly liquid capital has now to be understood to be an integral part of how a capitalist economy works. I think these are core devices in terms of how capital manages its value, so it is not surprising that they returned. What I think is more interesting is how they have returned not just in larger quantities but also in more diverse areas. Let me clarify. The most telling dimension of this derivative growth is not just that algorithmic trading is seeing more and more money churn through interest rate, foreign exchange and stock derivative markets – that is pretty clear to understand. But we see more and more sorts of commodities being traded in derivatives markets, expansions of weather derivatives, expansions of house price derivatives, and more and more derivative sorts of products coming into the market. Most significant, I think, has been the growth of mortgage-backed securities, and other securities backed by auto-loans or electricity and water bills. The reason I call these derivatives is that the security owner doesn't own the underlying auto loan or mortgage, they own an exposure to the loan; they own the income stream on the loans, but not the loan. In that sense, they're derivatives.

The process of securitisation signals that derivative markets are moving to engage household risk exposures. Embedded in securitised household payments on mortgages, cars, credit card debt, student debt and utilities payments are trades in household default risk, for these risks are transferred from the lender to the purchaser of the security. These risks are accordingly being priced and explicitly traded.

* Previously appeared at: https://senseofgfc.wordpress.com/2016/02/19/dick-bryan-january-2016/, 19 February 2016.

If you look at the quantitative data, household derivatives may not be the biggest derivative market but they are interesting because no-one was expecting them to grow. Indeed, their reputations were massively tarnished in the global financial crisis. At the centre of that crisis was the crash in the value of mortgage-backed securities as it was realised that households were defaulting at unexpected rates. The popular critics announced the end of securitisation. They couldn't have been more wrong! Not only did they return in the US, but they became the centre-piece of post-crisis US macroeconomic management. They were the key financial asset purchased by the US Federal Reserve in its Quantitative Easing (QE) programs, and now MBS sit on the balance sheet of the Federal Reserve as its single largest asset. Via QE the Fed came to hold (and continues to hold) more assets in MBS now than it had in total assets before the crisis. As Marxists we can't ignore this: there is something really big going on there; that household financial payments have become the foundational asset of financial stability. Does it not resonate with labour time being thefoundational unit of value in commodity production? What is this policy gravitation to assets backed by household mortgage payments a symptom of? I think Marxists should be probing this issue, looking for its meaning for class and for value theory.

You argue that from another angle that this is an escalating financialisation of daily life, that people are being re-organised as managers of their own portfolios of assets and activities. I say, isn't there a danger of over-stating the neatness of it? Education is said to be an investment, for example, but the correlation between that investment and its outcome is very loose.

I believe people are being framed as managers of asset portfolios. Mike Rafferty and I have referred to people being hedge funds of their own lives – the expectation that people will borrow (take on leverage) to acquire long-term assets, and to hedge those assets via a plethora of new insurance products. And indeed this sums to a financialisation of daily life. If you are asking me to put on a sociological hat and say that this describes each and every household decision, the answer is no! Clearly it is more complicated than all that. And of course some aspects and many decisions of life, such as your case of people paying university fees for reasons other than expected rate of return, don't comply with the proposition. But the proposition isn't a descriptive sociological one. We can have in Marxism a distinction between a working class and a capitalist class, but it doesn't describe all aspects of people's lives or the broad aspects of every individual's life. It exists at a different level of abstraction. So the test, if you like, is not whether individuals' circumstances are more complex than a hedge fund analogy, but what underlying trend we can see by so defining the financialisation process.

So let me explain briefly why I think we should frame households as hedge funds and the parallels with workers producing surplus value. The fundamental thing here is that just as workers produce surplus value, households absorb risk. Households in aggregate hold illiquid assets: their labour power, household items, perhaps a car and some home equity. This constitutes an incredibly un-diversified "portfolio" because these assets are the household's means of subsistence. (Rich households are much more diversified in their portfolio than middle class ones, especially those committed to home ownership.) Households also hold contracts on phones and utilities and various forms of subsistence. These too are part of the means of subsistence. If you add these together as the contractual basis of subsistence, it is clear households try not to default on these contracts, for they would then lose their means of subsistence. They absorb the contractual risk, if they possibly can, even when they are financially in the red (unlike companies which are protected by limited liability), and they do so to sustain their means of subsistence.

Securitisation of loans and other household contract payments then has to be understood as a risk trade. The risk that comes into households is systematically less than the risk on the securities built on household payments. Households absorb risk: there is a risk spread. Notice that surplus value is also a spread – the difference between the value of labour power and the value created by labour. This "production" spread and the "risk" spread have something in common: they add to profits. We know how surplus value does that, but clearly also the absorption of risk changes the risk/return profile of assets. It reduces the risk on any return. Securitised household payments look like safe investments for capital at a time when virtually nothing looks safe – not even Treasury bonds. And both spreads are systemic: they are part and parcel of being labour power – working for wages to purchase subsistence goods in the case of surplus value and consuming subsistence goods to produce the payment streams for financial assets in the case of risk transfer.

So, returning to an earlier question, not all household expenditures fit the hedge fund model, but not all labour produces surplus value. I think the proposition I'm depicting here is a broad class story, not an individual one. I know that the idea I've just expressed is heretical in Marxist terms: a source of surplus being created inside the sphere of what is traditionally called "circulation". But I think that axiom of Marxism needs to be challenged, for it is leading to obsessions about measuring declines in the rate of profit (to "prove" Marxist value theory) at a time when we should be re-thinking what "capital" is and where surplus comes from, so as to rethink capital at its frontier of development.

I think that the changes that come with financial innovation have to be incorporated into value theory. If the best we can say is simply that it speculative and unproductive, we may feel like good Marxists, but we will have lost contact with how capital is re-loading its engagement with the working class in a financialised way. And anyway, we are not being good Marxists; just conservative ones. I'm more interested in materialist method than canonical taxonomies of capital.

Isn't one of the points about the crisis in the USA that households didn't absorb the risk? Six million households lost their homes, but even that did not absorb the risk for the mortgage issuers and security packagers. To foreclose on a house is very expensive. The agency which absorbed the risks for the financial capitalists involved was the Federal Reserve.

Sort of. The point is fair, as far as it goes. Just to clarify on a technical point, the Fed was buying real, triple-A securities, not junk, and when they hold those securities to maturity, as the Fed decided it would do, the value of these securities in the market can never be tested. But the point you make is reasonable, though the question is whether sub-prime was the exception that clarified the rule.

These are means for capital to draw revenue directly from households. Marx wrote about it in his time. In the Communist Manifesto he writes, as soon as the exploitation of the worker is at an end in the workplace, the worker is set upon by the landlord, the pawnbroker, and so on. Put another way: what is the essential difference between these new forms and pawnbroking?

On the analogy between sub-prime and pawnbroking, I think they need different treatment. I'll get to that, but let's take on the issue as you posed it. The issue at the moment is not household debt, per se, for this has many thousand years of history as usury. The issue I'm focussing on, and which Marx could not have imagined, is that household debt is now being re-configured in the form of an asset. That is, debt generates a stream of regular repayments, and with securitisation, this stream of repayments is itself being framed as an asset, and on-sold into global markets. In that sense, that which is illiquid, like the house or the car, suddenly takes on a liquid form as an asset. Not that the car or the house become liquid – they can't – but the household absorbs the illiquidity of owning or renting those assets, and their payments on them become liquid assets, and they circulate globally. But the thing is that household contract payments have a life as capital beyond the financial "exchange" (the purchase of electricity, or insurance or part-purchase of the house or car).

That is a profound difference from debt per se, such as the pawnbroker Marx wrote about. What's significant here is that the household is not aware that their monthly payments are providing inputs into securities – they think they are just repaying loans and other bills. Perhaps it is just like workers thinking they are producing commodities, not aware that they are there to produce surplus value, and commodity production is just the necessary condition of surplus appropriation. In this regard, the pawnbroker or payday lender is different. There is no global market; the objective is not to trade in risk, but simply to charge interest. It is simply usury within a capitalist setting.

This creates a whole different dimension of capital. The usury of the pawnbroker and payday lender is primitive accumulation, because it is just a matter of taking a household as it is, ripping as much money as possible out, with no concern for the reproduction of the household. I think that with securitisation the form of capital has changed. It has to be understood as a kind of process of capitalist accumulation, where it treats the household as capital and its payments as an input into a capital asset, not just the extraction of an income stream. It is parallel to the way Marx depicted relative surplus value: the worker's incorporation into capital, rather than as just an object of capital as in absolute surplus value.

And here is where we see that the lessons of sub-prime are being learnt by capital. Just as absolute surplus value reached its limits of the physical sustainability of workers with a lengthening working day, so we see an awareness that ripping more and more money out of households by means like sub-prime lending reaches its limits, for it threatened the financial viability of workers. The goal is to make households sustainable payers, but paying as much as possible. Accordingly, the surveillance and management of household risk is now extensive; way more extensive than occurred under sub-prime mortgage lending in the early 2000s. There is recognition that default rates have to be managed. There is a concern to keep households on payment.

It's now a highly-developed level of management. It's about keeping massive data sets and massive monitoring of what are the triggers of household default, and taking people to the edge of default but keeping them from going over the edge. Well, actually, you can carry a bit of default risk. So you can, for example, accept 5% of people going over the edge, but no more than 5%.

The object here is not to avoid defaults. It is to price the default risk accurately. The world wants junk bonds. The world wants triple-B-rated securities, so long as there is a trade-off between the risk and return. A hedge fund doesn't mind if a product has a higher default risk, so long as the expected bond yield is high enough to match the default risk. So we need to add that extra layer of complexity to the story, lest it appear I am saying all securitised assets must be safe. The thing about sub-prime lending is that this financial junk was listed as AAA, when it clearly wasn't. What capital learned from sub-prime is that you've got to monitor that default risk carefully. Capital has learned a lesson, especially in the US, with the help of the state. And it's not about banning sub-prime: in the USA, the sub-prime market has moved to auto lending. Rather, it's about putting a whole package of policies around households to manage their capacity to repay loans. That's where the policy pressure is now: there are changes in bankruptcy laws, education around financial literacy, moral pressures, and monitoring generally, and changing in the US, the rights of people to challenge in court the process of asset seizures for (alleged) non-payment.

Notice what this is saying about financial regulatory agendas. Many on the left bemoan the lack of regulation of financial institutions. And of course, it is appalling. But that's not what the state is targeting in its response to the crisis. The US state is effectively saying that regulating financial institutions beyond a certain point is too hard, but it can, on behalf of capital, regulate the way that borrowers behave. The significant shift since 2007–8: capital has learned better how to price risk. Overall, capital has found a path to a sustainable source of "surplus".

I think default rates on housing loans and personal credit have gone markedly down in the US. We see Janet Yellen saying, "we are not going to increase interest rates until employment rates grow, wages grow and house prices grow". The Fed is actually consciously and systematically putting in policies to reflate households. But not all households. There are people who we would previously have called a lumpen class in relation to wage labour. There is now a lumpen financial class, people who are going to get left behind. They don't have jobs, they don't get loans, at least not loans that will go on to being securitised. They are excluded from accumulation in every sense. The St Louis branch of the Fed has a big research centre managing household financial risk. The head of that centre says that the key factor in the global financial crisis was "household financial viability risk" and that they need to rectify household financial viability. So all these tools, big data, profiling households, the ability to gather profiles of particular households in real time so they know what risks are is a massive development on capital.

Now, the story I have been telling is a US one, but not the story of Europe. The inability of the ECB to undertake QE is telling. They keep announcing QE, but they can't find any safe assets to securitise. In contrast to the US Fed which is attempting to reflate household budgets, the ECB hasn't been able to capitalise households. So in Europe QE keeps falling over. I'm telling the US version of QE and mortgage-backed securities on the positive side, of reflating households; I think we can see in Europe the same story being played out on the negative side: they can't reflate Europe because they can't find enough household payments to securitise. But let me not get further diverted by the issues of the ECB.

Do you think this process has become more effective in disciplining households? Are we living neoliberalism ourselves, regulating our households by financial disciplines, rather than neoliberalism being a policy the government has?

What I always find puzzling and disappointing in the narratives about "neoliberalism entering our souls" is that it shifts the analysis to a purely ideological level. I'm trying to talk about the material processes of capital accumulation that underlie it. We could talk about the experience of a working-class person through most of the 20th century was about soul-destroying alienation, and so on – and that's important, but it excludes an economic dimension. Some people might call this deterministic, and it could be framed that way, but it need not be and it shouldn't be. It just requires that Marxism undertake a serious engagement with financial innovation. I'm disappointed that so much Marxism, when it addresses finance, has had immediate recourse to this ideological critique of how we're being overwhelmed by finance, its greed, etc. And when people want to say simply that finance is "speculative" and hence unproductive, my response is that it's not as simple as this, and this easy branding may be rhetorically effective, but it is analytically stifling.

If we are going to think about a politics of resistance to financialised capital, how do we think about it not just in terms of moral fightback; how do you find the vulnerability within capital that is part of capital's generation of this culture of financial domination? To do that, you've got to get inside capital and the calculative logic of capital, just as, to be effective in the 20th century, unions had to get inside the logic of Taylorism and understand what its momentum was and what its vulnerabilities were.

One of the elements of the Marxist critiques of wage labour has always been that this is a stream of market transactions which exercises hegemony in the sense of a dull compulsion of economic relations through the very form of the transactions. The ideologies generated by the market transactions – a fair day's work for a fair day's wage, all labour being paid for – are not imposed by brainwashing but are generated by the transactions themselves. Are we seeing a similar process here, whereby different sorts of market transactions, other than the transaction between capital and labour power, are creating an ideological structuring through the market transaction itself?

I think that we are in a world where, by and large, it is impossible to survive without becoming an accumulator. By that I mean taking on a debt to buy a house or buying into a pension scheme. Your engagement with finance shifts from a 1950s–60s model where you would work and have a savings account at the local bank. If you were a middle-class person you'd get a mortgage but you'd pay it off as quickly as you could, because debt's a bad thing. We are now living in an environment where everyone carries debt and you're seen as a bit of a fool if you don't because you are excluded from access to asset price appreciation. In this era, if you just live by wage labour and a savings account, then you know that you're destined to be living in poverty in old age and have a low standard of living. Everything draws you into rapidly becoming a "hedge fund of your own life". Do you think that's right?

Not entirely. Take the housing market in Britain now: the biggest single form of tenure now is people who have paid off their mortgages. There are more of those than there are of people who are still paying mortgages.

And there are more people paying off mortgages than there are renting?

The latest figures are: a bit over 30% paying off mortgages, and fractionally more owning outright; about 18% private renters, fractionally fewer social renters. Recent years have brought a very rapid relative increase in the number of private renters, who for decades were a small minority. Thatcher tried to revive private renting; she failed, but 30 years later that drive has succeeded. Take student debt for another example of widespread imbrication of people in financial transactions. Students are 50% of the age cohort now, and almost 50% don't pay off their debt, although the government in designing the student loan scheme reckoned for a much lower percentage. The calculation and enforcement is much less efficient than it might appear. This might be transitional – but is it? Are the miscalculations and divergences a permanent factor for the foreseeable future?

If the student debt was owned by a private agency, you would find much tighter legal obligations on people to keep repaying. The impossibility of defaulting on student debt, the requirements of a guarantor on the loan would be much higher. It is also an Australian story. The UK version will have its particularity: it is a transitional process, the introduction of fees was highly-contested, having state-funded lending institutions at subsidised rates was a transitional mechanism to more fully-marketised versions. So was the state copping defaults at a higher rate, and people getting away with defaulting without getting the knock on the door and people saying "we've come to remove your kneecaps".

For the state, the financialisation or capitalisation of tertiary education – or of education, generally – has been awkward because of its inter-generational unfairness, and perhaps low levels of surveillance of student debt is a result. Young graduates being dragged off to debtors' prison due to legislation by people who had free university education would not look good. I would have thought that once we see this lending in private hands, sold off – and presumably the asset will sell off at a really low value, because the book is so crappy – things will change. The enforcement of education debt will get much more serious. But we'll see, and you and I should look again in 15 years' time.

CHAPTER 29

The Globalisation of Elites (January 2016)

Discussion with Hugo Radice

In 2012 you estimated that the German government was isolated in its hard-line budget-balancing stance, and that the EU would end up making concessions to Greece to keep it in the Eurozone.

I have to own up: I totally underestimated the determination of the Germans to force through their policies. I hesitate to think that this is just a matter of stupidity. I think we need to understand more about changes in German politics since unification. Before 1991, German politics were looking outwards, to see what other states were thinking of them, but there is a sense in which they always "had to be on their best behaviour" and keep everybody happy. Because otherwise they'd be back in the shit of the 20th century. Taking over East Germany wasn't just an economic exercise, it was a political and cultural exercise. It was like wiping the slate clean. It's as if they sat back after that and said, "right, that's it, we're a state again. Not half a state: a whole state". The other thing we did was to over-estimate the capacity of the European left to oppose this, to oppose the German imposition of debt repayment and austerity. It's partly because they were quite careful to focus exclusively on Greece, and keep the French and the Italians and the Spanish on side, to avoid them getting into trouble. I suspect when we have some historical perspective on this, and decent data, we will find that there were a lot of private assurances being given to Paris and Rome and Madrid that their needs would be taken care of one way or another during the crisis. We just had rather too simple an understanding of the nature of the problem and how it could be solved. It's quite clear that the first Syriza government shared the same over-optimistic viewpoint. They thought it was just a matter of presenting the facts and the reasonable case. Varoufakis very sensibly scarcely ever mentioned Marx, and gave a fundamentally Keynesian argument, which, to a Keynesian, sounds completely sound, logically flawless, supported by Stiglitz, Krugman, in this country Skidelsky and Blanchflower, plenty of intelligent people saying, yes, you're absolutely right, this is completely stupid, and the way to deal with this

* Previously published at: https://senseofgfc.wordpress.com/2016/02/19/hugo-radice-january-2016/, 19 February 2016.

is to recycle the debt, to have a new debt agreement that allows Greece longer to deal with the problem. So it's a familiar case of being too optimistic. We had the optimism of the will, but we forgot about the pessimism of the intellect.

Firstly, I think there is some evidence that there is something more deep-rooted and systemic in that. It's not the case that Germany can get whatever it wants in the EU. The refugee mess is an example of that. Germany has not only been unable to get its policy to prevail, it has been forced into shifting, itself, by pressure from, quite often, some of the smaller states in the EU. So this is not just a German thing. Secondly: look back at the G20 meetings. The first G20 after the Lehman Bros crash produced a communiqué which was quite non-specific. Its only specific element was "we will not use protectionist measures". And, on the whole, that held. That was really all. Then the Toronto G20 meeting in June 2010 had quite specific language to the effect that it was time to cut budget deficits and return to normal. Now, that certainly wasn't imposed on everyone else just by the German government. And Spain: in early 2015, the Spanish government was one of the most insistent that Greece pay. Why was this? I don't think it's that they got promises from Germany. It's that they were already signed up for cuts, already well into them; the government probably thought, "we're going to look like idiots if someone else can get away with not doing this". If the EU had given substantial concessions to Greece, the left in Spain would have said, "why is the PP government doing all this? They could have done differently", and it would have been an unanswerable case. As it was, the PP came out of the last election still the biggest party, because they could get the line out that there was no alternative to this. It was not because they had been given sweeteners, but because they had not been given sweeteners that they backed the hard-line position. On Syriza: I am sure there was optimism because I talked to John Milios in 2012. I said, what's your plan? He said – "there is a possibility that the EU won't give us what we want. Now, we have a plan B... but we can't say what it is." It can't have been a very effective plan B. Since then, Milios has become a critic of the Syriza government. If you compare what they did in 2012, when it looked like they might win the election, Tsipras went to Paris and Berlin to do large meetings organised by a section of the left. He went out to campaign to win a constituency in the left across Europe. In 2015 there was a lot of international theatre, but it was all about presenting Yanis Varoufakis as the man going into the negotiations. The left across Europe was called on to watch the negotiations and wish him well. He went around Europe, but only to talk to the finance ministers.

Let's just run through some of these points. You say it's not a German thing, but most of the difficulty is still based on talking about Germany did this, Spain did that: about countries. I think a much broader point is that over the last

25–30 years – or, since 1970 – there has been a globalisation not only in terms of the economics of capitalism; there has also been a globalisation of elites. This hasn't been studied enough. And part of the reason for that is that it is not a subject that elites particularly want studied. If people understood the common interests of the ruling classes of different countries, they would be less likely to be attracted to the nationalist trope in their rhetoric. That cuts both ways. Germany is clearly the economic dynamo of the Eurozone. But in the process of Europeanisation in the broadest sense of European integration over the last 60 years, there has been an interpenetration of elites. For example, German integration was not simply supported by the German elite, but also by those of other EU states: thus the new East European elites saw that they would benefit enormously from German unification because once East Germany was in, it was very hard for anybody to resist the logic of extending EU membership across the countries of Eastern Europe. This globalisation of elites means that when we say that the German ruling class thought this, or the Germany political and economic elite thought that, there is a kind of rider to that, which is that this is in the context of other interests and other opinions, which count. The situation is not like in the 1930s. The point about Spain that you make: I didn't suggest that there were sweeteners. The word I used was assurances: "if you back us on this..." – there was a carrot as well as a stick, in part because of the huge exposure of German banks to the Spanish property bubble. It was in German interests to keep the Spanish on side. It was a question of taking account of each other. Spain fulfilled its side of the bargain in terms of its rhetoric over Greece. And Ireland was the same, Enda Kenny saying, "we've been through this stuff, why can't everyone else"?

The point about the G20 is interesting: it surfaces for a couple of years and then disappears again. It seems to have had very little role since. The thing about the austerity call in 2010 – it was at the G20, yes. But in the Spring of 2010, when Osborne suddenly jumped up and said "austerity", when the Coalition came into office and announced it, the ground had already been laid. It had been laid at the Bank of England in terms of the international arrangements put in place alongside the extraordinary bank bail-outs in 2009. The Bank was reassured that its contingency mechanisms were in place and that if they could contain that crisis, they could contain anything. That call for austerity came not only from Osborne and the Bank of England, but also from the OECD, in the aftermath of the election. Gurria [secretary of the OECD] came and visited Osborne and publicly endorsed his plans. That has to be taken alongside what happened in 2012, which is that Osborne relaxed austerity and again his position was supported by the OECD. What this says is that the overall rhetoric is one of austerity, but the actual practice is that you make sure that if austerity doesn't work, or if there are side effects which are not politically sustainable, then you relax it. That is what the coalition did here, to great effect, when they perceived that the Labour Party was making considerable headway in the spring of 2012, which was confirmed in the local elections. So they started quietly back-pedalling and stepping up the political rhetoric against Labour to remarkably good effect.

On Syriza, I think you are right, they did expect to get a deal. And I hadn't picked up on that point on the difference between 2012 and 2015. I assume it is simply that in 2012 they had no expectation of winning power. It was close, but it was only as a result of getting close that they started to think, through that parliament, like a governing party.

I think that's the problem.

Clearly this is also the source of the eventual split and the departure of people like Lapavitsas, coming out strongly against the deal in Summer 2015, to the extent of forming a new political party.

Back in 2012 you said that "trade union movements have remained essentially trapped within a national Keynesian framework in each country... it would take a huge change... for trade unions to be willing to re-enter the political arena, after having abandoned it for most of the last 20 or 30 years". Evidently, we haven't forced through that change, and we're still working on it. How best to do that? And evidently it is not just trade union movements.

No, it is left politics generally. It is quite extraordinary how much we are still up against it, how hard we are finding it to get trade union and left movements to think beyond national borders. It reminds me of the struggle I had in the 1980s to get people to take globalisation seriously. You would hear people saying "we can't have an international working-class movement until we have a national working-class movement: it stands to reason". But it is only by having an internationalist perspective that you can construct a credible left politics. This is clearly what confronts the leadership of the Labour Party at the moment. They are under siege from the media: when, for example, John McDonnell is interviewed, he is presented with a caricature of his policies and the interviewer says "this is a hard-left position". Then when McDonnell comes back with his actual policies, he is told "so you're no different from the Tories"! The objective since Corbyn's election seems to have been – and this is shared across the media – that this is an extremely dangerous development and we are going to close it down. And in that context what the Labour leadership is having to do is firefighting. It's constantly on the back foot, and when things start to look a bit better, their opponents in the PLP will find some reason to attack.

The Labour Party report on the 2015 election, "Learning the Lessons from Defeat", is a really revealing document. There is no mention of trade unionism at all, and no mention of the international dimension. It is all treated as if this is just a British thing. The report is weak in all kinds of ways. It manages to talk about the 1983 election without mentioning the SDP! By way of reasons for the defeat, all it does it trot out what all the journalists have been spouting since May: Ed Miliband wasn't an inspiring leader... neglecting the core vote... failing to rebut claims, and so on. The point about all this, relating to the passage you quote: I think I was absolutely right in 2012. Public sector unions have shown a certain capacity for mobilisation in the face of the cuts. The GMB, in Leeds, is playing a major part in trying to open up the decrepit machine of local politics, open it up to the membership and articulate what the interests of ordinary people in Leeds are, as opposed to just the jobs and conditions of work of their members. GMB are probably the best example. Unison members have probably borne the brunt of the cuts so far. I am currently secretary of our local Labour party branch. There's an element of the new membership that nobody is talking about. People are talking about members who left over the Iraq war; and about all the young, new people coming to the Corbyn rallies, who did all the facebooking and twittering and all the rest of it. But there is a third demographic, who are public sector trade unionists in their 30s and 40s, and we've had a lot of them joining. And they're joining because there has been enough of a re-politicisation of public sector trade unionism which has centred on the idea that we have to get away from this utilitarian, sectional type of trade unionism if we are going to have any jobs left at all, if we are going to have any future, going to defend our pensions. So there were a number of rallies, local and regional rallies where trade unions played a major part. But what is still absent is any real discussion in the trade union movement of developing links, even within the public sector, to trade unions in the rest of Europe. It happens in the ETUC and in the EuroMemorandum Group, which is exemplary in its activity. They've always operated at the European level and they've managed to piece together resources, especially from the German labour movement. So there are signs of things changing, but labour market reforms and changes in trade union laws and collective bargaining procedures, right across Europe and the world, have hugely restricted unions and essentially de-politicised them. And it's a long job to change that. But then, it's a long job to fight the wider de-politicisation of society. It is part of this neglected cultural and ideological dimension of neoliberalism. We are still too attached on the left to what are very simplistic and mechanistic economic arguments, that people's material interests are basically defined by their position within the capitalist economic system, and that their stimulus to action basically comes from their direct economic experiences. We have vastly under-estimated the role played by culture and communications, and the media in the widest sense. That is one thing that I like about Gramsci, that he understands the importance of "common sense".

One of the interesting things, though, even among those who are politicised, even with the new leadership of the Labour party, with some of the unions, like Unite, which has been quite close to the new leadership, it is all in a national framework, apart from perhaps John McDonnell talking a bit to Yanis Varoufakis. Even in the context of the coming [June 2016] EU referendum, Labour's going to be arguing to stay in, there is some talk of "we're not just staying in on the basis of accepting the status quo", but there is no talk of "this is how we think Europe can be different, here is our international outlook". There is a problem of de-politicisation, of unions being pushed back to business unionism, but even amongst those unions which are politicised, whose leaderships are highly political, there is still this limitation to the national picture. It's not just Britain. Look at the national crisis in Spain, now. Podemos has put conditions for a new government. They are pretty much all about Spanish questions.

Youth culture in Spain is pretty internationalised. It's the same here: the youth wing of Corbynism is internationalised. In terms of the form of activity, these things are conducted at the elite level. So yes, McDonnell talks to Varoufakis, but how many rank-and-file Labour members, supporters of the new leadership, pay attention to what is going on in other countries? How much discussion is there? What we're trying to do in relation to Europe is instead of just holding discussions within the Labour Party, we are holding public meetings, and getting our MEPs to come along and make the case to us. We had Alan Johnson talk about the EU in September. He brought in an audience, and that was an open public meeting. We had a meeting up in Stokesley, with the Labour MEP Richard Corbett, and got an audience of 100 in a relatively small market town. These are the sort of steps you have to take and it's very difficult. If all I did was read the *Guardian*, I would know nothing about what's going on in Spain. There is no discussion of it. I think the whole social media oriented Momentum idea reduces politics to an ephemeral activity, passing spasms. I don't want to romanticise things. But in the 1980s if you were a Labour Party activist, there were constant political debates in meetings. Maybe around conference resolutions – but there were debates in meetings. We have gone up in our branch from maybe 70 in May to 200 now. But hardly any of the new members will actually come to a meeting of any kind. Even if it's meetings to discuss, "what shall we do?"

Or elsewhere you have lots of new people at the meetings, but they come into meetings where there is no culture of putting motions, having debates.

This reflects quite deep cultural changes. Essentially the whole mantra of "private good, public bad, individual good, collective bad" has just got into people's souls. So you imagine that a collective political activity has got to have the immediacy of the individual – hence this frenzy on social media. But actually it's the other way around. It's the process of debate, analysis, consideration, respect, a whole political process, a political culture that has to be rebuilt.

CHAPTER 30

The Great Recession Is Not Going Away (January 2016)

Discussion with Leo Panitch

In terms of the crisis we are still in, it is certainly a great recession. We are now in its eighth year – I count it as beginning in the summer of 2007 – and it isn't going away. At a global level, it is very uneven. Greece has been thrown into a great depression; the United States has kept itself in different territory, I think, by the stimulus that it co-ordinated in 2009–2010. The US has managed to bring down unemployment; but even there the description of secular stagnation is not entirely wrong. And given what is going on in the rest of the world, that is, the appalling mess the Europeans have made of managing this crisis, reinforcing all the limitations of fixed exchange rates, and then the almost inevitable cooling-off of the commodity boom, and now the tapering off of Chinese export oriented development previously realised in American and European markets, leading to what looks like a very severe downturn in the BRICS and other emerging capitalist economies.

So now many serious observers are asking whether, eight years into this crisis, we are facing new contradictions on the road to recovery – something like what happened eight years into the Great Depression, which began in 1929, when there was a second dip in 1937, even after all the New Deal measures. And you get mainstream economists, even most senior former members of the Clinton administration like Larry Summers, constantly writing in the *Financial Times* that what is needed is more fiscal stimulus, where the political conditions are not there in the US or in Europe to do it. So we're in for a serious long stagnation.

This partly has to do with the contradictions in the way the slump was limited by the US Federal Reserve acting as a global central bank, throwing liquidity into the financial markets, including into the European financial markets. They never advertised that. But Quantitative Easing 2 and 3 were undertaken very much with an eye to making sure that Wall Street would continue

* Previously published at: https://senseofgfc.wordpress.com/2016/02/19/leo-panitch-january-2016/, 19 February 2016.

overnight lending to European banks, which was crucial to keeping them afloat. The effect of keeping such low interest rates in the US was that money – not only hot money, but also pension fund money – was being invested in the corporate bonds in the global south, where there were more significant rates of return. And inevitably these were going to come a cropper when the Fed started even slightly raising its interest rates. Of course, in some respects, the really remarkable thing is how the American Empire has reproduced itself at the centre of global capitalism during this crisis. We also saw that happen in the 1970s crisis, when despite tensions with the Germans and Japanese as they were all trying to cope with the domestic class contradictions and the international financial system that pushed the US dollar off gold in 1971, they created the G7 by 1975 and collectively managed the ongoing crisis of that period until the Americans by the beginning of the 1980s could re-establish the US dollar as "as good as gold".

What's happened in this crisis is that the Americans have shown, and the world has agreed, that in terms of taking responsibility for trying to restrain the worst effects of a global crisis, they are the only ones who even really try to do it, and they're the only ones who have the institutional capacity to do it. The European Central Bank doesn't. The German Bundesbank doesn't want to. Its concern is indeed selfishly narrow, oriented to making sure that the euro plays the same role that the deutschmark used to in fostering German exports. The Chinese don't have the institutional capacity even to manage the liberalisation of their own currency. The capacity to manage global capitalism is not even on their horizon.

The BRICS bank and the Asian Infrastructure Bank were designed to give China some room for manoeuvre, but both of these are very small potatoes and in any case would still effectively require the countries that would go to them having a stamp of approval from the World Bank and the IMF. For reasons in part having to do with American MNCs being the leading ones around the world, the Americans take responsibility for managing global capitalism and its contradictions. They do this even if they have to hide it from the American Congress. If they had revealed that QE2 and QE3 were in part about getting money to European banks, Congress would have gone nuts under the Republicans! In the harrowing stand-offs about this, Congress always backs down; but it is difficult, it is full of contradictions. It is ugly, because it involves bailing out these rapacious financiers. It's very ugly; but it's what they do at the centre of global capitalism, and this crisis has proved that this is the nature of this Empire.

So the more grievous the contradictions, the more US hegemony is likely to be reinforced?

I think that's right. I shrink back a bit from the use of "hegemony". It was a term that became adopted by some Marxists who were trying to engage with mainstream International Relations people and didn't want to use the word "empire". I know how you're using the term; but the danger is that people think of hegemony as ideological. And I think of it as institutional. Ideologically, the gloss is off. It was already off under Bush. It came back briefly under Obama, but only briefly. Nevertheless there is global capitalist institutional dependence on the American state. And even the legitimacy that it still has in the eyes of the world's capitalists may not be primarily ideological: they rather see the US empire as the ultimate guarantor of their property. This is why the Chinese are still pouring funds into US Treasury Bills, and why there is the increased flow into Los Angeles real estate from Chinese capitalists. This US role as ultimate guarantor is not so much to do with American military prowess as people sometimes think. It is much more to do with the financial markets and the institutional determination of the Treasury and the Federal Reserve to bail out the system.

You once said you expected an evolution to a more directive oversight on the part of capitalist states, a social democratisation of globalisation in a sense; and there was a lot of talk about that, but mostly it looks like exactly the same sort of neoliberalism as before, apart from the monetary policies.

If what we mean by social democratisation is active states, then we have certainly seen active states, and they're oriented towards keeping global capitalism going. Almost twenty years ago, I wrote a piece in *Monthly Review* that looked at the World Bank's Development Report for 1997 and said that they had an agenda for the social democratisation of globalisation. Even there I pointed out that this involved more privatisation. It was a social democratisation in the sense of promoting an active state in job retraining, in education, etc., to the ends of securing national competitiveness in global capitalism. It was a certain Blairisation or Third Way-isation of globalisation.

After the first global crisis of the 21st century emerged, I did feel that the co-ordination of the fiscal stimulus after the crash was an indication of a certain social democratisation. I had no illusions that we'd see a social-democratisation of the kind we saw in the 1940s, nationalising some industries and so on, but I believed that the fiscal stimulus would continue; and instead, the fiscal stimulus has not been maintained, starting when Obama lost control of the US Congress in 2010. The Obama administration had been much more Keynesian than the British Conservatives or the Europeans, the Germans in particular. They had begged the Europeans to continue the stimulus. And they were not being radical in that respect. Many neoclassical economists are in favour of a sort of Keynesian fiscal stimulus today.

In June 2010, there was a G20 meeting which set targets for reducing the fiscal stimulus, targets for balancing budgets. That shift was very quick. There had been a slight recovery from the bottom of the slump in 2009. It was not just that Obama lost control; there was an official international communiqué much more specific than the ones were in the depths of the crisis in 2008–2009. The Germans successfully promoted balanced-budget constitutional amendments across Europe...

I don't know what that compromise was about in June 2010. It probably reflected domestic pressures in the USA, and certainly pressure from the Germans. There is an element here of the incompetence of Obama's administration. Their inability to get the Europeans off this balanced-budget line does reflect their incapacities as global managers. The Obama administration wasn't very good at managing Congress. You could say the same of the inability of Geithner, Bernanke, and more recently Jack Lew to convince the Europeans, as Summers or Rubin might have done in the 1990s. That's why I'm reluctant to use the term hegemony. The global structure is an empire, but not an empire with colonies. The states within it have relative autonomy. The Americans can't simply tell them what to do. By empire, what I mean is the internationalisation of the American state, so that it not only takes on responsibility for managing its own economy, but for managing global capitalism, with all the burdens involved. "Empire" does not mean the ability for the USA to force policies down others' throats, and this is what makes so contradictory the role of the American state in the extension and reproduction of global capitalism.

Of course, the short explanation for the return of a budget-balancing orientation is that it shows us the power of bond markets in the world today. They want states to give priority to paying them off, rather than to sustaining the livelihoods of poor people or paying out their pension obligations to workers. The bond markets want the top priority of every state to be paying off bond debt. This doesn't just come directly through bond markets. The pressure also comes from the regulators of pension funds, who are worried that given the low rates of return that pension funds get, states should give priority to fixing up their pension arrangements given low interest rates and much lower returns. The governments do neoliberal things like shifting resources into sustaining bond markets at the same time as they do other things like cutting back pensioners' rights. Some longer-term answers are to do with the strategic orientation of states like Germany and others who have been encouraged to follow its example, which is to have a currency which is favourable to their exports.

The deeper explanations require a much longer historical perspective. This is why Sam Gindin and I began our book *The Making of Global Capitalism* with a chapter called "The DNA of American Capitalism". We have to look at the way in which particular countries' bourgeoisies and states have been structured historically. That's why we're historical materialists. We need to understand the development of these particular capitals and these particular class relations through a long historical accretion of institutional capacity and institutional contradictions. That said, what must always be taken in account in understanding how these capacities and contradictions play out in any given conjuncture, including the current, is the balance of class forces, which is in this global crisis extremely unfavourable to the centre-left, let alone the left. One sees this in all kinds of ways. The way the media is incredulous at Jeremy Corbyn's economic policy, which is actually much less radical than the Labour policy was in the mid-1970s. Corbyn's not talking about nationalising five leading banks and several leading insurers, which was Labour policy back then.

Even where a shift in the balance of forces takes place, as in Greece, or Spain or Portugal, we see, and we Canadians understand this well, that the degree of integration of for example the Greek state means that it cannot just be a case of going back to the drachma. You would have to have import controls, If you had import controls you wouldn't be part of the EU. If you weren't part of the EU, what would happen to the budgets of departments which are dependent upon EU development funds, from health to education?

I am not adopting the position that "there is no alternative". I think we have to build the kind of capacity, institutionally, ideologically, that would allow us to address these facets of the crisis and build a new type of internationalism. If the Northern European working classes had been prepared to make some real movement... but there was no movement at all in France or Germany even to make some room for manoeuvre for the Syriza government.

I am in favour of pulling out of the Eurozone, and I don't think that this European Union can be reformed. It's been neoliberal in its DNA since the Treaty of Rome 1957. Its orientation was always to get to the point of opening up capital markets and to full free trade. But with that accomplished, it is not easy for any state, no matter who it's led by, to break with, given the depth of its integration into global capitalism. We need to find a new type of socialist internationalism, of labour internationalism. But that looks far away on the horizon, given the state of working-class institutions at the moment.

I don't want to leave this on a pessimistic note. I think that what the Corbyn phenomenon has indicated, like the rise of Syriza, Podemos, Sanders, or even events in Canada, where we have just managed to get rid of the proto-fascist Harper government by means of the Liberals running to the left of the social-democratic party and picking up a fiscal-stimulus kind of appeal. All these things are indicative of great potential, of maybe even a majority of people showing they are very capable of understanding what global capitalism subjects them to. The trouble is the heavy institutional demobilising weight of trade unions as they are currently organised, of social-democratic parties as they have evolved, of the lack of creativity in populist parties where they exist – it makes it difficult for this to be a generalised thing. And of course we also see, as soon as they do break through, the heavy weight of the media, social democracy, the old forces weighing on them.

I'm not as pessimistic as I sound. It's just that it's a very long struggle. Our institutional weakness at the minute means that it is the far right that is appealing to working people by virtue of attacking globalisation. The *Socialist Register* has just launched our 2016 volume on The Politics of the Right, and it focusses on the enormous dangers of these ideologically opportunist, and extremely ugly and nationalist and racist, movements on the right. But the nature of the bourgeoisies is a difference between now and the 1930s. Bourgeoisies trying to accumulate within the framework of highly internationalised capitalism rather than in the framework of the old inter-imperialist rivalries will be a brake on the far-right capitalist parties.

CHAPTER 31

A Protracted Transition (June 2016)

Discussion with Simon Mohun

In 2008 you could "not see how the neoliberal world order will be re-established", and you expected "a move to a much more state-managed economy". There was indeed a wave of nationalisations and of discussions for new regulations. Eight years later, though, governments are avid for new privatisations and new strippings of worker protections from the labour market, and the new regulations on banks and finance look weak. The IMF*'s Global Financial Stability Report (October 2014) finds that "most broad estimates point to a recent pick-up in shadow banking activity in the euro area, the United States, and the United Kingdom... In emerging markets, shadow banking continues to grow strongly, outstripping banking sector growth". Why do you think it is that neoliberal finance has proved so resilient and so able to fend off criticism and efforts to restrain it?*

In one sense you're right. At the same time I still think that I was right in saying that the 2007–9 crisis presaged the end of the neoliberal era. Only, as I already said back in 2008, any transition will be long and protracted. My evidence would be that the metropolitan advanced capitalist countries just haven't recovered from 2008–9. The only "Western" economy that has had a half-way decent recovery is the USA. Most people put that down to the Obama stimulus package, which dwarfed fiscal stimulus packages in other countries. Britain has been one of the worst performers, and that failure is laid at the door of Osborne's austerity policies. I think it's an open question, but a coordinated Keynesian stimulus might well have worked in around 2010. In any case, the advanced capitalist economies just aren't recovering. Even the US recovery has been much weaker than from previous downturns.

As a result, ideas that used to be considered anathema are being discussed in influential circles. The IMF Research Department has taken quite a progressive stance in suggesting more stimulus. The OECD has published reports on similar lines. The Bank of England has published research with ideas a million miles from conventional economic textbooks. In a whole range of institutions, there is the idea that current policies just aren't working. And so extraordinary

* Previously published at: https://senseofgfc.wordpress.com/2016/06/02/draft-questions-for-simon-mohun/, 3 July 2016.

measures are being considered, like helicopter money [the central bank printing extra cash to distribute free to households] or People's Quantitative Easing [extra cash printed directly to pay for investment in housing and public transport]. Adair Turner, who was chair of the Financial Services Authority from 2008 to 2013, has called for helicopter money to be considered as an option.[1]

My analogy would be the recovery after 1929–33. It really wasn't for another 13 or 14 years after 1933 that one could say that the US economy had recovered. Any analogy is obviously complicated by the facts of fascism and World War II in that period. But you see with Roosevelt's New Deal that he was making policy on the hoof. He'd try one thing, and if it didn't work he would scrap it and try another. He didn't have a very coherent strategy. It took a long time before a more or less consistent new regime of capitalist strategy emerged.

For now the alternatives are weak, and the transition will be protracted, but I would reiterate that the neoliberal era is dead. One indication that I would point to as significant is that rise of alternative political movements, of different stripes, which are united by contempt for the political establishment. In Spain, Podemos and the mayoral coalitions; in Greece, Syriza, though in many ways that's been a disaster; in the USA, the supporters of Trump and of Sanders, in their different ways; and in Britain, the support for Jeremy Corbyn, though here it is complicated by the widespread utter contempt for the whole political class ever since the parliamentary expenses scandal [of 2009]. Another and more dangerous indication of course is the rise of the far-right (for much the same reasons of frustration and "dead-endedness" that are behind the rise of the left).

But the contrast with the 1930s is that then there were relatively few "talking heads" proposing new ideas, and yet governments tried new policies. Now there are many such dissident "talking heads", and yet all governments and all official oppositions stick quite close to established neoliberal policies. In the right-wing populist movements ascendant in recent years – Ukip, the Front National, the BJP in India... – there is little social demagogy compared to their similars of the 1930s. Their promise is less that they will bring prosperity than that with them people will still be miserable but after all properly "British", properly "French", or properly "Hindu". And on the left, even before taking office in 2012, Syriza, with its Thessaloniki platform, had renounced any direct challenge to neoliberalism in favour of a promise to negotiate a better deal with the EU and distribute the proceeds in social alleviation.

1 https://www.imf.org/external/np/res/seminars/2015/arc/pdf/adair.pdf.

One issue that is under-theorised is this: what has been the point of public policy over the last eight years or so? The usual answer is that government have a responsibility to get the economy going again, and policy pursues that aim. But then you have to ask why Osborne doesn't see that his policy does not achieve that aim. The answer may be that the purpose of neoliberal policy has nothing to do with growth and expansion. It's to do with recasting the role of the state in the economy and an assault on the working class, as regards wages, the state underpinning of living standards (the welfare state), and job security. Specific policy aims are about changing the norm of what's expected for a reasonable standard of living. But changing norms is complicated and difficult. Different norms change at different speeds. The norms of how gay people are treated in our society have changed very dramatically and fast. Other norms (including I think what is expected of a reasonable standard of living) change very slowly.

There are other under-theorised issues. Finance capital, as the dominant form of capital, and very mobile internationally, does not really have a national home and therefore may not be particularly interested in what happens to the British (or any other national) economy per se. Also, in terms of profitability, capital has been doing pretty well right through the neoliberal era. One measure of that is the way that the big corporations are swimming in cash. Why aren't they investing the cash in new operations? Are they short of profitable investment opportunities? That does not seem convincing. Is it to do with the fact that investment costs less these days than it used to? For example take investment to do with computing power: falls in the cost of total investment do not correspond to falls in the amount of "stuff" that is invested.

Those are under-theorised aspects. I don't think the perspective of what I said in 2008 was wrong. But I do think the transition will be long and protracted. The big contrast here is with the late 1970s. The proponents of the neoliberal "revolution" knew what they wanted, and got it very quickly. That contrasts with today. Take Corbyn and McDonnell today. Do they have a coherent idea of the economy they want? Maybe, but I doubt it. Do they have a coherent idea of how they're going to get there? I don't think so.

In their books The Crisis of Neoliberalism *and* La Grande Bifurcation, *Gerard Duménil and Dominique Lévy suggest that the crisis may lead to neoliberalism being replaced by a new form of managerial capitalism. In fact, they propose that the labour movement should make an alliance with the managerial class to bring that about. What do you make of that idea?*

Duménil and Lévy have essentially a three-class model of society: capitalists, managers, workers. It's a reasonable one. In a recent article I've made estimates for the distribution of personal income in the US economy. In 2012, the capitalist class covers the top 1.4% of the income distribution, managers the next 15.6%, and working class the rest (the bottom 83%), which seems quite plausible [Mohun, 2016]. It is also plausible that in the 1970s and 80s the managerial class switched to support for finance capital. But the approach of Duménil and Lévy is a bit mechanical. The social-democratic regime was workers and managers against capitalists, neoliberalism is capitalists and managers against workers, and so a different future can only be workers and managers against capitalists again. If any new alliance is created, it won't be in the same form as before neoliberalism.

Hasn't neoliberalism and financialisation changed the composition and orientation of the managerial layers, too? These days, a vast number of workers with only modest supervisory duties, probably little different from those that a skilled manual worker would have over workers helping him or her a century ago, are labelled "managers", but at the same time higher managers have been brought closer to the capitalist class proper, and their orientation has been changed. The Wall Street Journal reported in 1998: "Ten years ago, a bedrock American company... wouldn't have dreamed of having an outsider as CEO. Today, they all do. Ten years ago, chief executive officers were rooted in one business and rarely strayed from it. Today, increasingly, they hopscotch around corporate America and across all industry boundaries... Call them the portable CEOs. They are the antithesis of the 1950s-style company man".[2] More recent figures confirm that picture. The turnover rate for CEOs was 16.5% per year in 1998–2005, up from 10% in the 1970s.[3] "In 2012, 27.1 percent of S&P 500 companies that faced a CEO succession hired an outsider for the top job...".[4] These managers, by training, by personal interest, and by culture, are as "financialised" as the financiers. They are surrounded by, and often are the same people as, the new flood of highly-paid non-executive directors. "A steady increase in the representation of independent directors on the board [of publicly-traded firms in the USA], from approximately 20% in 1950 to approximately 75% in 2005... Circa 1950, director compensation was low and sometimes nonexistent... As it became desirable for firms to put 'outsiders' on the board... significant compensation became common; indeed, it became increasingly lavish...", now around $200,000 a year in big companies.[5]

2 Article by John Helyar and Joann S. Lublin, *Wall Street Journal,* 21 January 1998.

3 Steven N. Kaplan and Bernadette A. Minton, NBER Working Paper 12465, August 2006.

4 The Conference Board: *CEO Succession Practices: 2013 Edition.*

5 Jeffrey N Gordon, The Rise of Independent Directors in the United States 1950–2005, *Stanford Law Review,* (59) 6, April 2007.

A significant number of managers have been coopted into identification with the capitalist class. The unequal distribution of income within the three main categories – workers, managers, capitalists – becomes more unequal as you move up from workers to capitalists, so that within the managerial class there is a very wide distribution of income. At the upper end very many will see themselves as identified with the capitalist class, or even likely to move into that class soon. At the bottom end some may see a unity of interest with the skilled working class; others may desperately fear slipping out of the managerial stratum and will have a different identification.

Another issue is to do with visibility. Britain is very unequal today, but to a considerable extent that's invisible. On the whole people compare their incomes to those whom they see as their peers or just ahead of them. We don't know how the top one per cent live. We don't come across them. They live in a different society. The world's top 25 hedge fund managers earned $13bn in 2015.[6] It's a figure so big it's difficult to understand.

Your research on the US economy indicates that the counterpart since 1979 of a decline in productive workers' wage share has been, not a rise in unproductive workers' wage share, but specifically a rise in managers' wage share. In some countries, notably Germany and Japan, top bosses' pay has risen much more modestly than in the USA.[7] How fundamental a trend in neoliberal capitalism do you think the rise in managers' wage share is?

Britain and the USA are significantly different because of their huge financial sectors. Britain is in a worse position, because the USA is still a significant manufacturing economy. Germany and Japan, of course, are also significant manufacturing economies. A manufacturing economy involves complex production processes and capitalists having to be concerned with skills, training, and education in the workforce. In Britain, none of that is true. The manufacturing sector is very weak. Education is neglected. The USA is more complicated in that respect because it has a huge university sector, which I think is something to do with being a not-very-old immigrant society with cultural norms that don't exist in Europe. In the USA there is a social recognition of the need for apprenticeships, education, training. In the UK the epitome would be Dyson, the vacuum-cleaner manufacturers. Its head office is near Swindon,

---

6 http://www.institutionalinvestorsalpha.com/Article/3552805/The-2016-Rich-List-of-the-Worlds-Top-Earning-Hedge-Fund-Managers.html.

7 Luis Gomez-Mejia and Steve Werner, *Global Compensation: Foundations and Perspectives*, London: Routledge, 2008, p.192.

but it employs people in this country only for administration and research and development. Its production is all outsourced in Malaysia.

Does that mean that Britain is the most "advanced economy", the model towards which Germany and Japan and others will move over time, slowly or fast? Or that Britain is an anomaly?

There are tendencies in that direction, towards the "British model", but tendencies in other directions too. And if neoliberalism is, at least in one sense, finished, then the trends towards extreme "financialisation" and decline of manufacturing are unlikely to work out in Germany and Japan as fully as they have in Britain or the USA.

In 2008 you argued that "relatively speaking, the US economy is in decline", though slowly. Do you think events since then have confirmed that judgement?

The USA has not been declining in recent years relative to the UK, Germany, or Japan. But its percentage of world output is falling. It is falling quite slowly, but other areas of the world are increasing their percentage quite fast, especially in south and east Asia.

Yes, the USA's share of world output has been on a falling trend for a long time, from 27% in 1950 to 18% more recently. The USA became a net importer of manufactured goods as long ago as 1983. But my question is really about whether the USA's hegemony in the world economy is declining, and that is a different question. Around 1971, when the dollar went off the gold standard, almost everyone interpreted that as a sign of a decline of US hegemony, a decline that would then accelerate. But that was wrong. In fact, up to the early years of the 21st century at least, the USA was able to increase its hegemony. The question is whether that trend has now reversed.

The significant event for US hegemony was the collapse of the USSR. When the Soviet Union existed, the US defined its imperialist ambitions in terms of countering communism, whether one puts it in inverted commas or not. Since the collapse of the USSR, it has been much more complicated for the USA to intervene. Look at the Middle East today. What would constitute a successful intervention in Syria today? US strategists don't know.

The USA intended its invasion of Iraq in 2003 to be a lever for the transformation of the whole Middle East to make it more secure for the USA and for capital. That failed dramatically, and surely that has weakened the USA in the aftermath. The question is whether that was an episode which will be overcome in time, or part of a new trend for US hegemony to decline. In hindsight we tend to see US hegemony before the 1970s as tidier than in fact it was. Actually in that era the USA failed, or did not even try much, to dominate many particular developments, and yet its overall hegemony remained robust. Maybe the same is still true.

When the dollar was decoupled from gold in 1971, most of the left was talking in terms of inter-imperialist rivalries. In retrospect, everybody massively underestimated the significance of the dollar remaining the world's reserve currency. That gives the US huge power relative to other countries. It enables it to run huge trade deficits indefinitely, without problems. As long as the dollar remains the world's reserve currency, any relative imperialist decline will be limited. In the early 2000s, many writers pointed to the fact that China was holding so many US Treasury bonds: China would only have to sell them for the USA to go into complete catastrophe. But China wouldn't sell them, because they would have as much or more to lose from a collapse of the price of US Treasuries. The left didn't really take on board what the dollar being the world reserve currency meant; and that is secure for the foreseeable future.

CHAPTER 32

Brazil and Neoliberalism (July–August 2016)

Discussion with Alfredo Saad-Filho

Neoliberalism: Nurtured by Dysfunction

Do the developments since 2008 tells us that dysfunction (only to a certain degree, of course, but to a substantial degree) is functional for neoliberalism?

In your 2011 article (Saad-Filho 2011) you write that: "Under neoliberalism, state capacity to allocate resources... has been systematically transferred to an increasingly globalised financial sector in which US institutions play a dominant role". Neoliberalism is an era of huge quicksilver world financial markets and fast-mutating global production chains, in which the regulating principle for each state is to make its territory accessible, secure, and attractive for globally-mobile capital. Dysfunction makes that imperative bite more sharply.

You wrote in 2011: "this is a systemic crisis in neoliberalism, but it is not a crisis of neoliberalism because, although the reproduction of the system of accumulation has been shaken, it is not currently threatened by a systemic alternative".

You add now (July 2016) that "neoliberalism is resilient, but of course it does have contradictions. It is resilient because it is an internally consistent (as far as capitalism is consistent) and self-reinforcing system of accumulation (in the sense of a stage, phase or mode of existence of capitalism). Interestingly, crises tend to reinforce the system, because they promote modes of behaviour and "discipline" that supports this modality of social reproduction: crises lead to "austerity", the rollback of the welfare state (thus reduce the social wage and make the workers more dependent on capital), impose discipline on the state itself, banks, capital etc, intensify competition, and so on. In addition to these general outcomes, neoliberalism has been very successful intensifying financialisation in the wake of the crisis. There are problems also, of course, shown in the rise of new movements of resistance, which we do not need to review. But the point remains: neoliberalism specifically, and capitalism in general, will not collapse spontaneously or even drift into a quiet sleep perhaps because the rate of profit keeps falling or whatever.

* Previously published at: https://senseofgfc.wordpress.com/2016/03/28/questions-to-alfredo-saad-filho/, 6 August 2016.

They will be disarticulated and driven to collapse only through mass movements led by the working class. There is no other hope for social change".

Generally, a crisis "in" some system means a weakening, a step towards a crisis "of" the system. The crash of 2008 threw governments into disarray; confounded and discomforted neoliberal doctrinaires; and stirred up opposition movements like Occupy (2011). But once the governments had recovered themselves, if only partially, the crisis indeed "tended to reinforce the system". As with the proverbial definition of insanity, dysfunction and crises in neoliberalism tend to make its people repeat and increase the dose, rather than seeking different ways. State pursue policies which ease or push the envelope of neoliberalism more readily when neoliberalism is relatively stable and thriving than when it is in trouble.

Some similar things happened with pre-Keynesian orthodox economics, with turmoil after World War I prompting the return to the gold standard around 1925, and many states responding immediately responding to the crash of 1929–31 by seeking to balance their budgets. And also with the "mixed economy" doctrines of the 1950s and 60s: the crisis of 1973–5 led initially to a stepping-up of "Keynesian" and "dirigiste" intervention. But those seem more a matter of ordinary ideological inertia than of dysfunction being functional to the regime.

There are several issues here. One is that modes of thought tend to persist even when they have become poorly adapted to the changed circumstances in the world. Two is that ideologies also persist. Three is that when a crisis threatens the hegemony of a particular configuration of capitalism, and the world order associated with it (the imperialist power structure, and the class relations which constitute it, and that are parasitical upon it) there is also a tendency to try and restore the status quo ante, by applying the same policies "as before", but more intensively, because the disequilibria is perceived to be larger. Often this works; sometimes it leads to further instability, and the aftermath of 1929 offers one example of the latter.

There are two levels, then, to see the specific problem of neoliberalism. At one level, capitalism (and neoliberalism as its contemporary form) has a degree of integrity or internal consistency. Unemployment tends to bring down wages and the value of labour power, and market processes can lead to the absorption of some of the unemployed for whatever reason into this or that sector. These are material processes; not merely ideological illusions: within limits, markets do work.

The current crisis offers another example: there is a crisis driven by financial processes, and "austerity" can both help to fund the banks and impose discipline on the workers and other social groups: all this helps to restore the usual functioning of neoliberalism. This is a crisis "in" neoliberalism. This could become a crisis "of" neoliberalism – and this is my second level of analysis – if the reproduction of the system of accumulation is fundamentally destabilised. In my view, this is only likely to happen if there is a challenge coming from mass movements led by the working class. Failing that, the instabilities and inequities generated within neoliberalism will still exist, but they will appear through unemployment, poverty, accelerating environmental degradation, and the degradation of the working class, through divisions, strife, racism, cumulative disorganisation, and so on.

The outcomes cannot be predicted, and there are no "structural tendencies" here: either mass organisations led by the left manage to succeed, and stem the tide of destruction and degradation wrought by capitalism in general, and financialised neoliberalism in particular, or they do not, with severely adverse consequences for the majority, and for the planet as a whole. We struggle on, with many defeats to show, but some important victories too.

1982 and Neoliberalism in Latin America

José Gabriel Palma argues that "neoliberalism has conquered [Latin America], including many in its left-wing intelligentsia, as completely (and fiercely) as the Inquisition conquered Spain" (Palma 2012). He dates that back to the debt shock of the early 1980s: "most politicians and economists interpreted the 1982 debt crisis as conclusive evidence that import-substitution industrialisation had led the region into a cul-de-sac". Is that another example of dysfunction being functional to neoliberalism? Neoliberalism has brought more financial crises than previous regimes of capitalism, but so far those dysfunctions (that 1982 debt crisis; the 1987 stock market crash; the US S&L crisis and collapse of the junk bond market in the late 80s and early 90s; the "Tequila crisis" of 1994; the "Asian crisis" of 1997–8; the "dot.com" crisis of 2000) have prompted a ratcheting-forward of neoliberalism rather than an easing or progressive dissolution of it.

First, I agree with Palma. Second, the 1982 crisis was part of the transition to neoliberalism, rather than a "typical" crisis in neoliberalism. It did trigger the collapse of import-substituting industrialisation across Latin America and elsewhere. It is also true that neoliberalism has been associated with increased (financial) volatility and a proliferation of crises in different countries.

Third, it is true that these crises have generally led to a ratcheting up, or forward, of neoliberalism.

Pushing the Envelope of Neoliberalism – and Its Limits

Should the Lula administration in Brazil, 2002–10, be seen as the biggest effort yet to push the envelope of neoliberalism in the direction of social easing? Government measures included Bolsa Família; bringing many "informal" workers into formal contracts; mass connections to the electricity grid; a rapidly rising minimum wage plus increases in pensions and benefits; better spending on the still-patchy health and education systems; and broadening university access. The Brazil Development Bank became the world's biggest development bank, outstripping the World Bank.

"Unemployment fell sharply… Inequality declined… The incomes of the bottom decile rose by 91 per cent between 2001 and 2009, while the incomes of the top decile increased by a more modest 16 per cent. Incomes rose by 42 per cent in the poorer northeast of the country against 16 per cent in the southeast… Female income rose by 38 per cent against 16 per cent for men…the income of blacks rose 43 per cent against 20 per cent for whites… The population below the poverty line fell from 36 per cent in 2003 to 23 per cent in 2008" (Saad-Filho and Morais, 2014).

As you note (Saad-Filho and Boito 2016), the PT government "maintained (with limited and temporary flexibility in implementation) the neoliberal… 'policy tripod' [a floating currency, inflation targeting and a primary fiscal surplus]". In other words, the PT stretched neoliberalism rather than challenging it. The PT also did little to change the state or the political system, and increased public infrastructure investment little. If, however, the PT had done a bit more on those fronts – within the spectrum defined by pushing the envelope of neoliberalism – rather than mobilising the working class to expropriate capital and start socialist construction – that might have been desirable, but would not have changed the overall shape of events.

Within that spectrum, it was a big and exceptional achievement to reduce inequality and expand workers' rights. The PT's record shows that such things can be done even within the broad constraints of neoliberalism. At least, they can be done by a determined government, in a resource-rich country, in a period of relative world capitalist prosperity. Events since 2011 also show how limited and fragile those achievements are.

The PT government failed also to make Brazil's economy more robust and productive. Brazil's deindustrialisation, which had started in the 1980s, continued apace. Manufacturing industry, which had risen from 20% of GDP in 1947 to 36% in 1985, has continued to decline since then, to just 13% of GDP in 2013. Brazil's average labour productivity, which rose from 20% of the USA's in 1960 to 27% in 1980, was down to 19% in 2010; productivity has lagged especially in manufacturing

(Palma 2015). The record is thus evidence both (1) that those self-proclaimed reformists who say that governments are helpless in the globalised economy, and only tiny modifications are possible short of out-and-out revolution, are only covering up their own timidity and subservience to bourgeois orthodoxies; (2) that limiting socialist aims to what can be done by pushing the envelope of neoliberalism is a course likely to end in political collapse and rout when world-market circumstances turn sour.

The administrations led by the PT have contributed to an improvement in the overall conditions of the working class in Brazil. There can be no doubt about that. But they did so within a broader neoliberal framework: there was a lot of employment creation, but mostly in services and these were largely very low paid jobs. Patterns of consumption increased, but they were funded by these badly paid jobs and by a ratcheting up of financialisation, with a very rapid growth of consumer debt. There was a significant expansion of social provision and benefits, but these were used as a lever to promote financialisation (for example, state benefits could be used as collateral for loans from the private banking system: the banks were great beneficiaries of the expansion of employment and social policy in Brazil!). What the PT governments did, then, is a form of neoliberalism – they never broke with the logic of neoliberalism – but looked for avenues to moderate its effects, to bring some gains to the workers, and so on. To a certain extent they were successful. There were worse alternatives. But the PT governments did not build the organisative capacity of the workers; they did not build alternatives to neoliberalism; they do not promote any kind of anti-capitalist vision in society. They did not even contribute to transcending neoliberalism or to the construction of a more humane form of capitalism. It was social democracy of the most moderate kind. So: important gains, no doubt, especially in a world where naked neoliberalism is the norm, but those gains were very limited and, as we can see now, they were not sustainable.

Brazil in the World Markets

You write (July 2016) that: "There was no meaningful attempt [by the PT government] to...transform the country's economic structure or its international integration". The government played a leading part in sinking (in 2005) the US-proposed Free Trade Agreement of the Americas, in developing Mercosur (founded 1991), and in launching the Union of South American Nations (Unasur, a grouping designed to move beyond regional trade agreements to wider cooperation on the model of the EU) in 2007. Yet Brazil's chief economic linkages remain outside

Unasur (with China, the USA, Spain, and other European countries), and the Mercosur-Unasur line has been a continuation of previous Brazilian policy rather than a new shift.

By 2009 China had displaced the USA as Brazil's largest trade partner, and investment from China in Brazil has also increased. From 1999 to 2011 Brazil's exports to China (primarily of soybeans and iron ore) grew at 47% per year and its imports from China at 38% per year. Manufactured goods rose from 12% of exports to 60% by the early 1990s, and then declined to less than 40% (2010). Primary products fell from 75% of Brazil's exports in 1970 to 22% in 2000, and then rose to over 40% (2010). Foreign direct investments both into Brazil and out of Brazil have been much higher (though volatile) since 1995.

All those shifts started before the PT took office. Is it fair to say that they weaken the previously dominant position of the USA in Brazil's trade, but they have not reduced Brazil's vulnerability to shifts in the capitalist world markets? The current slump in Brazil – containerised exports from China to Brazil were fully 60% lower in January 2016 than a year earlier – was triggered by faltering prices of primary commodities, which now dominate Brazil's exports, and financial fragility arising from post-2008 "Quantitative Easing" in the richer countries. "By some estimates... up to US$7 trillion of QE funds flooded emerging markets since the Fed began buying bonds in 2008... These funds were used...in Latin America...mostly to finance capital flight, a variety of deficits, M&A and all sorts of financial deeds" (Palma, 2015).

Brazil remains very vulnerable to the fluctuations in international trade. The country inserted itself in the global division of labour through a process of deindustrialisation and reprimarisation – returning to a priority of agro-exports and mineral exports targeting the Chinese market. This is short-termist, and it was destructive for Brazilian manufacturing industry, and for the better-paid jobs that that sector could have created. This is unfortunate, and it is another demonstration of the search for the easiest path which was typical of the PT administrations: avoiding confrontation, avoiding shaking up established interests, and so on, and trying to accommodate and oil the wheels of a slightly more benevolent form of neoliberalism, rather than confronting it and building sustainable alternatives.

How the PT Sacrificed the Movement for "Governability"

You write (July 2016): "The impeachment process is a class conspiracy to remove Dilma Rousseff, destroy the PT, and put Lula in jail. This is the domestic aspect. The international aspect is also interesting because we are now in the third phase of the global crisis. The crisis started in 2007, centred in the US *financial markets. Then it was kind-of-contained, and the second phase exploded in the Eurozone in about 2010. That was contained at least provisionally by 2012. Now the third phase is in the middle-income countries. They are all in trouble, perhaps with the exception of India – but the others, Brazil, Russia, Turkey, Argentina, etc. etc., are all doing badly. Even China of course, but the situation is very different in that case. There are reasons for this – especially capital flows going back to the leading capitalist countries, after the massive flows to the middle-income countries in the wake of* QE*. This has destabilised the middle-income countries as capital was flowing in, and also when it's flowing out. Also trade has not recovered, commodity prices are down, and so on.*

"The other interesting process in this regard is that the third phase of the global crisis has been associated with a 'new authoritarianism' emerging almost everywhere: India, Turkey, Brazil, almost the entire Eastern periphery of the EU*, France, Denmark, then Trump and* UKIP *and so on".*

That various populist right-wing forces would batten on the crisis was inevitable. The question is the ability or inability of the left to respond. In the Brazilian case, is the chief advantage for the right the way that the PT *leaders accompanied their entry into state and municipal, and then federal-government, office with gutting the internal life of the* PT*? That they substituted manoeuvres with other parties and with sections of the ruling class for the work of building a strong, democratic, active, well-rooted party?*

The PT *was launched in 1980 on the back of working-class revolt against the military dictatorship. It defined itself as revolutionary and socialist. It had an active membership and lively internal debate. But then "the political learning achieved by* PT *mayors in a wide variety of Brazilian municipalities" (Hunter 2011) plus the absorption after 2002 of many* PT *cadres into government positions led to "growing pragmatism over time". The party was unable to sustain itself as an active and independent force, to use the popularity which some of Lula's measures won it among Brazil's poorest to renew its activist base, or even to generate a media presence and reach capable of challenging the established right-wing media.*

There is no doubt that the PT sacrificed itself, as a mass left wing party, based upon social movements, in order to pursue electoral victories and "governability". They did so, partly as a condition of victory – they took people off the streets, disorganised their own base, demolished their capacity to lead mass movements – in order to create "confidence" that would support alliances with conventional political forces and sections of the bourgeoisie. They succeeded, and while the international economic conditions were favourable, the PT achieved important successes. But once circumstances changed, they could not mobilise significant social groups to defend their own governments, and the PT now risks being obliterated by the neoliberal reaction.

Fractions of the Bourgeoisie and the Old Program of the Brazilian Communist Party

You have written: "The political conflicts during the Workers' Party administrations led by Luís Inácio Lula da Silva and Dilma Rousseff have been driven by disputes between two fractions of the country's bourgeoisie: the internal and the internationalised bourgeoisie.

"Following Nicos Poulantzas, the first fraction may be called the large internal bourgeoisie. It includes the owners of large firms across manufacturing, construction, agribusiness, food processing, shipbuilding, banking, and other sectors. The main goal of this fraction is to shore up its own economic and political position within Brazilian dependent capitalism, which implies a relationship of cooperation as well as conflict with international capital and the internationalised fraction of the bourgeoisie. Although segments of the internal bourgeoisie may be more or less closely related to international capital (e.g., finance is especially close, while construction is more autonomous), the internal bourgeoisie as a whole demands (different forms of) state protection to shore up its command of domestic markets and support its expansion abroad, especially in the Global South.

"The internationalised bourgeoisie includes the representatives of economic groups owned by foreign capital and the domestic firms directly dependent upon them. It consists of international banks, insurance companies, large consultancy and accountancy firms, transnational and internationally integrated manufacturing capital, and – very important – the mainstream media. Although the media are almost entirely owned by domestic capital, they are committed ideologically to neoliberal financialisation and the transnational integration of the Brazilian economy and reject the notion of a 'national' development strategy" (Boito and Saad-Filho 2016).

Isn't this analysis vulnerable to the critique made of Poulantzas, that the "internal bourgeoisie" concept is really only a rewording of the old Stalinist concept of "national bourgeoisie", coined to serve apologetics for class-collaboration policies by way of inflating differences of political alignment within bourgeoisies (which certainly exist) into a picture of two bourgeoisies, one progressive and one reactionary? Or, to put it another way, although Abu-el-Haj's critique (Abu-el-Haj 2016) has an excessive proportion of assertion to evidence, isn't there in fact evidence for his assertions?

The dividing line between the fractions is unclear. Corporations like JBS *(one of the world's leading meat-processing firms), Gerdau (a big steelmaker), Odebrecht (construction), and Embraer (aircraft), benefited much from the* PT*'s expansion of Brazil Development Bank credit, and some of their bosses have been investigated or jailed during the recent agitation about corruption. You seem to classify them as "internal". Yet they are highly internationalised. Indeed, Brazil Development Bank credit helped them internationalise. On the other hand, the main media firms are "internal", and yet, as you point out, anti-*PT.

If the political conflicts so mechanically represented different economic fractions of the bourgeoisie, then the "internal bourgeoisie" should be dominant, since Brazil is a large country, less dependent than smaller ones on international trade, with most capital domestically-owned. Foreign-owned firms have no strong economic reason for opposing Brazilian capital's "national development strategies", since they are interested in the expansion of Brazil's internal market, and the policy supposedly representing the "internal bourgeoisie" (the PT*'s) has never done much to reduce Brazil's openness to foreign capital.*

The big fluctuations in political alignments cast further doubt on the theory. Lula had a 90% approval rating at the end of his period as president. Yet the internationalised bourgeoisie had not suddenly disappeared or shrunk: on the whole, Brazil's economy was more "internationalised" in 2010 than in 2002.

The internationalised bourgeoisie has always been hegemonic on your account, since you describe the reactions of the internal bourgeoisie as relatively defensive, but, if that were so, and if the internationalised bourgeoisie were so cohesive and self-aware a fraction, then it would be able to create a strong political party. In fact, the PSDB*, the nearest approach to such a party, is still weak: even after the "impeachment" coup, opinion polls show* PSDB *candidates scoring poorly for the 2018 presidential election, well behind the* PT *and also behind the populist but not coherently neoliberal Rede of Marina Silva (Folha de S. Paulo, 18/07/16).*

During the good years for the PT *administrations, almost all sectors of the population were willing either to support them, or to go along with them despite annoyances and resentments. For all sections of the bourgeoisie, these were competent, less-corrupt administrations; if they disliked policies favouring the poor, they themselves were still prospering. Now no-one much is prospering, and no quick end to the trouble is in sight. The base of the* PT*, progressively demobilised since the mid-1990s, lacks capacity to propose socialist struggle against capitalism as an alternative to the policy, now in trouble, of inflecting the distribution of the fruits of capitalist prosperity in a more "social" direction, so right-wing responses have a free field. The annoyances and resentments of the upper middle classes and many sectors of the bourgeoisie now have no dampener; for them, calls for a return to neoliberal basics and no more social experiments become* *more attractive. And a large part of the population is frustrated and available to be mobilised by catch-call cries against corruption.*

If this latter account is on the right lines, two things follow. The post-12-May government is weak, because it does not (or not yet) represent a solid, cohesive, social and economic bloc. And, both in Brazil and in other countries, to search for a separated-off "internal" bourgeoisie as an interim ally for progress is a policy which can only lead to disappointments and demobilisation of the labour movement.

There are several issues here. First, there are, and remain, important ideological differences between fractions of the bourgeoisie; they also have slightly distinct material interests, e.g., more focused on the internal market or more on the external market; more connected to finance or less so, and so on. Second, there can be links drawn to earlier forms of conceptualising the bourgeoisie, for example, it is plausible to say that the PT managed to build – in part! – and very imperfectly – the program of the old Brazilian Communist Party in the 1950s, focusing on a national developmental alliance. But this alliance was not led by the working class, and it did include many segments of agribusiness, which in old times would have been considered "feudal" and thus unacceptable partners. Third, corruption is an important but secondary issue. In the context of the ongoing political and economic crisis in Brazil, it is being used as a stick with which to beat the PT and the segments of the bourgeoisie aligned with it. They have been chased up, and attacked viciously by a judicial-media-right-wing conspiracy. This is a conspiracy, because the investigations stop when they stray away from the PT and from the segments of capital that fund the PT. So there is clearly a motive and a driving force here, and this is not to eliminate corruption or anything of that sort, but to destroy the PT and its sources of funding. This is what is really going on: it's a political offensive, not a legal process.

Afterword: 2016

Like every crisis, 2008's surprised. Some of us failed to see how turmoil originating in finance, and apparently in a limited area of finance to do with the US housing market, could have such great impact on factories and offices which were not booming, but still jogging along with tidy profits. Others saw those tidy profits as artefacts of inaccurate accounting, or illusory gains created by an unsustainable pumping-up of debt used to cover up inability to resolve previous crises. My own view is that 2008 was genuinely new: the profits of the years before it were real, but so was the imbrication of the capitalist world into a network of financial relations so taut that an apparently-local crash could disrupt it worldwide.

We wondered what shape of capitalism would emerge from the crash. Frequently in the history of capitalism, economic crises have broken the inertia of bourgeois wisdom and triggered political shifts or conflicts. Some saw 2008 as having fatally wounded neoliberal policy: a new turn might be slow in coming, but it was inevitable, and the left could hope at least to inflect it. Others reasoned that the governments had sought only, albeit by temporary methods contradicting their previous orthodoxies, to patch up the hegemony of globally-fluid finance capital, and so neoliberalism would be resilient unless the left gained great new strength.

As of late 2016, facts seem to confirm both strands of argument in part. There have been political shifts. So far, the great winner has been right-wing nationalist and populist forces. They do not denounce neoliberalism as such. Some of them, such as Modi in India, rather advocate it. The Front National in France increasingly speaks against "ultraliberalism" but not against "liberalism" as such: the word "liberalism" is often used in France to mean what would elsewhere be called economic neoliberalism. Donald Trump, as John Weeks puts it, represents not so much a rejection of neoliberalism as a climax of its drive to remove restraints on the abuses of capital (Weeks 2016). Trump says he favours free trade, he objects only to poorly negotiated trade agreements, and that, if left free to swagger and threaten, he, with his "art of the deal", can do better. But there is now a serious risk that this climax-from-within of neoliberal combativity could disrupt the whole world order of neoliberalism. At the same time, new left-wing mobilisations have developed: they have the potential to defeat the burgeoning right-wing backlash, but only if they can sharpen themselves politically.

The neoliberal capitalist regime since the 1980s emerged organically from the basic drives of capitalism and from the previous regime, but is inherently febrile. It generates a financial superstructure which is inherently febrile and crisis-prone, but organically and multifariously connected with the world of production. In 2008 the capitalist politicians who once shouted loudest in favour of "free markets" accepted hugely expanded state intervention in the economy. The government of George W Bush carried out the biggest nationalisations in history. Even before that, the notion of "free markets" was misleading. For a long time now, the giant enterprises which dominated the economy had, to a great extent, been "socialised" – organised on a vast, society-wide basis, with huge numbers of people working collectively and cooperatively, but under the control and in the interests of the capitalists, and dependent for their operation on public infrastructure.

The state intervention made a fundamental case for socialism – that the social economy, privately owned, needs to be socially owned and controlled. But it was "socialism for the rich". The governments intervened, and effectively, to socialise the economy's losses, so as better to continue to privatise its gains. The nationalised or part-nationalised banks did not stop paying their bosses huge salaries or repossessing the homes and ruining the lives of working-class people. The governments explicitly wanted the nationalised or part-nationalised banks to operate on a private-profit basis and to be re-privatised as soon as possible.

Since 2010 most governments have returned to undiluted versions of the neo-liberal course set since the 1980s: social cuts, marketisation, privatisation, stripping of labour-market protections. They have assumed that electorates will accept these measures as necessary or at least inevitable. The accompanying monetary policies (ultra-low interest rates, pumping-up of the monetary base, "quantitative easing") are different from those pursued before 2008, but in line with orthodox economy theory, and not incompatible with neo-liberalism.

Even the conservative *Financial Times* columnist Martin Wolf was moved by the 2008 fiasco to write: "Banks, as presently constituted and managed, cannot be trusted to perform any publicly important function, against the perceived interests of their staff [meaning their top bosses, not the ordinary workers]. Today's banks represent the incarnation of profit-seeking behaviour taken to its logical limits, in which the only question asked by senior staff is not what is their duty or their responsibility, but what can they get away with" (*Financial Times*, 2 July 2012). Banks have faced more critical scrutiny. Thus, the series of scandals spilling since 2008: about mis-selling of mortgage-backed securities, of payment insurance, of credit schemes, etc.; about rigging interest and currency-exchange rates; about tax avoidance and evasion (and banks' role in helping them), and tax havens. And thus, voluminous new regulations and legislation, like the USA's 2319-page Dodd-Frank Act of July 2010.

But the new legislation and regulations change nothing decisive. Partly this is because financial capitalists remain a concentrated and powerful lobby. "The financial industry ... is back on its feet now, punching its weight – or above – and showing precious little gratitude to the government that saved it ... The industry has proved to be a formidable foe of financial reform ..." (Blinder 2013, p. 454). As of late 2015, 36% of the rules required in order to put the Dodd-Frank Act into effect had not yet been decided, and of the other 64% many had been softened by bankers' lobbying. Republicans want to repeal Dodd-Frank altogether.

The system's immediate recovery from the deep slump of 2009 was relatively quick. It has been followed by, not a rebound, but only faltering growth, and much slower growth of world trade than before 2008. Frantic competitive cost-cutting, gross uncertainty of long-term markets, governments' focus on making their countries "safe to invest in", corporations' focus on quick cash returns and on remaining nimble-footed in a chaotic world by pumping up liquidity, all contribute to these trends. Financial assets are tickets to portions of future surplus-value. The 2008 crash was a warning that the expectations embodied in financial-asset prices then were false. Central banks and governments intervened to limit the crash in financial-asset prices. That intervention, to "stick", must provide some back-up for the claims on future surplus-value signalled by the financial-asset prices. In the capitalist long-term, that means boosting real output. In the short and medium term, it can mean something different or even contrary: governments squeezing the population through taxes and social cuts, and corporations anxiously holding on to cash or near-cash, in order to be sure of keeping up payments.

I can see no absolute block to a recovery to the growth rates at least of the period before 2007. However, it is not happening now, and the plagues of the current "chaotic regulation" (Husson 2009) are unlikely to be cured soon. A new crash may well intervene before conditions can be assembled for a larger recovery. In that new crash, or maybe as a political move preceding and triggering it, the elaborate checks and balances of the US-keystone neoliberal world order may well be disrupted from the right.

The USA remained hegemonic in the world capitalist economy after the loss in the 1960s of its industrial dominance, the collapse in 1971 of the Bretton Woods structure set up after World War II to organise the hegemony, and the turmoil of the 1970s. "The United States' structural power has, on balance, increased" (Strange 1987). The surge since 1989–91 of the global reach of organisations like the WTO, the IMF, and the G7, in which the USA is pivotal, confirms Strange's view of what happened from the 1970s right up to 2008 and its immediate aftermath.

The USA still has the biggest markets; US corporations lead in high technology; and "America has the ability to control the supply and availability of credit denominated in dollars, and thus to exert predominant influence for good or ill over the creation of credit in the world's monetary system" (Strange 1987. See also Panitch and Gindin 2013). The fiasco of the USA's 2003 invasion of Iraq has surely weakened the military and diplomatic hegemony of the USA. The events of 2008, and the big losses sustained in the crash, were apt to weaken New York's position as the centre of global finance. The IMF's resources (about $380 billion in late 2015) were revealed to be too small to "bail out" governments hit by the crisis. Sovereign wealth funds like the UAE's ($800 billion), China's ($750 billion), and Saudi Arabia's ($700 billion), are bigger. In 2014 China was able to launch the New Development Bank and the Asian Infrastructure Investment Bank, each with capital of $100 billion, both bypassing the USA.

Yet up to 2016 US hegemony has continued. Foreign holdings of US securities increased from $10,000 billion in June 2008 to $16,500 billion in June 2014. The billions of cash US dollars held abroad have increased, too. "When global financial markets get nervous, US Treasuries remain the ultimate safe haven" (Blinder 2013, p. 395). It will be a long time before gradual processes can decisively subvert US hegemony, and 2008 showed that some crises in US hegemony can actually end up reinforcing it. Any sudden sell-off of dollars or US Treasury securities will be countered not just by the US government, but by other governments and wealth-holders with large holdings of dollars and Treasuries. Yet that is not an absolute. The vast volume of holdings, and the vast size of the constant inflow of capital that the USA needs to balance its trade deficit on goods and services of over $500 billion a year, puts it within the range of possibilities that a sell-off could gather such momentum that some holders of US securities and cash, resisting the sell-off, would be overwhelmed, and others would opt for reducing their losses by trying to be among the first out of the door. Such an event would exceed the crash of 2008 in impact. It would collapse credit across the world.

Most notable in the left-wing responses to the 2008 crash have been the democratic and secular impulses in the Arab Spring of 2011; the rise of Syriza in Greece and Podemos in Spain; the Corbyn surge in Britain; the Sanders movement in the USA. So far, however, the temper and tone of that left-wing revival remains soft. It comes after a long period of capitalist triumphalism which has weighed down on the left, making "official" left parties conformist, and even activist left groupings unconfident. The leftish Tamarod movement in Egypt, which brought down Morsi's Muslim Brotherhood regime in 2013, was unable to resist, or even form a cohesive opposition to, the subsequent organisation of a military-dominated authoritarian regime by Abdel Fattah el-Sisi. Syriza had already before its January 2015 election victory reduced its program to a list of alleviations to be won through negotiating with the European Union, and when the EU leaders stood stubborn, it capitulated. Podemos, having made big gains in Spain's December 2015 elections, proposed a list of priorities for a new government which included nothing definitely anti-capitalist: adapting buildings for energy efficiency standards; banning ministers, MPs and their assistants from company boards in sectors which they have dealt with as politicians; an easing of VAT and social security burdens on small business; and a guaranteed minimum income of €600 a month. In Britain, Labour's new left-wing Shadow Chancellor appointed in September 2015, John McDonnell, has tried to placate the media by claiming that the difference between him and the Labour Party's previous milder-austerity policy is just one of speed: "Look, on domestic politics, there is virtually nothing between us, absolutely nothing, other than that some want to go faster than others" (McDonnell, 2015). Much of the avowedly-revolutionary activist left, most of the time, limits itself to advocating more militant tactics in pursuit of minimalist and defensive aims ("stop cuts").

Support for mainstream consensus parties has been eroded by the crisis and depression. So far, the bigger gains have gone to nationalist, sectarian, or "identity politics" groupings, mostly more or less right wing. The advance of political Islamism after the Arab Spring, especially with Daesh in Syria and Iraq; the BJP victory in India; the results of the European elections of May 2014; the Brexit vote in the UK on 23 June 2016; and the successive right-wing mobilisations in the USA (Tea Party, Trump) show that. In Europe, the right gained most in the richer countries, less hard-hit by the economic crisis, and left-wing or leftish parties gained most in the poorer and harder-hit countries.

Many discontented people, looking for a grand narrative and hearing only a weak message from the left, are receptive to a scapegoating story from the right which appeals to feelings of identity and territory. The right proposes to blame and exclude worse-off, insecure people who have no entrenched power. To soured and demoralised people, that sounds like an easier way of "doing something" than battle against remote-seeming, intangible-seeming, ostentatiously-mighty global capital. The far-right groupings offer less social demagogy than their equivalents of the 1930s. They promise not to solve social ills, or even to challenge global neo-liberal policies, but only to penalise immigrants or infidels. Noise about restoring national or religious identity and culture, about "taking back America", "restoring the caliphate", or "taking control of our borders", suggests that at least in that direction "something will be done".

A fascist seizure of power, as in the 1930s, would mean the crushing of the labour movement and the suppression of all free speech and debate. That is not round the very next corner. None of the far-right parties, except on a small scale Golden Dawn in Greece and maybe Jobbik in Hungary, has the militant street-fighting base that the fascists of the 1920s and 30s had. The more electoralist far-right parties might well, if they enter coalition governments, gravitate towards mainstream conservatism on economic policy, and distinguish themselves mainly by even more brutal anti-migrant policies. Yet one such right-wing mobilisation has already won a majority for the exit of Britain from the European Union; others may be triggering further dislocations of the EU; or even start a serious spiral of protectionist measures to re-raise economic barriers between countries. And then conditions for a full-scale fascist seizure of power could quickly be generated.

Those possibilities have been jolted closer by Donald Trump's victory in the 8 November 2016 US presidential election. Trump will surely hack back migrants', workers', women's, and civil rights; speed environmental destruction; and raise risks of war, especially with Iran. He may also disrupt the large trends which have allowed capitalist growth for 60 years.

A trade-liberalising, world-market-boosting trend, embedded in institutions keystoned by the USA, was launched in 1947 and has emerged from five major convulsions since then strengthened or intact. It survived the US dollar's breaking of its link with gold, in 1971, and the crises of the 1970s: in fact, global financial flows zoomed in that decade. It was accelerated by the global shift to neoliberalism in the late 1970s and the 1980s. When most of the Stalinist states collapsed, and China and Vietnam shifted to "market Stalinism", from 1989 onwards, the institutions set up to order the affairs of the "Western" side of the Cold War adapted smoothly to draw in new territories. Where the Kennedy Round of GATT in 1964–7 had included only 62 countries, the World Trade Organisation, GATT's successor from 1995, had 128 countries subscribing to the 1994 Uruguay Round, and has 164 today. China joined in 2001. In 2008, the first G20 statement after the crash stressed above all avoiding protectionism; and on the whole that has held. Between 2008 and 2016 many new trade restrictions were introduced, but none huge, and almost as many trade liberalisations (WTO 2016).

Since 2008 world trade has grown slower than world output for the first extended period since World War II, and global capital flows have slowed, too. Even that, however, does not necessarily signify a solid trend of "deglobalisation". Global trade is mostly in raw materials and (increasingly) manufactured and semi-manufactured goods. In most economies "services" dominate output (about 80% in the USA), while in global trade they are an increasing part but still only 21% (UNCTAD 2015). In an era where manufacturing employment is declining not just in the old industrial countries, but in Brazil, South Korea,

China, etc., the relative decline of manufacturing value-added can outstrip the relative increase in trading of services for a while without this signifying a general turn inwards and away from world markets. The world's governments have been unable to reach comprehensive new global trade agreements since 1994. The "Doha round" of WTO negotiations has produced nothing but the relatively slight "Bali Package" of 2013. The US–European TTIP, and the US–Asian TPP, looked unlikely to get concluded even before Trump's victory. And yet: further trade agreements would always be harder to reach once tariffs on most trade had been reduced to single-figure percentages (latest average applied tariffs on WTO figures: USA 3.5%, Japan 4.0%, EU 5.1%, China 9.9%: in 1931 the average applied tariff in the USA was 35%). About 80% of world trade is now transfers within the supply chains of multinational corporations: they show no wish to do other than keep those chains expanding. Long-entrenched, deeply-embedded interests sustain the world-market-oriented order, with all its inequities and instabilities and horrors and also with all its erratic dynamism.

And yet, and yet ... Trump has been specific about imposing high tariffs on the USA's main trade partners, Mexico and China; less specific, but threatening, about US withdrawal from the WTO. Even if more mainstream Republicans in Congress are horrified, he has much wider legal scope to impose tariffs and disrupt trade than presidents Obama and George W Bush had to push through tariff-reduction deals (Noland et al 2016). Possibly Trump's administration could produce what has been called an "aborted trade war", in which Trump's first protectionist measures produce such backlash and disruption that he quickly retreats, something like an enlarged version of Reagan's initial protectionist lurch. Possibly it could produce a still-largely-globalised world in which the USA is an exceptional rogue state, a counterpart to China, which, though the world's largest exporter, still has large (mostly non-tariff) barriers to trade.

Those limited outcomes, however, presuppose a controlled reaction by other states, in other words by a world system of states in which the keystone for decades, the USA, has gone rogue. The EU's difficulties in dealing expeditiously even with its own internal problems make it unlikely that it could become an alternative keystone. They presuppose that the Trump precedent does not snowball; yet his victory has given a boost to the Front National and Marine Le Pen in France. In April-May 2017 Le Pen will almost certainly enter the run-off vote for the French presidency, and current opinion polls are close enough that she could win. She promises a referendum to take France out of the EU, and in June 2016 polling showed 61% of the French (a greater percentage than of British: Pew Research 2016) had an "unfavourable" view of the EU. If France withdraws from the EU, nothing like the current EU's level of capitalist integration can survive: only some loose trade area, and maybe a much-reduced tighter

Eurozone. In other important EU countries (Italy, Netherlands, Austria ...), too, political shifts which could disrupt the EU now look possible.

A global slump, and ugly, regressive politics almost everywhere, would ensue, and probably strengthen the protectionist trends. And suppose that weighty "globalist" interests do deter or limit Trump, and the EU resists disruption. Even then a new crisis (which is likely to come soon for other reasons, independent of Trump or Le Pen) would find a political establishment whose repertoire of anti-crisis measures has been exhausted and discredited, and thus vulnerable to new and more aggressive right-wing surges.

The USA has always been an exception within the capitalist world order it has promoted and keystoned. Because of the USA's size, its relatively small (though increasing, from 10% in 1970 to 25% now) ratio of trade to GDP, and its status as home to so many multinationals, Alden remarks that: "The United States has not historically worried much about how to make itself an attractive location for investment geared towards exports" (in Card 2011, p. 12), though most other governments have worried greatly and increasingly about that. Brexit sentiment in Britain has been mostly about immigration, not trade: most Brexit voters (according to surveys) and Brexit leaders (according to their statements) want the UK to stay very open to trade, only they dislike immigration more than they like trade. In the USA, it has been different. There is much anti-immigrant sentiment there, but it is not overwhelming nor even necessarily increasing: as of 2016, 61% supported a path to citizenship for illegal immigrants, and that percentage had been stable for some years (Jones et al 2016). Skepticism about trade has been on the rise since the 1990s, both in public opinion and in Congress. Both George W Bush and Obama had to battle and cajole Congress for trade deals. The "fast-track" authority of the presidency to do trade deals, in effect from 1975, lapsed in 1994, was restored from 2002 to 2007 and then lapsed again; was restored in June 2015, but to little effect. By September 2010, in a poll 53% said free trade agreements "hurt" the USA, and only 17% that they "helped", where in 1999 there had been a majority for "helped" (Card et al 2011 p. 28). The USA has simultaneously been the keystone of a relatively free-trade world-market system, and often the most reckless and narrow-minded about the necessary capitalist give-and-take. This contradiction could now become deadly.

Trump promises to "make America great again", but very little specific to his plebeian voters. But for the left, the tactic of going for mild policies, advertised as capable of taming neoliberalism with consensus support, is not vigorous enough to undermine the populist right, and in any case will collapse unless those mild measures are subsumed into bolder policies, for a serious battle to create means of democratic control over economic life capable of countering the mechanisms which constantly re-establish the grip of capital: the wild and rapid gyrations of the global financial markets and the intensely competitive machinations of the "top one per cent" in the multinationals and the international banks. Even the relative successes of the Brazilian PT in modifying neoliberalism, 2002–10, are probably unavailable to piecemeal-reform policies in a country more fully tied into world markets than giant-sized Brazil, and in a period of general depression when even the PT in Brazil has floundered. Small-scale tinkering "in one country" is likely to bounce off resilient neoliberalism, and then probably collapse as abjectly as the economic policies of the once radical-left Syriza, or as the left-wing promises which French president Francois Hollande made before his election in 2012.

The economic question is not just, or even mainly, about techniques for promoting growth. It is about what sort of growth, for whom, controlled by whom, at the expense of whom. It is about whether collective and individual human endeavour serves "the economy" – in other words the given economic structures, or in other words again the constraints of profits; markets; enforced inequality, insecurity, alienation – or we build a realm of freedom by consciously reshaping economic life to serve human solidarity. As Lenin succinctly put it, the central question is "who, whom". Activists should create space for that question to be discussed.

In other words: instil, in dialogue with the new left-wing movements, ideas which will make the left a real and formidable alternative, and transform the labour movements so that they can become an effective counter to the resurgent right, and create governments willing and able to take on entrenched capitalist power.

Appendices

APPENDIX 1

Marx on Capitalist Crises

In 1858, when Marx set out his plan for what he meant to write on economics, he envisaged six books – Capital, Landed Property, Wage Labour, The State, International Trade, and, lastly, the World Market and Crises. Crises, the condensations of all the contradictions in the capitalist mode of production, could only be understood when the concatenations were elucidated.

Marx never came anywhere near completing that plan. His ideas on crises were left as scattered fragments, mostly in unfinished writings. "Here ... was no finished draft, not even a scheme whose outlines might have been filled out, but ... often just a disorderly mass of notes, comments and extracts. I had no choice but ... confining myself to as orderly an arrangement of available matter as possible". So Engels reported on the section of *Capital* volume 3 dealing with credit, one of the most important for Marx's ideas about capitalist crises. There is much to learn from Marx's notes and comments. But crises cannot be adequately understood – nor Marx loyally interpreted – just by slapping everyday facts into the framework of one or another of the abstract elements of crisis which Marx discussed at various points in his writings, and calling that abstract element "the Marxist theory of crisis".

Early on in volume 1 of *Capital* (Chapter 3, Section 2a) Marx argues that the possibility of crisis exists in any money economy. The "metamorphosis of commodities" – through sale and purchase, from commodity to money to commodity – implies that possibility. Those with money are under no immediate compulsion to buy. But if they don't, then those with commodities cannot sell. There is not just mishap or miscalculation and overproduction of one particular commodity, but general overproduction of all commodities. Marx expounds this as an expression of "the antithesis, use-value and value; the contradiction that private labour is bound to manifest itself as direct social labour; that a particularised concrete kind of labour has to pass for abstract human labour; the contradiction between the personification of objects and the representation of persons by things; all these antitheses and contradictions, which are immanent in commodities ..." Commodities are commodities only because they are equated with money. Money is money only because it is equated with commodities. Yet commodities and money are also distinct and separate entities.

In a crisis, unsold commodities pile up on one side, money remains idle on the other. The possibility of this is incipient even in the simplest money economy, because, contrary to the impression given by simplistic accounts, money is not just an intermediary in such an economy which vanishes once its job is done of transferring commodities from hand to hand. Money does not vanish. It only goes from hand to hand. "Circulation sweats money at every pore". At the end of market day, the population takes away at least as much money, unspent, as it brought to that day. A money economy necessarily includes at least some "incipient" hoarding. Nor should we suppose that only a population of crazed misers piling gold coins under their beds could produce a reluctance to advance money for commodities sufficient for a crisis. In the USA in the year 2000, the total stock of money on the narrowest definition (about $1100 billion) was enough to buy 40 days' net national output. On broader definitions (M2 and M3) the stock was enough to buy 180 days', and 250 days', output, respectively. A slight variation in the speed at which money is thrown into circulation can in principle produce a crisis. Yet all this – Marx emphasises – implies "the possibility, and no more than the possibility, of crises. The conversion of this mere possibility into a reality is the result of a long series of relations that, from the present standpoint of simple circulation, have as yet no existence".

Marx made his most comprehensive attempt to look at how – through what "long series of relations" – the possibility of crises becomes reality in *Theories of Surplus Value*, volume 2 (Marx 1963, pp. 492–535. Much the same argument is also developed in the *Grundrisse*, Marx 1993, pp. 401–447). His approach there suggests that he envisaged developing successive approximations, or successively less abstract and more complex expositions, through which the whole anatomy of crises would finally be presented. Thus, for example, when he points to the part played by the "intertwining and coalescence of the processes of reproduction or circulation of different capitals" in crises (essentially what Keynesians would later call the "multiplier effect"), Marx comments that "the definition of the content of crises is already fuller".

Marx polemicises repeatedly against two schools of orthodox economics. One is the followers of "Say's Law", the doctrine according to which, since every sale is a purchase, sales and purchases must balance, and general overproduction is impossible. "But ... trade is not barter, and ... the seller of a commodity is necessarily at the same time the buyer of another. This whole subterfuge ... rests on abstracting from money ..." (p. 532). Again, Marx's idea here is one later to be rediscovered by Keynes, and then again after Keynes by the economists of the "Keynesian reappraisal".

The other school against which Marx polemicises is those who, he says, reduce the question of crises to the mere possibility inherent in the separation of sale and purchase. "How insipid the economists are who ... are content to says that these forms contain the possibility of crises, that it is therefore accidental whether or not crises occur and consequently their occurrence is itself merely a matter of chance". Marx thus sets himself the task of explaining why capitalism develops much more than the mere possibilities inherent in simple circulation of money – which "come[s] into being long before capitalist production, while there are no crises" (p. 512) – and makes crises systematic. He does not complete that explanation in these pages, or anywhere else, but he gives some pointers.

Marx starts his discussion simply by pointing to empirical examples where general overproduction happens (pp. 494–496). In so doing he adds content to the discussion of the abstract possibilities of crisis in any money economy by introducing the concepts of capital and of time. "The immediate purpose of capitalist production is not 'the possession of other goods', but the appropriation of value, of money, of abstract wealth" (p. 503, emphasis added). Under capitalist conditions, a slowness of money-holders to exchange money for commodities may have nothing to do with any "miserly" reluctance to consume. The capitalists must at all times, with urgency, turn their commodities into money; their decisions to turn money into commodities ("to invest") are always dependent on prospects of profit. There is asymmetry.

Secondly, capitalist production necessarily has a dimension of time, time in which the future is always uncertain. "The comparison of value in one period with ... value ... in a later period is no scholastic illusion ... but rather forms the fundamental principle of the circulation process of capital" (p. 503). If conditions for immediate profit are poor (falling prices, for example), then: "Surplus-value amassed in the form of money ... could only be transformed into capital at a loss. It therefore lies idle as a hoard ..." (p. 494). Or: "A person [specifically, a capitalist] may sell in order to pay, and ... these forced sales play a very significant role in the crises" (p. 503). Prices are pushed down by these forced sales – and then despite their frenzy to sell the capitalists are still unable, or only just able, to meet the payments (supplies, debt interest and repayments, rent) they are already committed to on the basis of old prices. And: "Since the circulation process of capital is not completed in one day but extends over a fairly long period ... it is quite clear that between the starting-point ... and ... the end ... elements of crisis must have gathered and develop" (p. 495). If all capitalist decisions to order or commission buildings and equipment had instantaneous effect and were "tested" against the market immediately, the question of crisis would look quite different. But they are not.

Marx's point here is similar to Keynes's: "Our social and business organisation separates financial provision for the future from physical provision for the future", but with an added critical insight. The "provision for the future", financial or physical, is never correlated to future needs, but to immediate prospects of gain. Thus, in the boom, "excessive" physical provision for the future because profits are good and every capitalist wants to get in on the game; in the slump, "excessive" financial provision for the future because capitalists want to see a recovery of markets before they will transform their wealth from the "liquid" form of cash into fixed assets, or they are tied down by debts.

Once Marx has also introduced the "intertwining and coalescence of the processes of reproduction or circulation of different capitals" – the idea that overproduction in one major branch of industry, can, via that industry's reductions in wages paid out and supplies bought, depress the level of demand for other industries, and redefine those other industries' production as "overproduction", he comments that "the definition of the content of crises is fuller". All this, however, still demonstrates only possibilities, and does not show why crises should be more than accidental. In these pages Marx repeatedly refers to the possibility of crises being triggered by poor harvests or other such causes of crisis "accidental" relative to the basic mechanics of capitalism. Obviously he is far from thinking that every crisis must be the expression of some one Law of Capitalist Crisis.

As regards a general driving force, or mechanism, which will persistently, repeatedly, systematically trigger the possibilities, Marx writes this: "The whole aim of capitalist production is appropriation of the greatest possible amount of surplus-labour, in other words, the realisation of the greatest possible amount of immediate labour-time with the given capital, be it through the prolongation of the labour-day or the reduction of the necessary labour-time, through the development of the productive power of labour by ... mass production. It is thus in the nature of capitalist production to produce without regard to the limits of the market" (p. 522).

Or again, what happens is that "too much has been produced for the purpose of enrichment, or that too great a part of the product is intended not for consumption as revenue, but for making more money (for accumulation); not to satisfy the personal needs of its owner, but to give him money, abstract social riches, and capital, more power over the labour of others, i.e. to increase this power" (pp. 533–534).

All this is still very abstract. At least two problems are posed here for further discussion. First, Marx says flatly that: "permanent crises do not exist", and that the idea of "over-abundance [glut] of capital ... [as] a permanent effect" is wrong (p. 497). He is referring to Adam Smith's notion (shared, for example, by no less than Keynes) that capital may become no longer scarce in much the same way as potatoes may become no longer scarce, and thus may lie idle or yield little profit "permanently". It seems plain that Marx rejects the vision of capitalism sometime entering a "final" crisis, in which it must forever wallow until released from its agony by revolution. He refers in these pages, and elsewhere, to "the almost regular periodicity of crises on the world market" (p. 498). Crises are periodic. But nothing in the argument so far explains this periodicity. What does?

Secondly, Marx repeatedly refers to the relative poverty of the working class ("underconsumption") as an important factor in limiting the market. What is the role, and what are the limits of the role, of "underconsumption" in crises?

Marx's general argument here, however, does indicate that any "theory of crisis" relying solely on "commodity-side" relations must be unsound – and this applies, for example, to the "orthodox" Tendency of the Rate of Profit to Fall theories (based on the proportions in production between capital-stock, wage-bill, and surplus value) and to the usual "underconsumption" theories (based on the proportions in production between wage-bill and total product). Crises do not arise directly from such abstract "snapshot" proportions in production. They arise from proportions between production and markets (which are connected to proportions between different sectors of production) and from proportions between past, present and future.

To analyse those proportions, Marx must examine fixed capital and credit. He does that in *Capital* volume 2 Chapters 8 and 9 (also Chapter 16 Section 3 and, briefly, Chapter 20) and volume 3, Chapter 30. By its very nature, capital seeks maximum fluidity and the quickest returns; but equally, and also by its very nature, a large, generally increasing, proportion of it must be tied up in instruments of production which transfer their value to products only piecemeal and over a length of time, i.e. in fixed capital. In a period of strong capitalist expansion, fixed capital – new machinery and buildings, etc. – is expanded disproportionately. "The market is ... stripped of labour-power, means of subsistence for this labour-power, fixed capital in the form of instruments of labour ... and of materials of production, and to replace them an equivalent in money is thrown on the market; but during the year no product is thrown on the market [by the big projects of building new factories, installing new machinery, etc.] with which to replace the material elements of productive capital withdrawn from it.

"If we conceive society as being not capitalistic but communistic, there will be no money-capital at all in the first place, not the disguises cloaking the transactions arising on account of it. The question then comes down to the need of society to calculate beforehand how much labour, means of production, and means of subsistence it can invest, without detriment, in such lines of business as for instance the building of railways, which do not furnish any means of production or subsistence, nor produce any useful effect for a long time, a year or more, while they extract labour, means of production and means of subsistence from the total annual production.

"In capitalist society however where social reason always asserts itself only post festum great disturbances may and must constantly occur. On the one hand pressure is brought to bear on the money-market, while on the other, an easy money-market calls such enterprises into being en masse, thus creating the very circumstances which later give rise to pressure on the money-market. Pressure is brought to bear on the money-market, since large advances of money-capital are constantly needed here for long periods of time ...

"The effective demand rises without itself furnishing any element of supply. Hence a rise in the prices of productive materials as well as means of subsistence ... A band of speculators, contractors, engineers, lawyers, etc., enrich themselves. They create a strong demand for articles of consumption on the market, wages rising at the same time ... A portion of the reserve army of labourers, which keep wages down, is absorbed. A general rise in wages ensues, even in the hitherto well employed sections of the labour-market. This lasts until the inevitable crash again releases the reserve army of labour and wages are once more depressed to their minimum, and lower". (*Capital* 2 Chapter 16).

One element in "the inevitable crash" will be that a mass of commodities produced by the new factories and equipment comes on to the market while there can be no corresponding increase in wages, consumption by capitalists and their hangers-on, or productive-investment projects to create demand. On the contrary, as the big construction and re-equipment projects are completed, workers will be laid off, fees for engineers and lawyers will diminish, and so will demand for new construction or re-equipment.

"The cycle of interconnected turnovers embracing a number of years, in which capital is held fast by its fixed constituent part, furnishes a material basis for the periodic crises. During this cycle business undergoes successive periods of depression, medium activity, precipitancy, crisis. True, periods in which capital is invested differ greatly and far from coincide in time. But a crisis always forms the starting-point of large new investments. Therefore, from the point of view of society as a whole, more or less, a new material basis for the next turnover cycle". (*Capital* 2 Chapter 9, emphasis added).

Large fixed-capital projects would hardly be possible without credit. The credit system gives greater elasticity both to capitalist production – and to capitalist over-production. "The credit system appears as the main lever of over-production and over-speculation in commerce ... the reproduction process, which is elastic by nature, is here forced to its extreme limits ... The credit system accelerates the material development of the productive forces and the establishment of the world-market ... At the same time credit accelerates the violent eruptions of this contradiction – crises – and thereby the elements of disintegration of the old mode of production". (*Capital* 3 Chapter 27).

Marx also polemicises much against the follies of a "tight-money" school of thought influential in Britain in the mid-19th century, called the "Currency School". These people, notably Samuel Lloyd, later Lord Overstone, got a law passed in 1844 to restrict the Bank of England's issue of banknotes to a fixed proportion to its gold reserves. In 1847, recovery from a serious economic slump was made possible only by a special decision by Parliament to suspend that law and allow the Bank to issue more notes. Amidst dated references and polemics, however, some important ideas can be found in the chapters on credit of *Capital* volume 3.

In Chapter 30 Marx describes the typical pattern of the boom-slump cycle. "After the reproduction process has again reached that state of prosperity which precedes that of over-exertion, commercial credit becomes very much extended [i.e. trade credit between capitalist firms is easy and extensive] ... The rate of interest is still low, although it rises above its minimum ...

"[But] those cavaliers who work without any reserve capital or without any capital at all and thus operate completely on a money credit basis began to appear ... in considerable numbers. To this is now added the great expansion of fixed capital in all forms, and the opening of new enterprises on a vast and far-reaching scale. The interest now rises to its average level. It reaches its maximum again as soon as the new crisis sets in".

Marx has not yet indicated why, exactly, the "new crisis" sets in, but he continues: "Credit suddenly stops then ... the reproduction process is paralysed, and ... a superabundance of idle industrial capital appears side by side with an almost absolute absence of loan capital ....

"The industrial cycle is of such a nature that the same circuit must periodically reproduce itself, once the first impulse has been given. During a period of slack, production sinks below the level which it had attained in the preceding cycle and for which the technical basis has now been laid. During prosperity – the middle period – it continues to develop on this basis. In the period of over-production and exertion, it strains the productive forces to the utmost, until it exceeds the capitalistic limits of the production process".

But why do the contradictions express themselves in a sudden crisis and not in gradual corrections? Because a decline of credit is by its very nature self-multiplying – no capitalist can afford to offer easy credit when others are tightening – and comes at a point when many business failures or outright swindles have developed and remain hidden only because of easy credit.

"In a system of production, where the entire continuity of the reproduction process rests upon credit, a crisis must obviously occur – a tremendous rush for means of payment – when credit suddenly ceases and only cash payments have validity. At first glance ... the whole crisis seems to be merely a credit and money crisis .... But the majority of these bills [bills of exchange, or invoices, which cannot be converted into cash] represent actual sales and purchases, whose extension far beyond the needs of society is ... the basis of the whole crisis". (By "needs", here, Marx does not mean human needs. Elsewhere he has commented that by that criterion capitalism is a system of constant underproduction. He means effective demand).

Further indications on the suddenness of crisis are given earlier in Chapter 30. "The whole process becomes so complicated [with a developed credit system] ... that the semblance of a very solvent business with a smooth flow of returns can easily persist even long after returns actually come in only at the expense of swindled money-lenders and partly of swindled producers. Thus business always appears almost excessively sound right on the eve of a crash ... Business is always thoroughly sound and the campaign in full swing, until suddenly the debacle takes place".

And then again in Chapter 32: "It is a basic principle of capitalist production that money, as an independent form of value, stands in opposition to commodities, or that exchange-value must assume an independent form in money ... [Thus] in times of a squeeze, when credit contracts ... money suddenly stands as the only means of payment and true existence of value in absolute opposition to all other commodities ....

"Secondly, however, credit-money itself is only money to the extent that it absolutely takes the place of actual money to the amount of its nominal value. With a drain on gold its convertibility, i.e. its identity with actual gold, becomes problematic. Hence coercive measures, raising the rate of interest, etc., for the purpose of safeguarding the conditions of this convertibility. This can be carried more or less to extremes by mistaken legislation [here Marx refers to the Bank Act of 1844 – he would probably have similar comments on Paul Volcker's policies at the Federal Reserve in the early 1980s, or on 'monetarism' in Thatcher's Britain] ... The basis, however, is given with the basis of the mode of production itself. A depreciation of credit-money ... would unsettle all existing relations. Therefore, the value of commodities is sacrificed for the purpose of safeguarding the fantastic and independent existence of this value in money ... For a few millions in money, many millions in commodities must therefore be sacrificed. This is inevitable under capitalist production and constitutes one of its beauties".

On "underconsumption", Marx writes: "The replacement of the capital invested in production depends largely upon the consuming power of the non-producing classes; while the consuming power of the workers is limited partly by the laws of wages, partly by the fact that they are used only as long as they can be profitably employed by the capitalist classes. *The ultimate reason for all real crises always remains the poverty and restricted consumption of the masses* as opposed to the drive of capitalist production to develop the productive forces as though only the absolute consuming power of society constituted their limit" (*Capital* 3 Chapter 30, emphasis added).

But also (*Capital* 2 Chapter 20, emphasis added): "In proportion as ... the luxury part of the annual product grows, as therefore an increasing share of the labour-power is absorbed in the production of luxuries ... the existence and reproduction of [a] part of the working-class ... depends upon the prodigality of the capitalist class, upon the exchange of a considerable portion of their surplus-value for articles of luxury. Every crisis at once lessens the consumption of luxuries ... thus throwing a certain number of the labourers employed in the production of luxuries out of work, while on the other hand it thus clogs the sale of consumer necessities and reduces it. And this without mentioning the unproductive labourers who are dismissed at the same time, labourers who receive for their services a portion of the capitalists' luxury expense ... That commodities are unsaleable means only that no effective purchasers have been found for them, i.e., consumers (since commodities are bought in the final analysis for productive or individual consumption). *But if one were to attempt to give this tautology the semblance of a profounder justification by saying that the working-class receives too small a portion of its own product and the evil would be remedied as soon as it receives a larger share of it and its wages increase in consequence, one could only remark that crises are always prepared by precisely a period in which wages rise generally and the working-class actually gets a larger share of that part of the annual product which is intended for consumption*. From the point of view of these advocates of sound and 'simple' (!) common sense, such a period should rather remove the crisis. It appears, then, that capitalist production comprises conditions independent of good or bad will, conditions which permit the working-class to enjoy that relative prosperity only momentarily, and at that always only as the harbinger of a coming crisis".

Both italicised passages have been much-quoted – the first to prop up theories in which workers' "underconsumption" is presented as central to crises, and the second to knock them down. Both ideas here – that the relative poverty of the working class is central to crises, and that the immediate run-up to crisis is a period of relatively high wages – are repeated by Marx in many other places.

However, the preceding argument (not so often quoted) is identical for the two "contradictory" passages. Because the workers' effective demand varies within relatively narrow limits, continued capitalist expansion depends heavily on the capitalists' effective demand. When that sags – and generally it does sag first, before the workers' effective demand does – then it brings the whole process down with it. Crises are rooted in the general limitation of workers' effective demand, but not in a special limitation of it prior to the immediate point of crisis.

Marx's argument here is, however, deficient. Most of the capitalists' effective demand is for means of production, not for their own individual consumption. And the factual evidence is that often the decisive shortfall in demand at the onset of crises is a shortfall of demand for the elements of fixed capital. Many fixed-capital projects initiated in the boom have come on stream. Credit has become more expensive. It is the sudden changes in the credit system, due to the nature of that system, which make for a sudden downturn in demand. A downturn in capitalists' individual consumption (and in government expenditures on armaments, welfare, etc., which fall into the same category) may follow, and have repercussions, but is not the decisive first step.

Marx never wrote anything of any weight introducing the state or international trade into his discussion of crises – though his discussion of the 1844 Bank Act alone indicates that Marx thought that the state, and government policy, were factors of some weight. No cut-and-dried "Marxist theory of crisis" can be derived by exegesis alone. What we can do is learn from Marx's approach, and the important indications he gave for understanding the roles of capital, of time, of fixed capital specifically, and of credit in crises.

In *Capital* 3 Chapter 30 Engels adds a footnote repeating an idea which he also develops at the end of his 1886 preface to the English edition of *Capital* 1. Those brief notes are the only example in the writings of Marx and Engels of an attempt by them to analyse what seemed to be a shift from one era to another in capitalist development – in other words, to do work analogous to what we must do in understanding the great upswing from the late 1940s to 1973, and the subsequent "global turbulence". They are modest and tentative, rather than profound. Maybe it is from their lack of dogmatic preconceptions, and their willingness to take all levels of analysis seriously rather than reducing "the crisis" immediately to an expression of one or another contradiction of capital-in-general, that we have most to learn. "The decennial cycle of stagnation, prosperity, overproduction and crisis, ever-recurrent from 1825 to 1867, seems indeed to have run its course; but only to land us in the slough of despond of permanent and chronic depression".

In *Capital* 1 Engels attributes this to two things: international competition (yes, indeed, he does refer to competition and not to capital-in-general – "Foreign production, rapidly developing, stares English production in the face everywhere ..."); and a supposed inbuilt tendency for production to outstrip markets long-term ("While the productive power increases in a geometric, the extension of markets proceeds at best in an arithmetic ratio").

The second argument, despite the long reach of its influence in Marxist discussion, is wrong. Long-term, increased production means more wages paid out, more orders from suppliers, more surplus-value in the hands of capitalists – i.e. increased markets, to exactly the same extent. "Universal overproduction in the absolute sense would not be over-production, but only a greater than usual development of the productive forces in all spheres of production". Quoting this argument from capitalist "apologetics" in *Theories of Surplus Value* volume 2, Marx agrees that "this non-existent, self-abrogating overproduction", based on a general, uniform, long-term increase of production beyond markets, cannot exist. "Actual overproduction" does, because capitalism develops unevenly and sequentially ("there could be no capitalist production at all if it had to develop simultaneously and evenly in all spheres"). The unevenness, industry-to-industry and period-to-period, creates sectoral overproduction, and sectoral overproduction snowballs into (temporary) general overproduction.

Crises cannot be rooted in a static comparison – too much production here, too little money there. There is no ideal static balance between production and money. The relations are always dynamic.

Writing later, in *Capital* 3, Engels is more hesitant and considers more aspects.

1. Perhaps, he writes, the cycle is still there, but has become longer, not synchronised between different industrial countries, and for the time being less marked, oscillating between "slight improvement" and "indecisive depression". (But only for the time being – maybe "a new world crash of unparalleled vehemence" is coming).
2. "The colossal expansion of the means of transportation and communication" has done away with some old causes of crisis arising from the uncertainty of distant markets (English textiles in India).

3. "Competition in the domestic market recedes before the cartels and trusts, while in the foreign market it is restricted by protective tariffs".
4. He refers again to the fact that "the monopoly of England in industry has been challenged by a number of competing industrial countries". "Infinitely greater and varied fields" have opened up for capital. The conclusion, I suppose, is that this development, combined with the cartels, trusts, and tariffs, could dampen crises by making it likely that a downturn in Britain would be offset by expansion in Germany or the USA, or vice versa.

Certainly, capitalist crises are not a mechanical pattern. And, though "permanent crises do not exist", "permanent and chronic depression" (high unemployment, etc.) can very well exist. The fruitful suggestion by Engels, I think, is that the regime of crises and depression is shaped by the way capital is organised – within countries (how the state and big capitalist cartels or trusts deal with their difficulties) and between countries (industrial supremacy of one nation or competition of several, protection or free trade, etc.).

APPENDIX 2

Ruinous Competition

The first service of Robert Brenner's study of The Economics of Global Turbulence (Brenner 1998; Brenner 2006; page references here are to the 1998 text) is a demolition of the myth of unparalleled US prosperity in the 1990s. Output, investment, and productivity all grew unusually slowly for a boom phase in the regular boom-slump cycle. Wages mostly stagnated. The limited advances in profit rates, and their exaggerated reflection in the gaudy rise of the stock market, were only the flipside of a punishing war against labour, described well by Brenner.

Brenner's book also does two other major services. It presents a lot of information about the direct capital-versus-labour dimension of the various phases of the post-1945 economies as well as the capital-to-capital dimensions more usually documented by economists. It reflects a volume of research and reading possible only for someone who as well as being committed to active Marxist politics also holds a major university position and has a range of capable academic associates and assistants. And the book establishes a central idea for Marxist economic analysis, never before, I think, as clear as here: that analysis must proceed not from a blurred outline of a "typical" capitalist economy, but from the complex reality of a world economy with its own structure and within it national economies substantially different in pattern both from the global structure and from each other.

The book has greater ambitions. It seeks to be a comprehensive reworking of a Marxist theory of economic crisis and depression for our times, explaining the big picture of capitalist development over the last half-century in a way which orthodox economics does not even attempt. Brenner clears the ground with a criticism of the main Marxist theories previously advanced to explain world capitalism's lurch into trouble around 1970. The so-called "fundamentalist" school, which saw the root of the turmoil in the Tendency of the Rate of Profit to Fall discussed by Marx in volume 3 of *Capital*, is dismissed by Brenner abruptly, but, I think, with good reason. I will return to that argument later. Another argument, the "wage-push", was pioneered by Andrew Glyn and Bob Sutcliffe (Glyn and Sutcliffe 1972). They argued that it was the strength of the trade unions, and their ability to win wage rises higher than suited capital, that had squeezed profit rates in the 1960s to the point where even small disturbances would trigger crisis.

With their picture of an inexorably, ruinously falling rate of profit, both wage-push theorists and fundamentalists shared a view of a world driven by iron laws towards apocalypse. "The crisis" – they didn't differentiate much between cyclical downturns and longer periods of depression – was bound to climax soon in revolution or in ruinous trade wars or worse. The wage-push theorists gave trade-union struggle a central revolutionary role while the fundamentalists tended more towards socialist preaching, but the apocalyptic perspective was more or less common.

It didn't happen that way. In the last 30 years there have been many crises and horrors, but no single Big Bang. A third response, that of the Regulation School of French Marxists, has become more influential than either the fundamentalists or the wage-push theorists. For them, world capitalism's lurch into slow growth and repeated crisis after 1969–71 was the product neither of an apparently extraneous factor (wage-push) nor of mechanical true-for-all-seasons trends like the Tendency of the Rate of Profit to Fall. It happened because the productivity-improving potential of the "Fordist" mass-uniform-production paradigm was becoming exhausted in manufacturing, and because the not-yet-Fordist nature of most labour in the welfare state (health, education) was provoking financial crises for the state. The world was moving into another messy, floundering transition period in which no integrated "regime of accumulation" was established.

The Regulation School seemed to provide a more rounded and fluid picture of capitalism as a social as well as economic system, shaped by class struggle as well as by abstract economic laws. But, where the wage-push theorists and the fundamentalists were revolutionaries, the Regulationists leaned towards reformism. Their best-known writer, Alain Lipietz, a former "soft Maoist", has long been a leading figure of the French Greens. They tend to advocate an immediate economic program of re-regulation, not very different from left Keynesianism.

Brenner wrote a thorough criticism of the Regulationists in 1991 (Brenner and Glick, 1991) and in the new book Brenner also argues in detail that the picture of productivity-exhaustion in the late 1960s and early 1970s is false to reality.

Political choices always need much more than economic analysis, and, equally, almost always have to be made without clarity of economic analysis. But Brenner's aim in his book, if I've understood it right, is to construct an account of modern capitalism which both comprehends its fluidity and malleability in detail and shows the link between current economic turmoil and the basics of the private-profit system – an account which can help to inform a socialist politics which is revolutionary but free of mechanical "catastrophism". I believe that his aim is right, but this first shot has missed the target.

All the 1970s theories, fundamentalist, wage-push, and Regulationist, focused on contradictions burgeoning in an "average" or "typical" leading capitalist economy, each national economy being that average type written small, and the world economy being it written large. Brenner criticises that approach and explains the turning-point in capitalism around 1965–73, from "Golden Age" to trouble, from a change in the interactions between national economies: specifically, sharpened international competition in manufacturing.

The industrial growth of West Germany and Japan, and the freeing and cheapening of international trade, reached a threshhold above which their lower-cost manufacturers could suddenly step up their export drive into the US market. They did so by accepting their current profit rates, not trying to secure higher profit rates from their lower costs, and thus undercutting US firms. US manufacturers, with their huge resources sunk in equipment and in know-how, networks of suppliers and customers, etc., could compete with them by accepting lower profit rates. Instead of making 20%, say, on their whole accumulated investment, they could cut their prices and make just 20% on the capital investment necessary each year to maintain production on the basis of the huge already-acquired assets. The net result, though, was a lower average rate of profit and over-capacity across manufacturing.

The dip in profit rates would have been only temporary if in the longer term the US manufacturers either went out of business or re-equipped to establish costs as low as the Germans or Japanese. In fact great world-wide overcapacity in manufacturing has persisted since the 1970s. Government economic policies both expansionary and restrictive ("monetarist") have sustained it. The expansionary policies have allowed excess-capacity manufacturers to remain in their old line of business at the price of increased debt, which then makes any drastic switch to a new line more difficult. The restrictive policies, by depressing demand across the board, have inhibited capital from risky switches to new lines of business. The consequent deficiency of "exit" from manufacturing industries has been compounded since the 1980s by the dramatic "entry" of manufacturers based in Korea, Taiwan, China, etc. into world trade. Thus continued mutual ruin by competition.

Brenner's is a heroic effort to integrate a great mass of information (about capital-versus-labour battles as well as capital-versus-capital) into a coherent story, but I find it ultimately unsatisfactory both on how the increased competition reduced profit rates, and on overcapacity "sticking".

Any individual capitalist is likely to have to take a lower profit rate if competition in their market increases. It seems obvious, then, that increased competition overall means lower profit rates overall. But it does not. Suppose increased competition forces all capitalists to cut their prices by ten per cent. Then all capitalists' income falls ten per cent – but all their costs fall ten per cent too, unless workers are strong enough to make the ten per cent cut in the cost of all they buy into a rise of real wages rather than a cut in money wages. There is no drop in the share of profits in income unless it is due to a rise of real wages uncorrelated with a rise in productivity. For profits to fall, workers must gain a cut in the rate of exploitation, and do it in the less-favourable conditions for labour which must result from the increased competition, where the weight of other capitalists stands more solidly behind each individual capitalist in their disputes with workers, and workers suffer greater insecurity. Brenner responds that "conditions do not ordinarily exist that could enable capitalists to prevent workers from securing any gains from the reduced price ...", but why not?

If actual dollar prices are reduced, workers may be able to improve real wages without an autonomous shift in the general balance of class forces. It is harder for bosses to cut dollar wages than to resist an equivalent increase in real wages at a time of generally rising prices. Workers will have already absorbed the improved conditions arising from lower prices (at the same dollar wage) before the bosses attempt the wage cut, and, all other things being equal, will be stronger resisting the dollar-wage cut than they would be in pressing for an equivalent rise in real wages through an above-inflation dollar-wage rise. But in the late 1960s prices in the US were not generally falling. They were rising faster than they had done in previous years. The effect of international competition squeezing manufacturing prices was only to make the general increase in prices smaller than it would hypothetically have been without that competition. I do not see how that hypothetical comparison could shape wages. To suppose that the squeezed prices would not, all other things being equal, push up real wages, all we have to assume is that wage-bargaining based itself on actual price inflation and productivity.

Competition equalises profit rates. It does so more or less completely depending on whether competition is fierce across the board, or some firms have monopolised, rigged, or protected markets. Fiercer competition can wipe out the excess profits of firms with monopolised, rigged, or protected markets, to the benefit of the rest. It does not, however, tell you anything about the average rate of profit. Or, rather, longer-term, its tendency will paradoxically be to increase profit rates, by sharpening the capitalists' drive to cut costs. Especially so if it includes sharper competition between workers to sell their labour-power, as it has done since the early 1970s.

Brenner focuses on German and Japanese manufacturers with lower costs (essentially lower wages) entering the US market on a large scale in the late 1960s. US manufacturers reduced their mark-up to compete. But then US workers got cheaper cars, TVs and so on, and US manufacturers got cheaper steel and machine-tools. Profit rates for US manufacturers fell from 1965 onwards, but this can be attributed to the increased competition only if US workers were strong enough to use the turbulence to reduce their rate of exploitation at the same time as they were suffering loss of bonuses, short-time, insecurity, and increased management pressure because of the increased competition. Increased international competition alone cannot explain the development.

Brenner is as harsh against the wage-push theory as he is against the "fundamentalists" and the Regulationists. He argues in detail that wages militancy in the 1970s was more a response by workers to the crisis than a cause of it. If there was a heyday of autonomous wage-push in the USA, it was in the 1950s, and then the capitalists quickly managed to set countervailing forces in motion to keep profit rates up. His own account, however, in fact relies on wage-push. It relies on the implicit assumption that the workers "pushed" at least enough for the less-increased-than-otherwise prices brought by increased competition to produce higher real wages rather than less-increased-than-otherwise money wages, and for that to happen when increased competition was tilting the general economic determinants of the balance of class forces against labour.

Conversely, the detailed text of Glyn and Sutcliffe's book (and of later works on the same lines, such as Armstrong et al 1991) presents the squeeze on profit rates as a pincer-operation by wage-push and fiercer international competition, with the movement coming as much if not more from competition. The theory was "headlined" as wage-push less for strictly economic reasons than for political ones. It was a defiant reply to bourgeois arguments about wages militancy ruining capitalism. Yes, it was, and a good thing too! Paradoxically, Brenner's "ruinous-competition" theory is really a wage-push theory, and Glyn and Sutcliffe's wage-push theory was really a "ruinous-competition" theory.

Now, unlike increased competition, increased wages must cut profit rates, all other things being equal. Yet other things rarely are equal. Capitalists can and do respond to wage-push not just by accepting lower profit rates, but with new technologies and production methods which restore the rate of exploitation (ratio of surplus-value produced to outlay on wages) while leaving the increased real wages intact. Often the countries with the highest real wages – like the US from 1945 to the early 1970s, at least – also have comparatively high profit rates. Successful wage-push demands favourable conditions – low unemployment, full order books – which are also those favourable to the capitalist response. Long-term, real wages tend to rise, but so does the rate of exploitation. Short-term, wages rise in booms and fall or stagnate in slumps – but the ratio of wages to (much-increased) profits in booms is often lower than in slumps. Wages are more a dependent than an independent variable in capitalist accumulation – as Brenner's detailed examinations confirm.

In short, fiercer competition in the US and world markets, in the 1960s, from German and Japanese (or German and Japanese based) manufacturers would explain a trend to economic levelling between the US, Germany and Japan. But it does not explain lower global profit rates unless there was also wage-push. And there are both theoretical and empirical arguments against taking wage-push as a generally decisive autonomous factor.

German and Japanese manufacturers' profit rates also fell, from 1968, rather more sharply than US rates. Why? Brenner's explanation rests heavily on the effect of currency exchange-rate movements after 1971 (the dollar came to buy fewer marks or yen), but how could exchange-rate movements create rather than just redistribute a fall in profit rates?

Yet US manufacturing profit rates did fall sharply from 1965 to 1970. And they did so without any very sharp drop in demand. Capacity utilisation in manufacturing dropped from its very high level of 92% in 1966, but remained at boom-time levels, above 85%, until late 1969. Only in 1970–1, as the US government cut back Vietnam war spending, did it drop towards 76%. Before 1970, US manufacturing capital evidently managed to keep its production lines rolling, even if its output prices were squeezed.

Brenner's evidence suggests, to my mind, that there was an autonomous wage-push in the late 1960s. He records "a major increase in strike activity in these years", which he describes as "a lagging response on the part of labour to a spectacular increase in profitability between 1958 and 1965". This would not have been an independent factor sufficient to mark an epochal turn in capitalist development (as in the full-blown "wage-push" theory), but it was a response, an active intervention by workers with some autonomy from the movements of capital at the same time, which could have been sufficient to hinder manufacturing capital from making sufficiently quick adjustments to the onrush of international competition, and to prevent non-manufacturing capital from scoring increased profit rates from the lower prices at which they could buy manufactured supplies.

This reading, however, would reduce the sharpened-competition-plus-wage-push of the late 1960s to the status of an essentially episodic blow at the profit rate, due to be reversed (by re-equipment, closure of weaker firms, pressure against wages, and so on) unless other and more fundamental developments intervened.

The economic levelling between the US and Germany and Japan has generated movement of currency exchange rates. You get a lot fewer marks or yen for a dollar today than you did in 1968. Consequently, dollar wages in the US are now lower than dollar wages in Germany or Japan, rather than being twice or four times as high, as they were in 1968. Germany and Japan's low-cost advantage has disappeared. Brenner's graphs show that profit rates in the three countries as becoming similar, instead of Japanese rates being much higher than US rates, and German rates lower, as before 1965.

Profit rates evened out – but why did they do so at a markedly lower level, long-term? Why did profit rates decline and remain low after the early 1970s, recovering only to a limited extent? Because of wage-push? Hardly. Real wage rates have stagnated in the USA. Among the leading economies, they have risen most in Japan – which has also, until its 1990s slump, had the highest profit rates.

Brenner deals with this question by tracing in some detail the movements of currency exchange rates (which include many erratic ups and downs as well as the long-term trends), and successive government policies in the USA, Germany and Japan. The gist of his argument, if I've understood right, is that the "ruinous competition" which suddenly hit capitalism in 1965–73 then became semi-permanent. As the big capitalist manufacturing corporations sought to make good on their huge fixed assets, tangible or intangible; as governments and banks aided them by allowing a great rise in debt; as other government policies restricted home markets everywhere and sent manufacturers everywhere on a no-win chase to export to a consequently depressed global market; and as new manufacturing-export bases emerged in East Asia – as all these trends persisted, there were always lower-cost producers somewhere (where, at each moment, depended on the movement of currency exchange rates) pushing down prices, and higher-cost producers elsewhere ready and able to accept lower profit rates to stay in business. Thus "the further strategies individual capitalists found it best to adopt ... continued to bring about an insufficiency of exit and too much entry, exacerbating the initial problem of manufacturing overcapacity and overproduction". The competition was ruinous, but not (or not allowed to be) ruinous enough, and so it remained ruinous.

I see several problems here.

In the first place, impressionistically, if what has happened has not been ruin enough, what would be? We have had a quarter-century of "deindustrialisation". There were great waves of bankruptcies and closures in the USA under Paul Volcker's direction of the Federal Reserve in 1979–83, and in Britain under Thatcher simultaneously. Brenner documents "a vast restructuring" of Japanese industry after the oil shock of 1973 (which hit Japan especially hard). Everywhere there has been drastic economic and technological reorganisation. Although most Marxists in the early 1970s (including me) expected the economic turmoil to lead to increased tariffs and import controls if not trade wars, the actual development has been the opposite, to deregulation and freer-flowing trade. Capitalist governments have responded to ruinous competition – if that was the crux of the problem – not by trying to stifle it but by making large economic areas "free-fire" zones.

Secondly, in detailed statistics – as noted above, US manufacturing capacity utilisation remained at boom-time levels until late 1969. There was no overcapacity. Over the whole period 1967–96, capacity utilisation averaged 81.1%, only slightly down from its 1948–65 average of 82.4%. It does seem that changes in the system have prevented it from having booms as exuberant as the 1953 and 1966 war-economy peaks of 92% capacity utilisation; and some industries do have heavy overcapacity. Overall, though, it does not seem that the general problem for capital is that there are simply too many factories in proportion to other sectors of the economy.

Even if the official statistics are misleading, and there is chronic and aberrant excess capacity, it is not so obvious that it should generate depressions or crises. An economy running at 75% capacity is more wasteful and poorer than one running at 85%, but is it less stable or even slower-growing? Once it has settled down to running at 75% capacity, why should it have a downward trend of profits? The Stalinist economies from the 1950s to the 1970s almost never scrapped old factories or equipment, yet industry grew fast, and their crises then and more drastically in the 1980s did not stem just from excess capacity. China notoriously has great excess capacity in inefficient state factories, but its industry has grown fast.

Brenner alleges a "great ledge of high-cost, low-profit means of production" resulted from "the intensification of international competition". On one level this could be just a restatement of the fact of lower profit rates. If average profit rates are lower, then (unless the range of difference of profit rates between enterprises has narrowed in the same way as the range between average profit rates in different countries) there will be more factories operating at "low profit" (by any predetermined definition). But then the larger number of low-profit factories cannot be cited as the cause of the lower general profit rates. That the "tail" of low-profit factories comes to include some old-established US firms in place of German enterprises is not necessarily a cause of crisis.

If, on the contrary, the "ledge" of "low-profit" factories is not just the "tail" of the usual scatter of profit rates between more successful and less successful enterprises, but rather represents capital saved from bankruptcy, sell-off and scrapping only by deliberate government policy (like the Chinese state enterprises), then why is it a cause of crisis for the higher-profit firms rather than just a cause of irksomely higher supply prices and higher taxes?

At one point (p. 151) Brenner refers to "the survival of those high-cost, low-profit firms which perpetuated overcapacity and overproduction" and then in the next paragraph to "the unprecedented growth of debt of all types – government, corporate, and consumer – which kept up capacity utilisation". But what is an "overcapacity" which exists even when capacity utilisation is kept up? Is the idea that demand kept up by the growth of debt is "artificial"? It is, but then so is demand kept down by "tight-money" policies. The free-market "no gain without pain" course is no less "artificial" than the Keynesian one. The Keynesian expansion of debt may lead to a crash (the collapse of debt-financed demand, and the emergence of actual "overcapacity"), but it may not.

In some passages, however, Brenner seems to assume that a lower profit rate means that there are "too many" producers and "too much" competition in a particular line of business. In which case, don't the profit rates in non-manufacturing (consistently lower than in manufacturing, on Brenner's figures) indicate an even greater excess of producers and of competition there, too? If the lower profit rates do prove that there were "too many" firms in business and thus "overcapacity", then "too many" and "over" relative to what? Here, Brenner's careful initial argument about how competition becomes ruinous in certain circumstances slides over into far too general an argument about over-competition, overcapacity and lower profit rates being synonymous.

There are always established but out-competed capitalists preferring to hold on in their current line of business rather than up and off. There are always new competitors. Easy government policies always allow some out-competed firms to remain in business – while also easing capitalist entry into new lines. Tight government policies always tend to inhibit new businesses – while also clearing away out-competed firms. A narrative can highlight chosen aspects of these generalities in such a way as to create the appearance of an empirically-detailed, specific explanation – "in these-and-those years there was easy government policy, which allowed out-competed firms to survive; then in such-and-such years there was tight government policy, which depressed demand" – but it really does not explain why the overall outcome should be depression. "Slow-adjusting" individual responses do not necessarily make for greater global depression or crisis than a more "market-rational", "fast-adjusting" pattern where capitalists "exit" faster and "enter" more cautiously. The "fast-adjusting" pattern, by triggering a chain of demand cutbacks and of defaults, can very well convert previously "viable" firms into "unviable" ones and convert previously manageable competition into ruinous.

Brenner's picture is one of a world economy adjusting too "stickily" to the shock of fiercer competition brought by the freeing-up of world trade and the rise or revival of new industrial centres. Wages did not adjust downwards to lower high-competition prices; and then manufacturing capacity did not adjust downwards to more crowded markets. The question is, was adjustment really so "sticky"? In any case, doesn't "sticky" adjustment sometimes limit slumps, downturns or depressions, as compared to quicker free-market adjustment? If there were such "sticky" adjustment as to create a permanent pool of outdated capital subsisting only on subsidies, then that would produce a one-off slowdown in capital accumulation. But why should that pool have a depressive or crisis-producing effect long-term greater than, for example, the pool of outdated capital existing in Japan's notoriously inefficient agricultural sector throughout its tremendous upswing after 1945?

In the "Great Depression" of the late 19th century, capitalist firms and governments responded to "ruinous competition" by trying to stifle it (tariffs, cartels, etc.), and yet the system did adjust to the rise of new world-competitive firms in Germany and the USA. In the late 20th century, capitalist governments and business strategists worldwide have made a vigorous and varied set of attempts to "unstick" the adjustment of industry to sharper global competition – deregulation, subsidies to speed the rundown of old industries or to promote "sunrise" sectors, moves to smash union strength and break up large-scale nationalised industries, shifts to "greenfield" sites .... And yet, on Brenner's account, these policies add up to a "failure to adjust". They have even been counterproductive. Brenner speculates at the end of his book that the US industry may have finally established the conditions to escape depression, but that, apparently, would only be because even "sticky" adjustments get made eventually.

Either the bosses botched it drastically – different government policies would have speeded adjustment and averted the long depression – or late 20th century capitalism had no possible smooth (or at least relatively smooth) way of adjusting to fiercer competition. If the latter (and I suspect Brenner's view would lean that way), then we must explain the impossibility before we get into any of the details of different governments' policies. And the explanation cannot be that capitalism can never deal with fiercer competition.

It seems to me that Brenner's argument "overstates" the failure to adjust, and by doing so obscures the question of what it was in late 20th century capitalism that made its adjustments, failed or successful, so hurtful. Brenner paints a picture of capital as having become cripplingly inflexible, but has it not generally in fact become more flexible? – with its ill-health maybe due to an impossible-to-win race in which flexible productive capital tries to keep pace with always-more-flexible money capital?

What Brenner has done, however, is re-focus our attention, as we try to understand the trends of capitalist development, on the structures and patterns of the world market, and away from calculations about the evolutions of capital in a vaguely-envisaged "average" capitalist economy. That fact alone makes his work the most valuable and important in its field for many years.

APPENDIX 3

The Tendency of the Rate of Profit to Fall

In volume 1 of *Capital* Marx argued in some detail that capital would squeeze down living labour and replace it by machines, not just to reduce costs but also to increase its control over the process of production. This drive, wrote Marx, would produce an increasing ratio of c/v (outlay on means of production/outlay on labour-power). In his unfinished volume 3 Marx deduced, as a simple mathematical consequence of increasing c/v, that s/(c + v), the ratio of surplus value to total costs, would tend to decrease. Thus the Tendency of the Rate of Profit to Fall. Many have relied on this as "the Marxist theory of crisis", but I believe they are wrong.

Marx erred, I believe, in assuming too rapidly that the social tendency to squeeze down living labour would clearly reflect itself in a statistical trend (c/v, whose rough equivalent in available statistics is the capital/output ratio). He also erred in not seeing that what he cited as "countervailing tendencies" to the Falling Rate of Profit – increased exploitation (s/v) and cheapening of constant capital – were so entwined with the "tendency" as to annul it. The factual evidence confirms this. Over the whole of the last century, there is no clear long-term tendency for profit rates to fall.

Consider a capitalist making desktop computers, for example, who introduces a new technique cutting his costs. For a while he can sell his computers at the price established by the old technique, making super-profits. Then the new technique spreads, and he has to cut his prices and accept only an average rate of profit. The argument of the Tendency of the Rate of Profit to Fall is that the new average rate of profit will be below the old average, because of increased c/v. The individual capitalist's short-term profit-maximising decision cuts profits longer-term for all capitalists.

But if the new technique offers lower costs to the individual pioneering capitalist, then it must also, once generalised, cheapen constant capital (by enabling all capitalists to buy computers for their businesses cheaper) and increase the rate of exploitation (by reducing the labour-time required to produce the total of the commodities consumed by workers – including those desktop computers bought by workers – while workers' total hours of labour remain unchanged). And those effects must be sufficient to raise the general rate of profit. At any rate of profit lower than the super-profits won by the pioneer when he first launches his new technique, every other capitalist will enjoy a cut in the outlay (on means of production and wage costs) they must make in order to mobilise a worker's labour-power for a standard week. Either their profits are raised, or their capital-stock outlay is cheapened, or both. Their rate of profit rises above the old average. As the price of desktop computers falls, the super-profits of the pioneer are reduced, but the profit rates of other capitalists are raised. The point at which those two tendencies meet, and a new general rate of profit is established, must be above the old general profit rate.

This argument (the "Okishio theorem") can be formalised mathematically. It shows that profit-maximising technical innovation, in and of itself, cannot push down the general rate of profit. Even if increased real wages come with the technical innovation, as they usually will in periods of high-investment boom, the general rate of profit will be cut only if workers capture all the cost-cutting benefits of the new techniques plus a bit more. Profit rates cannot fall as a simple and direct result of profit-maximising technical innovation alone. If the technical innovation is in a line producing luxury goods, or armaments, consumed only by the capitalists or their state, then it has no cost-cutting effect for the rest of capital, and the new general rate of profit is the same as the old. All the cost-cutting benefits of the new technique are captured by the capitalists for their private consumption or by the military. But even then the new profit rate is not lower.

It may still happen that a development centred on technical innovation reduces profit-rates or leads to crisis. Innovating capitalists may make mistakes – from the point of view of profit-maximisation – in their urgent drive to outstrip their competitors or to gain greater control over labour through mechanisation. Capitalists may collectively "over-invest" in a particular sector when they see a new profit opportunity – without any individual making an obvious mistake – and thus drive a large number of the higher-cost businesses in that sector to bankruptcy and trigger a devastating chain of defaults. Generally, the industrial rate of profit derives from the ratio of surplus value to capital outlay only indirectly and after a series of deductions (taxes, interest, rent, fees, other unproductive costs, losses on goods unsold or sold cut-price, etc.), and thus may fall when that ratio rises.

Anwar Shaikh contends that the warlike character of capitalist competition means that capitalists will generally make massive investments in fixed assets which enable them to produce extra at reduced extra current cost and thus drive their rivals out of business but reduce their ratio of profit to total investment (Shaikh 1978). Shaikh, however, offers no empirical evidence that capitalists do this generally, rather than exceptionally. He assumes an "excessively" fast rate of innovation, while a large volume of socialist comment, from Marx onwards, has rather found cause to indict capitalism for failing to introduce new techniques which cut labour-time but may not cut wage-costs.

In any case, the pattern described by Shaikh, or that of innovation propelling a profit-rate-cutting rise in real wages, would develop only in a period of exuberant capitalist boom. The Falling Rate of Profit might then explain why that boom would slow down. It might explain a gradual downward drift of the rate of profit, but not the sudden downturn typical of a capitalist crisis. There is no "natural" rate of profit below which crisis kicks in. At an average rate of profit of 10% per year, capital will grow slower than at a profit rate of 20% per year, but it will not necessarily plunge into crisis.

Moreover, even in the "best" case for the advocates of the Tendency of the Rate of Profit to Fall, it is unlikely that the Tendency can bring the rate very low. The physical image of a vast mass of fixed assets overshadowing a relatively small workforce is an optical illusion. In value terms, at any time, all the recent additions to fixed capital are simply congealed portions of the previous few years' surplus value. If the mass of surplus value is increasing – and Marx, in his exposition of the Tendency of the Rate of Profit to Fall, explicitly expects that it will – then the value ratio of current surplus to the congealed portions of previous years' smaller surpluses cannot fall very low, however impressive the physical embodiments of those previous years' surplus value.

What then of the idea that the Tendency of the Rate of Profit to Fall is "the Marxist" explanation of economic crises? Without it, argues Shane Mage, "the central argument of 'scientific socialism'... would fall to the ground. There might still be a case for socialism, but it would have to be argued exclusively on a moral, not an economic, basis" (Mage 1963). But a moral basis is the right one for arguing the case for socialism, so long as "moral" is understood in the broad sense as "in relation to human history". "Logical" proofs that any economic model satisfying the general properties of Marx's theory of capitalism must break down are no help to working-class socialism. Whom are they meant to convince? Why should we accept the implication that humanity should scrap capitalism only if it breaks down irreparably and cannot be got to work at all, at any cost? In any case there is only one capitalist system, the actually existing one, and it can be "broken down" only by political action, not by logical demonstrations on paper.

Marx never referred to the Tendency in any writings that he completed for publication. Nor did Engels cite it in his *Anti-Dühring*, which was written in consultation with Marx as a summary of their common doctrine and which included a section on crises. In Marx's unpublished writings, the longest connected discussion of crises, in *Theories of Surplus Value* volume 2, scarcely mentions the Tendency. His discussion of the Tendency in his unfinished volume 3 of Capital notes that "it is only under certain circumstances and only after long periods that its effects become strikingly pronounced".

Almost all economists at the time reckoned that in fact the rate of profit did tend to fall. Adam Smith and David Ricardo both believed that there were iron laws depressing the rate of profit. (So did Keynes, in his *General Theory*). What is special to Marx, as against other economists of his day, is not that he saw a tendency of the rate of profit to fall, but that he saw the tendency as a social one, operating through and modified by class struggle, rather than an inescapable law of nature; and that he stressed the "countervailing tendencies". Marx was keen to derive further indictments of capitalism from a tendency which seemed to be established as solid fact by many other writers' work. He did not make his indictment hang or fall on that tendency, see it as his special role to demonstrate the tendency's existence, or present the tendency as the prime cause of all capitalist crises.

In volume 3 Marx does essay an account of the Tendency generating crisis through its specific effect on small capitalists, whose ruin, at a certain stage of the fall of profit-rates, unleashes a chain of collapses. This is, however, an unfinished speculation of Marx's, unintegrated with his other writings on crisis – and both theoretically and empirically unsound.

Plekhanov, Kautsky, Lenin, Luxemburg, and Trotsky never, as I far as I know, propounded the Tendency of the Rate of Profit to Fall as central to their Marxism. None of the early Communist International's accounts of the catastrophic crisis of world capitalism after World War I attributed it to the Tendency. The Tendency was referred to in works like Hilferding's *Finance Capital* and Bukharin's *Imperialism and World Economy*, but only in a subsidiary role. It became "the Marxist theory of crisis" only in the 1930s, under Stalinism.

Emile Burns's Stalinist primer (Burns 1935) gave over a big part of its space available for extracts from *Capital* to the section on the Tendency of the Rate of Profit to Fall from *Capital* volume 3, and included nothing else on crisis. The picture of capitalism as driven to ruin by a mechanical iron law, so that an alternative sufficiently powerful, stable, and "realistic" gained credit by comparison, suited Stalinism.

From the Popular Front period onwards, reformist or underconsumptionist accounts of crisis became more prominent in Stalinist literature; but the Tendency of the Rate of Profit to Fall remained as an esoteric doctrine for the "cadres", and it also became an icon for many Trotskyists. Many Trotskyists, too poor and ill-connected to produce their own literature, would have educated themselves on volumes like Burns's *Handbook*, spurning only the sections by Stalin. Also, the picture of an iron law of crisis suited the apocalyptic and millenialist perspectives of many Trotskyists who looked for their political isolation to be broken by an impending catastrophe in which the mass of workers would be hurled into revolt, the old bureaucratic leaderships of the labour movement would be put in disarray, and revolution would result just so long as the alternative leadership had built itself up sufficiently. When a new generation of Marxist economists, Trotskyist-inclined or at any rate anti-Stalinist, was formed in the early 1970s, the doctrine of the Tendency gained additional reinforcement. Research showed that in the run-up to the slump of 1973–5, the rate of profit had indeed fallen (since about the mid-60s) in the leading capitalist countries, and that the capital-output ratio (the best proxy in official statistics for the ratio of outlay on means of production to outlay on labour power) had risen. Behold the Tendency! Behold the secret Marxist explanation for the crisis, ignored by conventional thought! 1973 tended to get seen as "the" crisis, the archetype of all crises, and statistical discoveries of falling profits as the mark of Marxist insight.

List of Previously Published Articles

Part 1: After 2007

Fred Moseley – The long trends of profit. March 2008 – *Solidarity* 129, 20 March 2008.

Costas Lapavitsas – A new sort of financial crisis. April 2008 – *Solidarity* 130, 10 April 2008.

Leo Panitch – The crisis depends on the fightback. April 2008 – *Solidarity* 131, 24 April 2008.

Simon Mohun – An era of rampant inequality. May 2008 – *Solidarity* 132, 14 May 2008.

Trevor Evans – The imbalances are unsustainable. June 2008 – *Solidarity* 134, 26 June 2008.

Dick Bryan – The inventiveness of capital. July 2008 – *Solidarity* 135, 10 July 2008.

Michel Husson – A systemic crisis, both global and long-lasting. July 2008 – *Solidarity* 136, 24 July 2008.

Part 2: After September 2008

Michel Husson – The crisis of neoliberal capitalism. December 2008 – *Solidarity* 146, 12 February 2009.

Costas Lapavitsas – The debacle of financialised capitalism. January 2009 – online at www.workersliberty.org/node/11912, 26 January 2009.

Andrew Kliman – The level of debt is astronomical. December 2008 – online at www.workersliberty.org/node/11807, 12 January 2009.

Leo Panitch – The chain broke at the weakest link. December 2008 – *Solidarity* 145, 29 January 2009.

Fred Moseley – The bondholders and the taxpayers. December 2008 – *Solidarity* 144, 15 January 2009.

Simon Mohun – The neoliberal model is bust – January 2009 – online at www.workersliberty.org/node/12523, 4 June 2009.

Robert Brenner – The economy in a world of trouble. April 2009 – *Against The Current*, March-April 2009.

Dick Bryan – The underlying contradictions of capitalist finance. June 2009 – online at www.workersliberty.org/node/12683, 30 June 2009.

Part 3: After 2009

Barry Finger – The falling rate of profit. July 2011 – online at www.workersliberty.org/node/17123, 19 July 2011.

Leo Panitch – The banks' crisis and the left's crisis. August 2011 – *The Bullet, Socialist Project E-Bulletin* 536, 15 August 2011.

Michel Husson – Nationalise the banks! September 2011 – in English translation by Edward Maltby, *Solidarity* 218, 28 September 2011. French original at http://hussonet.free.fr/natibank.pdf, 15 September 2011.

Michel Husson – The endless bail-out of Europe. November 2011 – French original at http://hussonet.free.fr/bailout11f.pdf, 2 November 2011. Translated here by Edward Maltby.

Daniela Gabor – Europe: the bankers vs the people. June 2012 – *Solidarity* 249, 13 June 2012.

Part 4: After 2010

Hugo Radice – A turning point from neoliberalism? June 2012 – *Solidarity* 249, 13 June 2012.

Paul Hampton and Martin Thomas – The world of neoliberalism. October 2013 – *Solidarity* 298, 2 October 2013.

Barry Finger – An alternative view on the world of neoliberalism. January 2014 – at http://www.workersliberty.org/story/2013/10/02/world-neo-liberalism#comment-31438, 1 January 2014.

Andrew Gamble – The resilience of neoliberalism. June 2016 – at https://senseofgfc.wordpress.com/2016/06/19/questions-to-andrew-gamble/, 19 June 2016.

Part 5: After 2015

Michel Husson – The coming crisis. October 2015 – English translation by Edward Maltby, *Solidarity* 389, 13 January 2016. French original at http://hussonet.free.fr/crisequiv.pdf, 23 October 2015.

Fred Moseley – "Too much debt in relation to income". January 2016 – at https://senseofgfc.wordpress.com/2016/02/17/fred-moseley-26-january-2016/, 17 February 2016.

Andrew Kliman – "The situation had long been unsustainable". January 2016 – at https://senseofgfc.wordpress.com/2016/02/17/andrew-kliman-january-2016/, 17 February 2016.

Dick Bryan – "We become a hedge fund of our own lives". January 2016 – at https://senseofgfc.wordpress.com/2016/02/19/dick-bryan-january-2016/, 19 February 2016.

Hugo Radice – "The globalisation of elites". January 2016 – at https://senseofgfc.wordpress.com/2016/02/19/hugo-radice-january-2016/, 19 February 2016.

Leo Panitch – "The great recession is not going away". January 2016 – at https://senseofgfc.wordpress.com/2016/02/19/leo-panitch-january-2016/, 19 February 2016.

Simon Mohun – "A protracted transition". June 2016 – at https://senseofgfc.wordpress.com/2016/06/02/draft-questions-for-simon-mohun/, 3 July 2016.

Alfredo Saad-Filho – Brazil and neoliberalism. July-August 2016 – at https://senseofgfc.wordpress.com/2016/03/28/questions-to-alfredo-saad-filho/, 6 August 2016.

Bibliography

Abu-El-Haj, J., 2016: Brazilian Left Bonapartism and the Rise of Finance Capital. *Latin American Perspectives* 43 (2).

Acemoglu, D, and J A Robinson, 2012: Is This Time Different? Capture and Anti-Capture of US Politics. *The Economists' Voice* 9 (3).

Allen, F., and D. Gale, 2007: An Introduction to Financial Crises. *Wharton Financial Institutions Center Working Paper* No. 07–20.

Almunia, M, and others, 2010: Lessons from the Great Depression, *Economic Policy*, April 2010.

Armstrong, P, A. Glyn, and J. Harrison, 1991. *Capitalism Since 1945*. Oxford: Basil Blackwell.

Bain & Co, 2012: *A World Awash in Money: Capital Trends Through 2020*. At http://www.bain.com/Images/BAIN_REPORT_A_world_awash_in_money.pdf.

Balls, E., 2010: Bloomberg speech, at http://www.tom-watson.co.uk/2013/01/the-bloomberg-speech-by-ed-balls-27th-august-2010/.

Basu, D., and R. Vasudevan, 2011: Technology, Distribution and the Rate of Profit in the US Economy: Understanding the Current Crisis. *University of Massachusetts Amherst Economics Department Working Paper* no. 140.

Bates, T.W., K.M. Kahle, R.M. Stulz, 2006: Why Do US Firms Hold So Much More Cash Than They Used To? *NBER Working Paper* 12534, September 2006.

Bernanke, B, 2007: speech at Economic Club of New York, October 2007, reported at http://www.nakedcapitalism.com/2007/10/bernanke-i-would-like-to-know-what.html.

Blankfein, L, 2009: Remarks to The Council Of Institutional Investors, April 2009, at http://www.goldmansachs.com/our-thinking/archive/lcb-speech-to-cii.html.

Blinder, A., 2013. *After the Music Stopped*. New York, NY: Penguin.

Bloomberg, update of 9 August 2007, at https://cybercemetery.unt.edu/archive/fcic/20110310201441/http://c0181567.cdn1.cloudfiles.rackspacecloud.com/2007-08-09%20Bloomberg%20-%20BNP%20Paribas%20Freezes%20Funds%20as%20Loan%20Losses%20Roil%20Markets.pdf.

BLS (Bureau of Labour Statistics, USA), 2014: Consumer Expenditure Survey, http://www.bls.gov/cex/tables.htm.

Boito, A., and A. Saad-Filho, 2016: State, State Institutions, and Political Power in Brazil. *Latin American Perspectives* issue 207 43 (2).

Bowles, S., 1981: Technical change and the profit rate. *Cambridge Journal of Economics* (5), 183–186.

Brenner, R, 1998: The Economics of Global Turbulence, *New Left Review* I:229.

Brenner, R., 2006: *The Economics of Global Turbulence*. London: Verso.

Brenner, R, and M. Glick, 1991: *The Regulation Approach: Theory and History*. New Left Review I/188.

Bryan, D., and M. Rafferty, 2014: Financial derivatives as social policy beyond crisis, *Sociology* 48 (5).

Bryan, D., and M. Rafferty, 2005: *Capitalism with derivatives*. London: Palgrave Macmillan.

Bunn, P, and M. Rostum, 2014: Household debt and spending, *Bank of England Quarterly Bulletin* 2014 Q3.

Burns, E, 1935: *A handbook of Marxism*. London: Gollancz.

Card, A, and others, 2011: US Trade and Investment Policy. *Council on Foreign Relations Task Force Report* 67.

CoreLogic, National Foreclosure Report, at http://www.corelogic.com/about-us/researchtrends/national-foreclosure-report.aspx.

Crotty, J., 1985: The Centrality of Money, Credit and Financial Intermediation in Marx's Crisis Theory, in Resnick and Wolff, eds., *Rethinking Marxism: Essays in Honor of Harry Magdoff and Paul Sweezy*. New York: Autonomedia 1985.

Dallery, T, 2009: Post-Keynesian Theories of the Firm under Financialization, *Review of Radical Political Economics*, Volume 41, No. 4.

Daly, K., and B. Broadbent, 2009: The Savings Glut, the Return on Capital and the Rise in Risk Aversion. Goldman Sachs Global Economics Paper no.185.

Damodaran, A., 2001: *Corporate Finance*. Hoboken, NJ: Wiley 2001.

Degras, J., 1956: *The Communist International, 1919–1943: documents*, volume 1. London: Royal Institution of International Affairs.

Duménil, G, and D. Lévy, 2011: The crisis of the early 21st century: a critical review of alternative interpretations. Preliminary draft, at http://www.jourdan.ens.fr/levy.

Duménil, G, and D. Lévy, 2011: The crisis of the early 21st century: general interpretation, recent developments, and perspectives. Preliminary draft, at http://www.jourdan.ens.fr/levy.

Duménil, G., and D. Lévy, 2011. *The crisis of neoliberalism*. Cambridge, MA: Harvard University Press

Duménil, G., and D. Lévy, 2012. The crisis of the early 21st century: Marxian perspectives, at http://www.jourdan.ens.fr/levy.

Duménil, G., and D. Lévy, 2014. *La grande bifurcation*. Paris: La Découverte.

Dunning, J.H. and S. Lundan 2008: *Multinational Enterprises and the Global Economy*. Cheltenham: Elgar 2008.

Ellis, L, and K. Smith, 2007: The global upward trend in the profit share, BIS Working Papers No 231.

Evans, T., 2010: Five explanations for the international financial crisis. Institute for International Political Economy, Berlin, Working Paper 08/2010.

Friedman, M., and A. Schwartz, 2016: *The Great Contraction, 1929–1933*. Princeton NJ: Princeton University Press.

Gabor, D., 2015: The IMF's Rethink of Global Banks: Critical in Theory, Orthodox in Practice. *Governance*, vol. 28, no.2.

Gabor, D., 2014: Learning from Japan: The European Central Bank and the European Sovereign Debt Crisis. *Review of Political Economy* vol.26, no.2.

Gamble, A., 2009: *The spectre at the feast*. London: Palgrave Macmillan.

Gamble, A., 2014: *Crisis without end?* London: Palgrave Macmillan.

Glyn, A., and B. Sutcliffe, 1972: *British Capitalism, Workers and the Profit Squeeze*. Harmondsworth: Penguin.

Graham, J.R. and M.T. Leary, 2016: The Evolution of Corporate Cash (July 1, 2016). http://dx.doi.org/10.2139/ssrn.2805505.

Hagel, J., and others, 2013: *Success or struggle: ROA as a true measure of business performance*. Westlake, TX: Deloitte University Press, 2013. bit.ly/hagel-sb.

Hague, D.C., 1961: *The theory of capital*. London: Palgrave Macmillan.

Harvey, D., 2005: *A brief history of neoliberalism*. Oxford: Oxford University Press.

Hunter, W., 2011: The PT in power, chapter in Levitsky, S, and K M Roberts, *The Resurgence of the Latin American Left*. Baltimore, MD: Johns Hopkins University Press.

Husson, M., 2014: Towards a "long-lasting chaos", IIRE, 3th Economic Seminar Amsterdam, 14–16 February 2014, at http://hussonet.free.fr.

Husson, M., 2012: Le néoliberalisme: stade suprême? *Actuel Marx* no. 51, 2012.

Husson, M., 2012: Les salaires et la crise en Europe, at http://hussonet.free.fr.

Husson, M., 2010: The debate on the rate of profit, *International Viewpoint* no.426, July 2010.

Husson, M., 2010: La hausse tendancielle du taux de profit, at http://hussonet.free.fr.

Husson, M., 2009a: Les coûts historiques d'Andrew Kliman, at http://hussonet.free.fr.

Husson, M., 2009: Capitalisme : vers une régulation chaotique, at http://hussonet.free.fr/impa9web.pdf.

Husson, M., 2008: *Un pur capitalisme*. Lausanne: Page deux.

Jones, R.P., and others, 2016: How Immigration and Concerns about Cultural Change Are Shaping the 2016 Election: PRRI/Brookings Survey. PRRI.

Judson, R., 2012: Crisis and Calm: Demand for US Currency at Home and Abroad From the Fall of the Berlin Wall to 2011. Federal Reserve System International Finance Discussion Paper 1058.

Kincaid, J., 2016: Marx after Minsky: Capital surplus and the current crisis. *Historical Materialism* 24 (1).

Kliman, A, 1996: A Value-theoretic Critique of the Okishio Theorem, in A. Freeman and G. Carchedi (eds) *Marx and Non-equilibrium Economics*. Cheltenham: Elgar.

Kliman, A., 1997: The Okishio theorem: an obituary. *Review of Radical Political Economics*, vol.29 no.3.

Kliman, A., 1998: The Significance of the "Internal Inconsistency" Allegations. http://akliman.squarespace.com/writings/Signif-of-II-Alleg-web.doc.

Kliman, A., 2002: The Specter Haunting "Marxian Economics". http://akliman.squarespace.com/writings/Specter%20web.doc.

Kliman, A., 2011: *The failure of capitalist production*. London: Pluto.

Lapavitsas, C., 2006: Power and Trust as Constituents of Money and Credit. *Historical Materialism* 14 (1).

Lapavitsas, C., 2013: *Profiting without producing*. London: Verso.

Lazonick, W., and M. O'Sullivan, 2000: Maximizing shareholder value: a new ideology for corporate governance, *Economy and Society* 29 (1).

Mage, S., 1963: The 'Law of the Falling Tendency of the Rate of Profit': Its Place in the Marxian Theoretical System and Relevance to the US Economy, 1900–1960. PhD dissertation, Columbia University. At http://archive.org/details/MagesDissertation.

Mankiw, N.G., 2006: The Macroeconomist as Scientist and Engineer, *The Journal of Economic Perspectives*, 20 (4).

Marx, K., 1969: *Theories of Surplus Value*, Part 2. London: Lawrence and Wishart.

Marx, K., 1970: *Capital*, volume 1. London: Lawrence and Wishart.

Marx, K., 1972: *Capital*, volume 2. London: Lawrence and Wishart.

Marx, K., 1977: *Capital*, volume 3. London: Lawrence and Wishart.

Marx, K., 1993: *Grundrisse: Foundations of the Critique of Political Economy*. Harmondsworth: Penguin.

Mason, J.W., 2013: Strange Defeat. *Economic and Political Weekly*, 48 (32), 10 August 2013.

Mason, J.W., 2014: Debt and demand, at http://slackwire.blogspot.co.uk/2014/01/debt-and-demand.html.

Mason, J.W., 2015: Disgorge the Cash. Roosevelt Institute paper, at http://rooseveltinstitute.org/wp-content/uploads/2015/09/Disgorge-the-Cash.pdf.

Mason, J.W., and Arjun Jayadev, 2014: "Fisher Dynamics" in US Household Debt 1929–2011, *American Economic Journal: Macroeconomics* 6 (3).

McDonnell, J., 2015: Interview with *Holyrood* magazine, 14 December 2015. https://www.holyrood.com/articles/inside-politics/interview-john-mcdonnell.

McLean, B., and J. Nocera, 2011: *All the Devils Are Here*. London: Portfolio Penguin.

Mejorado, A., and M. Roman, 2013: *Profitability and the Great Recession*. New York, NY: Routledge.

Mian, A., and A. Sufi, 2015: *House of Debt*. Chicago, IL: University of Chicago Press.

Minsky, H., 1975: *John Maynard Keynes*. New York, NY: McGraw Hill.

Minsky, H., 2008: *Stabilising an Unstable Economy*. New York, NY: McGraw Hill.

Mirowski, P., 2013: *Never let a serious crisis go to waste: how neoliberalism survived the financial meltdown*. London: Verso.

Mohun, S., 2014: Unproductive labour in the US economy 1964–2010, *Review of Radical Political Economy* 46 (3).

Mohun, S., 2016: Class structure and the US personal income distribution, 1918–2012. *Metroeconomica* 67 (2).

Mongiovi, G., 2002: Vulgar economy in Marxian garb: a critique of Temporal Single System Marxism. *Review of Radical Political economy* 34 (4).

Montecino, J.A. and G. Epstein, 2015: Did Quantitative Easing Increase Income Inequality? PERI Working Paper 405.

Moseley, F., 2013: The US Economic Crisis: From a Profitability Crisis to an Overindebtedness Crisis. *Review of Radical Political Economy* 45 (4).

Nassif, A., C. Feijó and E. Araújo, 2013: Structural change and economic development: is Brazil catching up or falling behind? UNCTAD Discussion Paper no.211.

Noland, M., and others, 2016: Assessing Trade Agendas in the US Presidential Campaign. Peterson Institute for International Economics.

Okishio, N., 2000: Competition and Production Prices. *Cambridge Journal of Economics* (25) 493–501.

Palma, J.G., 2009: The Revenge of the Market on the Rentiers. Why neo-liberal reports of the end of history turned out to be premature. Cambridge Working Paper in Economics 0927.

Palma, J.G., 2012: Was Brazil's recent growth acceleration the world's most overrated boom? Cambridge Working Papers in Economics 1248.

Palma, J.G., 2015: Why corporations in developing countries are likely to be even more susceptible to the vicissitudes of international finance than their counterparts in the developed world. Cambridge Working Paper in Economics 1539.

Panitch, L., and S. Gindin, 2013: *The Making of Global Capitalism*. London: Verso.

Pew Research, 2016: Euroskepticism Beyond Brexit. http://www.pewglobal.org/2016/06/07/euroskepticism-beyond-brexit/.

Piketty, T., 2014: *Capital in the Twenty-First Century*. Cambridge, MA: Harvard University Press.

Quadros, R., 2008: Implications of The Global Financial Crisis For The Brazilian Economy, Institute of Development Studies (Sussex) briefing, 12 November 2008.

Romer, C., 2009: The lessons of 1937, *The Economist* 18 June 2009.

Saad-Filho, A., 2011: Crisis in neoliberalism or crisis of neoliberalism? *Socialist Register*.

Saad-Filho, A., and A. Boito, 2016: Brazil, The Failure of the PT and the Rise of the 'New Right'. *Socialist Register*.

Saad-Filho, A., and D. Johnston, 2005: *Neoliberalism, A Critical Reader*. London: Pluto.

Saad-Filho, A., and L. Morais, 2014: Mass Protests, Brazilian Spring or Brazilian Malaise? *Socialist Register*.

Schumpeter, J., 2010: *Capitalism, Socialism and Democracy*. London: Routledge.

Shaikh, A., 1978: Political economy and capitalism: notes on Dobb's theory of crisis. *Cambridge Journal of Economics* 2.

Simerly, R., 2000: The Global Economy and the New Role of Governments, *B>Quest 2000*, https://www.westga.edu/~bquest/2000/global.html.

Stiglitz, J., 2011: Rethinking macroeconomics: what failed, and how to repair it. *Journal of the European Economic Association*, 9 (4).

Strange, S., 1987: The persistent myth of lost hegemony. *International Organisation*, 41, pp. 551–574.

Tett, G., 2009: *Fool's Gold*. New York: Free Press.

Trotsky, L., 1938: The Transitional Program. In Matgamna (ed), How *Solidarity Can Change the World*, 1998, London: Phoenix Press.

UNCTAD 2015, *Handbook of Statistics*.

Weeks, J., 2016: Trump's victory represents the fulfilment of neoliberalism, not its failure. *Open Democracy*, https://www.opendemocracy.net/john-weeks/trumps-victory-is-fulfilment-of-neoliberalism-not-its-failure.

Wolf, M., 2015: *The Shifts and the Shocks*. London: Penguin.

World Trade Organisation, 2016, Reports on Recent Trade Developments, at https://www.wto.org/english/news_e/news16_e/trdev_22jul16_e.htm.

Index

America; American capital, central bank, economy, state, etc: *see* United States
Argentina 61, 125, 180, 184, 206, 274
Asian crisis (1997–8) 43, 270
asset (financial) prices 70, 130, 135–37, 213, 246

bail-outs 8–9, 102, 124–26, 147, 154, 157, 171–75, 184
Bernanke, Ben 6, 65, 69, 134, 258
Brazil 3–5, 39, 79, 204–07, 268–77
Brenner, Robert 35–37, 134–38, 140, 300–09
BRICS 4, 55, 79, 95, 96, 211, 255

Chicago Mercantile Exchange 60–61
China 3, 5, 66–67, 78–79, 92, 96–97, 143–46, 190, 217, 267, 273, 284
crisis, theory of 14, 16, 35–37, 56–57, 62–63, 92, 103, 141–44, 168–71, 191–97, 269–70, 289–313

debt 8, 46, 48, 107, 108, 116–18, 125, 126, 169, 174, 214–15, 225, 235–36, 246, 307
- bad 64, 69, 70, 118, 191
- consumer or household 24, 47, 49, 69, 91, 120, 126–27, 199, 224, 243, 272
- public 169, 171, 214, 215, 216
- securitised 80, 81, 199
- student 240, 247

derivatives, derivatives markets 43, 61, 64, 73, 80–82, 108, 113, 117, 149, 150–52, 240
dollar, US 53, 55, 58, 66, 78, 82, 84, 85, 96, 109, 110, 114, 127, 129, 281
dysfunction (and hegemony) 38, 39, 206, 211, 268–70

ECB, *see* European Central Bank
education 12, 25, 86, 105, 130, 241, 245, 247, 257, 259, 265, 301
emerging economies 3–6, 89, 91, 95, 96, 102, 109, 204, 212, 215, 217, 218, 219, 225, 255, 261
Engels, Frederick 30, 35, 289, 297, 298, 299, 312
euro 84–85, 129, 169, 173–86, 202, 204, 218
European Central Bank 8, 9, 52–53, 62–63, 76, 92, 169, 172–80, 185, 204, 245, 256
European Union 9, 38, 96, 103, 178, 180, 230, 259, 282, 283
Eurozone 11, 172, 173, 176, 177, 179, 180, 184, 185, 186, 203, 212, 218, 221–23, 231
exploitation, rate of 31, 33, 60, 89, 90, 158, 159, 161, 220, 238, 302, 303, 304, 310

Federal Reserve 2, 50, 52–3, 62, 65, 72, 73, 76, 109–11, 114, 135, 241, 243, 255, 257
fictitious capital 80, 108, 216, 217
financialisation 23, 25, 68, 71, 89, 90, 91, 105–11, 132, 138, 163, 164, 174, 241, 264, 266, 272

Gamble, Andrew 201–08
globalisation, social-democratisation of 101, 105, 119, 122
Greece 8, 11, 169, 171–73, 176–80, 184–86, 203–4, 231, 248, 249

Hampton, Paul 189–200
household debt, *see* debt, consumer or household
housing bubble 65, 70, 135, 136, 137, 139, 146
Husson, Michel 24, 28, 44, 89–104, 169–75, 212–23, 237

imperialism 35, 57, 94, 95, 140, 142, 188–98, 200
India 4, 5, 7, 39, 55, 67, 79, 95, 143, 211, 212, 262, 274, 278, 282

Japan 10–11, 57, 76, 77, 102, 103, 111, 113–14, 134, 135, 141, 143, 265, 266, 305

Keynes, Keynesianism, Keynesian policies 13, 18, 21, 22, 58, 83, 112, 132, 138, 139, 142, 149, 198, 290, 291, 292, 312
Kliman, Andrew 33, 34, 114, 116, 228, 230, 232, 234, 236, 238
Korea 134, 143–47, 207, 218, 302

labour 48, 68, 87, 88, 141, 154, 242, 292, 293, 300, 301, 302, 304, 305, 310
living 30, 194, 310
productive 48–49, 70, 159, 160
Latin America 103–4, 118, 211, 225, 270, 273
Lenin, Vladimir Ilyich 37, 121, 193, 286, 313
liquidity 11, 19, 62, 69, 83, 102, 106, 119, 176, 177, 178, 185, 192, 213, 216

managers, managerial classes 47, 241, 263–65
Marx, Karl 15–17, 19, 26–27, 30, 31–33, 43, 49, 47, 136, 238, 239, 243, 289–313
Minsky, Hyman 17–19, 43, 49
Mohun, Simon 68–71, 128–33, 261–67

neoliberalism 13, 37, 38–39, 102–03, 112, 128–133, 147, 166, 175, 183–89, 192, 196, 200–04, 211, 220, 226, 230, 231, 264, 265, 268–73, 278

Okishio, Nobuo 30, 35, 236, 237
overcapacity 36, 101, 134, 135, 141, 145, 302, 306, 307

Palma, José Gabriel 4, 5, 23, 29, 270, 272, 273
Panitch, Leo 58, 60, 62, 64, 66, 84, 120, 122–23, 164, 166, 168, 256, 258, 260, 281
Podemos 37, 253, 259, 262, 281, 282
profit 14, 22, 24, 26, 28, 30, 44–52, 56, 70, 94, 102, 104, 135, 138, 141, 151, 154, 160–62, 195, 197, 199, 221, 234, 235–37, 302, 310
average rate of 89, 159, 194, 303, 310, 311
falling rate of 26, 158, 159, 160, 161, 198, 300, 310, 311
rate of 26–36, 45, 47, 49, 90–91, 159, 194, 220, 234, 235, 236, 238–39, 304, 305, 310–13
replacement-cost and historic-cost rate of 28, 158, 234–37
profit share 27, 45, 47, 70, 302

Regulationists 301, 303
ruinous competition 35–36, 300–09

Saad-Filho, Alfredo 12, 268–76
Spain 9, 169, 171, 179, 184, 185, 203, 249, 250, 253, 259, 262, 273, 281, 282
Syriza 8, 37, 157, 179, 183, 185, 201, 202, 203, 204, 249, 251, 259, 262, 281

Trotskyists 17, 313
Trump 183, 207, 208, 262, 274, 278, 282–85

United States 55–67, 114–16, 121–22, 143–45, 190–92, 207, 257. *See also* Bernanke, Federal Reserve, Trump
unproductive labour 48, 49, 70, 158, 159, 265

wage-push theory 300–05
wage share 159, 219, 221, 222, 265

www.ingramcontent.com/pod-product-compliance
Lightning Source LLC
Chambersburg PA
CBHW070907030426
42336CB00014BA/2319
* 9 7 8 1 6 0 8 4 6 0 8 6 1 *